Stories Rabbits Tell

Stories Rabbits Tell

A NATURAL AND CULTURAL HISTORY
OF A MISUNDERSTOOD CREATURE

———•——

SUSAN E. DAVIS
MARGO DEMELLO

LANTERN BOOKS • NEW YORK
A DIVISION OF BOOKLIGHT INC.

2003
Lantern Books
One Union Square West, Suite 201
New York, NY 10003

Printed in the United States of America.

Library of Congress Cataloging-in-Publication Data

Davis, Susan E., 1961–
Stories rabbits tell / by Susan E. Davis and Margo DeMello.
p. cm.
Includes index.
ISBN 1–59056–044–2 (alk. paper)
1. Rabbits. I. DeMello, Margo. II. Title.
SF453.D426 2003
636.9'322—dc21
2003005191

Susan's dedication

To Phoebe (the rabbit), and Elmo, Maybelline and
Mr. Bop (also rabbits), for telling their stories;
and to Phoebe (the girl) and Harrison (the boy)
for showing me how deeply children understand
those stories.

———•+•———

Margo's dedication

To Blueberry: You were my Herman;
and to Melinda, Mouse, Wormguy, Hopper,
Mrs. Bean, Chester . . .
and all of the other special rabbits who have enriched
my life and inspired my actions.

ACKNOWLEDGMENTS

———•—•———

THIS BOOK WAS very much a labor of love for both Margo and Susan, but it could not have been written without a number of people whose time, expertise and assistance both supported and expanded the project.

Many people from the animal protection world provided us with information, contacts and historical background. Rachel Query, Elissa Bob, John Goodwin and Martin Stephens, all with the Humane Society of the United States, helped us frame critical issues and gave us crucial information and contacts. Christopher Heyde, with the Animal Welfare Institute, sent reams of material that contained much-needed context on several commercial rabbit industries. Roger Curran of the Institute for In Vitro Sciences, Sara Amundson of the Doris Day Animal League, John McArdle of The Alternatives Research and Development Foundation, and Alan Goldberg of the Johns Hopkins Center for Alternatives to Animal Testing helped us sort out the many complexities of the current debate on laboratory animals. Daniel Rolke mysteriously appeared one day with news (and footage) of the rabbit meat industry in Sweden. Marshall Smith of In Defense of Animals provided input on the world of USDA oversight and licensing, and Debra Howard of the Companion Animal Protection Society helped interpret the USDA APHIS Web site, a place into which no layperson should venture alone. Merritt Clifton of Animal People provided us with figures on America's charitable giving.

Joy Gioia of the St. Louis House Rabbit Society, Kirk Lowis of the Michigan House Rabbit Society and Sandy Koi, also of House Rabbit Society, shared their experiences and notes from their visits to commercial rabbitries. Susan Smith of the Wisconsin House Rabbit Society, Alvin Smith of Oregon State University and Jeff Bryan, DVM, rabbit vet extraordinaire, guided us to more accurate language on RHD and myxomatosis. Mary Dawson, with the Carnegie Museum of Natural History, shone light into the recesses of rabbit paleontology, and Barry Richardson, of the University of Western Sydney, helped us sort out our questions about rabbits in Australia. Dana Krempels, a biologist at the University of Miami and also head of Miami HRS, ran the numbers on the rabbit's amazing reproductive prowess.

In the commercial rabbit breeding world we are indebted to the many breeders and processors who took the time to talk and write to us about their operations and their perspectives, including Pat Lamar, Clyde Marsh, Dean Goforth, Bobby Martin, Jennifer Thorn, Corrine Fayo, Eugene Sadler, James McNitt, Steven Edwards and Mark Grobner. Dr. Louis Houdebine of France's National Institute of Agronomic Research also answered our questions on both cloned and glowing rabbits.

We wouldn't even have thought of this book if Marinell Harriman hadn't found a little spotted rabbit in her yard one day back in 1981. Marinell went on to found House Rabbit Society, to write the *House Rabbit Handbook* and to educate many thousands of people about the beauty of rabbits as pets. We also want to acknowledge the contributions of Dr. Carolynn Harvey, who pioneered many medical procedures for domestic rabbits. Without these two forward-thinking women, many of our own rabbits—and thousands of rabbits around the world—would not have lived to be cherished companions.

We are also grateful to Mary Lou Randour, of Psychologists for the Ethical Treatment of Animals, and Carol Adams, editor of *Animals and Women: Feminist Theoretical Explorations*, for initiating the chain of events that led to this book being published by

Lantern Books. We deeply appreciate Martin Rowe's acceptance of our proposal at Lantern, as well as the keen eyes, balanced perspective and enthusiastic support of Sarah Gallogly, our editor there.

A number of people helped us secure images for the book, including Lara Connor of the Australian Companion Rabbit Society; Nancy Freeman of the National Wildlife Research Center; Pam Nave of the Lindsay Wildlife Museum; John Turner, who helped us procure a transparency of a gorgeous Howard Finster painting; and Candace Frazee of The Bunny Museum, who graciously spent an afternoon with us, answering our questions and sharing her life's work. Paul Fussell donated photographs of Margo's rabbits to our work; we very much appreciate his time, skill, and patience with not-always-cooperative rabbits.

Finally, Susan would like to acknowledge her husband, Peter, who for many months put up with her late nights, vacant stares and rambling discourses on all things related to rabbits. Susan also thanks her parents, who taught her early on that pets are truly part of a family, and her children, whose patience allowed her to finish the book and whose impatience made her take much-needed breaks.

Margo thanks her husband, Tom, who has (mostly) graciously put up with living with hundreds of rabbits (not to mention dogs, cats, guinea pigs, rats and birds) over the years, with all the craziness that this entails, as well as her parents, who continue to support and feel proud of their obviously nutty daughter.

TABLE OF CONTENTS

FOREWORD xiii

INTRODUCTION xvii

Part One
PESTS, PETS AND PROFITS
The History of the Domestic Rabbit 1

1. "THE MOST GRACEFUL CUNICULI"
The Wild Rabbit 5

2. "TO SKIP AND GAMBOL LIKE A FAWN"
The Public Life of Rabbits 79

Part Two
WITCHES, WHORES AND TRICKSTERS
Rabbits as Cultural Icons 129

3. "LIKE A GHOSTIE O'ER THE FIELD"
The Rabbit in Ancient Belief 131

4. "TRIX ARE FOR KIDS!"
The Rabbit as Contemporary Icon 169

Part Three
HOPPING DOLLARS
Rabbits as Revenue 225

5. "WHY NOT RABBIT FOR DINNER?"
The Rabbit Meat Industry 229

6. "ERMINE FROM YOUR OWN BACKYARD!"
The Rabbit Fur Industry 265

7. "40 SMOKING RABBITS"
The Vivisection Industry 279

8. HOW MUCH IS THAT RABBIT IN THE WINDOW?
The Pet Rabbit Industry 305

CONCLUSION 327

INDEX 352

FOREWORD

———·•·———

EVEN AS A child, I always felt that an animal who lives in a cage in your house or yard is not your companion; he is more of a slave, confined and forced to live with humans against his will. This is especially true of rabbits, who usually live in backyard cages and historically have been not companions but "units," bred for their fur, or as food for humans or other animals, or to be used in medical or other experiments. Yet over the centuries, historical evidence shows, people have rebelled against this arrangement by bringing rabbits indoors, litter-box training them and allowing them to run free. I tried this myself with a series of rabbits, starting when I was about twelve years old. The house-breaking was surprisingly easy, but a new problem presented itself. All the wires in our house were consumed with consummate skill. This didn't make my parents happy, of course, but somehow we kept getting more rabbits—and losing more wires. Fifty years later, I now know that houses—and especially the electrical wires in them—need to be "bunny proofed," just as parents now "baby proof" their home for young children. But in the 1940s, I was constantly frustrated in my search for more information about rabbits. People just did not know that much about them. Here we are in 2003, and it has taken this long for the first book to be written about rabbits in all their glory, complexity and mystery.

Why has it taken so long? There are two key reasons. First, the limited and often contradictory notions about rabbits that are embedded in our culture (and which these authors explore so fruitfully in this book) have deemed the rabbit an animal unworthy of either respect or research. Second, few people have lived with rabbits in a way that facilitates an intimate understanding of the species. It's only when we live with rabbits the way that we live with cats and dogs—when rabbits sleep on our beds or sprawl out beside us on the floor, when they kiss our children or play ball with them—that we can see what they are truly like. That's because a rabbit who lives her life in a cage does not display much of her true rabbit nature.

It is that intelligent, feeling nature that Susan Davis and Margo DeMello show us so thoughtfully here—a portrait informed not only by the authors' considerable knowledge and experience of life with "house rabbits," but also by their extensive research on the history and habits of the domestic rabbit and its wild forebears. I did not realize, for example, how sociable rabbits naturally are, sometimes hundreds of them living in enormous and complex warrens. How much more lonely must life be for rabbits used in research, deprived of family and friends. Their loneliness may be more intense than what even humans experience, a deeply sobering thought.

Many people who read this book may not know that rabbits are also capable of loving us the same way that other "pets" do, or that rabbits have a sense of humor. As these authors note, rabbits like to get away with something they know we would not approve of. As naughty bunnies skip about, the authors say, "their actions look much like a full-body laugh."

I feel fortunate to have learned of this capacity for rabbit joy firsthand thanks to a rabbit named Hoppel Poppel who joined our family one day in 1997. A homeless man came to our door and said, with tears in his eyes, that he knew I loved animals, he could not explain, but he had to leave this rabbit with us, goodbye. The big white rabbit walked in, sized up the three astonished dogs, and then immediately began chasing the two terrified cats. He so exhausted himself that he flopped onto his side, panting from the exertion, and looked immensely pleased. He had found the right home. The dogs respected him, the cats gave him a wide berth and we were captivated by his charisma and presence. He loved lying in the garden with us, lazily taking in the sights. He also loved racing around the perimeter of the lawn, getting up to higher and higher speeds. (I learned from this book that hares could reach speeds of up to fifty mph, and I believe Hoppel Poppel was not far from that.) And when he finished he would leap crazily in the air for the sheer joy of it. He loved guests, human or otherwise. Nothing fazed him; nothing seemed to displease him either. He was a prince among rabbits, and when we had to leave America for New Zealand, the people who adopted him fell in love with him within days, such was his ability to project pleasure. People would come to see him from everywhere, and leave exclaiming, "I never knew a rabbit could be such fun."

Well, they can, and these two authors know that well and truly, and explain it in loving detail. If you already love rabbits, you will find much to delight you in this book. (You may also find much to make you sad, as the authors spent many months investigating conditions in commercial rabbit industries and the news, I'm afraid, is not good.) If you knew nothing about rabbits before, you may want to live with one. And if you were skeptical about the worth of "mere bunnies," you are likely to leave your reading converted. As Diane Ackerman notes in *The Moon by Whale Light,* ". . . in all honesty, there is no animal that isn't fascinating if viewed up close and in detail. I chose to write about bats, crocodilians, whales, penguins, and such because each would teach me something special about nature and about the human condition." Viewed up close, rabbits, too, are fascinating creatures. How just it is, then, that the rabbit should be presented for the first time, in extended form, in such a fascinating fashion. Read on. I can promise you that you will not be disappointed.

Jeffrey Moussaieff Masson, author, *When Elephants Weep*

Introduction

"A Book on Rabbits?"

A FEW YEARS ago, we met at Margo's house to discuss the whys and wherefores of a book about rabbits. Having lived a long time with these long-eared, short-tailed creatures, we felt we had a lot to say. We knew we were interested in the behavior of the domestic rabbit and how it derived from the behavior of the wild rabbit. (Scores of such books have been written about dogs and cats, but we had found no such books about our favorite species.) We also knew we wanted to write about rabbits living indoors, as true "pets" (as opposed to living outside in hutches, on the margins of petdom), and we knew we wanted to describe what affectionate, beautiful and playful companions rabbits can be.

But we realized that a book about the behavior of rabbits and their viability as indoor pets wouldn't capture everything we wanted to express. So we set up some low beach chairs in Margo's "rabbit room," where twenty-two of the rabbits that Margo fosters live together. This is always a special treat for Susan, who shares her home only with two rabbits, a mere pair compared to Margo's herd. A few rabbits hopped over to see what we were doing. But most of them ignored us, preferring to eat hay, nap with their friends or frolic in their cardboard tubes and houses.

Then Margo brought in banana muffins and tea to fuel our thinking. Suddenly twenty-two rabbit heads jerked up, twenty-two sets of ears tilted forward and twenty-two sets of rabbit nostrils twitched. Moments later, twenty-two rabbits came galloping across the floor to check out the snacks. Most rabbits love bananas, you see, and most rabbits have a sweet tooth, so a banana muffin pleases them as much as it pleases us.

Some rabbits were more assertive than others in asking for their share. Adolph and Jessie sniffed frantically about our legs and arms. Shannon and Maccabee tried to pull the muffins off the table. Trouble circled the group, trying to find a way to get to a muffin while avoiding Maccabee, who seemed intent on chasing him away. Bunilla, Norman and Lavender, all big white rabbits, tried to get their heads into the teacups to sample our tea, while the rest of the rabbits swarmed around our chairs and tried to climb into our laps.

Most people in our culture never experience the joy of sitting in the midst of a herd, gaggle or flock of anything. Our urban and suburban lifestyles sadly cut us off from such direct contact with other species. Many people might even shudder at the idea of being overrun, or perhaps overhopped, by a herd of rabbits clearly gripped by gluttony. But we found it to be a delightful experience, and, as we laughed at their antics, protected our muffins, carefully removed bunny heads from human cups and tried to discourage Maccabee from bullying his roommates, what we needed to write started to come clear. It wasn't just that rabbits are good companions, or that domestic rabbits still display behaviors developed by their wild forebears. It's that rabbits are truly fascinating creatures, with distinct personalities, behaviors and moods—and although rabbits are one of the most popular pets in the United States, few people have any idea what real rabbits are actually like.

In this culture, in fact, many people never come closer to a rabbit than buying a ceramic rabbit for the shelf above the kitchen sink, or reading a rabbity story to their child. Such items are mind-bogglingly easy to find. Gift stores teem with plush rabbits, rabbit figurines and rabbit-oriented clothing (e.g., slippers with rabbit ears and pastel-colored aprons adorned with happy bunnies). Many suburban gardens feature little rabbit statues, plaques or signs. Craft stores sell bunny pillows, bunny hats and bunny wall hangings. Kitchen stores sell bunny dishcloths, bunny pot holders and bunny magnets, and it is impossible to count the number of bunny-oriented books, toys, clothes and decorations marketed for infants and children.

Ironically, most people who buy rabbit *stuff* don't actually want a *real* rabbit in their homes. Rabbits, after all, have traditionally belonged in the barn, or the backyard at best. As Desmond Morris notes in *Dogwatching*, only dogs and cats are allowed to be indoor animals. While historically some farm animals were brought into the home at times for security, they usually were tethered or penned. And while people have long kept fish, birds and reptiles in their homes, they have almost always lived in tanks or cages, "still separated from us by glass or wire or bars," Morris writes. "Only cats and dogs have been permitted to wander from room to room and to come and go almost as they please. With them we have a special relationship, an ancient contract with quite specific terms of agreement."[1]

Yet in recent years, rabbits have become the third animal allowed the freedom of our homes. According to the American Pet Products Manufacturing Association, some 5.3 million pet rabbits now live within 2.2 million American households, up from 3.3 million in 1994.[2] By way of comparison, the American Veterinary Medicine Association, in its 2002 *U.S. Pet Ownership and Demographic Sourcebook*, estimates that the number of horses in this country is only about 4.0 million.[3]

Granted, the number of rabbits living indoors—or "house rabbits" as they're called today—is but a fraction of the total number of pet rabbits in this country. But people who live with indoor rabbits are beginning to realize that these creatures are really quite different than humans have thought for thousands of years—that rather than being "dumb bunnies," or the passive, depressed creatures we see in laboratories, pet stores or rabbit meat "growing" facilities, rabbits are capable of a whole range of behaviors and emotions. Once given their freedom, rabbits will jump, dance, groom, climb, fight, explore, lick, roll on their backs, love, play tag and in general behave in ways no one could imagine by observing them in cages.

Many people who cotton to rabbit kitsch—or even collect real rabbits—idolize the sheer cuteness of the species. But what most rabbit lovers don't realize is that most rabbits don't live particularly cute lives. The majority of the world's rabbits are either bred and slaughtered (for meat and fur) or kept in laboratories (to test everything from sleep deprivation to oven cleaner). Even as pets, rabbits often don't fare well. Typically kept alone in small outdoor hutches, these gregarious animals spend their lives deprived of exercise, medical attention, human or animal contact and, often, appropriate food. Many pet rabbits eventually wind up abandoned in parks, forests and by highways when their "owners," for whatever reason, tire of them; an uncountable number are euthanized in animal shelters for the same reason.

With the exception of protesting eye experiments on rabbits, however, animal protection groups have not done much to improve the lot of rabbits. This is because rabbits play an odd role in this culture. As domesticated "farm" animals, bred to provide a variety of products, rabbits can seem less worthy of concern than either the more "noble" wild animals or the more familiar "pets," like cats and dogs. Yet farm animal protection groups also eschew rabbit work, because, they say, the rabbit meat industry here is so small.

◆   ◆   ◆

Until the publication of Marinell Harriman's pioneering *House Rabbit Handbook*,[4] it's safe to say most people didn't know much about rabbits. They certainly didn't know that rabbits can live freely inside the home, that they can be neutered and litter-box trained, that they like to play, or that they can live, cheek-by-jowl, with other rabbits without fighting. Instead, what people knew of rabbit behavior and care came primarily from a large selection of books on home breeding or keeping rabbits as outdoor pets. Such books are full to the brim with erroneous information about domestic rabbits, because the authors had neither observed domestic rabbits living freely nor truly done their homework about wild rabbit behavior.

Scientific or veterinary materials on rabbit behavior weren't much better, as most were based on laboratory studies. Rabbits can hardly act naturally when caged and subject to constant probing, prodding and medication. In her book *In the Shadow of Man*, which is about the chimpanzees in Tanzania's Gombe National Park, Jane Goodall notes that trying to learn about chimpanzee behavior from a caged chimpanzee is similarly a futile exercise:

> Even those who work closely with (such) chimpanzees, such as zookeepers or research scientists, can have no concept or appreciation of what a chimpanzee really is, which is, perhaps, why so many scientific laboratories maintain chimpanzees in conditions that are appalling, housed singly for the most part in small metal barred cells with nothing to do day in and day out except to await some new, and often terrifying or painful, experiment. Sometimes I feel that the only way in which we might effect an improvement in the condition of most laboratory chimpanzees would be to take those responsible for their upkeep to see the chimpanzees of Gombe.[5]

Studies of wild rabbits provided some information about rabbit behavior, although most of those studies have focused on solving the near-plague levels of rabbits infesting some countries. Ronald Lockley's 1964 book *The Private Life of the Rabbit* is one of the few popular books written about the wild rabbit. Yet even some of his original observations came from his attempt to "exterminate" (in his words) the wild rabbits on Skokholm Island, off Great Britain, so that he could raise domestic, fur-bearing chinchilla rabbits there instead. Although his very zealous trapping, poisoning, ferreting and snaring extravaganza failed there, he later set up a rabbit observation system in Pembrokeshire, and wrote, very affectionately, about the wild rabbit behavior he observed.

Lockley provided valuable insights into wild behaviors like chinning, pellet marking, tunneling and circling—behaviors still evident in domestic rabbits. Lockley's work also illuminated life in and around a rabbit warren. But information on the behavior of solitary domestic rabbits (which is the condition of most pet rabbits), or even groups of domestic rabbits, remains sorely lacking. This paucity is particularly odd given the thousands of years that rabbits have shared a relationship with humans.

Popular culture is certainly no help. Even a cursory look at contemporary rabbit iconography reveals an animal that is generally cute, sweet, cuddly and fond of carrots. Some of these stereotypes are true: real rabbits are cute (or gorgeous), can be sweet, often like carrots and generally like to cuddle (but usually on the floor, not on the lap). But rabbits can be much, much more than that. They can be smart or dull, athletic or lazy, patient or impulsive, affectionate or aloof. They can be worriers like Big Bear or careful planners like Timothy. Bosco is a micromanager, always needing to have his paws in everything. Wormguy, a much loved angora, seemed like a Zen Buddhist monk, spending his time examining the nature of Mind. Maccabee, as we've seen, is something of a bully. Phoebe was very forgiving. Elmo was fiercely loyal to his humans. Maybelline doesn't like to be told what to do. Cocoa is a real ladies' man.

Can animals really have such personalities? There's strident debate now on whether or not animals of any species have any emotions at all. Those biologists who still hold that there is an essential difference between humans (who think and feel) and animals (who, presumably, cannot) would say no, that animals are governed entirely by their genes, with little room for individual agency or self-determination. But a whole gaggle of writers and animal behaviorists, including Jane Goodall, Vicki Hearne, Jeffrey Masson and Elizabeth Marshall Thomas are beginning to challenge this approach. Those authors are moving away from such generalizing statements as "chimpanzees are patriarchal," "dogs are hierarchical" or "rabbits are territorial" and focusing instead on the richness and variety of attributes that may be found within an animal species. This variety, in turn, is part of what we perceive as "personality" in an animal—and it's something people who live and work with animals take for granted.

❖   ❖   ❖

This has not been an easy book to write. Among friends and family, news that we were writing a book on rabbits was generally met with awkward silence, quizzical glances, and nervous smiles. One woman in Susan's writing group even burst out laughing when she heard the news. Later, she offered, snickering, "Well, rabbits like sex, and people like sex, so who doesn't like rabbits?" In fact, our hypothesis is that while almost everyone does like rabbits—or at least the more popular images of them—most people also deem these creatures unworthy of respect, compassion or study. As one friend who questioned the book's purpose noted, "I like rabbits. I've just never really cared about them."

Some of the research that went into this book was academic; we pored through scholarly studies of rabbits in the wild and carefully weighed the many arguments in the current debate on animal consciousness and animal welfare. Some of our research involved delving into the annals of popular culture—dissecting ancient symbols, reading rabbit folk tales, watching movies and cartoons with rabbit characters and analyzing children's books—as one of our goals was to look at the rabbit as a symbol, packed with cultural meaning, and its role in human society. Much of our research also involved gathering information on the commercial rabbit industries—by interviewing breeders and processors, searching historical records and monitoring industry group "chats" on the Internet.

A good portion of our research, however, involved old-fashioned animal watching (what Margo, trained in anthropology, calls "participant-observation" and what Susan, trained as a journalist, calls simply "hanging out with the locals"). That is, the majority of what we know about rabbits and their complex behavior comes from hours upon hours spent watching our own rabbits, whose every gesture, expression and vocalization tells us a story about the broad range of their personalities and histories. A skittish rabbit with sad eyes, found in a city park, for instance, tells us of the sorrow and terror of being abandoned in a wide-open, seemingly wild area. A confident rabbit, who hops up to us when we come home and lounges on the couch when we watch TV, tells us how secure and happy an indoor rabbit can become. A temperamental rabbit, who thumps when shooed from the closet, then leaps with joy at the sight of his food bowl, shows us that rabbits, just like humans, can have passionate mood swings. A sick rabbit, who struggles against being force fed but then licks our hands when we're done, shows that rabbits can feel grateful. An abused rabbit, who lunges to bite us, or chases us across the room, shows us that rabbits can fight back, that they can even hold a grudge. And when this same rabbit learns not to bite, discovering instead the joys of racing around the room, sprawling on the floor and feeling the touch of a human hand, she shows us that rabbits can learn to trust. All of these rabbits teach us that animals don't have to be the distant Other, but can be creatures who connect to us in very real, very profound ways.

◆　◆　◆

So, why a book on rabbits? Our primary purpose is to explain some of the roots and nuances of rabbit behavior, so that the reader can understand and appreciate what subtle—and interesting—creatures these animals truly are. We hope to deconstruct some misconceptions about rabbits, like the ideas that they are dumb, timid, only interested in mating, or that rabbits, like other animals, are incapable of experiencing emotions like jealousy, remorse, joy, terror, love or hate. We also want to reveal some of the history of the commercial rabbit industries, as well as the way that they operate today, in hopes that some practices can be improved.

In an article on animals and ethics, Linda Vance, a widely respected eco-feminist, writes, "A good narrative should give voice to those whose stories are being told."[6] How does one give voice to an animal who cannot speak? Research, observation, rumination and intuition all play a role in creating a worthy text. But, as Vance notes:

[T]he test, I think, for determining whether the voice we give to animals is accurate will lie in the behavior it calls forth from humans. If an animal's "voice" dictates action that serves human ends but compromises the animal, we had best try listening more carefully. . . . A good narrative should make us care.[7]

That is perhaps the very most apt answer to the question of why we would write so much on such a small, seemingly common mammal. We want people to care—and we know caring will only come through greater insight into this very beautiful, sensitive and mysterious animal.

Notes

1. Morris, Desmond, *Dogwatching* (New York: Crown Books, 1986), p. 1.
2. "2001–2002 National Pet Owner Survey," American Pet Product Manufacturing Association.
3. AVMA, "The Truth About Cats and Dogs: AVMA Study Uncovers the Nation's Pet Ownership Trends," April 24, 2002.
4. Harriman, Marinell. *House Rabbit Handbook: How to Live with an Urban Rabbit,* 1st edition (Alameda, CA: Drollery Press, 1985).
5. Goodall, Jane. *In the Shadow of Man* (Boston: Houghton-Mifflin, 1988), pp. 256–257.
6. Vance, Linda, "Beyond Just-So Stories: Narratives, Animals and Ethics," in Adams, Carol and Josephine Donovan (eds.), *Animals and Women: Feminist Theoretical Explorations* (Durham: Duke University Press, 1995), p. 182.
7. *Ibid.,* p. 183.

PART ONE

PESTS, PETS AND PROFITS

The History of the Domestic Rabbit

———·•·———

WILD RABBITS INHABIT a strange niche in the world's animal culture, at least as that niche is viewed through human eyes. While we respect most wild animals for their very "wildness," we tend to project pet rabbit qualities onto wild rabbits. Ronald Lockley, a British biologist who wrote a now-classic book on wild rabbit behavior, *The Private Life of the Rabbit*, even went so far as to equate the appeal of pet and wild rabbits. "Like children," he wrote, "the rabbits in garden, field and hutch endear themselves to us by their innocent, happy preoccupation with their simple way of living."[1]

Endearment doesn't guarantee much in the animal world, however. Humans may be instinctually attracted to these "happy," "simple" wild creatures, but they also kill them for their meat and their luxurious pelts. Wild rabbits are the primary game species in America and many countries of Europe; the wild rabbits killed for meat, fur or sport each year worldwide number in the tens of millions. Most farmers and many conservationists also despise wild rabbits. That's not because the rabbit is a lethal animal; bunnies don't kill livestock, maul humans in the bush or even knock over garbage cans. However, rabbits do have a love for vegetation, and when they're transported from their native landscape to a new one, they can become very invasive and very destructive. This capacity for destroying crops and trees has led humans around the world to try to eradicate this "endearing" creature altogether, via poisoning, trap-

1

ping, shooting, drowning, erecting giant fences—even by engaging in biological warfare.

This trio of wild rabbit roles—happy-go-lucky, endearing creature, valuable game species and invasive pest—has led to some odd treatment by humans. In Britain, for instance, the wild rabbit is protected as game yet reviled as a pest, and both government agencies and individual farmers have periodically waged campaigns of destruction against rabbit colonies.[2] In France, the man who introduced the deadly myxoma virus to the country's wild rabbit population was first fined by a hunters' group and then given a medal by a grateful foresters' group. Lockley himself praised rabbits for being "as curious and as stimulated by the actions of their own species as any other animal with a mammalian brain, including man";[3] later he added, "Rabbits are so human, or is it the other way round—humans are so rabbit?"[4] Yet he blithely killed tens of thousands of wild rabbits on his property when he wanted to replace them with domestic Chinchilla rabbits.[5]

There is another odd feature about the wild rabbit. Despite this culture's love of nature tales—whether they're in the form of televised documentaries, magazine articles or coffee table books and calendars—and despite our clear love of the idea of bunnies, it's hard to find information on the natural history of the wild rabbit. So far, no one has produced a nature documentary on the wild rabbit—perhaps because the animal is so common. Nor has anyone produced a coffee table book, although the potential exists for stunning photographs of wild rabbits in their many varied habitats. And although the scientific literature on wild rabbits is fairly voluminous, most of that research has been undertaken in Australia and the United Kingdom, where it is aimed at controlling the damage done to agriculture by rabbit populations run amok.[6]

What's more, anyone who defends the wild rabbit as an animal of interest in its own right—or who raises an eyebrow at the mass slaughters enacted periodically by various governments—is viewed as something of a sentimentalist. In his introduction to *The European Rabbit*, Henry Thompson writes that "there are always some voices to be heard in defense of rabbits, if only because of the small but persisting value of rabbit meat and pelts, and the lingering influence of Beatrix Potter."[7] Thompson's very academic book is the only one written in recent years about wild rabbits, and Thompson is widely respected as a scholar in the field of wild rabbits. Yet even he dismisses the idea that the rabbit might be worthy of respect or interest, beyond its status as a revenue producer and storybook hero. Similarly, when Susan was studying journal articles about wild rabbits at the Biosciences Library of the University of California, Berkeley, another library patron happened to walk by and notice a picture of a jackrabbit on one page. He looked down at Susan and said, "Awww, looking at little bunnies, are we?" It's hard to imagine someone taking a similarly condescending tone toward a researcher examining illustrations of, say, dinosaurs, wolves or snowy plovers.

But the wild rabbit, like most any wild creature, displays a variety of behaviors and characteristics that make it a fascinating creature in its own right: complex social systems, intricate communication methods, odd biological quirks and a tenacious ability to survive and reproduce despite the worst of odds. In fact, the wild rabbit can teach us plenty about how we as humans can simultaneously love, hate and be totally ignorant about one species of animal, and how those opposite reactions can lead to wildly contradictory human behaviors.

Notes

1. Lockley, R.M., *The Private Life of Rabbits* (London: Corgi Books, 1954), p. 13.
2. Thompson, Henry, *The European Rabbit: The History and Biology of a Successful Colonizer* (New York: Oxford University Press, 1994), pp. 93–97.
3. Lockley, *op. cit.*, p. 78.
4. *Ibid.*, p. 64.
5. *Ibid.*, p. 79.
6. Chapman, Joseph, "Introduction and Overview of the Lagomorphs," in Chapman, J.A. and John E.C. Flux (eds.), *Rabbits, Hares, and Pikas: Status Survey and Conservation Action Plan* (Oxford: International Union for the Conservation of Nature and Natural Resources, 1990), p. 4.
7. Thompson, *op. cit.*, p. xv.

1. "The Most Graceful Cuniculi"

The Wild Rabbit

———

All things that love the sun are out of doors;
The sky rejoices in the morning's birth;
The grass is bright with rain-drops;—on the moors
The hare is running races in her mirth;
And with her feet she from the plashy earth
Raises a mist, that glittering in the sun,
Runs with her all the way, wherever she doth run.

William Wordsworth, from "All Things That Love the Sun"

ON A HILLSIDE near Susan's home, a herd of black-tailed jackrabbits (*Lepus californicus*) has taken up residence. These are shy creatures, most often spotted as they bound up the hill, away from whatever perceived predator—biker, mother with stroller, canine—happens to be passing on the path below. But sometimes, early in the morning or around dusk, a still and patient observer can watch these creatures grazing, lying quietly or sitting up on their back feet to sniff the breeze, their long black-tipped ears arching gorgeously skyward, their dun-colored fur blending perfectly with the dry grass on this windswept hillside.

Last summer, as Susan crouched in the grass to watch the jackrabbits, a father stopped by with two young boys. "Look, Daddy!" shouted the younger one, who looked to be about five years

Figure 1.1. Like all members of the family Leporidae, the black-tailed jackrabbit is built for dashing away from predators. Photo by Elaine Friedman.

old. The sudden sound sent three jackrabbits leaping into the air and vaulting across the hill. "Bunnies! Can we catch one for a pet?" The father sternly replied, "No, we're not having bunnies as pets." Susan, moved by a maternal urge to make peace, added, "They're actually wild rabbits, so they're happier out here." And the older boy, who was perhaps eight, said, "Yeah, but they'd still make good pets."

It was a classic boys-see-pet, boys-want-pet conversation. But it was also indicative of a widespread confusion in our culture. Most Americans don't realize that the domestic rabbits kept as pets and the wild rabbits bounding about in local forests, meadows and deserts are very different creatures. In fact, the groups are barely related. The domesticated pet rabbit is of the genus *Oryctolagus* and the species *cuniculus*, and is commonly known as the "European rabbit," because it is native to that continent. The fourteen species of wild rabbits and the four species of hares in America belong to the genera *Sylvilagus* and *Lepus*, respectively.

Members of these three genera look very similar; most of them have long ears, fluffy tails and big back feet—although a few species, like the volcano rabbit (*Romerolagus diazi*) and the pygmy rabbit

(*Brachylagus idahoensis*), have rather short, round ears and short legs. But their lives are very different. The *Sylvilagus* species, commonly known as "cottontails," live in brush or rocky outcroppings while hares prefer open ground (like forest clearings or alpine meadows) and the European rabbit lives in complex, underground warrens. *Oryctolagus* even means "digging hare" in Latin (although the European rabbit is truly a rabbit, not a hare) and *cuniculus* means "underground passage."

The Romans used that same word to describe the underground passages and mines they built to attack city-states, but whether the Romans named the mines after the rabbits or the rabbits after the mines is unknown. We do know, however, that by the second century B.C.E., Polybios, the Greek historian, had described rabbits on Corsica as "the most graceful cuniculi."[1] We also know that all of today's vernacular names for rabbits in central Europe are derived from the Latin cuniculus, including the Italian *coniglio*, the Spanish *conejo*, Portuguese *coelho*, Belgian *konin*, Danish and Swedish *kaning*, German *kaninchen*, Old French *connin*, and Old English *conyng* and *coney*.[2]

Rabbits and hares also differ in that the latter are more adapted to running rapidly across open ground; they have longer legs and feet, plus wider nose openings, which helps them take in more oxygen. Hare babies are born with fur and open eyes, while rabbits are born naked and with eyes squeezed shut, which necessitates longer care in their nests.[3] In addition, hares tend to be bigger than either wild European rabbits or cottontails and have long, arched bodies. In addition, both cottontails and hares are solitary, whereas the European rabbit lives in social groups of two to three and is considered a "gregarious" animal.

Most laypeople also think that wild rabbits are rodents, due perhaps to their big, curved front teeth, which remind people of other gnawing rodents, like rats and beavers. But rabbits and hares belong to the Leporidae family, which is part of the order Lagomorpha. That order also includes the Ochotonidae family, which consists of twenty-five species of pikas: small, roundish mammals with short ears, most commonly found in Asia and western North America.

Linnaeus, the Swedish botanist who invented our modern classification system, was the first to say that rabbits are rodents. But biologists kicked rabbits, hares and pikas out of the order Rodentia in 1912, due to dental distinctions. That is, although rabbits, hares and pikas all have buck teeth, they also have a second set of incisors, called "peg" teeth, directly behind their upper front incisors,[4] which rodents don't have. This anatomical difference—albeit a small one— is just significant enough for rabbits, hares and pikas to merit their own taxonomic clan—although biologists continued to lump rodents and lagomorphs into a "super order" called "Glires."

But even that distant-cousin clumping may no longer be appropriate. In 1996, Dan Graur, a zoologist at Tel Aviv University, published a study in *Nature* showing that according to DNA analysis, rabbits are actually more akin to primates and tree shrews (order Scandentia) than to rodents. In fact, the article claimed, after tree shrews and flying lemurs, primates are closer to lagomorphs than to any other mammalian order. When asked about his findings in 2002, Graur was less definite, saying, in an email correspondence, that the evidence seemed to fluctuate and that he "wouldn't put too much faith at this point on molecular data since rabbits are quite underrepresented in that regard."[5] Still, the idea that lagomorphs could be genetically akin to humans is rather tantalizing, especially given this culture's love/hate relationship with these long-eared creatures.

The more recent origin and evolution of the European rabbit is somewhat murky, in part because this species is a burrowing animal, which means that its fossils are often found in deeper—or, in temporal terms, earlier—strata than would be the case if the animal lived and died above ground. In addition, rabbit skulls are light and easily crushed, and so only mere fragments—a tooth here, a shard of skull there—exist in most fossil records.[6] These can be harder to date, even using radiocarbon techniques, than larger skeletal pieces.

Conventional wisdom among lagomorphologists and paleontologists, however, is that today's hares and rabbits are descended from a rabbity-looking creature called Alilepus, which first appeared in North America in the mid-Miocene period. Eight million years later, Alilepus appeared in Europe and Asia, presumably having crossed land bridges to get to these areas. In Iberia, a bounty of rabbit fossils exists from the late to middle Pleistocene period, some 500,000 years ago. This puts rabbits hopping about during the Lower Paleolithic period, or the earliest period of human development, when pre-humans known as *Homo erectus* still subsisted as hunter-gatherers using very rudimentary tools. Records in southern France have been dated to 200,000 to 300,000 years ago, as have fossil records from around Swanscombe, Kent, in Great Britain.

The next records in England don't show up until the twelfth century C.E., during the Norman period. These rabbits had most likely been brought to the island by humans. This gap in wild rabbit populations has led some biologists to allege that a creature resembling the wild European rabbit lived throughout central and western Europe during pre-Pleistocene times, but that the creature probably died out during the last glaciation of the region, some ten thousand years ago, except for a small population that remained in Iberia, which was slightly warmer.

Written records about wild rabbits date back to three thousand years ago, when the Phoenicians first noted their abundance in Iberia. "Hispania," in fact, is the Latinized version of the Phoenician "Ishepan-in," which means "Land of the Shephan." The "shephan," in turn, is the Phoenician word for hyrax, an animal with which the Phoenicians confused the rabbit at first. The two animals actually aren't related—in fact, hyraxes are more closely related to elephants than they are to lagomorphs—but the name stuck and is the root, of course, of both "Hispanic" and "Spain."

Today, the family Leporidae includes ten genera and twenty-four species of rabbits, plus twenty-nine species of Lepus, or hare genera, and twenty-five species of pikas. The hares and rabbits themselves inhabit every continent from Africa to Australia, every climate from the equator to the Arctic and every altitude from sea level to the high mountains. And while many of the rabbits and hares behave in stereotypical rabbit fashion (e.g., they hop, they nibble and they twitch their noses), some behave in surprisingly unrabbitlike ways. The swamp rabbit, for instance, which is the largest cottontail and can weigh as much as ten pounds, has waterproof fur and can swim and dive with great skill. It was a swamp rabbit, by the way, that allegedly went after President Jimmy Carter in April, 1979, while he was fishing in Plains, Georgia. According to one press account, the big bunny "was hissing menacingly, its teeth flashing and nostrils flared and making straight for the president." Depending on which account you believe, the president defended himself valiantly—either by bonking the rabbit on the head with his paddle or splashing water at him. Poor Carter got a lot of ribbing about the story, as some cynics claimed rabbits can't swim and don't attack people—two statements even fanciers of domestic rabbits can tell you are false. To settle the question, Carter got the photo blown up to identify his assailant. This didn't help; when the press got hold of the story, it really blew up, with all sorts of columns and cartoons poking fun at the beleagured leader. Carter's press secretary, Jody Powell, who originally leaked the story to the media, wrote later that columnist George Will even linked Carter's timid response to the "killer rabbit" to the failed assault on the embassy in Tehran.[7]

Marsh rabbits, which are different from swamp rabbits, have no tails, but have extra large feet that allow them to move easily over marshland. (One subspecies of marsh rabbit, the *Sylvilagus palustris hefneri*, is even named after Hugh Hefner, who founded Playboy magazine and sent the Playboy Bunny leaping into the American male imagination.) Brush rabbits can climb trees, as can Audubon's cottontails and Nuttall's cottontails (the latter, in fact, are considered "semi-arboreal").[8] The fur of the snowshoe hare, the arctic hare, the white-tailed jackrabbit and the Japanese hare changes to white in the winter, so that it blends in with the snow. The snowshoe hare also has heavily furred toes that separate widely to allow it to run over fluffy snow.

While it seems like wild rabbits are everywhere (especially if you live in an area with a wild rabbit problem), some rabbit and hare

Figure 1.2. The marsh rabbit, which is slightly smaller than other cottontails, prefers to live in swampy or marshy land, or even flooded agricultural lands. Like the swamp rabbit, the marsh rabbit is a good swimmer. Photo by Scott Hein.

species are actually very rare. The volcano rabbit, for instance, lives in only three sites on the slopes of four volcanoes in central Mexico.[9] The Sumatran rabbit has only been seen once since 1916. The Hainan hare is found only on Hainan Island off the coast of South China. The black jackrabbit is found only on Espiritu Santo Island along Mexico's Baja Peninsula; the Tres Marias cottontail lives only on the Tres Marias Islands, also in Mexico.

Similarly, the New England cottontail is currently endangered, both because of habitat loss (as farms, with their brushy borders, are replaced by woodlands) and because hunters introduced the eastern cottontail into the New England cottontail's habitat in the 1930s, to provide more hunting game. When humans introduced the snowshoe hare in Newfoundland, it pushed the native arctic hare from its forest habitat.[10] The *hefneri* marsh rabbit and the swamp rabbit are both disappearing due to habitat loss and hunting, as is the hispid hare, whose range once stretched along the tall grasslands of northern India and southern Nepal. Those grasslands have been decimated by agricultural and forestry projects, as well as overgrazing.[11] The same is true for the pygmy rabbit, which lives in very dense sage-

Figure 1.3. The introduction of the eastern cottontail (*Sylvilagus floridanus*) is now endangering the native New England cottontail throughout much of the northeast. Courtesy U.S. Fish & Wildlife Service.

brush in the western United States, much of which has been wiped out for crops and livestock grazing.[12] (The U.S. Fish and Wildlife Service estimates that only 30 Columbia Basin pygmy rabbits, a subspecies found in Washington state, are still alive.) The most primitive lagomorph, the Amani rabbit in Japan, is also endangered, again due to habitat destruction. This rabbit is considered a "living fossil" because its shape is so similar to fossil species from the Miocene era.[13]

These are animals that most people have never heard of, in spite of their endangered status, and that very few mainstream conservation organizations have targeted as worthwhile subjects for conservation. As Ken Myers, a rabbit researcher in Australia, has written, "Lagomorphs are relatively small mammals and do not excite the curiosity and appeal of some of their larger kind."[14] Yet a number of researchers have determined that without the rabbit, which is a crucial prey species inhabiting the bottom of many food chains, entire ecosystems can get thrown out of whack. From an ecological perspective, then, wild rabbits are actually a valuable resource—not just a "happy" wild creature that's also fun to shoot.

A Morphology of Prey

Most rabbit and hare species actually look similar: they have longish ears, shortish tails and powerful hindquarters. These exaggerated features contribute to the animal's broad appeal in storybooks and bunny collectibles. But the truth is, much of that seemingly adorable shape is owing to the fact that rabbits, especially young rabbits, do indeed provide tasty snacks for a wide range of creatures the world over, including foxes, hawks, badgers, owls, eagles, cats and dogs. As such, their form has evolved to allow them to first perceive and then flee their many predators.

Indeed, life is a risky business for most wild rabbits. Mortality rates for warrens can reach as much as ninety percent annually.[15] The average life span for a wild rabbit is a mere two years, with death usually coming from predators, viral infections, injuries, disease and agricultural operations, like mowing and harvesting, which seem to be particularly hazardous for young rabbits.[16] Put another way, wild European rabbits between the ages of four and eight months have only about a fifty percent chance of surviving at all.[17]

The species partly compensates for its vulnerability with its infamous reproductive powers. Female rabbits (called "does") are "induced ovulators," which is to say that they don't actually ovulate until they have mated (and then usually not until about ten hours after copulation). This keeps them from wasting energy by releasing eggs that have no chance of being fertilized. It also means that they are technically fertile all the time.[18] Rabbit literature is full of reports of females that mate the same day—even the same hour—they give birth. Since gestation takes about thirty days, this means that a female potentially can have about one litter per month. In the wild, however, female rabbits have definite "breeding seasons" that correlate with the vegetative growing season and ambient temperatures. (Researchers believe the females need the estrogens found in green plants to both maintain their pregnancies and support their lactation, while high temperatures reduce the rates of conception, the number of litters and the number of "kitlings," or "kits," born alive.[19]) Those breeding seasons range from four months a year in northern latitudes to nine months in New Zealand, so it's more typical for wild European rabbits to have just three or four litters per year, although some do have more.

An average litter contains four or five kits, so a typical female can produce a grand total of twelve to forty-five young per year. Males (also called "bucks") and females reach sexual maturity between four and eight months of age, depending on their location. It doesn't take a rocket scientist (or a rabbit scientist, for that matter) to figure out that in one year, just one breeding pair can create a lot of rabbits. That is, if a female rabbit starts reproducing at the age of six months and bears one litter per month, she'll create, over the course of the first year, 36 female rabbits. At the age of six months, each of those female rabbits in turn, can produce another three females, each of whom will start reproducing at six months, so by the end of the second year you'd have 1,332 female rabbits (plus the original 37, of course). If all those rabbits lived to three years of age and reproduced as bunnies tend to do, by the end of three years you'd have 47,952 female babies. These figures are dicey, because lots of wild rabbits start reproducing at four months—not six—which makes for even more kits. But most wild rabbits don't bear young every month, which makes for less. Still, the general idea here is that the rabbit's ability to create more rabbits is breathtaking, if not a little spooky. (By the way, rabbits aren't the most prolific beasts in the kingdom; rats and mice can produce even more offspring.)

The fact that wild European rabbits are nocturnal—which means that they emerge from their warrens to eat and frolic from dusk until dawn, when their brownish or blackish fur is hard to see—also protects them from predators. (During the rest of the day they mostly nap, often with their eyes open.) The eyes are large, allowing them to see well in dim light, and placed high and to the sides of the skull (in contrast to our forward-placed eyes). This gives them close to 360-degree vision, which, combined with the fact that their long-distance vision is very acute, means that they can see predators coming from afar—whether it's a fox creeping up from one side or a hawk swooping down from on high. (Other lagomorph species—and most domestic European rabbits—seem to be "crepuscular" or most active at dawn and dusk.)

A very smart, small predator, however, would walk right towards a rabbit's nose, because rabbits have a blind spot of about ten degrees right in front of them. They also have poor depth perception. Rabbits make up for this visual weakness by bobbing their heads up and down when they see a new object, which makes an up-close object appear to move more than an object that is distant. This technique, called "parallax," allows rabbits to judge just how close that dog-shaped log is or just what sort of creature yon giant tractor might be.

Rabbits' long, funnel-shaped ears are built for detecting the sounds of predators. These ears can move around in many different directions—both ears pointing forward, both ears cocked backward, one ear pointing forward and the other one covering the rear, even one ear to one side and the other ear to the other side. The ears also serve as biological air conditioners, as they are the only body parts from which rabbits can radiate heat. (Rabbits don't pant like dogs or sweat like horses, so they need some other way of dispelling heat.) This mechanism is so efficient that, in Australia, rabbit ears actually grow longer in hotter seasons to facilitate heat control.[20]

Hares, by the way, have an exaggerated prey morphology—their ears are much longer than those of rabbits, their hearts are bigger, they have more dark muscle with myoglobin (which is better for sustained running), their eyes are larger and their legs are longer. This is because hares live on open ground, where they are more vulnerable to predation and so need to be able to see—and bound rapidly—across the terrain.[21] If you've never had the opportunity to see these hauntingly beautiful animals up close, "The Hare," painted by German artist Albrecht Dürer in 1502, perfectly depicts this animal's form. One of the first self-contained nature studies ever completed, this watercolor shows the long, lean lines of the hare's body, as well as its oversized ears, wild "agouti" coloring and powerful haunches. In that particular study, the hare's eyes are slightly closed, as if the

Figure 1.4. The gorgeous head and almost human-like eye of the hare inspired many ancient people to believe that hares had supernatural powers. Photo by Brian Murphy.

animal is relaxing, but its posture and ears remain alert—a common pose for wild and domestic rabbits alike.

Many species of rabbits and hares will "freeze" when they sense danger. That is, they'll flatten themselves against the ground, sometimes for as long as fifteen minutes. Yet it is the long hind legs and big back feet—both adapted to hopping and bounding—that most characterize the rabbit's prey status. According to biomechanist Rachel Simons, who has studied the gait of the rabbit, the hop is actually a "half bound," in which the hind legs come up together to overtake the forelegs, which then fall on the ground in succession. In fact, if you listen to a rabbit hopping across a wood floor, you can hear a 1–2–3 beat, as first the hind legs, and then one front leg, and then the next, strike the ground. In *The Tale of Peter Rabbit*, Beatrix Potter conveys this rhythm with the delightful "lippity-lippity"; in *Watership Down*, Richard Adams describes the rabbit's gait with the equally apt word "lolloping."

Using two big feet together allows for maximum acceleration, Simons says, which is important for prey animals. Rabbits, in fact, can go as fast as forty kilometers per hour (about twenty-five miles per hour) over short distances; hares can reach speeds of up to eighty kph (about fifty mph). The half bound also permits rabbits to change direction quickly in what appears to be a crazy zigzag pattern but is actually an excellent way of eluding a fox in the wild (or a human in the house).

Simons, by the way, is one of the very few researchers in the world who has studied the biomechanics of rabbits. She suspects there are two reasons for the dearth of information on the beloved hop. First, rabbits are a little hard to handle on a treadmill, where most animal gaits are studied, because rabbits can be high-strung. (She spent hours getting her rabbits used to a treadmill in her laboratory so she could accurately analyze their gaits.) And second, rabbits, being small mammals, are not as glamorous as horses, antelope or sheep—common objects of biomechanical study—nor are they as dramatic as creatures like millipedes, which have between ninety and three hundred legs to organize.

The cuteness of the hop belies the actual power that rabbits have in their long back feet and springy hindquarters. Some species of hares can leap twenty feet in a single bound; one observer claimed he saw cottontails leaping as far as fifteen feet while challenging a male intruder.[22] No reports of vertical leaping abilities seem to be available in the literature, but domestic European rabbits have been known to leap onto chair backs and over four-foot-high gates.

Unlike many other mammals, most rabbits and hares don't have several gaits from which to choose. Horses and dogs, for instance, have a distinct walk, trot and lope, in which the legs move very differently; horses also have a fourth gait, a gallop. On occasion, rabbits do a modified walk, or creep: they use their hind feet and forefeet separately to crawl under a table or fence or to investigate something threatening. The marsh rabbit doesn't hop at all; it moves by either walking or swimming. Some arctic hare populations can actually hop on their hind feet, like kangaroos[23]—although rabbits and kangaroos are not related, as rabbits are placental mammals and kangaroos are marsupials. But in general, rabbits have just two ways of moving: hopping and hopping very fast.

There is also what might be termed "hopping like crazy," which isn't a defense but is based on prey-like behavior—just as the rough-and-tumble play of dogs and cats is based on predator behavior. Wild rabbits who are happy channel all their excess energy into spurts of hopping, leaping, rolling and scurrying about in mad, seemingly spastic patterns. Sometimes they leap up in the air in a virtual capriole and then do a full-body shake before they land again; other times they spin or twist themselves halfway around in mid-air. One researcher observed that a whole warren of wild European rabbits twice started this frantic shimmying just before storms: "[A] kind of craziness seemed to permeate the whole population," he wrote. "Young rabbits would frisk and leap in the air, while others would hurtle headlong around the enclosure, scattering various groups to right and left; still others would be rolling on their backs in the sandy earth and kicking their legs in the air like playful dogs."[24] In *The Private Life of the Rabbit,* Lockley described similar behavior in one elderly male European rabbit: "The buck rabbit . . . suddenly frisked," he wrote, "gave a little jump into the air, twisting sideways so as to come down facing half backwards. He then ran easily in a wide circle around the warren. . . . [He] gave another jump into the air. He ran to some dry ash from the burnt stump of a tree and suddenly rolled in it, like a cat in dry earth."[25]

Because rabbits are prey, humans have coined a number of phrases that use the word "rabbit" as an insult. In the Middle Ages, for instance, the word "rabbit" referred to a fearful soldier. Leonardo da Vinci noted that rabbits are even scared of falling leaves. What's interesting is that the rabbit's shape—its powerful legs, its acutely sensitive sensory apparatus, its finely honed startle reflex and a flight pattern based on outwitting would-be predators—could be seen as an exquisite adaptation to prey status. But most things having to do with prey are not much valued by big, bold predator humans. Animals that fight, like sharks, bears and wolves, attract us; animals that flee, like rabbits and timid songbirds, repel us or attract us only by virtue of their seemingly "childlike" nature.

Rabbit Relations

Jumping about, lolling about and hopping about are all very rabbity things to do; most people would recognize that behavior as being bunny-like, although some might misinterpret rabbit shimmying as some sort of fit. But whether rabbits are getting ready to attack, to mate or simply to establish a territorial claim, they also communicate in far more subtle ways.

Much rabbit relating, for instance, occurs via scents emitted from glands under the chin and tail. Rabbits will often "mark" new territory by rubbing the underside of their chins on trees, branches, rocks, blades of grass and each other. This, action, called "chinning," makes a new place smell like home. Chinning also makes established turf smell more like the rabbit in residence—which is handy when an unfamiliar rabbit arrives on the scene. Males tend to have more secretions than females;[26] some males secrete so much, in fact, that their chins become yellow and matted.

Male rabbits seem to derive psychological "confidence" from chinning with their submandibular glands,[27] but just how often a male rabbit performs this behavior—and just how much scent he secretes—depends on several factors, including social rank, testosterone levels and reproductive activity. Female marking, on the other hand, depends on other factors, like day length and the gender of other rabbit markers. Studies have shown, in fact, that female domestic rabbits can discriminate between chin marks of different rabbits and that they respond more (i.e., they chin more) when confronted with the scent of unfamiliar animals.[28] Those of us who live with domestic rabbits have seen this behavior over and over again—a strange rabbit is brought into the home and the resident rabbits start chinning everything in sight, from shoes to chair legs, from doorjambs to toys, and from litter boxes to infant car seats. Some male rabbits even try to chin the female with whom they want to mate and will chase her around the room with their chin resting on her back.

Rabbits also have very powerful glands under their tails, from which they emit a musky odor when they're in the mood to mate. Rabbits use these same glands—which actually coat feces as they pass through the rectum—to mark territory. Evidence seems to show that rabbits with bigger anal glands, like rabbits with bigger chin glands, tend to have greater social status and to be sexually dominant.

Both male and female rabbits also mark their territory with urine and droppings. Rabbits actually have two kinds of droppings: "fecal" pellets and "cecal" pellets. The fecal pellets are the small, hard, round, brown droppings with which most people are familiar. The softer cecal pellets, also called night droppings, rarely make it to the ground, as the rabbit ingests these directly out of the anus.

Biologists call this seemingly unsavory act "coprophagy," and over the years it has gotten a pretty bad reputation. In the Bible, God tells Moses not to eat hares because, like rock badgers and camels, they chew their own cud but don't "part the hoof," which makes them unclean (Leviticus 11:4; Deuteronomy 14:7). But while we may not care to indulge, or even watch other animals indulge, there are sound biological reasons for this particular habit. Those grape-like clusters of cecal pellets, which are coated with a thin membrane, contain a rich mixture of B vitamins and protein. That means that even in poor feeding areas or difficult feeding times, rabbits can get the nourishment they need. And if rabbits need to lie low for long periods of time—whether it's due to bad weather or a lurking predator—the re-ingestion process allows them to essentially get two meals in one.

Here's how it works: after chewing, say, a big mouthful of native grass on a wild moor somewhere, the rabbit swallows the masticated vegetable matter, sending it to the stomach. There, the food gets mixed with gastric acid and passes into the small intestine, where protein and starches get absorbed. That still leaves a lot of undigested material, however, including cellulose (what we think of as fiber). That material travels on to the cecum, which acts like a big fermenting vat. Bacteria produce the B vitamins and digest the cellulose. The undigested fiber becomes the hard pellets; the cecal pellets go out through the anus and the rabbit eats them.

The cecal pellets come out about twice a day. The fecal pellets come out more often. Lockley brought new meaning to the term "bean counter" when he became one of the first researchers to bother to measure just how many of these little marbles come out in a day. Lockley removed and counted all the pellets an adult male European rabbit left in a 250–square-yard enclosure for forty days and determined that the rabbit deposited an average of 360 pellets a day.

Lockley went on to claim that to estimate the number of wild rabbits living on one acre, one need only multiply the number of fresh pellets collected within 48 square random yards by 101 (the nearest round number required to multiply 48 to 4840 yards, or one acre) and divide it by 360, the average pellet output per rabbit. Then he came up with an approximate pellet "decay rate" in nature; he decided that rabbit poop disintegrates in about two days in mild, wet weather and three weeks or even longer in dry, frosty weather. Since then, a number of researchers have counted pellets in given areas to estimate the population of wild rabbits there.

Some of the rabbits in Lockley's study were a special case: they had been gathered and put in large enclosures with fake warrens made of concrete tubes stuck in the ground, so that Lockley and his associates could observe them from underground chambers. (Picture an ant farm populated with rabbits, and you'll get an idea of what the researchers saw.) Those rabbits must have breathed a sigh of relief when they realized the only predator on their tails was a guy picking up their poops and analyzing how fast they disintegrated under various climatological conditions.

◆   ◆   ◆

Unlike most mammals, rabbits are relatively quiet animals—with four exceptions. All rabbits can growl, although it sounds more like a snort, a grunt or even a "hmmph" than the "grrr" we associate with carnivores. Most rabbit species also give very high-pitched screams when they are frightened or are being attacked. And rabbits in the mood for love make soft honking or oinking noses as they circle their beloved.

Rabbits, like gerbils, kangaroos and some species of rat and deer, also communicate, and quite noisily, by stamping or drumming their feet. Sometimes they do this to warn other rabbits; sometimes they do it when they're angry. Various studies show that this stamping also occurs after copulation, after returning to home ground, when frightened, when aggressive, after winning a contest or when females need to warn their young in the burrow below. The sound is quite effective, perhaps because rabbits actually lift both hind feet off the ground at the same time and then stamp them sharply and simultaneously on the ground—in contrast to the usual cartoon image (think Thumper, in *Bambi*) of the rabbit drumming just one foot in alarm. The rest of the rabbit's body remains very tense and alert during this motion, although the rabbit often moves his head from side to side as if looking for what's startling him.[29]

Living with rabbits, we hear these sudden thumpings in a variety of contexts. When we put rabbits down after medicating them, for instance, they'll sometimes dash across the room, then whirl around, stare at us, and thump in protest. Many rabbits thump when they're about to be picked up; some thump when they *think* they're about to be picked up, and some thump just because they see their pals getting picked up. Strange sounds in the middle of the night often prompt a chorus of thumpings, too. Breeders note that whole barnfuls of rabbits thump if they hear a predator—like a fox or coyote—outside.

Even small group thumpings can create quite a ruckus in a human household. One night when Susan, her two children and two rabbits were camped out in the living room (waiting for the recently cleaned bedroom carpets to dry), a neighbor's cat came onto the deck and started clawing at the screens on the sliding doors. All creatures great and small in the living room awoke with a frightened start, but it was the rabbits who were most alarmed. They leapt halfway across the rug, tore across the hardwood floors (scrambling like Fred

Flintstone in his foot-powered car), and ran under a bed. There they continued thumping for almost five minutes, until Susan got up and chased the cat away.

Doing It Like Rabbits

Wild European rabbits who are getting ready to mate use all of these communication strategies. The male will chin the female's back or ears to "claim" her and will emit a cloud of musky odor from his tail glands. The female will sometimes thump to express lack of interest. Or, if she is interested, she'll lie down next to the male, and the two rabbits will groom each other with their tongues. Sometimes the rabbits chase each other around in tight circles, in what Lockley calls a "kind of nuptial dance," with their tails up and ears pushed forward,[30] while making soft honking or grunting noises. Often the male rabbit lags behind the female rabbit, sometimes by as far as twenty yards, a sign that this isn't so much an aggressive chase as it is a flirtation.[31] The male will also exhibit "tail flagging," in which the tail is held flat against the back as he approaches and then retreats, stiff-legged, from the female. Researchers aren't sure if the male is emitting some sort of scent from his glands during this move or simply trying to arouse her with visual stimuli.

Many males also engage passionately in "enurination," a fancy name for peeing on one's intended. In fact, male rabbits seem to have excellent aim with this trick: they simply run toward the female, twist their hindquarters skyward, and emit a jet stream of urine at her—or they leap over her and pee on her as they pass overhead. (Some male rabbits also use enurination as an offensive move, as anyone who has been sprayed by an angry—or simply surprised—domestic male rabbit can attest.)

The sex act itself, once the female accepts, is startlingly to the point. The female lies with her chest on the ground and pushes her hindquarters up into the air. The male mounts her from behind by wrapping his forepaws around her flanks and then inserting his penis. Some males will bite the female or pull out large mouthfuls of her hair. The male then shakes like a jackhammer for about half a minute, gives a screech upon having an orgasm, and usually falls off to one side. This is not exactly a swoon of ecstasy—slow-motion photography of copulating rabbits shows that the male's hind feet are actually off the ground at the moment of orgasm; he falls off simply because he can't keep his balance anymore.[32]

The female's uterus has two horns and two cervices, which theoretically means she could carry fetuses from two different males, although it's generally thought that only the European hares can execute such "superfoetation" feats. (That's not the weirdest sexual anatomy in the animal kingdom, however. Female kangaroos, the rabbit's hopping brethren, have two vaginas, and the male has a split penis to accommodate her.)

Whether European rabbits are monogamous or polygamous is open to debate. It appears that males and females do form long-lasting—even lifelong—bonds. But ample evidence exists, too, that males will mate with any attractive female rabbit that happens to hop along or may even engage in what Americans call "serial monogamy."[33] These variations in pair bonding may be driven by warren size. In smaller warrens, males and females may form exclusive pairs, while in larger warrens there may be more "swinging" going on, simply because there are more rabbits with whom to consort. It's also possible that the female bonds not with the male, but with her burrow, which means that if her regular mate dies or leaves, and a new male moves in, she'll take up with him.[34] In all cases, however, male rabbits ignore their offspring, making parenting a strictly female affair. Even that parenting can be less than what we see with other mammals—the females generally visit and nurse their young just once in a twenty-four-hour period, presumably to keep predators from noticing the very vulnerable kits.

Warren Life

Most of the members of the family Leporidae live in the brush or among rocky outcroppings, or they simply rest in small "forms" dug into the dirt. The European rabbit, however, creates very large and sophisticated warrens. (The word "burrows" refers to single-entrance holes. "Warrens" refers to multi-entranced, multi-chambered living quarters.) In Canberra, Australia, for instance, one six-year-old warren had a total tunnel length of 517 meters and boasted 150 different entrances. Researchers estimated that 30 cubic feet of soil had been dug out.[35] Inter-rabbit relations within the warren are also the most complex of the Leporidae family,[36] as European rabbits, unlike hares and cottontails, are very gregarious and so depend on large groups (up to one hundred rabbits per warren) for safety and well-being.

In general, rabbits dig their warrens in sandy soils—since these are easier to dig than clay soils and drain better, too, thus reducing the risk of drowning or hyperthermia.[37] Warren life offers a number of benefits, including climate control (warrens are typically much cooler than the outside air) and protection from predators. This penchant for dark and protected spaces has continued down the line to domestic rabbits today, many of whom like to sleep under beds and chairs or inside cardboard tunnels and boxes, and most of whom will dig when given time and access to dirt—or even, sometimes, to plush carpet.

The warrens have many different "rooms," which are primarily used for sleeping, resting and nesting. Rabbit babies are born at the least advanced stage of development of any newborns in the Lepidorae family; they have no fur, they can't move and their eyes are shut, so they need considerable protection from predators. Just before birth, pregnant rabbits line the nesting chambers with grass and fur plucked from their abdomen to keep their kits warm. Hares, cottontails and some submissive female European rabbits, however, leave their young in "stops," or yard-long pits in the earth, instead of full-fledged nesting chambers. These, too, are lined with vegetation and fur. To protect those pits, the mother simply digs dirt and lays leaves over the young when she's done nursing them.[38]

Even in elaborate warrens, most of the house-building work is done by the females, who get especially "diggy" after rain or during pregnancy. (Males sometimes help, but it's a sporadic effort.) Given the need for protection for the young, it's easy to see why females "nest" this way. Mothers sometimes house more than one litter in the burrow; in one case a mother kept five litters from one breeding season in one warren. Each litter had its own chamber and a separate tunnel leading to the outside. This may sound like a mammoth maternal undertaking, but rabbit mothers generally nurse only one litter at a time and then let the other litters stay around for several months. As Lockley noted, "From many hours of watching the behavior of the adults and the young . . . it was clear that the rabbits enjoyed a family life below ground. Buck and doe accepted their progeny in the home for long after weaning time and all through the neutral season—July to October—the growing youngsters might sleep by day in contact with adults."

Warrens are precious commodities in the rabbit world; both males and females will protect their geographic territory against invaders, be they other rabbits, foxes or big birds. (Males are also territorial about their females, especially during the breeding season.)[39] Females are especially solicitous of their own burrows, as they are vital to the survival of the kits. Dominant females will often chase away submissive females who get too close.[40] When there isn't enough warren space—as when rabbit populations get too high— those submissive females suffer in other ways, too. They may have fewer litters, or fewer of their kits will live long enough to emerge from the burrow, or those who do survive may be malnourished and show behavioral differences.[41] During hard times—as when population densities are high or when green food is scarce—some dominant females even kill off the young of submissive does, and both dominant and submissive does can "resorb" their embryos to keep populations down.[42]

Like dog packs, a rabbit warren, which often consists of up to a hundred rabbits, is governed by dominance, with one buck ruling over a number of subordinate males and females. Within those ranks of minions, there may be any number of "consorts," rabbits who are sexual partners or "just friends" and who sleep together (rabbits nap for much of the day), eat together, frolic together and groom each other. (Rabbits wash themselves the same way that cats do—using their moistened front paws as washcloths—but help their buddies with the hard-to-reach spots, like behind the ears and on top of the head).[43]

Some rabbits—especially young male rabbits—may be ejected from the warren if space gets tight, especially at the beginning of the breeding season, when more kits will be born. Those rabbits may continue to live a solitary existence, or they may live as a "satellite" to another bonded pair.[44] Fans of *Watership Down* may remember that the group that left the original warren contained several of these unattached male rabbits.

Just who gets to be dominant and who remains submissive is worked out via aggressive encounters—the dominant rabbit consistently patrols his territory and chases away the others, not the other way around—but once the pecking order is established, it affects individual rabbits in a fairly profound way. The average heart rate for a rabbit is two hundred to three hundred beats per minute, but submissive rabbits typically have a higher heart rate than dominant rabbits, probably because dominant rabbits have freer access to limited resources and get to initiate the aggressive encounters. If a submissive rabbit reaches a dominant position, however, his heart rate will drop accordingly.[45]

When hostilities or challenges do arise, rabbits can be truly vicious. Fights occur over a number of different issues, including territory, sexual partners and choice grazing spots. The levels of aggression, however, vary according to several factors, including population density and the number of escape routes available. That is, denied the ability to flee, rabbits will fight. Adults raised in high-population areas are generally more aggressive than those raised in low-population areas.[46]

Aggressive behavior can start fairly mildly, with males running up and down the boundaries of their territory, chinning, urinating and marking with pellets to make sure the boundary is well defined. Aggressive chasing may ensue, at which point hostility ends if the submissive rabbit flees. If he doesn't flee, however, rabbits challenge each other by lunging, stamping their back feet, growling, tail flagging or mounting (which is a gesture of aggression or domination as well as a sexual position). Wild hares in North America also tend to box and chase rival males.

Once the real rabbit fighting starts, it's as bad as a cat or dog fight. Rabbit teeth are very sharp. The back claws are also strong and sharp and can tear out large chunks of flesh. Typically rabbits roll on the ground like schoolboys, bounce chests like sumo wrestlers, leap over each other like capoeira dancers and try to eviscerate each other with their hind claws. Sometimes they lie on their sides, belly to belly, and spin around in a circle as they rake at each other with their feet and hold on with their teeth. The fight usually doesn't stop until one of them wins by either chasing the opponent away or wounding him so badly he gives up.

Sound like an exaggeration? Consider the following account by Lockley, who observed a fight between two males whom he dubbed Bold Benjamin and Big Boss. Lockley had removed Big Boss from an area called "Plain," in which he was the dominant bunny, to an area called "Wood." After Bold Benjamin usurped Boss's dominant position in "Plain," Lockley put Boss back into his old territory, just to see what would happen. He writes:

[The two rabbits] met somewhere below [ground]. There was a thudding noise and they emerged together, rolling on the bare grass in a confused clinch. Separating, they leaped or pranced around each other for a few seconds, as if awaiting the moment to thrust home a telling bite or kick.

Then Benjamin darted in, bowling Boss over sideways, and sinking chisel-teeth into his neck.

Boss screamed, kicking out. Benjamin hung on, so that Boss half-dragged his enemy for a little distance before Benjamin lost or released his grip, tearing out as he did so a mouthful of Boss's fur. . . .

The bucks grappled, each seeking to bite the head and neck of the other. They fell together sideways, bellies exposed, and scrammed with all four armoured legs . . .

The painful drumming on the belly and flanks threw up a cloud of white fur. Big Boss rolled away to save his entrails. But Bold Benjamin hung on to his neck with a locked grip of the teeth. Screaming fearfully, the anguished Boss struggled free—at the cost of a severe wound at the base of his ears. He ran back towards the tunnels leading to Wood.[47]

Unfortunately for Boss, the humans had sealed off the tunnels leading back to "Wood," a place that had been an exile but now, Lockley admits, must have seemed like a sanctuary. As Boss ran frantically up and down the fence line looking for a way to escape, Benjamin followed him doggedly. Boss survived and remained in Plain, but lived in fear for the rest of his days. The "artificial experiment," Lockley declared,

> . . . served its purpose. It indicated that possession of a warren, when enjoyed for even a short time by a strong buck, gave him the confidence and courage to defend it with full vigour even against a larger buck who, returning as an absentee and with morale lowered by failure to dominate elsewhere, was psychologically ill-prepared to fight.[48]

In most cases, just who wins the fight appears to have more to do with who "owns" the territory than with who is bigger, older, stronger or, perhaps, capable of making a bigger stink with his anal glands or a nastier hit with his urine stream. In one study of wild and domesticated European rabbits, Robert Myktowycz found that wild rabbits will defend their homes (in this case, a nest box created to simulate a warren) but become inhibited on another rabbit's territory. In fact he found that the "home boys" were aggressive in seventy-six percent of the tests and "won" the fight in eighty percent of the cases.

In that same study, females proved to be just as aggressive as males, perhaps because the amount of space available to females has a strong bearing on their reproductive success (in that a burrow provides both shelter and a place to give birth, and overcrowding can lead to embryo resorption and kit death). While sex may not affect aggression, domestication and artificial selection may: when Myktowycz put domestic New Zealand White rabbits together with the wild rabbits, he found that the wild rabbits were generally more aggressive. He attributed this to the fact that humans have bred New Zealands to be less vicious so they'd be easier to handle.[49]

That rabbits can be fierce warriors often surprises people attached to the image of rabbits as either cute and cuddly or shy and retiring. But that ferocity is actually another very successful adaptation to the rabbit's status as a prey species. The term, after all, has always been "fight or flight"—not simply flight! The fact that rabbits can fight—and not simply run away—and that they can kill each other's litters, wreck each other's burrows and tear out each other's insides gives them more depth, we think, than the traditional idea of bunnies trembling in the face of falling leaves.

The Rabbit as Pest

Because of an early attraction to rabbit meat and fur, humans began "farming" wild European rabbits as a game species long before domestication began. Neolithic settlers, for instance, brought rabbits to Menorca around 1400 B.C.E.[50] Both the Phoenicians and the Romans, who were great fans of rabbit meat, also brought wild rabbits to areas around the Mediterranean, including North Africa. Some of those rabbits were no doubt released in the wild so they could be hunted. But in his book on the history of agriculture, *De re Rustica*, Roman author Marcus Terentius Varro (116–27 B.C.E.) also described how wild rabbits could be caught and then allowed to run free with other creatures (including hares, doormice, bees and snails) in so-called "leporaria," or walled enclosures.[51] Some of these

enclosures were as large as four kilometers in circumfere
roofs to keep out predators.[52]

By the Middle Ages, the French, British and Germans v
keeping wild rabbits in similar "rabbit" gardens that were prov
with crops, hay and watchful rabbit keepers. Some rabbits were eve
kept on islands in lakes or rivers to facilitate keeping and capturing
them.[53] But the European rabbit only arrived in continental Europe
because humans carried it there. As such, the wild rabbit spread
across Europe over a period of several hundred years—far faster
than it could have done in the course of a natural migration, even
taking into account factors like massive forest clearance, overgrazing
and agricultural development, all of which created wonderful conditions for the burrow- and vegetable-loving rabbit.[54]

Though these rabbits were enclosed, they were not "domesticated." The term "domestic" only refers to those animals that can be
forced to breed in captivity, because that's what allows humans to
start selecting for various traits. Instead, the "leporaria rabbits" were
wild rabbits living in semi-freedom and getting very fat on human
food. Unlike hares, who are unable to breed in captivity but are
hunted for their meat, the wild rabbits did reproduce, but they did it
completely on their own, not under the guidance or coercion of
humans. In fact, natural selection probably would have favored
those wild rabbits that were less tame or interested in humans, as the
more placid strains would have been the first to be caught and
killed.[55]

Historians have found many references from the second to the
seventeenth centuries to rabbits being kept in large enclosures by
European monks, peasants and the feudal gentry. One twelfth-century book, *Conejeria de Toledo*, even focused specifically on the rabbitries of Toledo. References to a robust rabbit trade exist as well. In
1148, for instance, the abbeys of Corvey (in Germany) traded rabbits
with Solignac (in France); in 1221, six thousand rabbit pelts were sent
from Castile to Devon.[56] (There were so many warrens in England, in
fact, that today you can still find place names like "Coneygarth,"
"Warren" and "Conigree."[57]) In the sixteenth century Queen

Figure 1.5. "Frightened, the hares dive into the traps." Gaston Phoebus's fifteenth-century *Book of the Hunt* described methods for killing and butchering many species. He suggested several techniques for hunting rabbits and hares, including driving them into nets (shown here) and chasing them down with greyhounds and ferrets. (BNF, FR 616) fol. 26v Gaston Phoebus, Courtesy Bibliothèque Nationale de France, Paris.

Elizabeth of England kept "rabbit islands" and King Henry IV of France had a leporarium that was large enough for hunting. Just outside Berlin, Frederick Wilhelm started a "Kaninschenwerder," or rabbit island, in 1683.[58]

Not all Europeans favored rabbit hunting—whether it was inside or outside of rabbit gardens. Numerous artists depicted hares and rabbits enacting their revenge on hunters. One engraving by the sixteenth-century artist Virgil Solis shows a group of rabbits eagerly roasting a hunter. These rabbits look quite human, or rather quite diabolical; some stand on their hind legs and others wield tools, like bellows, a hunting horn and a skewer. George Penez, a sixteenth-century German, was quite renowned for his engravings depicting rabbits executing hunters. In 1665 another German artist, Johan Schaper, even created an enameled glass in the style of Penez: that is,

Figure 1.6. Like his other still lifes, Jean Baptiste Simeon Chardin's "Rabbit, Copper Cauldron, Quince, and Chestnuts" illuminated ordinary objects in familiar domestic scenes: in this case, the ingredients for a meal, including a wild rabbit. Courtesy National Museum, Stockholm.

one that showed clothed hares, with very human-like features, leading a hunter to the gallows to be hung.

(More than three hundred years later, American folk artist Reverend Howard Finster would play on a similar theme in a 1981 painting called *Us Poor Rabbits*. Less vengeful than sad, Reverend Finster's rabbits still protest their status as human hunters' prey. In the painting, two baby rabbits walk through a forest with a mother rabbit. The caption reads, "Us poor rabbits have it hard when we get shot and get all crippled up we don't have any doctors or nurses we hafto just lay around and suffer for nights and day for weeks till we die while our enemies sleep well and a lot of times we get burned out of our home." Another caption on the mother rabbit's skirt reads

Figure 1.7. This seventeenth-century enameled glass cup shows hares reversing the tables on hunters. Johan Schaper Cup, gift of Edward Drummond Libbey, The Toledo Museum of Art, Ohio.

"don't just shoot us for sport you will kneed us soon let us multiply for the bad day ahead." The mother carries on her back a bag filled with people, and on the bag is written "In 1931 people lived on us but now we should be free.")

From the seventeenth to the nineteenth centuries, wild rabbits were nurtured for meat and sport in England, primarily for the gentry, although by the late nineteenth century land tenants could also kill rabbits on the landlord's property. In France, rabbit warrens also belonged primarily to the gentry, who sought to protect their property by legislating that no new warrens could be created and no old ones could be enlarged. This became a key point during the French Revolution, when control of the warrens was taken away from the upper classes. Still, rabbits weren't allowed to run free (that is, beyond the boundaries of aristocracy's warrens) until 1862, when Napoleon finally claimed that rabbits were "game."

Eventually some of the captive rabbits in Europe escaped their enclosures—rabbits are famous for that—or were released to be

Figure 1.8. Howard Finster's *Us Poor Rabbits* depicts the suffering he felt wild rabbits experienced at the hands of humans. Collection of Jane Braddock, Joelton, Tennessee.

hunted as game. But the fact that the "wild" rabbit in continental Europe was actually transported there by humans has led some commentators to claim that the only true wild European rabbits are those still living wild in Spain and that all the other wild rabbits on the continent are actually "feral." (One author has even suggested that the species should have been dubbed "Feral Rabbit," rather than the more official *Oryctolagus cuniuculus*.[59]) These commentators raise an interesting point. Once wild animals have had persistent contact with humans, they're not really wild anymore, because domestication by definition means that the animals can be bred and sustained in captivity and can't survive in the wild. The rabbit garden rabbits were an odd case. They weren't being "domesticated" per se, but they were being "kept" by humans. This relationship was sufficient enough to dull some of the rabbits' wild instincts. The consequences of this "half domestication" are especially clear in Germany, where rabbit warrens were started in the 1100s, but no wild rabbit colonies were mentioned until 1423. Rabbits undoubtedly broke free of their warrens during those three centuries. Some may have even been freed when their keepers tired of tending them. But it probably took all of three centuries for the released domestic rabbits to redevelop the wild behaviors that would protect them from both elements and predators.[60] Even then, the "wild rabbit" in Europe retained the larger body size that so often accompanies domestication.[61]

◆   ◆   ◆

The wild European rabbit was not only introduced throughout Europe. The British also brought domestic European rabbits to Australia and New Zealand throughout the 1770s and 1780s. (Captain James Cook was the first to leave domestic rabbits in New Zealand.[62]) For about seventy years, those rabbits pretty much stayed within the colony settlements there, probably because the land hadn't been cultivated and natural predators could easily wipe out domestic rabbits that wandered into the bush.[63] But in the mid-nineteenth century, colonists developed "acclimatization societies" aimed at importing and then releasing game, fish and songbirds in Australia and New Zealand, including wild rabbits. The goal, according to an 1882 report by the society in Victoria, was "to enrich (the country) by stocking its broad territory with the choicest products of the animal kingdom borrowed from every temperate region on the face of the globe."[64]

The country did indeed become enriched with wild rabbits. By 1879, there were so many rabbits in Western Victoria that farmers had to abandon their land. By 1887, farmers were able to kill ten million rabbits in New South Wales in just eight months.[65] By 1888, an Intercolonial Commission on Rabbits had declared that the rabbit was a pest and the country should be rid of the species.[66] Two years later, the rabbit population had reached twenty million and had begun spreading rapidly, probably due both to the development of agricultural lands and the eradication of rabbits' natural predators, like dingoes, native cats and eagles.[67] By some estimates, the wild rabbit spread across Australia at a rate of about 54 kilometers, or 33.5 miles, per year. That's about as fast as the European starling, another famously invasive species, spread across North America. In the Northern Territory, however, the rabbits spread as fast as 390 kilometers (242 miles) per year.[68]

Likewise, in New Zealand, populations of imported wild rabbits exploded in the nineteenth century. By 1876, the House of Representatives had declared that the "mischief done is most serious, is increasing, and unless some effectual remedy be adopted, is likely to increase."[69] European settlers also brought European rabbits to South America in the mid-eighteenth century, again to use as game, although the animals didn't become established there until the 1930s. Here, too, the spread was phenomenal: just four rabbits resulted in thirty million rabbits within seventeen years in Tierra del Fuego.[70]

European colonists also released wild rabbits on islands, to serve as a living source of meat for sailors and castaways. Those rabbits colonized those areas, too, so much so that by some accounts they are the second most successful island colonizer in the world after *Rattus rattus* (more commonly known as the house rat, roof rat, black rat or ship rat). Today, at least twelve "Rabbit Islands" exist in New Zealand, thirteen exist in the Falklands, and some eight hundred islands in the world's major oceans house the wild European rabbit populations. None of these populations is native.[71]

The fact that rabbit populations could grow so quickly should not have come as a surprise. Humans had been commenting on rabbits' explosive reproductive potential since at least 30 B.C.E., when Strabo, a geographer, wrote about an overpopulation of rabbits in the Balearic Islands. According to Strabo, settlers there were so unhappy about the rabbits (who were all descended from one original couple!) that they asked Emperor Augustus to either send a Roman legion to clear the land of rabbits or give the settlers other land elsewhere. Pliny the Elder, in his *Natural History*, discussed the "famine" that rabbits caused in these islands, as well as the way that rabbit warrens were undermining the ramparts of Tarragone.[72]

Rabbits spread so quickly because they reproduce quickly, and because when the going gets tough, rabbits get going. That is, given habitat difficulties, like food or water shortages or new predators, rabbits migrate to new areas. And because rabbits thrive on a varied diet, can convert food efficiently and can live almost anywhere that provides soil to excavate, they adapt fairly readily to their new homes. In the process, they tend to wreak a lot of damage: they dig for roots and to create burrows, and munch on all manner of plants—from cultivated crops to tree bark to seaweed, all of which contribute to erosion, loss of native plants and the subsequent disappearance of native fauna. Plowing under forest or native grasses to create crop lands or pastures, as was common in Britain, Australia, Europe and New Zealand, just makes it easier for the rabbits to move in.[73] So too does cultivating wild rabbits for game by both feeding them and eradicating their potential predators—as remains common in every country where wild rabbits have become a pest.[74]

One of the more famous examples of the ecological damage wrought by rabbits occurred in the 1420s, when Portuguese settlers had to leave Port Santo because a single female rabbit and her litter had created so many progeny. Alfred Crosby, author of *Ecological Imperialism: The Biological Expansion of Europe: 900–1900*, hypothesizes that in the wake of the rabbits eating both crops and native plants on Port Santo, native fauna died off as well, leaving only "empty eco-niches" to be filled with weeds and animals the settlers brought from the mainland. "The Port Santo of 1400 is as lost to us as is the world before the Noachian flood," he concludes.[75] But, Crosby notes, to vilify the rabbit is wrongheaded. The settlers, he writes, were "defeated in their initial attempt at colonization not by primeval nature but by their own ecological ignorance."[76]

According to Lockley, wild rabbit numbers in England, at least, stayed fairly stable for about six hundred years after their introduction during the Norman period, primarily due to natural predation and human trapping. But in 1880, the Ground Game Act gave tenants the right to "take" the rabbits on the farm they rented. This turned out to be so lucrative that tenants starting laying out "gin"— or leghold—traps to catch the rabbit's predators, thus sending rabbit populations soaring. Lockley writes that this

> caused intolerable damage to agricultural production of cereals, kale, roots and grass crops, damage estimated, in the twenty-five years up to 1953, to be at the rate of forty to fifty million pounds annually. Against this the direct income from rabbits received by agriculture was only about two million pounds a year . . . .[77]

While European farmers lived with wild rabbits for centuries before they became a problem, Australia's problems accelerated within only a few short decades, and it is widely considered one of the most devastating examples of an exotic species invasion known. The rapid increase in Australia's rabbit population led to an increase in the European red fox and feral cats (also introduced species), which in turn contributed to the extinction or reduction in number of several indigenous birds and mammals, including kangaroos, burrowing bettongs and bandicoots.[78] Rabbits in Australia also cost the agricultural industry some $600,000,000 a year, as they eat cereals and other crops and reduce the forage available for sheep and cows (it's estimated that ten rabbits eat as much herbage as one sheep).[79]

In the long run, it would be nice to think that humans would learn from the rabbit mistake. It was humans, after all, who brought rabbits—what Henry Thompson calls "one of the classic and best-known examples of an invading species"[80]—to new lands in the first place, just as it was humans who brought the European starlings to Central Park, the ice plant to California, the cane toads to Australia. What's ironic is that in their native landscapes, rabbit populations stay in check naturally. In Spain, for instance, which is the European rabbit's native hopping ground, the species has never been much of a pest, because natural controls, like climate, vegetation, predation and terrain control the rabbit populations.[81] When populations get high or food gets scarce, high rates of embryo resorption and disease, combined with low rates of conception, bring the population down; then it slowly rebuilds again.

Conversely, in areas where humans have altered the natural environment—by both replacing woodland with cropland and eradicating native competitors and predators—the highly adaptable rabbit will reproduce quickly and mightily. In Australia, only three mammals and thirteen birds of prey rely on rabbits for food; in Spain, seventeen mammals and nineteen birds of prey hunt rabbits (and rabbits comprise forty percent of the diet of six of those mammals and eight of those birds).[82] "In its ancestral home the rabbit is an essential part of a complex natural environment," one researcher notes. "Only when it is removed from the demands and constraints of that environment does the ecological opportunism which allows it to survive at home turn it into a pest elsewhere."[83]

Pest Controls

Some researchers claim that if humans hadn't carried the wild European rabbit out of Iberia several thousand years ago, it would either have stayed there (given the formidable oceans and mountains that ring the region) or gone extinct.[84] But humans did carry wild rabbits out of Iberia, the rabbits did spread, and humans, being human, didn't care to have natural processes interrupt their plans— even those natural processes had been brought into play by the humans themselves.

As such, dozens of strategies for getting rid of rabbits have been tried, with varying degrees of success. One of the most common techniques is to bring in rabbit predators, like ferrets, dogs, cats, stoats and weasels, which either flush the rabbits from their burrows so hunters can shoot or net them, or attack them directly. This strategy often causes more problems than it solves. One lighthouse keeper on Berlenga Island used cats to get rid of rabbits, but once the rabbits were gone, the cats (who were only doing their jobs, after all) simply starved to death. Wildlife officials on Sable Island in Canada likewise brought in cats to kill the wild rabbits, then brought in foxes to kill the resulting overpopulation of cats, and then had to gather humans together to kill the excess foxes. The humans, presumably, left the island on their own.[85]

Trapping—whether by snare or steel trap—has been used for centuries, but even people who don't like rabbits agree that trapping is inhumane. Gin traps—which seize the animal's leg in toothed jaws and have been described as "diabolical" instruments[86]—have been one trap of choice, although they tend to catch sheep, weasels, foxes, pheasants, woodcock, sheepdogs, cats and cow lips—in addition to the rascally rabbits. England banned the use of gin traps in 1954; since then, dozens of other countries—although not the United States, Australia or New Zealand—have also banned these traps.

Many people, including Indians in North America, have also driven hares and rabbits, usually by the thousands, into nets (as long as forty feet across) or corrals (with V-shaped fence "wings" stretching as much as two to three miles out) and then beat them to death with sticks or clubs. In California, starting in the late nineteenth century, jackrabbit drives were fairly common and popular enough to be considered a "gala" event. Hundreds of people from across the countryside would gather and start to flush out the hares—chasing them on horseback, on foot or in cars. As one participant of an 1893 drive in Fresno described it, the participants would get a good group of hares together and pursue them:

> Now hundreds of the poor creatures are easily discerned as the fences appear on the left and right. . . . Many try the back track only to meet death in the attempt. . . . Great numbers of rabbits dash in every direction in front of the advancing hosts, and far ahead the long ears of hundreds more can be seen racing for life, occasionally crouching and then starting ahead again, but still surely advancing into the inevitable death trap. . . . The fence on each side is closing in fast, and although still some distance from the corral the

Figures 1.9a, "A Jack Rabbit Drive Near Fresno, CA," and 1.9b, "Result of the Grand Army Rabbit Drive at Fresno, CA." The Australians are not the only ones to hunt down lagomorphs en masse. In the late nineteenth century, farmers and ranchers in California, especially, often participated in "rabbit drives" to rid the countryside of jackrabbits that were destroying their crops, vineyards and fruit trees. From *The Jack Rabbits of the United States*, by T.S. Palmer, M.D. Washington: Government Printing Office. 1896. Courtesy USDA National Wildlife Research Center.

screaming of the poor creatures can be heard as they find their retreat cut off.

The climax of the drive is now at hand. . . . The screeching of the rabbits can be heard above everything, and the ground is covered with dead rabbits by the dozen. . . . The result of the drive at Fresno was 20,000 dead rabbits.[87]

More labor intensive, and certainly less spectacular, is the poisoning method. Sometimes the rabbit eradicators put out poisoned carrots and jam. Other times they spray gas from the air or directly into the warrens. Sometimes they poison watering holes, although indiscriminate poisoning can kill rabbit predators, which just allows the rabbit population to rebound again. Fumigation, usually with cyanide powder, is considered by some to be more humane for all creatures involved, but it has to be followed up with "warren ripping," or digging up the burrows, to make sure all the rabbits have been killed.[88]

Many attempts have been made to simply fence rabbits out, most often out of paddocks and pastures. Australia was the first to try fences on a grand scale, when it built thousands of miles of wire netting, called the Great Barrier Fences, across New South Wales, Queensland and Western Australia around the turn of the century. At the time, this was the longest fence in the world and stretched three times as far as the Great Wall of China. Yet the rabbit population in the southeastern half of the country continued to spin out of control as rivers washed out fences and rabbits found ways to get through and under the barriers. Some photographs show the rabbits piled three feet deep against the fences as they try to get through in search of food and water; older Australians still recall looking out over their paddocks and seeing the ground rippling with the movement of herds of rabbits.[89] The fences still exist today, and in some areas are used to control sheep and dingoes.

In his description of his own attempts to eradicate his land of wild rabbits, Lockley provides a macabre microcosm that demonstrates the sheer difficulty of the task. In his first winter, he writes, he

Figure 1.10. For more than a century, "conventions" of wild European rabbits have been a common sight in Australia, especially around water. This photo was taken in 1961. Photo by C. Bettmann. Courtesy CORBIS.

and some trappers "trapped, snared, and ferreted 2,415 rabbits, then had to stop because the burrows were invaded in February by thousands of shearwaters, a kind of albatross . . . " The next winter, his team trapped 2,908 rabbits, "again leaving a substantial minority alive—though some of them had only three legs left."[90] At that point, Lockley gave up on the steel-jawed traps for good, as they were too "inefficient and inhumane"—not because the traps were maiming rabbits, but because they were killing wild birds. Long-nets and snares didn't work because there weren't enough flat areas on which the rabbits could run; ferrets didn't solve the problem because the rabbits had never seen such predators and so refused to bolt from their warrens.

When the 1930s depression hit, Lockley gave up on his dream of setting up a Chinchilla farm altogether, as no market existed for the furs. But in 1938, he agreed to try calcium cyanide dust to kill the rabbits as a demonstration project. Within a few months, the population of rabbits on his island dropped from ten thousand to several

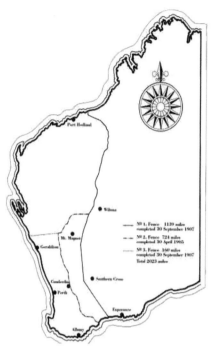

Figure 1.11. Map of Rabbit Proof Fence. It took more than four hundred men and eight thousand tons of material to build the two-thousand-mile long Great Barrier Fences from 1904 to 1906. Courtesy Darling Downs-Moreton Rabbit Board, Queensland, Australia.

Figure 1.12. Today's rabbit fences control not only Leporidae but also emus, dingoes, feral goats and kangaroos.

hundred. Sixteen years later, he wrote, "the rabbits are as numerous as ever on Skokholm."[91]

It was perhaps New Zealand that took the most holistic approach to eradicating rabbits within its borders. During the late nineteenth and early twentieth centuries, the New Zealand government tried the usual techniques: releasing predators, setting traps, erecting fences, night-shooting with the aid of large spotlights and using various kinds of poison. Finally, in 1947, the New Zealand legislature passed the Rabbit Nuisance Amendment Act, which established the ominous-sounding Rabbit Destruction Council, which, again, advocated using poisoned carrots and jam, guns, dogs and aerial gassing—but this time their goal was to totally wipe out, rather than simply control, the country's wild rabbits.

The first chairman of the RDC was a man named Bart Baker, who was passionately opposed to the foreign lagomorphs now inhabiting his country. As one researcher writes admiringly,

> A South Island farmer, Bart Baker combined organizational skill with a rare understanding of his fellow farmers. He was absolutely dedicated to the cause of rabbit destruction, particularly to "getting the last rabbit." He promoted this belief with religious zeal and expected others to do the same. He had little sympathy for science or scientists unless work was directed strictly towards better methods of killing rabbits. With a less committed man, rabbit control could have foundered again in the 1950s.[92]

Stringent as the RCD's policies were, however, they were stymied by one minor problem. Even as the government was trying to wipe out the wild rabbit population for the sake of the farmers, many members of the human population were making tidy profits off the fur and meat of those same wild rabbits. Between 1900 and 1945, in fact, the country exported some twelve million wild rabbits to other countries.[93] The government wisely realized that the only way to reduce the supply of pesky rabbits was to reduce the demand for

DARLING DOWNS - MORETON RABBIT BOARD

RURAL LANDS PROTECTION ACT

IT IS ILLEGAL TO KEEP RABBITS IN QLD

Rabbits destroy the environment. The cost to the economy
of Australia exceeds $600 million per annum.

*MAXIMUM PENALTIES
FOR*

1.	Introducing rabbits from Interstate	$7500
2.	Keeping rabbits	$3750
3.	Selling rabbits	$3750
4.	Releasing rabbits	$7500

**Should you require further information
contact the Clerk of the Board on
(07) 4661 4076**

Figure 1.13. Although the Queensland government fears that domestic rabbits could worsen wild rabbit problems, many citizens keep domestic rabbits surreptitiously as pets. Courtesy Darling Downs-Moreton Rabbit Board, Queensland, Australia.

game and pelts. While the Rabbit Nuisance Amendment Act established just the kind of bureaucratic bother one might expect from such legislation (including the establishment of subsidies, rates and authorities), it also mandated a brilliant "de-commercialization" of rabbit skins. First they were reduced in value by ten percent, then completely in 1956, making them worthless as an exportable commodity. As a result, the number of skins exported from New Zealand dropped from 13.5 million in 1948 to 0.8 million in 1954; the number of carcasses (for meat) dropped from 4.9 million to 0.4 million during the same period. The export of any carcasses was banned after 1954, and by 1960 only hospitals, zoos and research centers could keep live rabbits at all.[94] In 1958, the Council also banned the sale of rabbits as pets—for fear that pet rabbit genes might make wild rabbits "even more fecund," as Professor Barry Richardson, of the University of Western Sydney puts it. "It is rubbish but the argument is still on."[95] Since 1980, it has been legal to raise domestic rabbits in New Zealand, and the country's wild rabbit populations have been kept in check by a combination of predation and traditional control methods. (It is also illegal to keep rabbits as pets in Queensland, Australia, although in recent years some citizens have advocated for a lifting of that ban. "The truth is, rabbits are already Queensland's most popular illegal pet," one rabbit rescuer in Australia says, "so the ban no longer makes sense.")

New Zealand is not the only country where the profits of hunting and trapping wild rabbits have collided with attempts to control them. Today, most countries overdosing on wild European rabbits use a combination of techniques to exterminate them—including snares, traps, poisons and hunting with beagles and ferrets—even as the rabbits are cultivated as hunting stock. In some countries, hunters still build artificial warrens for wild rabbits to both help them reproduce and protect them from predators. French hunters, for instance, release about 500,000 wild rabbits per year; the rabbit is the number one game species there. Yet the rabbit is still considered the country's second-worst pest, after the wild boar. British hunters, some of whom make their living solely by the trapping and sale of wild rabbit meat and pelts, still take out insurance policies to reimburse farmers whose crops are damaged by the rabbits.[96]

Bugs for Bunnies
When it comes to controlling rabbits, national governments are faithful proponents of the time-worn adage "If at first you don't suc-

ceed"—and in the case of rabbits you almost never do—"try, try again." As each mechanical strategy has failed to control wild rabbit populations, government workers have tried ever more severe—and bizarre—techniques. Indeed, some of the most gruesome, and failed, attempts to eradicate rabbits have been in the form of biological warfare: namely, introducing fatal viral agents into rabbit habitats.

The myxoma virus was the first biological control agent used by humans against rabbits. Highly contagious and very lethal, the virus is spread via the mouthparts of fleas and mosquitoes and creates myxomatosis, a disease characterized by swelling of the eyes, ears, nose, genitals and mouth, and, in some cases, high fevers, seizures and hemorrhage. Death eventually results from diseases ranging from pneumonia to liver infection, or simply from the blind and deaf rabbit either stumbling into the road and getting hit by a car or succumbing, defenseless, to a predator's attack.

The myxoma virus was first identified among domestic European rabbits in Brazil in 1896. It then appeared in breeding establishments in California, where it caused severe decimations in numbers and probably came from the brush rabbit (*Sylvilagus bachmani*). News of the virus's potency piqued the interest of the Australian government; researchers began suggesting that the government release the virus among wild European rabbits on that continent in 1918. Other researchers, however, protested, because they weren't sure if the disease would affect other species—and they knew that trapping rabbits for meat and fur was a very profitable endeavor.[97] It wasn't until 1950 that the Australian government imported the virus to use on that continent.

Getting the virus and infecting the rabbits are two different tasks, but the Australians came up with some pretty ingenious ways of spreading the disease. They put out gin traps that contained needles covered with the virus. They caught wild rabbits and used an abrasive powder to rub the freeze-dried virus on the rabbits' eyelids. They even shot arrows tipped with glass vials of infected fleas at the mouths of the warrens. Initial attempts were incredibly successful, with ninety-nine percent of the wild rabbits dying in areas where the virus was released. Likewise, in Tierra del Fuego, a deliberate release of the virus killed ninety-seven percent of the region's thirty million rabbits within three years.

Myxomatosis didn't exist in Europe until 1952, when an enterprising French pediatrician by the name of Armand DeLille procured the virus from a colleague at the Laboratoire de Bacteriologie in Lausanne and released it on his farm. DeLille assumed that the virus would stay within his six-hundred-acre estate; he was unaware that the disease was spread by mosquitoes, who can, after all, fly over walls. Within three years, ninety-eight percent of the wild rabbits in France were dead, as were some forty percent of the country's 140 million domestic rabbits.[98] The disease then spread to other countries, including Spain, Belgium, Holland, Germany and England.

French hunting groups were outraged; in 1954, their annual catch was only two percent of what it had been before the virus arrived. They took DeLille to court, where he was convicted of illegally spreading an animal disease and fined all of one franc. Foresters and farmers, however, were delighted with the change, as agriculture and sylviculture production skyrocketed once the rabbits were gone. The foresters even gave DeLille an award "in recognition of services rendered to agriculture and sylviculture."

In Britain, too, the virus elicited a variety of reactions. Although the government had formally chosen not to introduce the virus, at least one farmer took matters into his own hands by bringing an infected rabbit from the continent into England. Soon many farmers were collecting the corpses of infected rabbits from other farmers and scattering them about to get the virus going locally. Some members of the general public were horrified at the fate of the infected rabbits in their country, however. As Lockley writes,

> [T]he appearance of the affected rabbits, with swollen heads, blind and deaf, and wandering helplessly along roads and fields, aroused a national indignation and outcry. "Mercy squads" of men and women, chiefly from the towns, were set up by the Royal Society for the Prevention of

Cruelty to Animals and other humanitarian organisations, to go forth and shoot or cudgel these dying rabbits to a more speedy death.[99]

The New Zealand government tried to introduce the myxoma virus in the early 1950s. That attempt failed because the country lacked both the fleas and the mosquitoes that spread the disease. In the 1970s and early 1980s, farmers in that country asked the government to try releasing the appropriate fleas, but in 1987, after some debate, the government ruled that myxomatosis wasn't needed in the country, both because the rabbit populations were fairly stable there and because the public probably wouldn't accept the spread of the disease.[100] In all areas where myxomatosis wiped out rabbit populations, however, crops and livestock flourished once again. In parts of Australia, stock numbers increased twenty-five to one hundred percent following the myxomatosis epidemic, and wool and meat production increased by thirty-four million pounds. In England, rabbit damage to crops practically disappeared after myxomatosis swept through. Farmers were able to cut twice as much hay and to take in bumper harvests of many crops.[101]

Today, myxomatosis has spread all over Europe and killed millions of wild rabbits, making it the most important wildlife disease in Europe in the twentieth century.[102] It infects, but doesn't kill, hares and wild cottontails in the United States; it does kill pet rabbits here. As a naturally spreading virus, it's quite effective, initially. But as a control technique it's problematic. Besides being cruel, one major problem with using the myxoma virus as a control agent is that the relationship between host (rabbit) and pathogen (myxoma virus) can change. In Australia, for instance, after the virus initially killed off ninety-five to ninety-nine percent of the rabbits, it became less powerful, and the rabbits developed some genetic resistance to it. Suddenly there was, if not detente, a considerably diluted effect: sometimes only fifty percent of the exposed rabbits died in an outbreak.[103] When the Australians also neglected to eradicate the surviving rabbits, either by ripping out warrens or fumigating them, rabbit populations rebounded. Introducing the rabbit flea as an additional vector in 1966 helped bring the populations down again.

Conversely, as a virus that is spread by two rather voracious vectors, myxomatosis can initially wipe out rabbits—including those in commercial rabbitries—too fast. Britain decided not to use the virus as a weapon against pest control in 1950s for these reasons. Nevertheless, when that ambitious farmer introduced the disease in 1953, it spread all over the country within two years.[104] Myxomatosis can wipe out wild rabbit populations so fast that entire ecological chains may be affected, simply because many predators, including weasels, foxes, coyotes and large birds of prey, eat rabbits. In Spain, two of the most endangered species in Europe—the Spanish lynx and the imperial eagle—depend on rabbits for food. In England, after the virus wiped out some ninety-nine percent of the entire wild rabbit population in the 1950s, herbs, grasses and flowers, including rare species, flourished. Buzzard clutch sizes, however, diminished, as did those of the tawny owl, because there were fewer bank voles and wood mice; predators like foxes, stoats and weasels, who missed their usual rabbit snacks, were eating them. Stoat numbers also dropped, due to a loss of rabbit prey, while weasel numbers soared, due to the proliferation of grasses, which boosted vole and mouse numbers.[105] The large blue butterfly *Maculinea arion* also went extinct, for rather complicated reasons. The butterfly's larvae feed on thyme and then are captured by the *Myrmica subuleti* ant. In the ant's nest, the butterfly's larvae feed on young ants while producing a secretion on which the ants feed. But the ant only lives in turf that is less than one centimeter in height, and when the rabbits were wiped out, the turf grew, and both the ants and the butterflies disappeared.[106] In Spain, populations of hares, partridges and pheasants dropped after myxomatosis wiped out the rabbits, because hunters had turned their attention to these animals as game.

Two vaccines for myxomatosis do exist and have been used especially in France. During the 1950s, in fact, tens of millions of the vaccines were sold each year to protect domestic stocks. Today, they are mostly used on breeding stock. The myxomatosis vaccine is also available in England. The myxoma virus in the United States is different, however, and a vaccine that is effective and safe is not yet available.

In Australia, researchers have also considered using other biological controls. The most controversial one has been rabbit hemorrhagic disease (RHD), which the Australians call rabbit calicivirus (RCV), and which is sometimes known as viral hemorrhagic disease (VHD). This disease was first spotted in a herd of German rabbits imported by China in 1984; researchers suspect that it may have originated in wild hares in that country. Since then, it has been reported in more than forty countries, including the United States, and has wiped out populations of wild and domestic rabbits in Cuba, Mexico, Italy, France, Germany, Spain and Austria, among other countries.[107] The virus is highly contagious, as it spreads by contact (not through an indirect vector, like a mosquito), and it can live a long time both on non-biological surfaces and in the tissues of rabbits. (One study found that the virus lived for two weeks in pig tissues.) That means that the virus can be carried and spread on shoes, tires and rabbit hair, on flies or birds that eat the carcasses of infected rabbits, and on rabbit meat, cages and trucks. In China, researchers believe, the virus spread via bicycle messengers carrying rabbit wool from one rabbitry to another.

The disease appears to spread and kill very quickly. "Once the rabbit is exposed it dies within one or two days," says Dr. Alvin Smith, a professor of veterinary medicine at Oregon State University and head of its Laboratory for Calicivirus Studies. "So the incubation period isn't even a couple days long. Even ebola virus takes about a week to kill its host." Symptoms vary, but many rabbits show no signs of infection for as long as a day, and then become quiet, develop a fever and/or start breathing heavily. Autopsies show that the rabbits develop blood clots in their internal organs, which then hemorrhage when the blood's clotting material runs out. During the virus's initial run, it can kill up to ninety percent of the animals in a population.

RHD supporters say the virus creates minimal suffering.[108] But many rabbits bleed from the mouth, nose or anus before actually dying; some die screaming, and many, according to one witness, are found with their heads thrown back, "as if they have been unable to breathe," Dr. Smith notes. Indeed, the deaths of the rabbits in some European commercial establishments were so bizarre and so rapid that some people attributed it to Chernobyl radiation or other pollution.[109]

So far, no government has formally released RHD within its borders. Australia considered releasing the virus in the mid-1990s and set up an experimental station on Wardang Island, off the coast of South Australia, in the fall of 1995.[110] There the disease did not spread particularly well; usually no more than one or two out of ten rabbits died in each pen. But before they could even finish their research, the disease suddenly cropped up in—and wiped out—rabbit populations on Point Pierce, about five kilometers across water on the mainland, and in a national park about two hundred kilometers inland. Just how the virus jumped from Wardang Island to the mainland is unknown, but many people believe that government researchers deliberately spread the disease. Whatever the cause, within eight weeks, ten million rabbits were dead. And while local hunters were quite unhappy, local farmers were quite excited; rumor had it that a dead or dying calici rabbit could fetch one hundred pounds, because it could be used to spread the virus further.[111] The government now allows the release of RHD within its borders and is considering releasing RHD in baits. To date the disease has wiped out some ninety-five percent of the wild rabbits in dry areas; in wetter areas, the disease "has had absolutely no effect," says Barry Richardson.

The New Zealand government also considered releasing the virus but decided against it. In 1997, however, farmers in Mackenzie Basin imported it and spread it around. For a while, in fact, farmers in that country cooked up their own "home brews" of RHD poisons by grinding up the corpses of infected rabbits in their kitchen blenders—an act that was foolhardy, at best. Unable to stop the practice, New Zealand legalized the spread of RHD that same year.

In that country, too, RHD has been extremely deadly—at least so far. At one sheep station in New Zealand, for instance, ninety-five percent of the rabbits (that's 600,000 rabbits in a six-hundred-square kilometer area) died within two weeks.

Aside from its cruelty, the primary controversy around RHD centers on whether or not the virus could mutate and infect other species, including humans. Caliciviruses are known for being unstable and for being able to mutate rapidly. Researchers have tried to test the adaptability of RHD by injecting all sorts of critters with the virus, including mice, guinea pigs, golden hamsters, Chinese hamsters, chinchillas, horses, donkeys, mules, cows, buffalo, sheep, goats, dogs, cats, rats, geese, short-tailed bats, chickens, ducks, native birds, wombats, koalas, reptiles and moles. They have taken the uteri out of pregnant pigs, removed the piglets, deprived them of colostrum (the antibody-rich fluid that they would normally drink in the hours after birth, before the mother's real "milk" arrives) and then shot the virus up their noses, all to see if the piglets could get the virus. None of these animals has come down with the virus.[112]

Critics of the studies note that the Australians never tested primates, which would seem important if one was concerned about the disease spreading to humans. Moreover, most of the animals who were injected with the virus were watched for only two weeks before being destroyed. When a kiwi bird, the sacred bird of the Maoris, was watched for a full month, it did develop antibodies to the virus—although antibodies are not the same as an active infection.[113] Hares inoculated with the disease have also developed antibodies, and when rabbits were injected with liver tissue from these hares, the rabbits died.

Other viruses have jumped species. The equine morbilivirus, which originated in bats, jumped to a horse and then eventually infected and killed two humans. Both SARS and monkeypox also originated in animals (the civet and giant Gambian rat, respectively) and then infected humans. Some researchers believe that RHD originally jumped from some other species to rabbits in China in the 1980s, which means it could jump again.[114]

In the United States, documented outbreaks of RHD have appeared only three times so far, although these outbreaks are so disjointed that many people believe the virus has been here for some time and just wasn't recognized or reported. The first outbreak occurred near Ames, Iowa in April 2000. Twenty-seven rabbits died. Then in August 2001, about three hundred rabbits died from the disease in Utah, but federal officials ended up killing about four thousand rabbits altogether to try to stop the spread of the disease— including rabbits that had been shipped to Illinois, Idaho and Montana to be slaughtered. (Mexico also used this so-called "ring slaughter" technique in the late 1980s to eradicate RHD; 160,000 rabbits were slaughtered over several years, of which only 65,000 actually had the disease.) After receiving a shipment of rabbits from the Utah facility, one breeder and dealer in Illinois noted that she could actually see the virus move from rabbit to rabbit around her barn and that "[Each] breed dies different, Rex would waste away, the New Zealand would scream for about 15 minutes before dieing [sic]. You could hear them at nights. The chinchilla would bleed for days before dieing. Does would die with babies still sucking."[115] The third U.S. outbreak occurred in December 2001, when eight rabbits died at a petting zoo in the Queens Zoo in New York.

A vaccine does exist for RHD, but the USDA's APHIS division is currently concerned that importing vaccines might actually spread, rather than stem, the disease. The vaccine is also produced by infecting live, healthy rabbits with the ground-up livers of infected rabbits, which raises serious ethical questions about killing rabbits to save rabbits (vaccinating all five million pet rabbits in this country would require the death of about five thousand rabbits). In addition, if RHD breaks out in a herd where some of the rabbits are vaccinated, it will be nearly impossible to figure out where the infection originated and which rabbits have been exposed. And feline calicivirus is already rearing its ugly head again—despite the vaccine's having been available for some thirty years. This only shows that viruses can and do mutate despite vaccination efforts.

Some people have suggested that the United States should immediately ban all imported rabbit meat and rabbit fur products (including clothing and cat toys), especially from China, but also from Australia and European countries where RHD has been found. Some believe the United States should even institute a quarantine policy for bringing in live rabbits. Unfortunately, the USDA, which would normally be in a position to make that regulation, doesn't cover rabbits, because rabbits aren't technically "livestock," although the agency does take charge of ring slaughters and quarantines. The USDA did not respond to our requests for information about the disease or the agency's policies.

While most people with pet rabbits don't know much about RHD, many breeders are terrified about the implications of the disease. "If there's an outbreak in your herd, the USDA's policy is to eradicate it completely," says Corinne Fayo, who breeds and shows Netherland Dwarf rabbits in upstate New York. "Meat rabbit growers could go out and get new animals, but my herd represents years of hard work. It would be heartbreaking if I lost the rabbits; I would never be able to duplicate those lines. I don't even know if I could stay in business it would hurt so much."

Concerned breeders and rabbit enthusiasts have been unable to exert sufficient pressure on the government to force a change, in part because of the lack of cohesiveness between the many rabbit-oriented groups in the United States. The country's estimated five million pet rabbit caretakers are hard to reach, as few of them belong to either the American Rabbit Breeders Association or House Rabbit Society. People interested in rabbits as pets don't communicate much with rabbit breeders; some animosity, in fact, exists between some rabbit rescuers (who think breeders exploit animals), and some rabbit breeders (who claim all rabbit rescuers are radical—even terrorist—animal rights activists). The meat rabbit "growers" move in still different circles—or no circles at all, as the industry has never been truly organized. "I feel pretty helpless," Fayo says. "If RHD breaks out here, there's pretty much nothing I can do to prevent losing my entire herd."

❖   ❖   ❖

Given the dangers of biological controls, the startling lack of research into how they work and whom they affect, and the chance for suffering, both among rabbits and other species, releasing these viruses seems rather shortsighted. Indeed, with the exception of reducing demand for rabbits, most of the controls used to reduce supply are inhumane. Most of them are also inefficient: either they don't get all of the rabbits, or they also get other animals, or, if they do wipe out most of a rabbit population, the remaining populations reproduce all the more rapidly to get their numbers up again.[116]

What would the real solution to wild rabbit overpopulation be? The answers aren't easy. Richardson told us he can "think of no rational or evenly faintly effective alternative" to the RHD strategy, except to "poison every rabbit inside a rabbit-proofed fenced area, rip up all the warrens and clear all the harbor on the surface (logs etc). This would need to be done again every year as they break through any kind of system." Smith has suggested that the farmers in Australia and New Zealand simply convert from sheep farming to rabbit farming and let the rabbit populations find their own balance—a suggestion that brings guffaws from other analysts.

Researchers in Australia are touting a new birth control option for wild rabbits: inserting reproductive genes into the DNA of the myxoma virus, which is then released via mosquitoes or fleas. In the process of developing antibodies against the virus, the female rabbits produce antibodies against their own eggs, thus making them immune to fertilization.[117] The result? In an ideal world, it would be rabbits who are still alive, but sterile. But given that most biological controls have gone awry in the past—often by being spread illegally—it seems quite possible that something would go wrong with this procedure, that hares and cottontails, for instance, who get a very benign form of myxomatosis now, might also get exposed to the virus and become sterile, or that entire commercial rabbitries might be affected. "When people start messing around with infectious agents, they're cruising for a bruising," Smith says. "This is insanity."

Surely the ultimate goal of any eradication program should be to develop a sense of stewardship that acknowledges the dignity of human and animal alike. One solution might be to manage habitat more carefully, so that farmers aren't encouraging rabbits. Such methods do exist. One study found that electric fences can scare away sixty to sixty-five percent of wild rabbits—and that they only need to feel a shock once to stay away from the fence for good.[118] Other studies have found that removing brush from agricultural areas also discourages wild rabbits, who generally want some vegetative cover, as does filling in old quarries, in which rabbits might want to build their burrows,[119] and wrapping fruit tree seedlings with aluminum foil or plastic guards, to keep the rabbits from destroying the bark.[120]

The idea of controlling wild rabbits brings up quandaries for those who respect animals, because it requires us to balance the needs of humans against the suffering of animals. That something must be done is indisputable: there are too many competing demands—both from humans and other species—to allow the rabbits to spread unchecked. But even Henry Thompson, who seems to have had little sentimental love of wild rabbits, insisted that "control is not a euphemism for killing."[121] If control is going to entail killing, then, as history seems to indicate, the humans involved must at least understand that our own species made a terrible mistake in transporting the European rabbit to new countries in the first place—and that any form of killing is likely to create widespread suffering among both the targeted and other species.

Domesticating the Rabbit

The fact that domestic rabbits, wild American rabbits, wild European rabbits and hares are continually jumbling in the popular mind is not surprising. The names are confusing: jackrabbits, for instance, are actually hares, while both domestic Belgian hares and some wild "hares" (like the hispid hare and the African rockhare) are actually rabbits, albeit of different species. These animals also look similar—although if you place a long, lean hare next to a roly-poly

French Lop, a meaty Flemish Giant or a neatly belted black-and-white Dutch, you'll see that domestication has had its effect. This hasn't stopped generations of illustrators from placing cute little white bunnies in the fields and forests of children's books. Nor has it stopped many zoos and wildlife centers from displaying domestic rabbits in exhibits about "wild" rabbits, both of which no doubt confuse the public—especially the young public—even more.

Animal domestication probably began with our Neolithic ancestors, who lived during the latest period of the Stone Age. They most likely domesticated the wolf first, somewhere between fourteen thousand and twelve thousand years ago in the Near East, and then sheep and goats. Cattle and pigs were domesticated in Asia approximately nine thousand years ago; horses, camels, water buffalo and fowl followed shortly thereafter; and between four thousand and three thousand years ago cats were domesticated in Egypt. The New World saw, during this same ten-thousand-year period, the domestication of alpaca, guinea pigs and llamas in South America, and turkeys and dogs in North America.

This was no small step for humankind. Widely considered the third most important development in civilization (after tool making and the mastery of fire), this "Neolithic Revolution" (which included both the cultivation of crops and the domestication of animals) made possible a stable food supply, which, in turn, ushered in the beginning of settled life, after centuries of nomadic wanderings. Domestication also had fateful consequences for the nonhumans. Once humans began controlling the *who, when* and *where* of animal reproduction, they also began controlling the very *what* of the animals themselves. Today's dairy cows produce a thousand times as much milk as their wild ancestors. Today's pug dogs look little like their wolf progenitors. Today's Angora rabbits may have a body shape that resembles a wild rabbit, but the "big" hair of the Angora nearly masks the rabbit that lies beneath.

Put another way, the domestication of animals, combined with the agricultural revolution, paved the way for a totally new relationship with animals. According to James Serpell, a scholar of animal-human interactions, traditional hunter-gatherers typically viewed the animals that they hunted as their equals. Once animals were domesticated, this relationship changed to one of property and owner, as all aspects of the lives of domesticated animals were controlled, from birth to sex to feeding to death.[122]

Humans first controlled wild European rabbits in "leporaria" or rabbit gardens. True domestication, in which rabbits were bred for size and form, was a parallel development that began somewhere between 500 and 1000 C.E., in French monasteries. The monks initially became interested in keeping wild rabbits because they thought that rabbit fetuses and newborn babies, called *laurices*, were aquatic and so could be eaten during Lent and other fasts, when meat was forbidden. (By some accounts the monks picked up this practice from the Romans, who liked to eat newborn rabbits, too.)[123]

The monks kept the rabbits in walled, paved courtyards, where the young were very easy to capture.[124] Early domestication attempts probably focused on breeding for tameness and size, but not for color. Breeding for color probably began around the middle of the sixteenth century; records from that time specifically mention piebald, white and black rabbits.[125] One hundred years later, monks and others began breeding for fur, and deliberately creating white, black, "blue" and the distinctly collared Dutch rabbit for pelts. Such an early rabbit appears in a 1587 painting attributed to Hans Hoffman, called simply *Hare*. This was painted in the style of Albrecht Dürer's hare studies, but it clearly shows a rounder, brown lagomorph with white markings that seems more like a rabbit than a hare. By 1700, seven different colors had been deliberately created—non-agouti, brown, albino, yellow, silver and spotted.[126]

Why domesticate rabbits and not, say, hares? Or raccoons? Or tigers? While it seems as though humans have domesticated a lot of animals, we've actually domesticated very few. And we've only domesticated those whose social hierarchies fit well with our own (that is, those that are gregarious and have linear dominance structures that would allow a human to be the head of the animal household), those who actually like living in close quarters, and those who are relatively easy to take care of. Dogs, horses, sheep and rabbits fill these requirements; tigers, raccoons, giraffes and beavers do not. In addition, rabbits, like dogs, sheep, goats and horses, are scavenging (or crop-robbing) animals, who naturally tend to live near human settlements. This in itself can be one step in a long process of adaptation and domestication.[127]

Another reason in favor of the domestication of rabbits is that they were thought to be good animals for women to take care of, since they were small, fairly easy to care for and even fairly easy to kill; one fourteenth-century French manuscript shows women hunting rabbits with bows and arrows, clubs and small dogs.[128] Such husbandry responsibilities were nothing new. Women throughout history have been in charge of the family's small animals (like poultry) and other livestock kept close to the house (like cows and pigs), as these chores could be done with small children, while men worked in the fields,[129] and the products of these labors (e.g., milk, eggs, wool and meat) could supplement the family's income. This gender division lasted until the industrial period in Europe and America. In post-industrial rural America, women have continued to be the primary caretakers of the family's small animals, and women very much dominate the worlds of rabbit breeders, rabbit rescue organizations and rabbit collectibles.

The rediscovery of Mendel's work on dominance and selection and gene combinations fueled rabbit breeding in the late nineteenth and early twentieth centuries. Since then, dozens of rabbit breeds have been created, ranging from the pure white New Zealand to the coal black Satin, from the patchwork Harlequin rabbits to the polka-dotted English Spot, and from the massive, silver-colored Giant Chinchilla, prized for its pelt, to diminutive dwarf breeds, prized for their tiny size. There are now "lop" rabbits with long floppy ears (including the English Lop, whose ears are so long they drag on the ground), and Angora rabbits that produce long dense "wool" used for knitting. In the commercial rabbit world, humans breed rabbits to be good breeders and mothers, to have lots of meat, to be docile

Figure 1.14. Woman and rabbit in a courtyard, New Orleans, sometime in the 1920s. Women have long been responsible for the keeping of rabbits. Library of Congress, Prints and Photographs Division. [Reproduction number LC-G391-T-1150]

in laboratory experiments, even to glow under ultraviolet lights (as part of a scientific effort to "tag" embryos).

❖ ❖ ❖

In the last hundred years, rabbits have also been bred to be pets. The exact history of this practice is hard to trace. This is partly because the history of rabbit breeding is so heavily dominated by commercial interests and partly because women, who cared for rabbits historically and may have been most likely to develop bonds with them, had fewer opportunities to write than did men. But it seems clear that some rabbits were cherished as personal companions—at least by women—even before the nineteenth century. Roman rules forbade residents of the British Isles to eat rabbit (as well as hare, chicken and goose), but Julius Caesar noted that the Britons could "keep these animals for pleasure."[130] Many centuries later, in 1387, William of Wykeham exhorted his nuns to "presume henceforward to bring to church no birds, hounds, rabbits or other frivolous things that promote indiscipline,"[131] which implies that the nuns had a personal bond with their small charges. In Renaissance times, women whose rabbits died are reported to have created tombs and funerary odes for them.[132]

True pet keeping of a variety of species began in the eighteenth and nineteenth centuries. According to the editors of *Companion Animals and Us*,[133] until the early modern period, Europeans viewed animals "as irrational beings placed on earth solely for the economic benefit of mankind, and most scholars would have insisted that affectionate relationships between people and animals were not only distasteful but depraved." Humans, including indigenous people, had certainly kept pets before this period. But modern pet keeping—which consists of domestic animals, with names, living indoors with humans—started in earnest in the eighteenth and nineteenth centuries, with the rise of an urban middle class that had little contact with either working farm animals or wild creatures and so tended to romanticize both nature and animals.[134] The Victorians became much enamored of companion animals, and it was during this period that pet keeping—or catering to pet keepers—began to take on more commercial tones, as pet supply companies began distributing booklets offering pet care advice. The first mass-produced pet, according to historian Katherine Grier, was the goldfish.[135]

William Cowper, the eighteenth-century poet, letter writer and scholar, was one of the first to write about living—and bonding—with lagomorphs. Cowper lived with three young hares (known as "leverets") while he lived in Buckinghamshire, England. Depressed and suicidal, Cowper undertook their care with a passion, naming them Puss, Tiney and Bess, and building them a set of "apartments" to sleep in. In one 1784 letter, Cowper writes that Puss:

. . . grew presently familiar, would leap into my lap, raise himself upon his hinder feet, and bite the hair from my temples. He would suffer me to take him up, and to carry him about in my arms, and has more than once fallen fast asleep upon my knee. . . . Thus Puss might be said to be perfectly tamed, the shyness of his nature was done away, and on the whole it was visible by many symptoms, which I have not room to enumerate, that he was happier in human society than when shut up with his natural companions.[136]

Cowper also wrote at length of Tiney and Bess. Although neither seemed to enjoy the close relationship with the author that Puss did, each "had a character of his own," Cowper wrote. "Such they were in fact, and their countenances were so expressive of that character, that, when I looked only on the face of either, I immediately knew which it was."[137]

Cowper's feelings towards his three hares also led him to take an unusual (for that time) stand against blood sports. In a piece for *Gentlemen's Magazine*, Cowper wrote:

You will not wonder, Sir, that my intimate acquaintance with these specimens of the kind has taught me to hold the sportsman's amusements in abhorrence; he little knows what amiable creatures he persecutes, of what gratitude they are capable, how cheerful they are in spirits, what enjoyments they have of life, and that impressed as they seem with a peculiar dread of man, it is only because man gives them peculiar cause for it.[138]

The eighteenth-century European introduction of fancy breeds is also an indication that people were beginning to see rabbits as more than just food. The English Lop, with its extraordinarily long, dragging ears, for example, is one of the oldest breeds of domestic rabbit (the lopped ear started as a genetic mutation) and has been found in images and accounts dating back to at least 1700.[139] Pet rabbits—or at least meat rabbits with whom the family felt a bond—also appear in paintings throughout the nineteenth century. One painting by Sir Henry Raeburn (1756–1823), the leading Scottish portrait painter of his period, shows an upper-class boy with his arm affectionately encircling a small, domestic rabbit. German genre artist Felix Schlesinger (1833–1910), whose rustic, sentimental paintings typically showed cherubic children bonding with equally cherubic animals (a favorite theme of the Victorians) created several paintings showing children playing with domesticated rabbits. *Feeding the Rabbits* shows two children in what looks like a barn. The girl holds a small rabbit on her lap; the boy appears captivated by two rabbits eating from his hands. In one of Schlesinger's "pet rabbit" paintings, a young boy sitting on a bale of hay cradles a very sweet-looking rabbit in his arms. In another painting with the same title, a young girl feeds a rabbit next to her on a bench, as she holds him with one arm. Schlesinger's *Children and Beauties* shows four rosy-cheeked children feeding two rabbits (one of which has lop ears), again in a barn. These rabbits all appear relaxed with, even affectionate toward, the children.

The same is true with *Pets*, by the English painter George S. Knowles, also a genre artist of the Victorian era. *Pets* shows two girls in a barnyard clearly enchanted with two white rabbits in a basket, one of whom looks like it might be licking her. Similarly, *Children and Rabbits*, by Sir Edwin Landseer, shows two upper-class children in a barn holding two large rabbits, while gazing fondly on a wooden bowl full of baby rabbits. (The pet dog in this painting looks rather dejected, as if the rabbits have usurped his position). *Little Timidity* and *Her Favorite*, both by Frederick Beaumont, also emphasize the potential love between child and bunny; both paintings feature a young girl looking up shyly, while cuddling a small gray and white rabbit close to her chest.

Although many of these rabbits may have been destined, ultimately, for the family stew pot, the fact that many of the titles emphasize the rabbits' status as "pets" shows that the idea of child–rabbit affection, especially, was already developing by the Victorian period.

Indeed, Victorian parents and moralists did encourage bonds between *children* and pets, as this seemed a good way to cultivate middle-class virtues, like kindness and self-control, in young people. A number of popular magazines sprang up that were aimed at children and chock full of poetry, advice, fiction and pictures about pets. Relationships with animals were thought to be especially helpful in counteracting boys' tendencies to be violent. "Pet keeping, an activity long interpreted and tolerated as a personal indulgence, was transformed into a morally purposive act," Grier writes.[140] As this movement gained strength, she notes, "parents were advised to provide their boys with coops of pigeons, cages of songbirds, hutches of bunnies, and rollicking dogs."

One text, in particular, used a story about a twice-abused rabbit to bring home a moral point. *Master Henry's Rabbit*, a small paperback children's book published around 1840, told the story of an eight-year old boy who adopts a rabbit who had been injured by some village boys and their dog. His uncle, Mr. Dalben, tells the boy he can have the rabbit as long as he takes responsibility for him, yet Henry takes care of the rabbit only until his new kite distracts him. His uncle sternly reprimands him: "You are greatly to blame, Henry. You would have done better, to have destroyed the little creature at once when you found it in the warren, than to keep it to perish with hunger. Go, careless boy, feed your poor rabbit now; and, in order that you may be able to feel for the poor animal another time, I shall deprive you of your dinner today." Grier writes, "The punishment meted out by Henry's uncle was intended to foster empathy—in this case through a similar experience of relatively harmless pain—and to encourage self-regulation through self-examination. Young Henry 'humbled himself before God for this sin, and prayed earnestly for a better heart.' "[141]

Wicked Tim, written in 1917 by New Zealand author Harry Rountree, continued this theme, with a harsher ending. In this book, Tim is actually a cranky little rabbit, "the youngest and wildest of

"Bother errands," said he, banging
the door angrily behind him, and
paying little heed to Mother Bunny
as she cried to him to be good and
return safely home.

TIM simply could not be good;
and soon he was playing pranks
with the wind, and the umbrella Pa
had lent him, spinning merrily along

Figure 1.15. The 1917 children's book *Wicked Tim* used a mischievous little rabbit to teach children about the dangers of being naughty. Published by Charles E Graham & Co.

the Bunny family, who hated going on errands . . . who simply could not be good." His mother sends him out to do errands anyway and Tim starts playing with his umbrella, which ends up getting carried away by a gust of wind—young Tim still attached. His "poor, half-frozen paws are unclasped," and he falls into the sea. Tim manages to crawl up onto a log, where he arrogantly chuckles, "Just my luck," and strips off his clothes to dry. The log then floats to a "desert island," where Tim pelts the local penguins with eggs. "And while they screamed with rage, he screamed with laughter," Rountree writes, "till the sport grew a little stale." Improbably, Tim then befriends one of the penguins and rigs up a little saddle so he can ride it, but the penguin loses patience and jumps, with Tim still astride, off a cliff and into the sea. When Tim's body washes up on the shore, the penguins take pity on him and bear him "tenderly away to a grassy knoll," where they bury him. True to his rabbit nature, Tim burrows out of his grave and, we can assume, will be up to no good again soon.

During this same period, people were developing or buying more and more fancy breeds of rabbits. The Dutch rabbit, which was first developed in the Netherlands, perhaps as early as the fifteenth century, was first brought to England in 1864. The Harlequin, English Spot and Havana were all created in the late nineteenth century. The nineteenth century also witnessed the development of organized rabbit shows and specialty clubs, giving "fancy" rabbit breeders an opportunity to show off their rabbits and further spreading the breeds throughout the world. That some of these animals were pets seems inevitable. According to the American Rabbit Breeders Association (ARBA) guidebook, few rabbits and rabbit clubs existed in the U.S. prior to 1893; those rabbits that existed were evidently "children's pets" and tended to be white, Dutch or spotted.

All that changed in the 1890s, a period known as the "Great Belgian Hare Era." Like many fancy rabbits of the time, the Belgian Hare (which is actually a rabbit bred to look like a wild hare) was developed in Belgium as a meat rabbit, but, after the breed standard was written in 1882, it became a popular show rabbit. In 1888, a Belgian Hare was first brought to the United States and exhibited at small shows throughout the country. This ushered in one of the first specialty clubs in this country, the National Belgian Hare Club of America, later the National Pet Stock Association, which eventually became ARBA.

Part of the craze around Belgian Hares had to do with the plethora of buy-back schemes associated with the breed. Belgian Hare breeders sold the pedigreed animals for everything from $25.00 to $1,000.00, all the while promising great riches from the sale of the rabbits' meat—or, sometimes, from the buy back of stock. As the breed gained popularity towards the end of the nineteenth century, at least six hundred Belgian Hare rabbitries sprang up in the Los

Figure 1.16. Domestic rabbits now come in all shapes, sizes, and colors. First Row: (l to r) Baron is a Dutch, Lucille is an English Spot, Corey is a New Zealand. Second Row: (l to r) Callie is a Harlequin; Pugsley is a Dwarf/Himalayan; Sugar is a Californian. Third Row: (l to r) Velveeta is a Rex; Jeffrey is a Florida White; Alexander is an Angora. Fourth Row: (l to r) Henry is an Angora; Snookie is a Flemish Giant; Hector is a Holland Lop. Fifth Row: (l to r) Felicity is a Lop; Claude is a Silver Marten; Diana is a Mini Lop. Photos by Ken Mark.

Angeles area alone. By 1900, more than sixty thousand Belgian Hares were being raised in Southern California.[142]

Beatrix Potter is one celebrity who was bitten by the Belgian Hare bug; her enormously popular *Tale of Peter Rabbit* was inspired in part by her two Belgian Hares, Benjamin Bouncer (known as Bounce) and Peter Piper. Potter purchased Benjamin in 1889 and wrote, "I brought him home (surreptitiously—if that's the way to spell it)—from a London bird shop in a paper bag. His existence was not observed by the nursery authorities for a week." She used Benjamin as a model for the first commercial drawings that she sold, a set of Christmas cards. When she received her pay for the cards, she writes, "My first act was to give Bounce (what an investment that rabbit has been in spite of the hutches), a cupful of hemp seeds, the consequences being that when I wanted to draw him next morning he was partially intoxicated and wholly unmanageable." She soon sold more cards, but noted that she was sometimes impeded by Benjamin, "who has an appetite for certain sorts of paint."[143]

Potter allowed both rabbits to live at least part time in the house with her. "Both were fond of the fire, and one used to lie inside the fender," she wrote, noting that one even slept "under the grate on the hot ashes when the fire had gone out."[144] Peter Piper, who learned to do tricks, also had "an old quilt made of scraps of flanel [sic] and blue cloth which he always lay on." When Peter died at nine years of age, Potter wrote, "Whatever the limitations of his intellect or outward shortcomings of his fur, and his ears and toes, his disposition was uniformly amiable and his temper unfailingly sweet. An affectionate companion and a quiet friend."[145]

After the Belgian boom died down, other breeds were developed, including the American, the Checkered Giant, the Dwarf, the Hotot, the Flemish Giant and the Rex, as were a whole host of specialty clubs on both sides of the Atlantic Ocean. Today, more than one hundred breeds of rabbits exist (although only forty-five have been recognized by ARBA), and thousands of rabbit breeders worldwide cater to the pet market, the show community and the commercial rabbit industries.

Figure 1.17. Beatrix Potter, a skilled naturalist and sketch artist, based her first commercial drawings on her house rabbit "Benjamin Bounce." Here she takes Benjamin for a walk in September 1891. Courtesy of a private collection, reproduced by Frederick Warne & Co.

❖   ❖   ❖

Humans generally create "breeds" to fulfill a commercial or aesthetic need—whether it's a rabbit with a high flesh-to-bone ratio for producing meat or a rabbit with ten-inch-long ears that drag on the ground (versus the three-inch average for a wild European rabbit), simply for the sake of interesting looks. But domestication does odd things to deeper physiology, too. The face and jaws get shortened, the teeth get smaller, an extra layer of fat develops, and the domestic version of the wild progenitor often retains the juvenile or even fetal characteristics of their species.[146] The domestic version also develops a strong dependence on humans, as the behaviors needed to survive in the wild are forgotten.

These processes change the animals far faster than they would ever evolve in the wild, where natural selection favors behaviors and physical characteristics that boost an animal's chance of survival.[147] This is a critical fact that people who release their pet rabbits (or who "liberate" laboratory or meat rabbits) into "the wild" don't understand. Over the last ten years we've met rabbits who were left on beaches, roadsides and railroad tracks, in parks, parking lots and playgrounds, and in backyards, apartment buildings and woodland lots. The releasers often think their pets will frolic their days away like the happy-go-lucky wild (and domestic) bunnies in children's storybooks, or that they'll somehow develop the street smarts that stray dogs and cats develop. But dogs and cats survive (when they do) because they're predators and because they have been domesticated longer than rabbits and know how to get what they need from us. Domestic rabbits have lost their instinctual defenses against predators like raptors, dogs or cats. Most of them have also lost the earth-colored, wild coloring that would help them hide from predators.

In fact, domestic rabbits, who have been affiliated with humans for only 1,500 years—or some two hundred to three hundred generations—inhabit a strange purgatory of domestication. They're not really wild anymore, but they aren't so integrated into our human habits that they know how to dig through garbage, scratch at back doors, beg passersby for food, or find water. (Most domestic rabbits in the wild, in fact, are the devil to catch, because they can't tell that their would-be rescuers are trying to help them.) Instead, released rabbits often perish from starvation, from exposure, or from being attacked by larger, more aggressive animals. Yet people who see a white or spotted domestic rabbit in the wild may blithely assume the animal was either wild to begin with or will happily adapt to its new wilderness home. This species that is so entwined with human history—as pest, pet, and cultivated product—remains as mysterious to us as far more rarified creatures.

Notes

1. Fox, Richard, "Taxonomy and Genetics," in Manning, Patrick, et al. (eds.), *The Biology of the Laboratory Rabbit*, (New York: Academic Press, 1994), p. 4.
2. Thompson, Henry, "The Rabbit in Britain," in Thompson, Henry (ed.), *The European Rabbit: The History and Biology of a Successful Colonizer* (New York: Oxford University Press, 1994), p. 65.
3. Corbet, G.B., "Taxonomy and Origins," in Thompson, *The European Rabbit*, p. 2.
4. Chapman, Joseph and John E.C. Flux, *Rabbits, Hares, and Pikas: Status Survey and Conservation Action Plan* (Oxford: International Union for Conservation of Nature and Natural Resources, 1990), p. 1.
5. Email to Susan Davis, August 29, 2002.
6. University of Florida Hall of Fossils Web site, www.flmnh.ufl.edu/fossilhall/library/lepus/leapinglepus.htm
7. Strege, Dave, "Hail to the Angler," *Orange County Register*, August 14, 1997.
8. Nowak, Ronald M., *Walker's Mammals of the World*, online at www.press.jhu.edu/books/walker
   Chapman, Joseph, "The Cottontails," in Chapman and Flux, *Rabbits, Hares, and Pikas*, p. 98.
9. Fa, J.E., "The Volcano Rabbit," in Chapman and Flux, *Rabbits, Hares, and Pikas*, p. 143.
10. Flux, John E.C., "The Hares and the Jackrabbits," in Chapman and Flux, *Rabbits, Hares, and Pikas*, p. 62.
11. Bell, Diana, et al., "The Hispid Hare," in Chapman and Flux, *Rabbits, Hares, and Pikas*, p. 128.
12. Dobler, F. et al., "The Pygmy Rabbit," in Chapman and Flux, *Rabbits, Hares, and Pikas*, pp. 112–113.
13. Nowak, *Walker's Mammals of the World*, www.press.jhu.edu/books/walker.
14. Myers, Ken, "Foreword," in Chapman and Flux, *Rabbits, Hares, and Pikas*, p. iii.
15. Chapman, Joseph, "Introduction and Overview of the Lagomorphs," in Chapman and Flux, *Rabbits, Hares, and Pikas*, p. 3.
16. Rogers, P.M., "The Rabbit in Continental Europe," in Thompson, *The European Rabbit*, p. 46.
17. *Ibid.*, p. 44.
18. Reed, C. "The copulatory behavior of small mammals," *Journal of Comparative Psychology*, Vol. 39 (1967), pp. 185–206.
19. Patton, Nephi M., "Colony Husbandry," In Manning, et al., *The Biology of the Laboratory Rabbit*, p. 32.
20. Myers, Ken, "The Rabbit in Australia," in Thompson, *The European Rabbit*, p. 118.
21. Flux, *op. cit.*, p. 62.
22. Mowery, William, "The Mystery of the Big Hop," *Audubon Magazine*, July–August, 1953.
23. *Ibid.*, p. 69.
24. Southern, H.N. "Sexual and aggressive behaviour in the wild rabbit," *Behavior*, Vol. 1 (1948), p. 181.
25. Lockley, *op. cit*, p. 26.
26. *Ibid.*
27. Myers, Ken, "The Rabbit in Australia," p. 121.
28. Hudson, Rogyn, et al., "Spontaneous and odour-induced chin marking in domestic female rabbits," *Animal Behavior* (1992), 43, pp. 329–336.
29. Black, Stephen L. and C.H. Vanderwolf, "Thumping Behavior in the Rabbit," in *Physiology and Behavior*, Vol. 4, (1969) pp. 445–449.
30. Lockley, *op. cit*, p. 46.
31. Southern, *op. cit.*, pp. 173–184.
32. Patton, *op. cit.*, p. 31.

33. Gibb, John A and J. Morgan Williams, "The Rabbit in New Zealand," in Thompson, *The European Rabbit*, p. 183.
34. Lockley, R.M. "Social Structure and Stress in the Rabbit Warren," *Animal Ecology*, Vol. 30 (1961), page 408.
35. Myers, Ken, "The Rabbit in Australia," p. 129.
36. *Ibid., p. 129.*
37. *Ibid.*
38. Nowak, *Walker's Mammals of the World*, www.press.jhu.edu/books/walker.
39. Myers, Ken, "The Rabbit in Australia," p. 121.
40. Southern, *op. cit*, p. 187.
41. Myers, Ken, "The Rabbit in Australia," pp. 121, 130.
42. *Ibid.,* p. 127.
43. Gibb and Williams, *op. cit*, p. 183.
44. Myers, Ken, "The Rabbit in Australia," p. 122.
45. Eiserman, K., "Long-term Heartrate Responses to Social Stress in Wild European Rabbits: Predominant Effect of Rank Position," *Physiology & Behavior*, Vol. 52 (1992) pp. 33–36.
46. Myers, Ken, "The Rabbit in Australia."
47. Lockley, *op. cit*, p. 55.
48. *Ibid.,* p. 57.
49. Mykytowycz, R. and E.R. Hesterman. "An experimental study of aggression in captive European rabbits," *Behaviour*, 52, (1975) pp. 104–123.
50. Flux, John E.C., "World Distribution," in Thompson, *The European Rabbit*, p. 8.
51. Thompson, *op. cit*, p. 64.
     Clutton-Brock, Juliet, *A Natural History of Domesticated Mammals* (Cambridge: Cambridge University Press, 1999), p. 180.
52. Thompson, *op. cit*, p. 64.
53. Flux, "World Distribution," p. 8.
54. *Ibid.*
55. Zeuner, Frederick E., *A History of Domesticated Animals* (New York: Harper & Row, 1963), p. 412.
56. Flux, "World Distribution," p. 28.
57. Thompson, *op. cit*, p. 63.
58. Zeuner, *op. cit.,* p. 412.
59. Chapman, *op. cit.,* p. 117.
60. Flux, "World Distribution," p. 9.
61. *Ibid.*
62. *Ibid.,* p. 11. Gibb and Williams, *op. cit.,* p. 159.
63. Flux, "Exotic Populations," in Chapman and Flux, p. 147.
64. *Ibid.*
65. Australian Museums and Galleries Online, "Run Rabbit Run: The Story of Rabbits in Western Australia," http://amol.org.au/guide/stories/rabbits/timeline.asp.
66. Hinds, Lyn A., et al., "Rabbits—prospects for long-term control: mortality and fertility control," Paper prepared for the Prime Minister's Science and Engineering Council, Australia, 1996.
67. Gibb and Williams, *op. cit.,* pp. 158–160.
68. Flux, "World Distribution," p. 11.
69. Gibb and Williams, *op. cit.,* p. 159.
70. Flux, "World Distribution," p. 13.
71. *Ibid.,* p. 14.
72. Rogers, *op. cit.,* p. 27.
73. Thompson, *op. cit.,* p. 97.
74. Rogers, *op. cit.,* pp. 28–29.
75. Crosby, Alfred, *Ecological Imperialism: The Biological Expansion of Europe, 900–1900* (Cambridge: Cambridge University Press, 1986), p. 75.
76. *Ibid.*

77. Lockley, *The Private Life of Rabbits*, pp. 143–144.
78. Hinds, *op. cit.*
79. *Ibid.*
80. Thompson, Henry, "Editor's Introduction," in Thompson, *The European Rabbit*, p. xiii.
81. Rogers, *op. cit.*, p. 35.
82. Myers, Ken, "The Rabbit in Australia," p. 131.
83. Rogers, *op. cit.*, p. 57.
84. Chapman, "Introduction and Overview of the Lagomorphs," in Chapman and Flux, p. 2.
85. Flux, "World Distribution," p. 16.
86. Thompson, *The European Rabbit*, p. 70.
87. Palmer, T.S. M.D., *The Jack Rabbits of the United States* (Washington, D.C.: Government Printing Office [USDA], 1896), p. 51.
88. Thompson, "Editor's Introduction," in Thompson, *The European Rabbit*, p. 36.
89. Australian Museums and Galleries Online, "Run Rabbit Run: The Story of Rabbits in Western Australia," http://amol.org.au/guide/stories/rabbits/timeline.asp.
90. Lockley, *The Private Life of Rabbits*, pp. 17–19.
91. *Ibid.*
92. Gibb and Williams, *op. cit.*, p. 163.
93. Flux, "Exotic Populations," p. 148.
94. Gibb and Williams, *op. cit.*, p. 163.
95. Email correspondence.
96. Rogers, *op. cit.*, pp. 30–35.
97. Fenner, Frank and John Ross, "Myxomatosis," in Thompson, *The European Rabbit*, p. 205.
98. *Ibid.*, p. 230.
99. Lockley, *The Private Life of Rabbits*, p. 130.
100. Gibb and Williams, *op. cit.*, p. 167.
101. Thompson, "The Rabbit in Britain," p. 92.
102. Fenner, *op. cit.*, p. 205.
103. Hinds, *op. cit.*
104. *Ibid.*, p. 73.
105. Thompson "The Rabbit in Britain," p. 79.
106. *Ibid.*, p. 85.
107. United States Department of Agriculture, "Rabbit Calicivirus Disease, Iowa, April 2000 Impact Worksheet," http://www.aphis.usda.gov/vs/ceah/cei/rabbitcal.htm.
108. Hinds, *op. cit.*
109. Rogers, *op. cit.*, p. 56.
110. Hinds, *op. cit.*
111. "The Bunny Bug: Friend or Foe?" Aired on Radio National, Sunday, April 21, 1996 in Australia.
112. Hinds, *op. cit.*
113. "The Bunny Bug: Friend or Foe?"
114. *Ibid.*
115. RHD in the United States Coalition Web page, http://www.vhdcoalition.org/victims-account.html.
116. Hinds, *op. cit.*
117. *Ibid.*
118. McKillop, I.G., et al., "The behaviour of free-living European wild rabbits at electric fences," *Crop Protection* 18 (1999) pp. 193–197.
119. Boag, B., et al., "Reduction in numbers of wild rabbits due to changes in agricultural practices," *Crop Protection* 6 (1987) pp. 347–51.
120. Moran, S. "Non-lethal control techniques against damage by vertebrates in Israeli agriculture," *Israeli Journal of Zoology* (1999), 45(2): 316.
121. Thompson, "The Rabbit in Britain," p. 93.

122. Serpell, James A. *In the Company of Animals*, 2nd (revised) edition (Cambridge: Cambridge University Press, 1996).
123. Rogers, *op. cit.*, p. 47.
124. Clutton-Brock, *op. cit.*
125. Zeuner, *op. cit.*, p. 413.
126. Fox, *op. cit.*, p. 5.
127. Carlson, Laurie Winn, *Cattle: An Informal Social History* (Chicago: Ivan R. Dee Inc., 2001), p. 29.
128. Zeuner, *op. cit.*, p. 412.
129. Tilly, Louise A. and Joan W. Scott, *Women, Work and Family* (New York: Methuen, 1987).
130. Ezpeleta, Alicia, *Rabbits Everywhere* (New York: Harry N. Abrams, 1996), p. 22.
131. Flux, "World Distribution," p. 9.
132. Ezpeleta, *op. cit.*, pp. 91–94.
133. Podberscek, Anthony, Elizabeth Paul and James Serpell, "Introduction," in Podberscek, Paul and Serpell (eds.), *Companion Animals and Us* (Cambridge: Cambridge University Press, 2000), p. 1.
134. Jasper, James and Dorothy Nelkin, *The Animal Rights Crusade: The Growth of a Moral Protest* (New York: The Free Press, 1992), p. 17.
135. Grier, Katherine. "Childhood Socialization and Companion Animals: United States 1820–1870," *Society and Animals: Journal of Human-Animal Studies* Vol. 7, No. 2 (1999).
136. Milford, H.S. (ed.), *The Poetical Works of William Cowper* (Oxford: Oxford University Press, 1975).
137. Reprinted in Purchase, Barbara, *Rabbit Tales* (New York: Van Nostrand Reinhold, 1982), p. 97.
138. Quinlan, Maurice James, *William Cowper, A Critical Life* (Westport, CT: Greenwood Publishing Group, 1970).
139. Crook, Sandy, *Lop Rabbits as Pets* (Neptune City, NJ: TFH Publications, 1985).
140. *Ibid.*
141. *Ibid.*
142. Lane, C.H., *Rabbits, Cats, & Cavies* (Edinburgh: Colston & Co, Ltd., 1903).
143. Taylor, Judy. *Beatrix Potter: Artist, Storyteller, and Countrywoman* (London: Frederick Warne, 1986), p. 51.
144. Potter, Beatrix, et al., *The Art of Beatrix Potter* (New York: Viking Press, 1981).
145. Taylor, *op. cit.*, p. 61.
146. Clutton-Brock, *op. cit.*, p. 36.
147. *Ibid.*, p. 30.

2. "To Skip and Gambol Like a Fawn"

The Public Life of Rabbits

———————

A Turkey carpet was his lawn,
Whereon he loved to bound,
To skip and gambol like a fawn,
And swing his rump around.

William Cowper, from "Epitaph for a Hare"

A FEW YEARS ago, Susan heard about two baby rabbits who had been dumped in a park near her house. One windy, foggy evening just before dusk, two tiny, caramel-colored rabbits came bounding out of a stand of bushes and onto the grass. They were clearly domestic; they didn't have wild rabbit coloring and there was no breeding population of rabbits in that park. It was also clear that they hadn't been handled much, or hadn't been handled well, as they scooted away as soon as Susan approached.

Susan returned to the park every evening with pellets and greens for almost a month. (The park had a lot of shrubs and the rabbits were very skittish, so it was very hard to catch them.) People who saw her with the rabbits sometimes paused to watch; some even asked if they were her rabbits, brought out to "play." Most people, however, simply passed by; they probably saw only a woman sitting on a hillside every night, talking to two rabbits eating grass. From the looks on some people's faces, they probably thought Susan was a lunatic. But there was no craziness here, only the delicious sanity of "reading" the subtle interactions between the two rabbits and a trustworthy human.

Because few people live with rabbits in their homes, few know a rabbit's full range of behaviors. People who keep rabbits in hutches in the back yard don't get to know a rabbit's true repertory—there's just not enough stimulation or physical space for the rabbit to really let go, and the keeper rarely has enough time to really observe the animal's behavior. This is one primary reason that most people approach rabbits as if they were stuffed animals: cute, but not capable of much except, maybe, eating carrots and twitching their noses.

Of course, rabbits can be very cute (or very beautiful, as anyone who has seen a giant-sized rabbit sprawled by the hearth can attest). Rabbits often eat carrots and they often twitch their noses. But they're capable of much, much more than that, and it's only by truly sharing space and time with a rabbit that a human can begin to learn the sounds, postures and movements that signal fear, happiness, contentment, rage, affection, greed, lust and, most afternoons, a delighted indulgence in sloth.

Take the case of the park bunnies, whom Susan, noting their warm coloring, named Butterscotch and Pudding. Within only a few days, it became clear that Pudding, who was slightly smaller and rounder, was the braver of the two; he came bounding out of the woods first every evening and was the first to discover the pile of pellets left for him beneath a small sapling. Butterscotch, on the other hand, was small, lean, and very shy. She would peek out carefully from behind her special bush before emerging; she didn't seem to realize that Susan could see her peering out. Even then she'd take a tortuously circuitous route to get to the food, keeping as much room between her scrawny little body and Susan as she possibly could.

Pudding communicated his curiosity by bounding up close, staring intently at Susan, and then dashing away. After a while, he grew brave enough to bump Susan's foot with his nose, which is a rabbit's gentle way of saying, "Hey, what's going on up there?" As he got to know Susan (and her food), he sometimes raced around on the grass when he saw her arrive, or leapt into the air, kicking his hind feet above him, then shaking his head goofily after he landed. This is the "shimmy" that Southern noticed, or the "frisk" that Lockley described. Among domestic rabbits, it's referred to as a "bunny dance" by some and a "binky" by others. It looks sort of like an epileptic fit—but it's an unmistakable gesture of joy.

Butterscotch too started doing binkies when Susan arrived, although she did them very carefully, at a safe distance. And although neither rabbit would let Susan get close, they eventually allowed her to sit by them as they ate. Susan couldn't pat them or sneeze; she could hardly even blink without their dashing into the shrubs for cover. But Pudding danced when he saw her or heard her calling his name, and Butterscotch would take a good roll in the dirt after she ate, waving her little paws merrily in the air and then sprawling out on the grass, gazing adoringly at her new human friend. Susan knew the friendship was sealed when Butterscotch ground her teeth at the sound of her voice. Tooth grinding is like a rabbit's purr. A slow crunching expresses contentment; a rapid chattering, so the whiskers wiggle vigorously, expresses irrepressible joy.

The two young bunnies—who were probably littermates—communicated with each other too, of course. When Pudding wanted to play, he ran in circles around Butterscotch, which is a bunny's way of saying, "Let's play tag," or "Let's make love!" When Butterscotch wanted to play, she crouched in front of Pudding or danced back and forth, shaking her head. After the two had eaten and were lounging about in the grass, they would snuggle up and groom each other, licking each other's ears, noses and backs. When Butterscotch heard the jingle of a dog's collar coming, she'd race off into the shrubs; when Pudding heard the same sound, he'd get up on his back feet, sniff the air tentatively, then thump his foot hard on the ground to warn his friends. Then he too would run pell-mell into the woods. He was a good guard; he often heard dogs coming long before Susan did.

After about four weeks, Pudding stopped coming out. For five days only Butterscotch greeted Susan, who worried that maybe Pudding had been killed or maimed by a dog, or had eaten something poisonous. But on the fifth night, Susan looked up and saw Pudding sitting on a ridge, staring down. He looked like a ghost; he was much thinner than he had been and his face exuded a weary misery. As Susan looked closer, she saw that his left eye was swollen. She called to him, and he flattened himself against the ground. When she clucked to tell him she had food, he hopped slowly up to her. As he approached, it was clear that he had developed a serious eye infection.

Now the levels of communication deepened dramatically and very suddenly. As Pudding ate next to Susan, she automatically put out her hand to touch his thin, dry coat. Because he was blind on one side, he didn't spook at the sight of that hand; because Susan was gentle (and perhaps because he was tuckered out), he trembled, but didn't bolt, at its touch.

Susan was deeply saddened by Pudding's injury, but Butterscotch seemed elated. She came bombing out of the woods, ran in circles, kicked her feet up in the air and then began dashing in and out between Susan's legs, tossing her head flirtatiously every time Susan talked to her or looked her way. When Butterscotch got too close to Pudding, he'd chase her and try to bite her; he obviously didn't feel well. She just shook her head at him then sped over to Susan again, dancing so vigorously she nearly lost her balance.

This was puzzling behavior. A cynic might say that Butterscotch didn't give two figs about Pudding's sore eye. But that made no sense in the context either of the relationship between these two siblings or their relationship to Susan. Was Butterscotch happy because Pudding had finally come out and was eating? Did Butterscotch somehow know that Susan would try to help Pudding? Was she relieved to have bunny company on the lawn again? Butterscotch still wouldn't let Susan touch her, but it seemed clear that this little female rabbit was trying to tell the female human something. Susan just couldn't get it.

Susan scooped Pudding up that night (it's pretty easy to catch a half-blind rabbit), but Butterscotch fled and couldn't be grabbed. Sadly, Pudding had to be euthanized several days later; it appeared that he had a severe infection in his facial bones. But Butterscotch was still out there, and since rabbits bond very deeply, Susan feared that the orphaned rabbit would grow depressed, or overly fearful, if left alone. Yet the next night, Butterscotch came bounding out to see Susan and seemed to have left huge fecal pellets around Susan's usual sitting spot. These were much larger than her usual pellets, and she had never left them out before. It was almost as if she was saying that she was still there, that she was healthy, and that she shouldn't be forgotten. After sitting with her for about half an hour, Susan felt that this was the time to catch her, so in the brief second that Butterscotch turned her back, Susan muttered a quick prayer, thrust out her hands and grabbed her. Quite a struggle ensued as Butterscotch fought tooth and nail to avoid being stuffed in the carrier, but at last Susan got her in and shut the door, relieved that she could finally get the rabbit to safety.

Rabbits in new environments display their nervousness in all sorts of ways. Some crouch in the corner of their pen or cage. "If I don't move," they seem to think, "no one will see me." Some try to hide behind objects, even if it's just a litter box or a bunched-up towel, using the toddler logic of "If I can't see you, you can't see me either." Susan expected Butterscotch, who had been so shy and skittish in the park, to tremble and cower once put in a pen at Susan's house. Instead, the little stray rabbit hopped in and out of the litter box a few times, then promptly rolled over on her side, peering up with half-closed eyes and grinding her teeth at the sound of Susan's voice. Then she fell asleep.

Rabbits in the Home

That rabbits can feel safe in houses—and bond deeply with their human companions—is a relatively modern concept. (That animals can have emotions and express them is an even more modern concept, one that makes some philosophers and scientists apoplectic, but that people who live and work with animals consider a no-brainer.) Historically, humans' primary use of—and relationship to—rabbits has been one of production, with most rabbits living only a few short months before being slaughtered. These months are often spent in cages, an environment that considerably constrains both natural behavior and interactions with caregivers. Most pet rabbits have lived longer, but have also remained caged throughout much of their lives. In the last few decades, however, humans have learned that free-running rabbits can fit quite well into human households, just as free-running cats and dogs do—and rabbits have learned that life in such households can actually be a pleasure, rather than a threat.

The strongest push to keep rabbits indoors as pets came when Marinell Harriman published the *House Rabbit Handbook* in 1985. Just four years earlier, Harriman had come home to find a black and white baby rabbit sitting in her backyard. She scooped up the little rabbit, and, thinking it a boy, dubbed it "Herman." For lack of a better place to put him, she spread some newspapers out in the kitchen, and let Herman—who later turned out to be a female—hop around there.

Harriman had grown up on a farm that regularly slaughtered rabbits for meat. She had been allowed to keep just a few of these rabbits as pets, but had never had one in her home. By the time a month had passed, she was as surprised as anyone to realize that the rabbit was generally peeing and pooping in one place. Harriman put a litter box in that corner, Herman promptly used it, and on that day, the word "house rabbit" was born, as Harriman discovered that rabbits, like cats, could be litter-box trained.

Herman died in 1983. Harriman was so devastated by her death that she decided to do advocacy work for rabbits, including writing a book about living with "house rabbits." When she put up posters in the Bay Area, asking for stories of people living with litter-box-trained, indoor rabbits, she was overwhelmed with responses. Harriman might have coined the term "house rabbit," but it was clear that others had been living with such creatures all along.

Marinell and her husband, Bob, published the first *House Rabbit Handbook* in 1985—complete with black and white photos of rabbits living, loving and lounging in human households, stories of how rabbits and humans get along together (Harriman interviewed more than thirty people with house rabbits), tips on how to

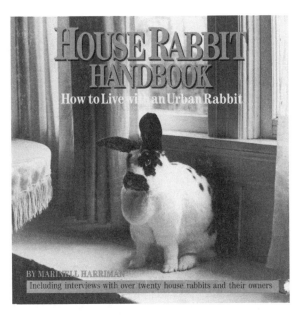

Figure 2.1. Cover of *House Rabbit Handbook*. *The House Rabbit Handbook* was the first book to acknowledge that rabbits were viable indoor pets. Photo by Marinell Harriman, design by Bob Harriman, courtesy Drollery Press.

feed, litter-box train and procure veterinary care for this newest lagomorph set, and thoughts on how to "bunny-proof" a home (so bunny teeth wouldn't destroy electrical wires and books) and how to "read" a rabbit's body language. Friends and family, Harriman recalls, "thought I was crazy, but my brother was actually my first convert. After watching me play with my rabbits he said, 'I'll never eat rabbit meat again.' "

The public response to the book was phenomenal. Hundreds of people wrote letters to Harriman sharing stories and begging for more information. Then, in 1986, Marinell received a phone call from a reader of the *Handbook*, who said that four rabbits at a local shelter would be euthanized unless someone rescued them. This led Marinell and Bob Harriman to begin the rabbit rescue efforts that would eventually lead to the formation of House Rabbit Society (HRS) in 1988.

The goal of HRS was to rescue and find homes for abandoned rabbits, as well as to educate people about humane and appropriate rabbit care. Since that time, a small group of rescuers in the Bay Area has developed into a national organization with thirty-two chapters in twenty-two states (as well as educators and fosterers in an additional eleven states, plus Canada, Asia and Australia), and a membership of eight thousand. In twelve years of work, House Rabbit Society volunteers have rescued more than ten thousand rabbits, counseled thousands of rabbit owners, been interviewed for hundreds of newspaper and magazine articles, and hosted an all-rabbits veterinary conference in 1997. In 2000 the organization opened a rabbits-only adoption and education center in Richmond, California.

Since the founding of HRS, advances in veterinary medicine have made indoor rabbits even more viable as pets. Veterinarians have discovered safe ways to spay and neuter rabbits, for instance, which eliminates the risk of unwanted baby rabbits and reduces the risk of uterine cancer, aggressiveness and territorial marking behavior. Veterinarians have also learned how to treat pain in rabbits, which is key to helping them pull through both minor and major illnesses, and determined which anesthetics and antibiotics could and couldn't be used on the species. An equally important development, notes Dr. Carolynn Harvey, a veterinarian in Oakland, California and one of the pioneers in rabbit medicine, is that "Until recently, all the research on rabbits focused on how to 'grow' them, short-term, for the market. Now we have a better understanding of strategies that promote long, healthful life." Domestic rabbits today, in fact, can live to twelve years of age, where twenty years ago they were expected to live only a few years at best.

The idea behind a "house rabbit" as opposed to a "backyard hutch" rabbit is this: rabbits in hutches in the backyard are vulnerable to predators, like raccoons, opossums, dogs, cats and birds of prey. Even the sight of such a predator can be dangerous to some rabbits; anecdotes abound about rabbits who have broken their backs or legs in their efforts to flee a predator outside the hutch or who have gone into shock because they simply saw one in the vicinity. Rabbits in the backyard also aren't as cherished as animals inside the house, because they don't spend as much time with the humans and therefore don't get as much attention. That lack of attention, in turn, can cause depression in rabbits and may mean that nascent illnesses aren't caught early enough to receive proper care.

Today, some people keep their indoor rabbits part-time in cages, letting them out daily to run around, play and generally get the exercise they can't get in a cage. Other people keep their rabbits in large pens or in just one or two rooms. Still other people, like Margo and Susan, let their rabbits run "free-range" in the house, just as a dog or cat would. The rabbits are able to do this because they have been trained to use litter boxes and because objects that can be chewed on—like books, electrical cords and shoes—are kept out of the rabbits' reach, at least most of the time. To people who have kept rabbits indoors for some time, it seems perfectly normal to see a rabbit frolicking on the living room rug, sleeping on the bed, investigating a clothes basket or searching for crumbs on the kitchen floor. To people who have never seen such a sight, it seems like magic. In fact, when Susan first went to Margo's house in 1995 to get her first rabbit, she stepped into the living room, looked towards the kitchen and whispered to her husband, "There are *rabbits* in there." Margo graciously ignored the comment and allowed Susan to bring home a gorgeous Giant Chinchilla named Phoebe.

◆   ◆   ◆

Domestic rabbits fit so well into human homes in part because, like their wild brethren, they are gregarious animals who thrive in the presence of other beings. Moreover, domestic rabbits, like wild rabbits, develop hierarchical dominance structures—this is one reason they were easy to domesticate. As such, rabbits can easily fit into a household where one human takes the position of the warren "leader." In Susan's household, for example, the rabbits very definitely see her as the dominant animal—she cares for her rabbits with kindness, but they understand that she is the source of food, water, household rules and a certain moral authority. (That Susan is also mother to the children in the household probably bolsters her leadership, as the rabbits see her caring for and directing these small creatures as well.) The rabbits ask Susan for food in the morning (by crowding around her feet or sitting up on their haunches near their food bowls and staring at her earnestly). They look up guiltily when she walks into a room and catches them doing something they're not supposed to be doing—like chewing on a book or rummaging in a closet. They nestle next to her for pats and they respond to her voice commands (e.g., "Come in off the porch," or "Out of the closet!" or "Time for vegetables!"). Conversely, if Susan's husband tries to direct the rabbits, they look at him as if it's the first time human language has been spoken in their presence.

As creatures of habit, rabbits also fit well into human schedules—they know when it's time to eat, when it's time to sleep, when people come home from work, even when people kick back and relax. Susan's Phoebe would come loping out every evening to join the humans in the living room. When Elmo, a Mini Lop, was brought home to be Phoebe's friend a few months later, he picked up the same habit, and the two would come out, "lippity-lippity," as Beatrix Potter would say, every night around eight p.m. to loll on the carpet, chase each other around the couch, scavenge for crumbs and enjoy some attention. Those two rabbits have since died, and Susan and her husband have added two young children to the household mix, so the evening routine has changed. But Susan's current rabbits, Mr. Bop, also a Mini Lop, and Maybelline, a mixed-breed rabbit, frequently join her and her two small children during bedtime story hour. The rabbits lie on the floor within easy reach of patting hands and have even come to enjoy gentle good-night kisses from both children.

Rabbits and children aren't always the best combination—especially if the parents aren't rabbit-savvy enough to teach the children how to properly handle and care for their pet. But as Victorian painters intuited, rabbits and children can get along together beautifully. In Susan's home the rabbits enjoy being talked to by the children, batting their toys around and snatching snacks from their small hands or small tables. They don't have heart attacks when a child screams or cries; in fact, Maybelline dashes out to get Susan when a

Figure 2.2. Rabbits can be as curious about children as children are about them. Here Elmo investigates the newest member of his household. Photo by Susan Davis.

child cries, and Mr. Bop leaps merrily across the room when the toddler bellows "Bop! Bop! Bop!" every morning from his crib.

Because the children have been taught to handle the rabbits gently—and never to pick them up—the rabbits trust them. But, because they are free-range, the rabbits can also "vote with their feet." That is, if a child gets too loud or too rough, the rabbits scamper off, whereas a caged rabbit could only flatten itself in a corner or decide to come out swinging the next time the cage door opened. That's not to say the rabbits only use flight to take care of themselves. If a child is in Maybelline's way, she gently nips to get the small person to move. Mr. Bop has been known to try to push a child out of the way with his nose, although that isn't quite as effective.

Such a system wouldn't work if Susan hadn't schooled the children carefully in rabbit etiquette and taught the rabbits that her household was generally safe. But once those foundations were laid, the children and the rabbits developed their own relationships. Now the unspoken agreement seems to be that if the children are gentle, the rabbits will lie still, and if the rabbits lie still, the children will pat them. Maybelline also has an arrangement with Harrison, the toddler, in which he puts his head on the ground in front of her and she licks it, while he giggles with delight. This is something Harrison learned to do by himself—no grown-up told him that rabbits greet each other by presenting their heads in a submissive position. And no grown-up has ever warned Maybelline not to nip this tiny person's head. The two creatures—one a non-verbal mammal and the other a pre-verbal mammal—have simply worked this game out for themselves. These aren't agreements the rabbits have with every child, however. When "strange" children come over, both rabbits often hide under a bed because, presumably, they know these children don't know the rules of the household and so aren't to be trusted.

A Range of Expressions

Contrary to the image of a "boring" or "passive" rabbit sitting in a cage, rabbits can show their affection for their human caregivers in a wide variety of ways. Most rabbits "bump" human feet and ankles with their noses to get attention or say hello, just as wild rabbits "bump" hello in their warrens. Many domestic rabbits also tug on human pant legs, shoes and socks with their teeth to be more insistent; others follow their humans from room to room or run around in circles when their humans come home. Maybelline, so named because she looks like she's wearing badly applied eye make-up, gallops after Susan when she moves through the house, then leaps in the air with joy if Susan turns to speak to her. Still other rabbits show their affection by licking human hands, faces, clothing or feet—a form of grooming that bonded rabbits in the wild also show to each other—or by sitting up on their haunches and very gently laying their front feet on the human's leg, an imploring gesture with which dog lovers may be familiar.

Within one group of rabbits, the different personality of each comes through in his or her style of greeting. Donna, who volunteers to come by weekly to clean Margo's foster bunnies' cages, finds that Bosco is always the first to approach her. This is partly because she cleans his favorite cage first. It's also because he likes his world to be very organized, and her arrival always throws everything into disarray, with towels, sponges, spatulas and litter boxes everywhere. So he runs circles around her as she cleans, getting in her way, sniffing her tools and making sure that she does everything to his satisfaction.

Next, Maccabee, a Mini Lop, arrives in a flurry, grabbing rubber gloves and kicking through her pile of cleaning items. Maccabee likes to show that he's the boss (although he's not), and he does this by monopolizing Donna's attention and generally showing off. If she doesn't pay attention to him, he bites her shoes, or the legs or seat of her pants. The other rabbits acknowledge Donna's presence by watching and sniffing her. Once they've ascertained that she carries no snacks, they generally leave her alone for the rest of the evening.

Some rabbits are more conservative with their affections, reserving them for members of their own species. Margo's rabbit Samantha actively disses her by turning her back—or so it seems—whenever Margo walks into the room. Mouse's brand of affection involves *not* running away from Margo when she walks up to pet him. Sometimes, if he's in a *really* good mood, he may even grind his teeth a bit when Margo touches him. Contented rabbits often "flop" over onto their sides when they're especially relaxed. Margo's fifteen-pound French Lop, Helga, hits the floor so hard the room shakes; Mr. Bop flops over when he hears Susan singing to her children (he is especially fond of *Baby Beluga*). Some rabbits even roll all the way over onto their backs, with their feet dangling in a silly way in the air.

But rabbits are not simply long-eared puppy dogs. They also can convey rather formidable disdain. Thumping with the back foot is meant to warn someone off; an indignant snort or a full-body shiver shows disgust. The Hind Foot Snap, in which a rabbit forcefully flicks his back feet while hopping quickly away, as if to shake off something despicable, shows the rabbit was offended by what you just did (whether it's putting drops in his ears or offering him food that's not to his liking). Rabbits are also quite skilled at giving the same kind of cold shoulder a cat can—by simply turning away from the offending human and staring at the wall.

Figure 2.3. Some rabbits do chew books (so they're best kept on higher shelves), but Helga just likes to rest near them. ©2002, Paul Fussell. All rights reserved.

A frustrated rabbit can push a patting hand away with his head; this is sometimes followed by a warning growl or bite (especially when the human didn't notice the initial clues). Belligerent rabbits often swish their tails back and forth. Sometimes they do this when another rabbit is bugging them, as if to say, "Temperature's rising there, buster, so back off." They also use this behavior with humans. If Mr. Bop has been handled too much recently, he'll sometimes greet Susan with an affectionate head bump, but then swish his tail and flick his feet a few times, as if warning her not to get too familiar. Mrs. Bean, a paralyzed Holland Lop, shows *her* disdain by using her wheelchair to roll away from Margo when she wants to pet her. Before she had her cart, she was unable to move when anyone wanted to pet or hold her, so for a basically unfriendly rabbit like Mrs. Bean, the cart was a godsend in more ways than one.

Domestic rabbits also communicate through sounds, just as wild rabbits do. Most domestic rabbits still know how to growl, although it sounds more like a wheeze or a cough than the "grrrr" of a dog or the "rrrrraaaaarrrrrr" of a cat. Rabbit growls can be especially formidable when accompanied by two front paws boxing the air (or you) in front of them. Sexually aroused rabbits make a charming, nasal honking sound as they circle their intended. Phoebe, who had a big appetite, used to grunt as she ran up to her food bowl every morning. Some female rabbits whimper loudly when they're being courted, and Mouse, like a lot of rabbits, snorts loudly when eating a piece of banana.

More disturbing is the rabbit's shriek or scream, emitted during severe pain, when terrified and sometimes upon death, whether it's violent or peaceful. (Hunters, in fact, carry "rabbit in distress" calls to attract coyotes and other predators.) Some rabbits shriek when they just *think* they're going to die. Ramona used to scream when she was caught at the end of the day because play time had ended and it was time for all rabbits to go inside. Melanie, a small white rabbit, wailed loudly whenever she got a shot, which was unnerving even for her veterinarian. Elmo used to make a sound like a bawling calf when Phoebe chased him around the room.

Domestic rabbits, like wild rabbits, also can express unhappiness through what we call "offensive peeing" and what the biologists call "enurination." This can sometimes happen almost involuntarily—as when a human grabs an unsuspecting rabbit or asks him to do something he doesn't want to do. Other times the peeing strategy is more, well, premeditated. One night after giving Elmo some medicine, Susan brought him out to the living room, to avoid disturbing her husband. She lay down on the couch and pulled a comforter over her. Elmo, who was feeling neither well nor grateful, hopped over to the hearth and lifted his tail, a sure sign that a rabbit's about to relieve his bladder. "Elmo, don't pee there," Susan said in a warning voice. He looked at her, leapt across the room, jumped on the couch and peed all over the comforter—giving Susan a good soaking in the process. That's probably not the sort of intelligence that scientists can measure in a laboratory, but it shows rather startling powers of interspecies communication.

Games Rabbits Play

A few years ago, a woman called Susan because, she said, she had "the rabbit from hell." The rabbit was a tiny, two-year-old

Netherland Dwarf named Joe, who, it was said, loved people and was "just the cutest thing." But his caretaker was ready to give him up because he was so destructive.

The woman proceeded to list Joe's nasty habits: he dug his litter out of his box and threw it all over the floor; he chewed newspapers left on the couch; he pulled her toilet paper tubes out of the waste-basket and flung them behind the toilet; he ran around in fast tight circles every night at midnight, waking her and her husband; he chewed holes in her clothes when she left them on the floor—and just the day before he had "stolen" a pair of her balled-up socks and gone racing through the house.

To a rabbit lover, Joe sounded like a quite a guy, but this woman was clearly upset. "What have you tried to do?" Susan asked, and the woman said simply, "I've shouted at him and I've shut him in his cage. Now I'm at my wit's end." "Have you given him any toys?" Susan asked. And she replied in a rather cold tone of voice, "Of course he has no toys. He's a *rabbit.*"

Joe's list of crimes did sound daunting; no one wants a pet who destroys one's house and home. But Joe wasn't trying to be destruc-tive. He was just having a good time in the only way he knew how: by running, chewing, digging and playing little games with his guardian. It's the kind of behavior rabbit lovers enjoy seeing in rab-bits, as long as it's channeled in non-destructive routes. It's also the kind of behavior most people are surprised to see when they visit a rabbit home, because a rabbit in a cage by himself doesn't play much. He may flop on his side when he feels relaxed. He may run in circles when he's excited—if the cage is large enough. He may even pop a binky—if the cage is high enough. But without stimula-tion, most caged rabbits become lethargic and depressed. Many also develop serious physical problems, including obesity, foot sores and fur chewing.

Free-running rabbits, on the other hand, enjoy a lot of games, with themselves, with their rabbit friends and with their human com-panions. In fact, even grown rabbits can be as playful as kittens. And there's something about a roly-poly, lop-eared rabbit galloping eagerly across the floor, with his long ears flopping up and down and his head hanging slightly low, that looks distinctly like a silly puppy and is distinctly irresistible.

The categories of rabbit games can be broken into some of their more common wild behaviors. Rabbits are pretty famous for chewing, for instance, but they don't just do it because it's fun to destroy Aunt Mildred's embroidered ottoman. Instead it's because rabbits are "grazers" in the wild—that is, they need to keep a constant supply of food moving through their gut. It may also be because they're bored. Give a rabbit some wicker baskets, some newspaper or some apple branches to chew on and he'll happily gnaw on those instead of your favorite antiques. Elmo, in fact, used to take on whole chewing projects: he'd sometimes spend an hour ripping up a litter bag and then flop down contentedly in the middle of his mess, as if congratulating himself on a job well done.

Sometimes the solutions to destructive behavior are more creative—and ambitious. Deborah, a friend of Margo's, found her rabbits, George and Gracie, chewing up her upholstered velvet chairs—from the inside out. Like many rabbits, they had shimmied beneath the chairs and then worked their way up through the stuffing and springs. Deborah came up with the idea of stuffing the space underneath her couches and chairs with the daily junk mail. This gave her rabbits a satisfying project to work on (burrowing through the paper), kept her furniture safe from their teeth and kept the toys (i.e., paper) hidden from sight.

Rabbits also enjoy digging. Outside, some rabbits dig in the grass, the flower bed or the dirt. Inside, some rabbits dig at the carpet, in the litter box or even at linoleum. To help the rabbit satisfy that urge, some people provide "digging boxes," filled with sand or shredded newspaper, so the rabbit can play a pretend game of burrowing without destroying the human's property. Other people give their rabbits long cardboard tubes (for pouring concrete), so the rabbits can pretend they actually live in a hole. Stuffing the end of the tube with newspaper gives them something to do, as they work feverishly to get the paper back out of the burrow.

Figure 2.4. Chester grooming himself. Rabbits groom themselves just as cats do and tend to be just as fastidious. © 2002, Paul Fussell. All rights reserved.

Many rabbits are ardent decorators: they like to move objects from one place to another, or turn things upside down, or scoot an area rug around until it suits their fancy. Moving a towel across a smooth floor, first bunching it up and then stretching it out, can be especially rewarding for a rabbit, as can smoothing out wrinkles in the bed linens with their front paws until they are organized just right. Many rabbits can't lie down comfortably, in fact, without first rearranging the bedding, whether it's a human's comforter, a rabbit's rugs or the pillows on the couch.

Flat-out running can also be a fun game. When Maybelline was younger, she enjoyed racing down a long runner in one of Susan's hallways. Sometimes she got going so fast that when she hit the wood floor, she would slide into a wall or door. It always sounded like she'd given herself a concussion, but she would just shake her head and run back the way she'd come, throwing in a jump or a full-body shake along the way. Other times she would run circles around the living room as fast as she could, looking like a dirt bike as she leaned in on the corners.

Figure 2.5. Rabbits and cats often develop close friendships, as shown here by Bunch and Adolph. Photo by Margo DeMello.

A surprising number of domestic rabbits, especially young ones, like to climb, too—onto desks, chairs, beds, table tops, laps, even into bathtubs and sinks. Many rabbits know this is forbidden, yet the taboo seems to only add to the deliciousness of the adventure. Phoebe used to get so excited when she jumped onto the couch that she'd race back and forth, coyly shaking her head. She actually was allowed on the couch, but she thought she was being naughty and she got a kick out of it. Elmo used to jump up on Susan's desk and clamber around on the piles of books and papers there, knocking many of them off in the process.

Rabbits also like to play games with each other. One perennial favorite is "Chase the Bunny," where one rabbit chases another rabbit up and down the hallway, through the concrete tube, into a cage and out again, or around and around one particular piece of furniture. The chaser could probably easily catch the chasee, but they just run around for the fun of it. Other rabbits derive immense pleasure from the game "Chase the Cat." It's evidently even more fun when it ends with the rabbit catching—and biting—the cat. Margo's cats, however, don't share the rabbits' enthusiasm for this game, and have learned to jump onto furniture whenever a rabbit approaches with too "friendly" a look on his face. (That's not to say that rabbits and other animals can't get along. Many house rabbits have developed close relationships with dogs, cats and other species.)

Another fun game is "Explorer," in which one rabbit—sometimes followed by a couple of bunny buddies—ventures into uncharted territory, like that exciting space behind the television set, a bathroom with a slippery linoleum floor or up on top of a house guest's luggage. A simple "Hey rabbit!" will generally bring the perpetrator merrily scrambling out again. For allegedly passive, timid creatures, rabbits actually display amazing powers of curiosity: they crawl under couches, leap onto chairs, riffle through closets, nose through files, "help" their caretakers clean litter boxes by jumping in and out of them, push small toys around and generally poke their noses just about anywhere they can get them, including the dustiest corners of the house. Pammy, a smoky gray rabbit Margo picked up in the woods, once tore through twenty-five bags of litter, looking for a between-meals snack. One by one, she ripped a small hole in each bag, hoping that maybe *this* time there might be some food inside. Maybelline thumps her feet in frustration when she finds Susan's closet door shut; she's enamored of its dark recesses. Elmo liked to jump on the bed every morning around five a.m., just to see what his humans were doing, and Margo once found Benjamin, a big charcoal gray rabbit, on top of her desk, eating his way through the library books.

Even rabbits with physical disabilities like to play. Mrs. Bean used to travel to the House Rabbit Society shelter with Margo every week. Once in her cart, she rolled around the building, teasing the boarding rabbits in their pens by coming very close to them through the wire and then quickly rolling backwards, as if to show them that while they were confined to a six-foot-by-four-foot pen, *she* could travel where she pleased. (This is a startling insight into the fact that rabbits know when they, or other rabbits, are caged.) Then she would proceed to the bags of food and hay for sale in the store and rip into them, eating happily from whatever she wanted.

How people respond to rabbits' games can spell life or death for the human-rabbit relationship. People who hit, yell at or cage a rabbit to punish her for her explorations will generally end up with a frightened or aggressive rabbit. But greeting the antics with cheer, patience and alternatives tends to have good results. Little Joe, the dwarf "from hell," didn't need disciplining; he was just doing what came naturally to him, and amusing himself in the process. What he really needed was toys—like baskets to fling and chew, tubes to explore, piles of newspapers to shred—and maybe some permission to be his own silly and rambunctious self.

Love and Friendship

Domestic rabbits, like wild rabbits, are gregarious creatures who thrive on social contact with their own kind. Domestic rabbits who have rabbit buddies often spend much of the day together—they'll eat together, sleep together, groom together, play together, even hop in the litter box at the same time to poop together. Rabbit friends comfort each other during stressful times (like a car ride or just having the vacuum cleaner turned on) and they often nurture each other when they're sick.

In the wild, rabbits choose mates. As pets, most domestic rabbits traditionally haven't had that choice: they've either had no mates or have been confronted with a strange rabbit suddenly thrust into their hutch. This generally results in either a violent fight or, if the rabbits are male and female, a lot of little rabbits. Breeders have long known that when it's time to make two rabbits mate, the best tactic is to bring the female to the male, because does are so territorial they will fight—even try to kill—a male introduced into their territory. But for many decades, pet rabbit keepers have thought that rabbits simply couldn't have friends, because the risk of violence or progeny was too high.

That perception began to change about ten years ago, as veterinarians fine-tuned the art and science of spaying and neutering rabbits, which eliminates the risk of both baby rabbits and hormonally charged aggression. Even altered rabbits can fight, however. Marinell

Harriman was the first person to explore ways to help rabbits avoid fights via behavioral adjustments. By observing courting and rejecting behaviors, she was able to create matchmaking rituals that allowed pet rabbits to get to know and establish relationships with other rabbits. This was another key milestone in the growing concept of the house rabbit, because it meant that rabbits could have friends, just as they do in the wild, and not just be delegated to solitary cages.

With a newly neutered male, the first date will often begin with the realization that the animal in front of him is not only a rabbit, but a female rabbit. Sometimes it takes a younger male a while to discern this, but when he does, the dance of love begins. He will sometimes begin with "foreplay," or circling the female, honking, oinking and sometimes spraying her with urine. Other males forego these niceties and proceed to try to mount the female right off the bat. Most, however, have no clue about the details of female anatomy, and will start out by humping her head or climbing up her side.

If the mounting continues, the male will eventually get it right, and begin vibrating on top of the female like a jackhammer. If he's lucky (i.e., if he has time to reach orgasm), he'll emit a sharp squeak and then fall off, panting vigorously, just as wild European rabbits do, and giving her a chance to finally run away. Most females are not crazy about this ritual; some actively fight back, biting their new paramour viciously. This behavior is understandable, because often the "sex" is very rough, with the boy biting off huge mouthfuls of her hair while trying to get a grip on his date. But thanks to the miracle of modern veterinary medicine, a neutered male will find that his desire to mount his new girlfriend wanes sharply after the first few days together, and the girl is allowed to regain some of her dignity.

Within this basic outline, there are many, many variations in rabbit relationships. Indeed, each new pairing develops according to the individual rabbits involved, their personal histories, their likes and dislikes and their personalities. Most of the time one rabbit ends up being dominant, but sometimes dominance is shared, with one partner getting all the licks and the other being first at the chow bowl, or perhaps with the rabbits equally sharing grooming duties.

Some rabbits are so bonded that they spend every waking and sleeping moment together—eating together, following each other around the house, snoozing and exploring together. Others seem to just tolerate each other, while still others constantly bicker (via butt biting, grunting and chasing the other away from the snacks). Some rabbit relationships, like some human relationships, are generally good, but have trigger points for conflict. One rabbit may not want to share his litter box, for instance. Another may be very greedy with her food, to the point of taking the biggest mouthful possible from a food bowl and running into a corner to eat it alone. Some rabbits remain bonded for life; other pairings are so brittle that the second a younger, handsomer rabbit comes along, a rabbit will leave her mate—just as happens in the wild.

Humans can strongly influence the nature of rabbit relationships. Some people are very hands-on during the introductions, others allow the rabbits to work things out more or less on their own and some, alas, do more harm than good. Many people, when bringing home a new partner for their rabbit, want the original rabbit to be the dominant one in the relationship, probably because they feel guilty about bringing a "new baby" home in the first place. That may not be what the rabbits are working out, however, and can lead to conflict and confusion. If the human constantly reprimands the new rabbit for bossing the old rabbit around, the rabbits will never be able to find a relationship that feels natural to them and hence may never get beyond the fighting stage.

Other times, the caretakers are sensitive enough to let the rabbits work things out for themselves. A woman named Mary brought Jack, a Giant Chinchilla, to Margo after his girlfriend, Boo, died. Boo had been the more outgoing of the two, and after she died, Jack crawled into a shell emotionally and wouldn't come out. Margo and Mary both agreed that Jack would do well to have a new friend (preferably another outgoing girl like Boo) and that it was time for him to meet some new rabbits.

Jack was not an entirely willing partner in this dating adventure: when Mary brought him over to the couch where the introductions would occur, he was so scared he wouldn't come out of his carrier, and Mary had to pull the top off. Even then, he scrunched down as low as he could get, as if hoping that this nightmare would end and he would wake up at home.

Margo and Mary tried a few girls with him, and he never even looked up; instead, he just hunkered as much of his ten pounds down into the bottom of the carrier as he could. The ladies were not impressed. But then he met Cody, a recently neutered, four-month-old male. Cody loved Jack. He climbed all over his prone body, licking his ears and chewing his eyebrows, trying to get Jack to show some interest in him. Jack's eyes got wider, but he didn't move. Cody continued to treat Jack like a jungle gym, climbing, pushing, pulling and experimentally humping him, all to no avail. Finally, he just flopped down beside him, legs extended, panting happily, inside the open carrier.

Mary and Margo looked at Jack's big, meatloaf-shaped body and Cody's slim, stretched-out posture, and decided that since at least one of the two liked the other, it was a start. Mary took them both home, where their relationship blossomed.

Melinda, a peach-colored Angora, was more aggressively picky about her mates. Her first boyfriend was Wormguy, a submissive Angora with a gentle personality. When Wormguy died, Margo thought Melinda might like Mouse, a big agouti half lop, so she unceremoniously moved him into the room where Melinda slept. Melinda did not, in fact, like Mouse. She tore after him, biting big chunks of fur, and a bit of flesh, from him whenever she caught him. Lucky for Mouse, Melinda had scoliosis, and he quickly learned that the best way to escape her was to jump up on the bed. Since she couldn't follow him, she just circled the bed, breathing hard.

After a couple of days of this, Margo took Mouse away and tried Captain Pooper. Melinda didn't like Captain Pooper either and gave him so many bites (he never did figure out Mouse's jump-on-the-bed maneuver) that he had to be taken away, too.

Finally, Margo tried Mr. Lunch, a young, active, spotted rabbit. For some reason, Melinda didn't find Mr. Lunch as offensive as she

Figure 2.6. Many indoor rabbits live as bonded trios or even quartets. Here Blueberry, Raspberry and Dairy Queen get comfort from their close proximity. Photo by Margo DeMello.

did Mouse and Captain Pooper, and she accepted him relatively quickly. Mr. Lunch was devoted to Melinda, but sadly he died a few short months later. At this point, Margo decided to give Mouse another try. We'll never know why, but Melinda finally decided that Mouse wasn't so bad after all. While he was a bit wary around her at the beginning, perhaps remembering her treatment of him the last time, Melinda and Mouse soon became fast friends, and their relationship lasted until she died.

Although rabbits are gregarious creatures, many domestic rabbits who are raised in isolation have no idea how to be social with another rabbit. This was certainly the case with Maybelline, a six-month-old rabbit Susan picked up in San Francisco's Golden Gate Park one morning. Susan meant for Maybelline to be a new mate for Elmo, whose friend Phoebe had died a few weeks earlier. But their initial introductions were rather violent. Elmo made it clear from the start that he liked the new girl: he lay down next to—or on top of— her cage, and spent hours simply staring at her. When she was let out of her cage, he ran over and promptly tried to hump her. She sub-

Figure 2.7. Maybelline and Mr.Bop cuddle on the rug. Rabbits who have rabbit friends are often happier and more confident than those who live alone. Bop also displays a contented "flop" here. Photo by Susan Davis.

mitted, for a moment, and then leapt up and tried to fight with him. Once the rabbits were separated, Elmo hopped peacefully to a corner and rolled contentedly over on his side, as if he knew relationships could be rough in the beginning, but he was still glad to have some female company.

This continued for five weeks. Every time Elmo and Maybelline were put together, she would race over to him, touch his nose with hers and then attack him. It was almost as if she had no idea what the benefits of a rabbit relationship might be. Elmo continued to defend himself against her attacks—and these were out-and-out brawls—but always took the time to take a nap between rounds.

It wasn't until Elmo started attacking Maybelline first that the new little female rabbit started to back off. Soon Elmo had only to move one small white paw at her to make her run off in the other direction with her ears flat and her eyes rolling. Now it was clear that Elmo was going to be the boss. Susan patted them and talked to them and tried to restrain Elmo's temper. For a while, the rabbits simply ignored each other. Then Elmo began to charge Maybelline without actually attacking her. Finally they began to lick each other. The bond was sealed.

For the next two years, Maybelline was completely enchanted with Elmo. She followed him from room to room, leapt into the litter box with him, groomed him incessantly and investigated every move he made. Sometimes she'd lie down parallel to Elmo and arrange her body just like his, as if to say, "OK, he's rolled onto his right hip and his right leg is kind of tucked up just so . . . oh, that *is* comfortable!" Other times she'd experiment with ways to snuggle up to him, like a teenager just learning to spoon her boyfriend. She also was very protective of her new love. If Susan picked Elmo up, Maybelline followed faithfully behind, anxiously circling Susan and tugging on her pant legs to make sure Elmo was all right.

Many people whose rabbits fight upon first meeting often give up, and end up either keeping the rabbits separate (which is stressful for the animals and a lot of work for the humans) or giving one of them up. But with some coaxing, and a good dose of patience, even feuding rabbits can learn to be friends. And two rabbits who are in love are easily four times as interesting as a rabbit alone.

Rabbits with physical disabilities often have relationships that are different from those of able-bodied rabbits. Margo recently rescued two disabled rabbits in one day: Smokey, a large gray rabbit with rear end paralysis, and Willow, a lovely Holland Lop with limited use of her rear legs. Margo put the two rabbits together into their new space in her dining room, and they took to each other immediately. Whether it was because they both entered Margo's home on the same day, and so had no territorial issues to work out, or because they recognized in each other a kindred spirit, their relationship began immediately and continued until Smokey's death.

Soon after Smokey died, Margo brought home Pippin, who was paralyzed due to mishandling at the local animal shelter, and introduced him to Willow. Just as before, Willow and Pippin took to each other immediately and bonded quickly. Pippin, who had just arrived from the shelter scared and confused about the loss of his legs, sought solace in Willow, who seemed to calm him down, to assure him that he would be okay in his new life.

Figure 2.8. Providing disabled rabbits like Pippin with small carts allows them to retain both mobility and dignity. Photo by Ken Mark.

On the other hand, Hopper, a quiet and happy Dutch rabbit who was also disabled, came into Margo's home about two years ago. For about six months, she tried to introduce him to a variety of rabbits. No one had any interest in giving up their freedom to spend time with Hopper, who was primarily bed-bound. Some, like Michelle, a pushy French Lop, attacked Hopper, perhaps threatened by his sickly condition. Eventually, however, Mrs. Bean, arrived. Similarly disabled, she seemed like the perfect friend for Hopper.

Unfortunately, Mrs. Bean, who like Pippin had become paralyzed due to an accident at an animal shelter, was full of rage upon arrival, and her anger did not lessen with time. Worse yet, Mrs. Bean took her anger out on Hopper, chewing on him incessantly. While Margo tried to monitor their activities, she constantly found Hopper with new scabs on his back and legs from Mrs. Bean's bites. This behavior went on for weeks, with Mrs. Bean seemingly blaming Hopper for her newly impaired lifestyle.

What finally changed their relationship was Margo's purchase of a custom cart for Hopper and Mrs. Bean to share. Mrs. Bean (who was physically much stronger than Hopper) took to it immediately, rolling around Margo's house and office all day. As soon as Mrs. Bean got her freedom back, she began to soften in her behavior towards Hopper (whom she still slept with when not in the cart), and her chews and bites soon turned into licks. Unfortunately, Mrs. Bean died only a few months after her new life began. Hopper died only two months later; we assume it was from sadness.

Grief and Mourning

Grief, mourning and depression have long been recognized in horses, chimpanzees, dogs and cats. Because domestic rabbits have rarely been able to form long-lasting pair bonds in captivity, their capacity for grief has gone unrecognized. Yet sadness, even mourning, is one of the very basic emotions that a rabbit experiences, and it can be so profound that, as happened with Hopper, a surviving rabbit can die of grief when his or her mate dies.

Benjamin and Melinda were friendly acquaintances who lived with two other rabbits in Margo's bedroom. When Benjamin became paralyzed from a viral disease, Melinda began to spend more time with him, grooming him, taking care of him and even letting him prop himself up by leaning on her back. Their relationship was heartwarming. When Melinda suddenly died of liver failure following the discovery of cancer in her stomach, Benjamin went into deep shock. Without anyone to lean on, either literally or metaphorically, Benjamin stopped eating and quickly went downhill. Margo tried to syringe-feed him, and propped him up on rolled-up rugs in the shape of Melinda's body, but nothing worked. He simply died of a broken heart.

Jake, an angry Dutch rabbit, had also lost a lot of friends. He outlived three girlfriends, and his way of dealing with the loss of each one was to take it out on those around him. After he lost his first two girlfriends, Ramona and Georgette, within a short period of time, it seemed like he lost his grounding. Ramona, a bossy, pushy Netherland Dwarf, had structured his life; after she died, he didn't have her to make the decisions for him. So he blindly lashed out at the other rabbits in the group, fighting with whoever made the mistake of coming near him. It got so bad that Margo had to remove him from the group and put him into a separate space. When Rosita, a baby Dutch, arrived not much later, Margo thought it might be worth introducing someone to Jake again. The two hit it off, not only becoming fast friends but soon welcoming Abe, a six-year-old, one-eyed Netherland Dwarf, into their circle. Margo even began to trust Jake enough to later introduce his threesome to the threesome in the bedroom, which had been run by Mouse. Yet when Rosie suddenly died, Jake reacted just as he had when his first two friends had died—with anger. He began to attack his new friends (none of whom was as close to him as Rosie had been), chasing Mouse, Big Bear and Abe from him whenever they got near. When he died, Jake still had not calmed down, lashing out at the others until the end.

Many rabbit caretakers leave a dead rabbit out for a few hours so that the other rabbits can understand what has happened. Like elephants, rabbits respond to these dead mates in many different ways: they may lick the body, lie down next to it, bite it or mount it. Some rabbits thump when they see their dead mate; others ignore it completely. When Dairy Queen died a few years ago, all of her friends reacted differently to her body. While some rabbits cautiously came by and smelled her, most of her closest friends did more than that. They seemed to take turns lying nestled against her, and, in some cases, directly on top of her. Baby, her only female friend, dug at her body and then mounted her. Most heartwrenching of all was the behavior of her newest friend, Wormguy, who had never had any real friends before Dairy Queen allowed him to join her clique. Wormguy stayed as close to her body as he possibly could and refused to leave her side.

Sometimes the loss of a mate can result in a long-term change in a rabbit's personality. When Phoebe died, Elmo lay next to her for a few minutes and licked her eyes and face. Then he ignored her. But he immediately went from being a spunky, active, playful rabbit to being subdued and sleepy, as if depressed. Sadder still, Phoebe had set up the daily schedule in Susan's house—playing in the office in the morning, sleeping under the bed in the afternoon and romping in the living room in the evening before retiring to the bedroom again. Phoebe had always led the way on these expeditions, and Elmo had followed eagerly behind her. For a full week after her death, Elmo seemed unsure of where he was supposed to be at any given hour.

Once Maybelline came to be his mate, Elmo began to perk up again. And once they bonded, he started playing in the living room at night and getting up on the bed again in the morning. But he never returned to his former levels of liveliness—he never ran laps around the bed at dawn or raced up and down the hallways at dusk. Phoebe's passing seemed to have sobered him permanently, even though he got over his initial depths of despair.

Just as humans may take on different roles, or display different aspects of their personalities, in different relationships, rabbits too seem to change subtly as they change partners. Elmo, it seems, matured. Jake, on the other hand, turned with the death of each girl-friend toward something safe and familiar—his anger. Willow, even with the loss of two mates, maintained her equilibrium based on her friendship with a group of part-time playmates. How a rabbit mourns is as individual as the rabbit himself. But the fact that rabbits *do* mourn raises real issues about how we treat them. What effect, for instance, does taking a three-week-old baby rabbit from its mother and littermates, to be sold in a pet store, have on the baby? What effect does it have on the mother? What happens when a familiar human dumps a rabbit, by itself, out in the wild? What grief does a rabbit feel when it hears its littermates being butchered for food or fur? What levels of sorrow, in other words, do rabbits feel that humans have never acknowledged?

War Games

Rabbit emotions aren't only about joy, love, grief and games. In fact, if you want to see the true range of rabbit behavior, try introducing one rabbit to another. On occasion, they'll fall in love at first sight, as evidenced by bumping noses, licking, tooth grinding and dancing around like flighty adolescents. More often, it's "hate at first sight" (although they may grow to love each other) and the would-be love-birds launch into each other like pit bulls. Many people are surprised to see their sweet little bunny tear into the flesh of the unsuspecting newcomer. But given the propensity of wild rabbits to fight, the fact that our domestic rabbits can also be vicious makes perfect sense.

As in the wild, many domestic squabbles center on territory. When one rabbit meets another rabbit for the first time, it is typically in one rabbit's space. Like gang members, suburbanites who live in gated communities, and other wild animals, rabbits don't appreciate invasions of their turf. It's understandable—most of us would react heatedly if a stranger walked unbidden into our living rooms as well.

Rabbits also have to work out who's going to be the top bunny. Just how important this is will vary from rabbit to rabbit, or relationship to relationship. For some rabbits, who is going to be on top is the most pressing question, and the relationship won't really "stick" until that issue is worked out. Two very dominant bunnies will usually have to fight to establish the relationship. When one or both rabbits are submissive by nature, on the other hand, the relationship will be much easier, as the more submissive rabbit will "present," or drop his head, to the other rabbit. As long as the second rabbit accepts this show of submission (and doesn't, say, bite or hump the other's head), a fight will be averted.

Sometimes it's not territory or dominance so much as the individual personalities and experiences of the two rabbits involved that lead to a fight. Some rabbits who have never had a friend before, for instance, have very little experience socializing with members of their own species and are either unable or afraid to react to the new rabbit in an appropriate manner (so they attack first, ask questions later). This was the strategy employed by Maccabee when he arrived in Margo's home. The problem was compounded by Maccabee's belief that he should be the dominant bunny in an already established group, a feeling that was not shared by all the other rabbits. As a result, Mac and some of the other boys suffered several injuries, though the greatest wound was probably the one to Maccabee's ego.

On the other hand, rabbits can pick fights with their friends, too, and it's often difficult for the human to tell what set it off. Sometimes it's as simple as smell. If one rabbit had to go to the veterinarian, especially if he had to stay overnight, his partner may not recognize his smell when he returns, and will attack him. For this reason, some people who live with rabbits will bring a rabbit's bonded mate with him to the veterinarian. That way they both end up smelling like antiseptic, antibiotics and the dreaded people in white lab coats.

Sometimes rabbits will fight if there is a change in one rabbit's status, or if the rabbits are of different ages and one reaches a different stage in his development. This happens most often when one rabbit hits adolescence before the other. But it can also happen if one rabbit hits middle or old age as well. Just as human friendships sometimes falter when one person marries or becomes successful, so too do rabbit relationships falter when interests or strategies diverge. In those cases, the relationship has to shift to reflect the change, or fighting will ensue. For instance, a rabbit who has been submissive for his entire life may decide that it's time for a change, and will challenge his partner's dominance, leading to a fight. Wallace, a very submissive young lop, once went to live with a Dutch named Poppy. Wallace and Poppy bonded right away and, the adopter reported, spent all their time together. After they had been together about three weeks, however, Wallace evidently ventured into Poppy's "special" room, which had been her private territory before Wallace arrived. A big fight broke out, and rather than back down, as was his habit, Wallace fought back, sending Poppy to the hospital for stitches.

What probably happened was that Poppy only liked Wallace when he kept to his proper place—both his literal place (out of her room) and his figurative place (submissive to her). When he challenged that by entering her room, she attacked him, and since he didn't back down, it signaled the end of their relationship. If Wallace had realized his "error" and run back out of the room, the relationship would have survived. Instead, a combination of territorial defense on Poppy's part and Wallace's challenging his submissive position led to the end of a previously close friendship. (Wallace is now living happily in a different home with another rabbit, Sophie, whom he dominates.)

Fights can also occur for what seem to be petty reasons, such as when rabbits fight over snacks. Usually these are minor tiffs, but if one rabbit is mad enough the squabble can turn into a full-blown war. Fragile relationships are especially prone to such mishaps, and sensitive rabbits can hold a grudge if their nose is gashed once or if they are unceremoniously chased from the room. That grudge can erupt into an all-out brawl at a later date.

Sometimes too, a fight between one pair of rabbits can set off another pair, as if the tension is contagious. One week, a rabbit named Dusty Miller, who lived in Margo's large group, began picking fights with Trouble, a rabbit who had been his friend. Margo never figured out what precipitated the fighting, but she does know that after about a week of off-and-on fights with Dusty Miller, Trouble turned around and started picking on Maccabee. Margo finally had to pull Dusty Miller from the group, because she was afraid that his problem with Trouble would eventually spread to everyone else, leading to gang warfare.

While domestication may have made rabbits easier for humans to handle, it hasn't quelled rabbits' desire to fight with each other. As in the wild, the signs of impending domestic rabbit hostility are unmistakable. The tail goes up, the ears go back (or sometimes forward), the shoulders hunch, and there may be growling, thumping and an angry look in the eyes. Some rabbits thrust their nose and chin forward; others sniff agitatedly. If one rabbit doesn't back down, or a person doesn't intervene, this is usually followed by the preliminary moves: circling (sometimes followed by humping), chasing, boxing, lunging and jaw-snapping. The fight itself often moves so quickly that it just seems like a blur of feet kicking and fur flying, but there are some distinctive moves. One rabbit may leap over the other, then turn around and attack again. The opponents may lie on their sides, latched onto each other with their teeth, spinning around in a circle. The rabbits may tumble across the floor. They may hold onto each other with their teeth while viciously kicking with the back feet. (Some rabbits use this same move when struggling with humans, too.)

Sometimes, if one participant is not as committed to the fight as the other, rabbit fights don't engage so fully. One rabbit may chase the other rabbit around the room, for instance, with his teeth attached to the fleeing rabbit's rear. Other times one rabbit will try to submit, constantly lowering her head to the charging opponent, hoping he'll choose to lick her ears rather than bite them off. As in wrestling or boxing matches, the combatants also sometimes take breaks between rounds to refocus their energy. The rabbits may flop down in separate corners, panting with exertion. Or they may sit and busily groom themselves, smoothing their own ruffled feathers before they dive in again.

Wild rabbits will fight to establish dominance, to keep newcomers out of their territory and (for females) to protect their young, so fighting serves an important social function, and it usually continues until one rabbit runs away. But domestic rabbits can't settle disputes this way—they have nowhere to flee to, after all—and fighting can lead to nasty wounds. Over the years, house rabbit aficionados have discovered that the trick to introducing rabbits is to start slowly and on neutral ground (i.e., a place neither rabbit has claimed as its own). When a fight breaks out, squirting water at the rabbits, shouting loudly or clapping to get them to separate is helpful. In some cases, the rabbits may need to be permanently separated. In other cases, they simply need more time and patience. How much humans are willing to do depends a lot on their own levels of tolerance and patience and the ability of the rabbits to handle the stress. If rabbits could choose their mates from a large group—as they do in the wild—these introductions would probably go more smoothly. But such choices aren't available to all people with pet rabbits, and we need to guide the matchmaking with care.

Given the potential volatility of the early meetings, the first signs of acceptance, or even tolerance, can come as a great relief. When the combatants retreat to separate corners rather than attacking each other; when they chase each other but stop short of actually catching or hurting the other; when they flop out near (but not touching) each other; or when one rabbit begins the first tentative "well, maybe we could be friends" sniffs or initiates the first little lick of the nose (that's not followed by a retaliatory bite), a friendship is in the making. When they indulge in their first full-body snooze, a serious relationship has been born.

Bunnies Who Run with Wolves

Rabbit aggression can also be turned on humans. Rabbits display their anger in a number of different ways. Some nip at the human's hand or feet. Some use their front feet to "box." Some rabbits bite hard enough to bruise, but not hard enough to break the skin, which shows great restraint. Others chase humans across the room or latch their teeth onto a hand, arm or calf and refuse to let go. The most severe bite occurs when the rabbit hangs on with her teeth and kicks at the offending limb with her big back feet.

What causes such "aberrant" behavior? Often the rabbit is just trying to communicate. Nipping and an occasional bite, for instance, are good ways of expressing annoyance or pain, as when the human is holding the rabbit too tightly or blocking the doorway through which the rabbit wants to pass. The more serious bites, when rabbits dig in with their teeth, are often related to hormones or terror; the rabbit is either so horny or panicked he can't control himself.

It may also be that the rabbit is smart and has just had it with humans behaving inappropriately. Unfortunately, because so few people understand rabbits, they often end up offending them— whether it's by sticking their hands in their cages, dangling their hands in their faces, doggy-greeting style, speaking too sharply to them or teasing them with food. A rabbit who is very sensitive or who has a strong sense of right and wrong may very well turn "mean" with frustration.

Aggressive rabbits aren't incurable, but many of the cures traditionally suggested don't do much good. Some people, for instance, advocate hitting rabbits on the nose when they bite, which probably won't help a rabbit relax much. Other breeders tell rabbit caretakers to euthanize an aggressive rabbit. This is a sad decision. Many biting rabbits, like many biters in other species, are smart, outgoing and expressive; they're just fed up with human behaviors. Once they're treated with respect and taught some ground rules, they often turn out to be boisterous, affectionate and happy bunnies.

When Maccabee (named for the famous Jewish warriors of Roman times) first arrived at Margo's house, he had already bitten his previous fosterer on the throat, sending her to the hospital for stitches. She was at her wits' end. As it turns out, Maccabee had a lot of problems, but they weren't really caused by aggression as much as they were related to having been abused and badly neglected by his previous owner.

Maccabee's primary issue was that he was very concerned about not getting enough food. When Margo brought out snacks for the rabbits every evening, Maccabee raced around in circles, madly attacking every rabbit he encountered and sometimes getting in some ugly scuffles. Margo realized that Maccabee needed to know that he was going to get fed, and that no one was going to take his food away from him. After a couple of months, he finally began to mellow out at snack time, and his once-scary charges turned into aggressive requests for attention.

Margo also took to gently but firmly pushing Mac's head down very low to the ground when he charged, and following it with heavy petting (so to speak) down his head and his back. He really enjoyed this and began to associate Margo's hand not with hitting, but with petting. Maccabee is now an extremely affectionate rabbit. He still, on occasion, will bite for what he wants, or will lash out when he thinks he's getting ripped off, but for the most part, his emotions and his behavior are well under control.

A young caramel and white Dutch by the name of Spike also had a touch of the fighting Irish in him. Whenever Margo used to go into his pen to clean or to feed him and his sisters, she had to bring a broom for protection. On a good day, Spike satisfied himself with attacking the broom, but often that wasn't good enough, and he went for human flesh instead. Margo often wound up trying to fend

Spike off with the broom while he worked himself up into a lather trying to bite something fleshy and soft. The game ended when either he bit Margo or she finished her work and hopped out of the pen, whichever came first.

Then Margo discovered that Spike was only aggressive when he was in his own play area with his family, where he was in charge. Outside of the play area, when he was in Margo's arms or on the couch, he was a different rabbit entirely. This made Margo think that his aggression could be managed by being moved into the larger area with more rabbits. He couldn't get adopted anyway as a biter, so Margo hoped the new environment, without his family, would destabilize some of his territorial activities.

Sure enough, Spike became much sweeter after his move. After a few days of being chased by the bigger bunnies, Spike realized he was no longer in charge and that he needed to defer to others. Yet rather than making him depressed or fearful, this brought out a new, more positive side of his personality. He became curious about Margo, climbing up her back when she was cleaning cages—without biting her. He also became more playful with his toys, and didn't dig into the carpet all the time. Spike seemed to feel a sense of relief at not having to be in charge of everything, since there were now other rabbits to do that. Authority, one might say, had been delegated.

Working with aggressive rabbits often takes time, sensitivity and no small measure of courage. A few years ago a woman called Susan because her lop rabbit was an erratic biter. Susan suggested she try a few things—not picking him up, not chasing him around the house, not reaching in his cage, and always greeting him with affection no matter how cranky he seemed. (Saying "Hello, you little pumpkin head" to a rabbit who is streaking across the room with his fangs bared isn't easy, but it works like a charm.) The woman said she had tried them all. Susan made a few more suggestions, and the woman said, "Look, I've tried everything you people suggest, so now what am I supposed to do?" Her mistake was thinking that a single formula could solve an animal behavior problem. There are no formulas. The trick is to observe the rabbit even more closely, figure out what's bugging him and then determine how to alleviate the condition.

When Susan adopted Elmo, it quickly became clear that he was overly hormonal and sick of humans. His previous owner had wanted to euthanize him because he was "mean." This was a good description. Elmo would circle Susan's ankles, bite her feet, leap in the air to attack an offending sleeve or seize her hands with his teeth if she moved anything on the floor. He was particularly annoyed by the sound of a rattling newspaper and would launch himself at Susan, teeth first, if she dared to open one in his presence.

The two hit bottom one day when Susan was cleaning his cage and he sank his teeth into one of her fingers, nearly reaching the bone. The pain was acute, and as Susan tried to yank her hand away (never a good response, but a natural reaction), he just held on tighter, until he was dangling from her finger, about three feet up in the air. When Susan slammed her hand down, he still didn't let go, and began kicking at her arm with his back legs. When she finally unhinged his jaws with her other hand, he lunged after her hands, feet and legs, sending her leaping into a rocking chair.

Friends and family thought Susan was nuts to keep him after this episode; her doctor even suggested she get rid of Elmo, "because there are plenty of other rabbits around." No doubt Elmo was something of a public health threat at the time. But Susan was already intrigued by this little rabbit, so she made a list of all he had been through. He had spent most of his life living in a hutch in the yard of a woman who didn't like him. He had then been moved to Susan's house, where he was living indoors for the first time, with the barrage of sights, sounds and smells that that entailed. Soon after arriving, he spent a night at the vet's, so he could get neutered. He had a slight complication from the surgery, so he had to have warm cloths pressed on his testicles every night, even though he was terrified of being picked up. Elmo had clearly had enough.

Susan decided the key would be getting Elmo to see that humans, and especially Susan, were actually an OK lot. She walked back and forth across his room repeatedly, while wearing high rubber boots for protection, so he'd get used to the movement. (He quickly switched from attacking her feet to hopping along behind her with a puzzled look on his face.) She fed him grapes with tongs so he'd get used to things coming at his face. She talked to him and sang to him whenever she was in the room. When he tried to bite she pressed her hand on his head and when he did bite she shrieked "eek" to let him know it hurt. And every time he came at her with bloody murder in his eyes she babbled baby talk to him. That stopped him up short. It took about a month—and the neutering no doubt helped—but he finally turned into a kinder, gentler bunny.

Some rabbits bite only in some contexts. Phoebe, for instance, had been a pretty aggressive rabbit until Margo worked with her. By the time Susan adopted her, she was very sweet and mellow, *except* when strangers or children were in the house. In those cases, she would jerk her head up and give Susan a look that clearly expressed mounting frustration. At a certain point, if the people didn't leave the room, she would lunge. Some people can live with that kind of contextual aggression; others can't.

A truly aggressive rabbit can be a scary sight. But even in the midst of a lunge, a bite or a chase across the room, it's good to remember that rabbits bite to express themselves. It's their only way of saying, "Get away from me," or "I need space." Such behavior generally isn't acceptable in human households, especially those with children, as no one wants to live in constant fear of being bitten. But rabbits who attack other rabbits (or the family's cat or dog, or humans) needn't be deemed only "rogue" creatures deserving only abandonment, euthanasia or a quick smack on the nose. Sometimes a vicious rabbit—like an angry dog or a cranky horse—is actually a puzzle waiting to be solved, an unhappy animal waiting to be made happy again, a misunderstood creature waiting to be understood.

Group Living

Humans "kept" groups of wild rabbits in wild rabbit gardens for centuries before they began to experiment with characteristics like color, size and form. Once the process of domestication began,

Figure 2.9. Group living. Groups of domestic European rabbits create the same hierarchies and sub-groupings that groups of wild European rabbits do. ©2002, Paul Fussell. All rights reserved.

humans most likely began to keep rabbits apart, so they could more easily control the partners and timing involved in the breeding. Today, accounts of domestic rabbit behavior are generally based on rabbits living alone as pets or as laboratory animals, or consorting in pairs during commercial breeding. As a result, most people don't even realize that domestic rabbits are social creatures.

A handful of people across the country, however, have experimented with keeping relatively large groups of rabbits together, in warren-like situations. Such arrangements aren't for everyone. Few laypeople have the space or the time to keep up with a herd of rabbits. But for those who do, hosting a herd can yield valuable information on just how closely domestic rabbit behavior can mimic wild rabbit behavior.

In Margo's home, the rabbits live pretty much free-range. A cherished few are allowed into her living room and kitchen, but the rest of the rabbits sleep inside, in "rabbit rooms," at night and spend the day going inside and outside as they please via a cat door. That means her rabbits don't actually live in warrens or burrows; they make use of a built environment. But they're allowed the freedom to go where they please and do what they like throughout the day.

Many of those activities match what rabbits might do in the wild. Although Margo discourages the digging of underground tunnels, the rabbits do have a variety of tubes and tunnels (primarily made of plastic and cardboard) in which to play, run and sleep. In addition, they have children's play structures, supplemented by cat and rabbit playhouses that feature more tunnels, as well as levels, overlooks and hidey-holes. This way the rabbits can sit on, under or inside of most of their structures, experiencing the security of "underground" and enjoying a variety of "rooms" for different activities and as elevated lookouts from which to survey their world.

Besides their very different physical environment, domestic rabbits living in groups also differ from their wild brethren in that they don't have to compete for food, nor do they have to worry about reproduction. But other features of wild warren life—territorial behavior, social structure and non-reproductive mating—are still prominent features of domestic life.

Over the years, Margo's warren has ranged in size from fifteen to sixty-five rabbits. As the individuals in the group have changed, the group dynamics have changed as well. But the basic social unit has always remained the same: a couple or a clique, each with its own leader. In the past, there have been one or two dominant leaders who ruled not only their own clique, but the entire group. At other times, there seems to be no single leader. Instead, a handful of strong figures command respect from the others who circulate around them.

In comparing the social structures of dogs and cats, Elizabeth Marshall Thomas writes that the canine structure is analogous to a ladder, with a single leader on top and all the subordinate dogs falling underneath the leader in a hierarchy. Cats, she claims, have a wheel-like structure, with the leader in the middle of the wheel and all the subordinates occupying the spokes around the perimeter. In this scenario, the lesser cats are all subordinate to the leader, yet equal to each other.[1] A rabbit hierarchy contains multiple, overlapping circles, with a leader in each, along with a number of unattached individuals who don't fit with one group but come and go between the groups. The groups themselves are arranged hierarchically, with some groups—and their leaders—dominating the others.

Margo's rabbits pick territories (in the house and the yard) and fight to protect them. Needless to say, just as the "cool" tough kids in high school stake out the spot where they like to hang out, the most dominant cliques in a rabbit group pick the best territories and the lesser cliques stay away. In a previous house and yard, the redwood picnic table in the corner of the yard was taken over by the dominant group, led by Dairy Queen. All seven rabbits in her group (including the submissive Wormguy, who somehow found himself in the cool clique) spent their days on and around the table. In Margo's current setup, one particular plastic play structure has become the focal point of the rabbit room, and Amelia or Praline gets to lie on it every night, sometimes with a friend. Others, like frail Trouble, wouldn't even try to sit there.

Another feature of territorial behavior is "competitive peeing and pooping." As they do in the wild, domestic rabbits use urine and feces to mark the boundaries of their territory. When indoor rabbits live alone, or with one or two other rabbits, they are usually pretty good about their litter-box habits. At Margo's house, the pee and poop situation is a little harder to control, as all the rabbits are marking all the time to sort out the overlapping territories. Some of the rabbits even pee on newcomers (that's new rabbits, not new humans) to mark them as territory, too.

In wild warrens, the "chief" rabbit is generally male. In domestic groups, the dominant rabbit is often female. In fact, the females are generally the more aggressive and territorial rabbits in Margo's warren, even though they are all spayed and not protecting any young. Dominance, however, appears to be based on a number of factors. Generally a dominant rabbit must be fearless, outgoing and smart, and must have some history within the group. Size is not always important. These days, Amelia is one of the most dominant

Figure 2.10. Angie through a tunnel. A play structure in Margo's backyard provides tunnels and protected areas in which the rabbits can rest, romp and work out domestic arrangements. ©2002, Paul Fussell. All rights reserved.

rabbits in Margo's group: she keeps most of the other rabbits in the large group under control, constantly slips out of the main group to harass the Angoras who live in the next room and demands the first, best and largest servings of snacks. Yet Amelia is a small rabbit, a Silver Marten, who is dwarfed by almost all the other rabbits in Margo's home.

Another small leader, from a few years back, was Ramona. Ramona was a Hotot—a small white rabbit with black rings around her black eyes. She was the leader of a gang of five rabbits— Georgette, Big Bear, Potato and her number one man, Jake—and she tolerated very little slack from her obedient charges. She was aggressive and overly confident, and threw her (small) weight around, forcing the others in her group to do her dirty work for her. Ramona was like the girl in high school who wore jeans that were too tight, blouses cut way too low and a lot of mascara, and hung out with the smokers behind the school. No one messed with Ramona, and until she died, no one messed with her friends.

New rabbits bear the brunt of the territorial behavior in a domestic group, just as they do in the wild, but luckily, over the years, Margo's group as a whole has become more tolerant of newcomers. Interestingly, even as the individuals in the group have completely turned over in the twelve years since Margo has had a warren, the group itself has evolved, the result being that the transition time after a new rabbit is introduced has shortened from at least two weeks to much less than a week today. Because the aggression toward newcomers is milder and shorter-lived, the newcomers, in turn, appear to learn the group dynamics, daily structure and other important social facts in a much shorter time.

◆   ◆   ◆

Konrad Lorenz and other animal behaviorists have long asserted that "animals have no culture." But plenty of people who live with, work with and think about animals now believe that animals do have culture, if culture is defined as the transmission of behaviors from one generation to the next. According to primatologist Frans de Waal, "Culture simply means that knowledge and habits are acquired from others—often, but not always, from the older generation—which explains why two groups of the same species may behave differently."[2] The classic example of these socially transmitted behaviors is found in the Japanese macaques' tradition of washing potatoes, in which one macaque named Imo began, in the 1950s, carrying her dirty potatoes to the water to wash them; soon the others in her group started washing their potatoes. Even after all the original potato-washing macaques had died out, the band continued—and continues today—to wash their potatoes.

In rabbits, cultural transmission can be seen in examples as simple as Phoebe teaching Elmo to sleep under the bed, and Elmo sharing his new knowledge with Maybelline, who then passed it to Mr. Bop. Another example is the way that Puddles and Muddles, Margo's two Angoras, taught Puffy (a Jersey Wooley) and later, Helga, to sneak out of their room in search of a disabled rabbit, whose snacks are easy to steal. But the transmission of culture can also be more abstract and complex—as evidenced by the fact that Margo's large group of rabbits seems to have a group understanding that new rabbits will periodically enter and that, unlike ten years ago, there needn't be a huge territorial battle each time this occurs.

Mealtimes and bedtimes have also become much more organized and less chaotic than in previous years. When Margo lived in a different house, with a group of thirty to forty rabbits, the rabbits slept in her garage but spent their daytime hours playing in the backyard. Because Margo had no easy access to the backyard, the rabbits had to travel every morning from the garage through the living room, around the corner in the hallway, into the bedroom and up a ramp to her bedroom window, where they would then go down another ramp into their yard. Evenings the trek would be reversed, and three dozen rabbits would be asked to run up the outside ramp, down the inside ramp and back through the house to their beds and dinner. While the group ran outdoors in the morning without much fuss, getting them indoors at night often took an hour. As soon as Margo came out to begin the evening's activities, the smartest and the hungriest rabbits would immediately run up the ramp and head inside (and some, like Baby, would be waiting at the top of the ramp for Margo to let them in!). But most of the group took much longer to climb up the ramp, and some, like Jerry, Jake and Ramona, actively evaded Margo for what seemed like hours every night. Sometimes they never did go up the ramp, and the only way Margo got them indoors was by catching them and forcing them through the window against their will.

Years later, the minute the rabbits in Margo's current group hear her coming into their room (which thankfully has a cat door leading directly to their play yard) at dusk, the vast majority of them immediately race into their room for their dinner. Even newcomers like Angie, Bert and Ernie, who arrived very recently, quickly learned the evening routine and come in with the others at dinnertime.

Mealtime etiquette has evolved, as well. After the rabbits have gotten their fresh vegetables, Margo fills four to six bowls of pellets every evening and places them on the floor for the group to share. Years ago, the rabbits would clamor anxiously (and sometimes aggressively) for the bowls, fighting to get their heads into the first bowl placed on the ground. By the time Margo got the fourth or fifth bowl down, she usually had to push a few rabbits from the over-crowded bowls to eat out of the last bowls. Eventually, a couple of the smarter rabbits started to realize that if they simply waited till Margo put down the last bowls, they could save themselves the stress of fighting over the first bowls, and could instead eat at one of the last bowls, perhaps all by themselves. Finally, with time, all the rabbits seemed to realize there would always be enough food for all. Today, there is less jostling over the bowls, and the rabbits are more evenly dispersed throughout the room at dinnertime.

◆　◆　◆

One of the odd things about rabbits living free-range or in groups is the reaction they get from people who have only met rabbits in cages. People who come to our houses are often stunned, for instance, to find two rabbits lying contentedly side by side ("They really love each other! That's so cute!") or to see a rabbit madly dashing through the dining room ("Oh, look! She's in a hurry! That's so cute!") Some people are moved to inquire further—about whether the rabbits are affectionate; if they mate; if they really use the litter box. When we tell them the truth (yes, they're affectionate; no, they don't mate—they're altered; and yes, they have excellent litter-box habits), the guests look puzzled. If we tell a few anecdotes about the rabbits—how Mr. Bop flops over on his side when he hears the song *Baby Beluga* or how Maybelline sneaks up behind Susan and nips her socks to ask for a pat—they look at us like we're nuts. Such antics would raise no eyebrows if the subjects were dogs or cats or horses, but because they're about rabbits, our stories seem worthy of suspicion.

Figure 2.11. Rabbits are easily litter-box trained. Putting hay in the box encourages rabbits to hop in and use the box, as Mr. Bop demonstrates here. Photo by Susan Davis.

Oddly, even some people who raise rabbits don't know about the full range—or roots—of rabbit behavior. In September 2002, one breeder posted a question to an Internet listserve dedicated to the meat rabbit industry. He had been debating whether or not to let his rabbits run in an enclosed turkey coop. Another breeder noted that they would become "wild" (i.e., hard to catch and possibly vicious). "I want to be able to pick up my rabbits without getting torn apart," the advisor wrote.[3] The original poster then replied that he used to let his rabbits play in the goat yard while he cleaned the hutches. "Even after several hours of being out they displayed more wild behavior," he claimed.[4] That wild behavior, sadly, probably only meant rolling around, popping binkies, running in circles, and playing games. If the rabbits evaded capture, well, perhaps they knew they were going to be put back in their cages—or worse. In safer environments, free-range rabbits may be high-spirited or feisty (or, on the other hand, indulgently lazy), but they don't become danger-ous "wild" animals. They become autonomous creatures who display as many moods, preferences and communication styles as more familiar, more beloved pets, like cats and dogs. They may not leap into our laps or beg to play ball (although rabbits have been known to do both), but they interact with humans as effectively and profoundly and affectionately as their other pet brethren.

Notes

1. Marshall Thomas, Elizabeth, *The Tribe of Tiger: Cats and Their Culture* (New York: Pocket Books, 1994), p. 71.
2. Quoted in Friend, Tim, "Culture's Not only Human," *USA Today*, June 5, 2001.
3. September 23, 2002.
4. *Ibid.*

PART TWO

WITCHES, WHORES AND TRICKSTERS

Rabbits as Cultural Icons

———•◦•———

THIS BOOK IS about rabbits. But it is also, in part, about what people think about rabbits, because rabbits, for better or for worse, exist both as living, breathing animals and as elements within our culture's popular imagination. That is, besides inhabiting forests, fields, backyards and homes, they inhabit the realm of representation—in folklore and photos, on television and film, in gift stores and in literature. These fabricated rabbits may not tell us much about the lives of real rabbits, but they do tell us a great deal about how we *think* about rabbits and their place in society. As such, the kinds of rabbit images we have in our culture influence how people treat the animals themselves. As Stephen Baker, coauthor of *Picturing the Beast: Animals, Identity and Representation,* writes, "[T]he representational, symbolical, and rhetorical uses of the animal must be understood to carry as much conceptual weight as any idea we may have of the 'real' animal and must be taken just as seriously."[1]

Humans are, of course, enamored of rabbits. These soft animals, with their big ears, big feet and fluffy tails, have long been a subject of tapestries, paintings, jewelry and sculpture. Today you can find rabbit decorations and rabbit clothing everywhere from high-end museum gift shops to home craft catalogues. And these images are not limited just to material culture. The quaint, cute, smiling and funny bunnies in our gift and children's stores are related to the celluloid rabbits of the Looney Tunes cartoons and Disney animated films, as well as the very sexualized image of rabbits portrayed by the

129

Playboy Bunny. Going back even further, these icons have their roots in the folk tales and myths told about rabbits in cultures around the world.

How do we account for the multiple uses—and meanings—that surround the rabbit, both in the United States and worldwide? Real rabbits have traditionally served as both childhood pet and family meal, as both highly prized show animal and hunted pest. In "texts" that range from ancient myths and stories to motion picture images and fuzzy slippers, imaginary rabbits have been portrayed as both innocent and sexual, clever and stupid, timid and brave. The fact that one animal occupies so many contradictory positions in our popular imagination both reflects and shapes the ways that we have viewed and treated real rabbits throughout history, for good or for ill.

Notes

1.   Adams, Carol and Stephen Baker, *Picturing the Beast: Animals, Identity and Representation* (Chicago: University of Illinois Press, 2001), p. 10.

3. "Like a Ghostie O'er the Field"

The Rabbit in Ancient Belief

In the black furrow of a field
I saw an old witch-hare this night;
And she cocked a lissome ear,
And she eyed the moon so bright,
And she nibbled of the green;
And I whispered "Whsst! Witch-hare,"
Away like a ghostie o'er the field
She fled, and left the moonlight there.

Walter De La Mare, "The Hare"

THROUGHOUT HISTORY, AND all around the world, various cultures have used rabbits as religious symbols. A "symbol," in this case, is simply something that mediates religious experience or translates between two realms—the sacred and the profane. A symbol makes comprehensible that which is incomprehensible, and puts the sacred realm within the reach of ordinary humans. As such, a symbol is both a physical representation of something that cannot be put into words and, when found in ritual or myth, a container for much more, as it evokes powerful feelings within believers. Most symbols are also "polyvocalic"; that is, they can signify multiple, abstract concepts all at once, not all of which can be easily articulated in words.

The use of rabbits (or hares[1]) as religious symbols is especially notable in the ancient cultures of India, Greece, Egypt, China, Japan, Rome, the British Isles and Native America. Often rabbit symbols have to do with the real qualities that rabbits possess. Rabbits are quick; they zigzag from place to place, and they have to rely on their quick wits to survive. In Chinese astrology, people born in the Year of the Rabbit are said to be quick and clever, and to have trouble finishing what needs to be done (or, depending on the source, to be virtuous, intelligent and highly skilled).

Rabbits also often sleep with their eyes open, which makes them look as if they can see (and understand) more than other animals can. (In real life, rabbits' short-range vision is actually quite poor, though their long-range vision is good.) This has given the rabbits a reputation for vigilance. Rabbits' open eyes also gave them such a reputation for intuition and prophecy that the ancient Egyptians, Romans and Britons used them for divination (or fortune telling).[2] The ancient Britons would let a hare run loose on the fields to plan an attack on another tribe; the direction in which the hare ran indicated the best route to take.[3] Similarly, the Algonquins (a Native American tribe) refused to hunt rabbits, as they were seen to be the keepers of life's secrets and a key to the afterlife.[4]

Other times, the qualities attributed to rabbits are less directly related to their actual physical or behavioral characteristics. In both the United States and China, rabbits are a sign of good luck, perhaps because they are so fertile. But another theory holds that rabbits are considered good luck because if you catch one in a trap, it's a sure sign that other small game are also in the area. According to this theory, the rabbit's foot, (i.e. the part that generally got caught in the trap) was seen as especially lucky. From this tradition sprang that of uttering "Rabbit, rabbit," or "white rabbit, white rabbit, white rabbit" or any variation on this theme, on the first of every month to garner good luck. (Some people try to be the *first* to say "rabbit, rabbit" in order to "win" the good luck. The person who was not quick on the rabbit draw is then said to have been "rabbited.")

While the origins of some of these traditions are unclear, we do know that as far back as the sixth century B.C.E., people carried hares' feet, as the practice was thought to provide good crops, many children and prosperity. (A left rear foot that was removed from a rabbit killed during a full moon by a cross-eyed person, and then carried in the left pocket, was considered most lucky.) The Welsh also believed that rubbing a rabbit's foot all over a newborn ensured the child's fortune.

Conversely, rabbits are the harbingers of bad luck in some cultures. Early European cultures believed that meeting a hare would bring misfortune, because hares were thought to portend madness. (The expression "mad as a March hare" refers to the "madness" displayed by a male rabbit when sexually aroused.) One variant of this belief states that if a fisherman meets a hare on his way to fish, he will not catch anything that day.[5] According to another, if a hare runs along the street of a village, a fire will start there.[6]

People also used to burn hares in May Day rituals in medieval Europe because, like cats, hares (white ones in particular) were thought to be the incarnations of witches. Ironically, some people believed that carrying a rabbit's foot or head actually acted as a protection against witchcraft[7]—simply because the rabbits themselves were associated with forces of evil. The Celts thought that rabbits lived underground because they had netherworld connections; medieval Hungarians believed that the appearance of a rabbit foretold a terrible accident; the Vikings thought rabbits were as frightening as sea monsters.

A number of artworks express the terror that some humans had of hares. One twelfth-century frieze on the collegiate church of Königslutter, Germany, shows two hares tying up a prostrate man. A thirteenth-century stone carving of *The Last Judgment* on the Chartres Cathedral shows a demon in the form of a rabbit attacking a woman. Another relief on that same cathedral shows a panicked soldier running away from a hare.

Many of these negative associations may have derived from beliefs that hares were sexually abnormal. Aristotle thought that rabbits were "abundant in semen," as demonstrated by their hairiness (he postulated that especially hairy men were also more sexually virile). Other early writers, including Pliny and Aelian, believed that hares were hermaphrodites.[8] Aelian also reported a story of male hares giving birth. The fact that hares were considered filthy didn't much help their reputation. One Middle English poem, *The Names of the Hare*, called the animal a "soillart," or "filthy beast."

◆   ◆   ◆

The primary use of the rabbit or hare in the myths and rituals of ancient cultures, however, was to indicate a set of themes related to womanhood, including fertility, sexuality, fecundity, the moon and rebirth on the one hand, and innocence, passivity and virginity on the other.

People have long believed, for instance, that the hare is a highly libidinous animal that mates frequently and indiscriminately. As such, the hare has been associated with lust and sexuality in the myths and practices of many cultures, especially in the spring rituals of ancient Greece, Rome and the British Isles. Greek and Roman artists also depicted hares as an attribute, or sacred accessory, of Aphrodite (or Venus), the goddess of love and fertility. The association was so strong that these cultures frequently sacrificed hares to this goddess, and many people thought that eating hare had an aphrodisiacal effect. The association between rabbits or hares and love and sex continued for centuries, as can be seen in the variety of surviving superstitions, love potions and spells using rabbits or hares. According to one spell, the way for a woman to break a man's love is to return one of his gifts and wear the left hind foot of a graveyard rabbit. Another superstition holds that the number of times a rabbit runs across your path indicates the number of years until you will marry.[9] The ancient Greeks presented rabbits to each other as symbols of love; the ancient Romans believed that eating rabbit meat would help cure sexual problems and Pliny mentioned that many people believed that eating hare meat would make them attractive for nine days.

Closely related to sexuality is fertility, and real rabbits are famous for their fecundity and large litters, and for being among the first animals to bear young each spring. (The Egyptian word for hare was actually "Un," or "open/to open/the opener," which referred not only to the fact that hares are born and sleep with their eyes open, but also to the hare's association with springtime, fertility and renewal.) This remarkable fertility has endowed the rabbit with an almost universal divinity. In ancient Greece and Rome, women desirous of becoming pregnant often sacrificed hares to the gods in exchange for fertility. Hares were also considered sacred to the goddess Diana in her aspect (or alternate form) as Lucina, the goddess of childbirth. Rabbits played a role in the fertility rites of other cultures as well, including Native America, ancient Saxony and Britain, Medieval Europe, China and Japan; tapestries from medieval and Renaissance Europe also include rabbits as symbols of fertility.

On the other hand, according to some superstitions, seeing a hare can sometimes be dangerous to a pregnant woman. One modern European superstition holds that if a pregnant woman sees the white tuft on the end of a rabbit's tail, her child will be born with a harelip. In other variations of the myth, it is the sight of a hare's head, or stepping over a hare's body, that leads to this unfortunate condition in the child.[10]

Many cultures believe that the moon rules a woman's reproductive cycles, and rabbits (and their fertility) are commonly associated with the moon or the moon goddess. In western astrology, which has been practiced in cultures as diverse as ancient Babylonia, Egypt, pre-Roman England, pre-Columbian Central America, the Greco-Roman world and throughout medieval and Renaissance Europe, the moon is almost universally feminine and is associated with virginity, purity and childbearing.[11] By the same token, the rabbit is often depicted with the moon. Cultures such as Japan, ancient Saxony, Mayan Mexico, parts of sub-Saharan Africa and China all worshipped a moon goddess represented either as or with a rabbit. In ancient China, the hare, a yin animal, was the attribute of the moon goddess Gwallen, and mixed for her the elixir of immortality.[12] In fact, images from the East showing a hare or rabbit with a mortar and pestle are explained as either pounding the elixir of immortality, making rice flour or making rice cakes known as *mochi*, which also means full moon in Japanese.[13] In Egypt the hare was associated with Osiris in his aspect as moon god (an unusual case in which the moon deity was male). Teutonic legends hold that torch-bearing hares follow Harfa, the moon goddess. In Sanskrit, the word for moon is "cacadharas," which means "one who carries the hare."[14]

The Chinese varied the theme slightly by incorporating the Buddhist notion of self-sacrifice. According to one myth, the Buddha placed the rabbit in the moon to thank him for his selflessness: when Buddha was hungry, the rabbit sprang into a fire and cooked his own flesh, thus symbolizing total sacrifice of the self.[15] The rabbit then got to live in the moon palace, where he became the Jade Rabbit. Another Chinese legend (derived from India) has Buddha taking the form of a hare and encountering Brahma, a sky god. Here again, Buddha/the rabbit leaps into a fire to become food for Brahma, pleasing the sky god with his sacrifice so deeply that Brahma paints his image onto the moon.[16]

Even when the legends vary within a culture, the rabbit–moon connection is constant. In one Far East legend, for example, a female hare gets pregnant by running across water under a full moon. In other versions she becomes pregnant either by staring at the moon or by licking a male's fur when the moon is full.[17]

These rabbit–moon connections show up frequently in the artwork from cultures in the East and the West. Japanese figurines and silk screens; Chinese paintings and bronzes; Dutch engravings; Mayan vase paintings and other ceramics; Syrian, Arab and Indian manuscript illustrations—all include examples of rabbits on, in or with the moon or a moon goddess. One explanation for these connections is that the rabbit has long been thought of as nocturnal (even though some species are "crepuscular" or most active at dawn and dusk); another is that the rabbit's gestation period is one (lunar) month long. The link may also have to do with the fact that some people believe they see an actual image of a rabbit on the moon (just as others see a "man in the moon"). As one scholar writes:

> Representations of a hare or rabbit on the moon are found in the art of ancient China and in Pre-Columbian Mexico. Mythologies of both areas also place a rabbit on the moon. Although such linkage might appear to be arbitrary, a comparison of the visible surface of the full moon with the silhouette of a rabbit does reveal a degree of congruence. Not only the distinctive ears of the rabbit but also other features appear to be delineated on the moon's surface.[18]

Since the moon was thought by many cultures to bring rejuvenation or regeneration (hence the traditional practice of planting under a waxing moon), the association between hares or rabbits and the moon and birth extends to include dawn, beginnings and rebirth as well. One seventeenth-century Saxon illustration, *Idol of the Moon*, shows a goddess wearing a rabbit costume (including a hat with rabbit ears) and holding a moon in front of her stomach, representing pregnancy or rebirth. This is both a derivative of images of the goddess Diana and her hare and, as we shall see,[19] a striking precursor of our own culture's Playboy Bunny.

"Here Comes Peter Cottontail"

Of course, the greatest example of the link between hares (and later rabbits) and rebirth or regeneration is in our own springtime ritual of Easter. At first blush, the fact that our contemporary Easter revolves both around the story of Jesus' resurrection and the story of the Easter Bunny is a little confusing. There are no stories of magical bunnies distributing baskets of eggs in the Bible, after all, and most Easter cards are decorated with cute bunnies and chicks, not graphic scenes of the crucifixion. But both the ancient observance of Easter, which celebrates Christ's rebirth after his sacrifice for humankind (reminiscent of the hare's sacrifice for Buddha), and the

Figure 3.1. Images of women dressed as rabbits date back to ancient times. This illustration from *A Restitution of Decayed Intelligence*, a book that glorified Saxon culture and was written by antiquarian Richard Verstegan in Antwerp in 1605, depicts the Saxon idol of the moon. Courtesy Rare Books Division, The New York Public Library, Astor, Lenox and Tilden Foundations.

modern celebration, which has become more secular, have traditionally included rabbits.

This springtime holiday originated as a pagan feast held by pre-Christian Europeans to celebrate the spring equinox. Even then, the hare was associated with this celebration, as it was an attribute of the Teutonic moon goddess Ostara, as well as the Anglo-Saxon moon goddess Eostre.[20] It was Eostre, in fact, who gave her name to the celebration (a name that is also related to "estrus," which further links women's cycles to this lunar holiday). Both of these goddesses were often depicted in the guise of a hare, or with the head of a hare.

Hares were sacrificed not only to goddesses of love and fertility but, as Christianity spread throughout Europe and co-opted pagan

Figure 3.2. Easter imagery often incorporates both egg and rabbit themes, as well as the themes of fertility and sexuality associated with rabbits. C Hulton-Deutsch Collection/CORBIS, 1935.

rituals, at the Eucharist as well. As religious scholar Beryl Rowland writes,

> Totemistic rituals always involved the sacrificing and eating of the animal at the major festivals so that its strength might pass into the celebrants. The strength of the hare became characterized as an aphrodisiac. . . . [F]rom such rituals came the observances associated with the Easter myth, with Christ as a surrogate for the hare, and with the hare still being eaten both as a Eucharist and as a confection.[21]

The Council of Nicaea's declaration in 325 C.E. that Easter was to be celebrated on the first Sunday after the first full moon of spring further reinforced associations between springtime, rebirth and the moon—and, less directly, the ancient associations between springtime, rebirth, the moon and hares.

The idea of an actual Easter Bunny seems to have originated in Germany in the sixteenth century, with the belief that the Easter Hare laid the Easter (Pasche) eggs. In this tradition, children built a nest in which the hare would lay her eggs.[22] This belief, in turn, may have originated in a German folk tale about an impoverished mother who painted eggs for her children as a present for Easter, and hid them in the woods. The children found the eggs by following a rabbit into the woods, leading them to believe that the rabbit had laid the eggs. The Easter Bunny arrived on the shores of the New World when German settlers arrived in Pennsylvania Dutch country in the seventeenth century. Children eagerly awaited the arrival of the *Oschter Haws* and believed that if they were good, the magical rabbit would leave a nest of colored eggs.[23]

Eggs, in fact, have a long and rich symbolic tradition, symbolizing the origin of the earth in cultures ranging from Egyptian to Chinese, Hindu, Japanese, Central American and Greek, and symbolizing resurrection in a number of other traditions, including Christianity.[24] Eggs used to be forbidden during Lent, so parents brought them out on Easter morning, often colored red to evoke the joy of the Resurrection.[25] Both eggs and rabbits also symbolize the virgin birth—the egg because chickens can lay eggs without the aid of a male, and the rabbit or hare because in some cultures it was held to be able to conceive without a male, and even to give birth without losing its virginity.[26] This made eggs and rabbits ideal symbols for a holiday associated with the birth—or re-birth—of Christ.

Ironically, although the Easter Bunny is supposed to be a benign creature, it has been known to strike fear in the hearts of young children. Often depicted wearing clothes and walking upright, the Easter Bunny is endowed with the ability to fly (or hop very fast) around the world, to sneak in and out of homes without waking the sleeping inhabitants, and to know which children have been good and which have been bad. Add to that characterization the association

Figure 3.3. Both eggs and rabbits have been associated with spring festivals for thousands of years. This Easter decoration combines the two symbols by showing little bunnies popping out of an egg carton. Courtesy The Bunny Museum. Photo by Margo DeMello.

with the spooky—albeit joyful—story of Christ's resurrection and the Easter Bunny seems not just like a happy little bunny, but more like a creature that is part human, part supernatural being and perhaps part monster, as well.

The Dark Side of the Moon

Once rabbits were introduced to Britain in the thirteenth century, they took on that culture's symbolism of the hare, along with that animal's association with sex, femininity and fertility, often to negative effect. Rowland notes that the Latin and English words for rabbit came to emphasize this connection:

> The Latin words *cunnus* (the pudendum) and *cuniculus* (rabbit) developed into *conin* [from which the old English word for rabbit, coney, is derived]. Thus, an animal prized for its fertility became the perfect symbol for woman as a whole and for a specific part of her anatomy.[27]

Indeed, *cuniculus* means "underground passage," demonstrating yet another link between women's genitalia (i.e., the vaginal passage) and rabbits. Even the word "hare" has sexual connotations: in

Figure 3.4. Madonna and Child with Saint Catherine. At first glance, this 1530 painting by Titian appears to simply show Mary showing a rabbit to Jesus. An alternative interpretation is that she is trying to control her own sexuality. Courtesy Bibliotheque Nationale de France.

Middle English, terms like "harlot," "whore," and "hare" were frequently used interchangeably.[28]

Medieval and Renaissance artists often placed white rabbits in paintings, and often in the company of the Virgin Mary, to indicate her victory over sexuality. In Titian's *Madonna and Child with Saint Catherine*, what looks like Mary's friendly grasp on a small white rabbit can be interpreted as an iron grip on her own sexuality. Other paintings from this same period depict rabbits actually tempting saints with their sexuality. Francesco del Cossa's fresco "Allegory of April: Triumph of Venus," in the Palazzo Schifanoia in Ferrera, Italy, clearly shows both humans and rabbits in sexually flirtatious poses, as if they had all caught the March hare madness. It seems that through the ages rabbits have been subject to the same virgin/whore dichotomies as human women have been.

Women and rabbits have been linked in other ways, as well. In many cultures the moon rules not just women's reproductive cycles, but also women's emotions, which are also thought to be controlled by the womb (or in modern terms, "hormones"). This isn't an entirely benign influence. In western astrology, the moon is associated with nurturing and sensitivity, but, because of its swift motion in the sky, moving rapidly from constellation to constellation and house to house (in astrological terms), it is also said to be changeable, finicky, moody and cunning. The same qualities have been associated with women and with rabbits. The word "cunning," in fact, is derived from the Latin word for "to know," *cunnan*, which is related to the word for rabbit, or *cuniculus*.[29] Yet "cony" (or coney), which is the old English word for rabbit, also means a fool or a dupe, and a "cony-catcher" is a cheater, turning the cunning aspect slightly on its head.[30] Both cuny and cunny are slang terms for a woman or her genitalia. (This association is so strong that the pronunciation of Coney Island, which once rhymed with money or honey, was changed in the Victorian era to the current "coney" because its original sound was too easily confused with slang for female genitals.[31]) From these words comes the extremely derogatory term both for woman and her genitalia, "cunt," which dates back to the eleventh century.[32] By the early twentieth century, "bun" meant prostitute; in England today, "coney" and "bunny" can still both mean vulva.

These negative associations between female sexuality and rabbits go one step further in the rabbit's final mythological attribute: prey. That is, even as the rabbit has been worshipped throughout history by men and women for its remarkable reproductive powers, it is simultaneously sacrificed so that the worshipers can garner those generative powers for themselves. Hares were portrayed as traveling with Diana, goddess of the moon and the hunt, and Venus, goddess of love, and were sacrificed to both. In the ancient world, images abound of rabbits depicted in hunting scenes, images that continue on into the Middle Ages and the Renaissance. Here, perhaps, lies the ultimate irony of the rabbit's exalted position as sacred animal: regardless of the attribute for which the rabbit is worshipped—fertility, sexuality or rebirth—she eventually ends up sacrificed to fulfill human needs.

Rabbit Tales

Folk tales, unlike myths and religious symbols, are essentially entertaining. Filled with fantastic creatures, animals that speak and magic of all kinds, these stories are told for amusement around the fire, during playtime with children and to pass the time while traveling long distances. Yet folk tales have a serious purpose, as well. Many contemporary folk tales contain fragments of ancient myths, even from religions that disappeared long ago. Others are educational, in that they explain why certain things are they way they are. Still others, like the fable, impart a moral lesson.

Just So Stories

Folk tales that use animals as the main actors are called "animal tales" by folklorists. Such stories exist in almost every culture in the world. One common type of animal tale is the "just so" or explanatory story. Native American tales include a number of "just so stories" that explain how the rabbit got to be the way he is. The Sioux legend "How the Rabbit Lost His Tail," for instance, tells why rabbits have such stubby tails. According to this story, the formerly long-tailed rabbit, arrogantly overestimating his own strength, interlocked his tail with the tails of three wolves, who pulled so hard that they broke the rabbit's tail in half. An Iroquois tale called "Rabbit and Fox" has an explanation for why the rabbit's nose is so short. In this story, Rabbit, in attempting to evade Fox, once masqueraded as a tree. The fox, sensing the deception, broke off a "dead limb"— actually the rabbit's long nose.

Just so stories are not just found among Native Americans. The Yoruba story "Rubber Girl" tells why rabbits have long ears (because the rabbit retained the tips of his ears when all the other animals cut theirs off); the Angolan version of the same tale explains why rabbits sleep in holes (to keep away from the leopard). African-American tales, themselves descended from West Africa, also include just-so aspects, such as the Uncle Remus tale "How Mr. Rabbit Lost his Fine Bushy Tail" (and ended up with a short one instead). This was retold as "Why the Rabbit Has a Short Tail," a story that also explains the rabbit's long ears. Other just so stories featuring rabbits explain how certain other animals came to be the way they are, such as the Sioux tale "The Rabbit and the Bear with the Flint Body," which explains that there are so few bears because the rabbit killed them all. (Ironically, many Native American tales, such as those of the Micmac and the Sioux, show the rabbit as a hunter, perhaps because of his swiftness, patience or excellent hearing.)

Still others explain other features of the natural world, such as the Creek tale "How Rabbit Brought Fire to the People." According to this story, in the beginning, the Weasels were the only ones who had fire, and the people asked the animals if they could get some. Rabbit was the only animal brave enough to steal it; he used his cleverness and speed to do so.

A Wabanaki story called "How the Rabbit Lost His Tail" explains the derivation of a whole host of the rabbit's distinctive traits—his long hind legs, short tail, split upper lip and white winter coat—by focusing on the travails of Ableegumooch the Forest Guide. In this story, Ableegumooch the Rabbit used to be a "very different animal than he is today. His body was large and round, his legs were straight and even, and he had a long bushy tail. He could run and walk like other animals, not with a hop-hop-hop as he does today."[33]

Ableegumooch loses his tail when he uses it to help Uskool the Fisher get out of a deep pit into which he had fallen. The exertion also lengthens his rear legs, forcing him to hop instead of walk. Later, when making a dress for Uskool's wife, he twists a piece of caribou skin between his teeth so hard that it splits his lip. "He twisted and twisted, and he twisted it so hard the cord snapped out of his teeth and split his upper lip right up to his nose! And now you see why it is that rabbits are hare lipped!"[34] Finally, Ableegumooch gained his white winter coat as a gift from the fisher's bride, who wanted to thank him for his troubles.

When Ableegumooch realized with a shock how strange his new body was, he went to Glooscap, creator of all animals, for help. Glooscap pointed out to Ableegumooch the benefits of his new features, such as the ease with which he'd be able to find clover with his cleft lip, how quickly he'd be able to hop with his very long legs, and how his short tail would never again get tangled with brambles, or get in the way when escaping from Wolf. "Why—with my new legs, my cleft lip, and without my long tiresome tail, I'm a better rabbit than I was before!"[35]

Just so stories do not simply explain the derivation of natural phenomena. They also entertain, impart moral lessons and contain elements that we recognize from mythology. The Micmac tale "Rabbit and the Moon Man" tells not only how the rabbit developed some of his distinctive characteristics, but also why the Man in the Moon looks the way he does, and why the moon disappears for a few days every month. Similarly, the Thompson River Indian legend "The Moon and his Younger Sister" explains the origin of the rabbit on the moon.

The animal tales that we know best in the West include literary fables, medieval animal tales and oral legends, all of which have become intertwined throughout history. While most of us have become familiar with such tales through the collections of Aesop or the Brothers Grimm, a large portion of European folk tales are not European in origin at all. Instead, they probably descended from both the twelfth-century Hindu collection of stories known as the *Panchatantra* and the *Jataka*, a collection of Buddhist tales from the fifth century B.C.E. The original version of "The Tarbaby and the Rabbit" (Aarne-Thompson type 175[36]), for instance, comes from the *Jataka*, and has been found in 250 versions around the world. The best-known version is part of the African-American Brer Rabbit series popularized by Joel Chandler Harris.

Rabbits who play a leading role in animal tales usually are cast because they have a certain set of characteristics that other animals do not possess. But the symbolic properties associated with the rabbit in folk tales differ markedly from those that are typically found in myths and ritual practice. While rabbits represent sexuality, fecundity, the moon and rebirth in religions around the world, they represent far less serious themes in folk tales. Even these attributes, however, change according to the culture. An animal's attributes seem to lie very much in the eye of the beholder.

Fools and Cowards

European tales usually portray the rabbit as a foolish, arrogant or cowardly animal, who relies only on his speed, not his intellect, to survive. This makes sense: rabbits and hares are prey species in real life and rely on running for protection. In some Aesop fables, such as "The Dog and the Hare," "The Hare and the Hound," "The Lion and the Hare" and "The Hares and the Lions," the rabbits simply run from larger, stronger animals who would eat them, emphasizing their status as prey. In "The Hare and the Hound" a goatherd remarks, upon seeing the hound chasing the rabbit, that the rabbit is a better runner. The hound replies, "You do not see the difference between us: I was only running for a dinner, but he for his life." Other Aesop's tales not only show the rabbit being pursued by other creatures, but demonstrate that very few animals are willing to help them. In "The Hares and the Foxes," the hares are at war with the foxes and ask the eagles for help. They reply: "We would willingly have helped you, if we had not known who you were, and with whom you were fighting."

It's just a short hop from the theme of rabbit as prey to that of rabbit as coward. In tales of this type, rabbits demonstrate their fear of other animals. (Rabbits, more so than hares, signify timidity not only because they live at the bottom of the food chain, but because they burrow underground, making them look especially cowardly.) In the Aesop fable "The Hares and the Frogs" ("More Cowardly Than the Hare," Aarne-Thompson type 70), the hares are so tired of being the most timid of the animals that they decide to kill themselves by throwing themselves into a lake. But when the sound of the hares approaching the lake scares the frogs into jumping into the water, one of the hares called out: "Stay, my friends, do not do as you intended; for you now see that there are creatures who are still more timid than ourselves." This theme is repeated in a Sioux version of Aarne-Thompson type 70 known as "Story of the Rabbits." In still other versions, the hare laughs so hard upon finding an animal more afraid than he that he splits his lip (Aarne-Thompson motif A2200, A2343). This makes the "Story of the Rabbits" a just so story, too.

The rabbit's alleged cowardice also appears in the Aarne-Thompson tale type 2033: "The End of the World." This folk tale is best known through the story of Chicken Little, who thought that the sky was falling when she was hit on the head by an acorn, and told all the other animals about it. But rabbits frequently show up in this type of tale, too, most likely because rabbits (and hares) stomp their feet at the sign of danger, which can make them seem overly timid or reactive. In the Indian tale "The Timid Hare and the Flight of the Beasts," a hare hears the sound of a vilva fruit falling on a palm leaf and thinks that the earth is collapsing. As with the Chicken Little story, all the animals in the forest eventually join with the hare in flight, and are only saved by the actions of the Bodhisattva.

> Alarmed at sound of fallen fruit
> A hare once ran away,
> The other beasts all followed suit
> Moved by that hare's dismay.
> They hastened not to view the scene,
> But lent a willing ear
> To idle gossip, and were clean
> Distraught with foolish fear.
> They who to Wisdom's calm delight
> And Virtue's heights attain,
> Though ill example should invite,
> Such panic fear disdain.[37]

The Tibetan story "Plop" follows the same path as "The Timid Hare and the Flight of the Beasts," except for the fact that the rabbits who heard the fruit fall into the lake did not interpret the sound ("plop") as the sound of the sky falling or the earth collapsing, but were terrified anyway, telling all the other animals that "Plop is coming!" until a wise lion showed them otherwise.

The Arrogant Rabbit

Conversely, another theme common to rabbit lore is the rabbit's supposed arrogance. In these tales, although everyone knows rabbits are prey animals, the rabbit thinks himself bigger, stronger or smarter than he really is, and usually pays for his folly. The best known example of this kind of tale is Aesop's "The Tortoise and the Hare" (Aarne-Thompson type 275), which goes like this:

> The hare was once boasting of his speed before the other animals. "I have never yet been beaten," said he, "when I put forth my full speed. I challenge anyone here to race with me."
>
> The tortoise said quietly, "I accept your challenge."
>
> "That is a good joke," said the hare. "I could dance around you all the way."
>
> "Keep your boasting until you've beaten," answered the tortoise. "Shall we race?"
>
> So a course was fixed and a start was made. The Hare darted almost out of sight at once, but soon stopped and, to show his contempt for the Tortoise, lay down to have a nap. The Tortoise plodded on and plodded on, and when the Hare awoke from his nap, he saw the Tortoise just near the winning-post and could not run up in time to save the race. Then said the Tortoise: "Plodding Wins the Race."[38]

Hundreds of variants of this story exist in the folk tales of countries in Africa, Asia, Europe and the Americas. All of these tales feature contests between mismatched contestants (like a fox and a snail, a fox and a crab, a tiger and a frog or a tortoise and a stag); many involve rabbits or hares. The Grimm collection alone, for instance,

THE HARE AND THE TORTOISE

No use to run, except you start betimes.
Let Hare and Tortoise prove it in my rhymes.

'I wager,' said the Slowcoach sturdily,
'You don't make yonder goal so soon as I.'
    'You!' answered Lightfoot in a pet,
'Gossip, you're raving – take four grains
    Of hellebore to clear your brains.'
    'Raving or no, I make the bet.'
'Done.' By the goal their stakes were set
(Though what they were's all one to me,
    Or who was named as referee).
To gain the post, four steps sufficed the Hare

Figure 3.5. This version of "The Hare and the Tortoise" is a take-off on the Aesop's fable. Illustrated by by R. de la Neziere, it appears in *Fables* by Jean de La Fontaine, originally published in 1926.

includes at least two variants of this tale: "The Hare and the Porcupine" and "The Hare and the Hedgehog." Multiple African versions exist (such as "Tortoise and Hare" and "Elephant and Hare"), as do a number of African-American variants, including "Brer Rabbit Finds His Match" or "Mister Rabbit Finds His Match at Last." There's even a Romanian tale in this category: "Why does the Buffalo Walk Slowly and Tread Gently? The Race of the Buffalo and the Hare."

Most versions of this story follow the plot of the Aesop fable, in that the hare, overconfidently underestimating the intelligence of his opponent, naps in the middle of the race, allowing the opponent to win.[39] In other versions, however, the tortoise/hedgehog/porcupine opponent actively tricks the hare, thereby winning the race. In the Grimm tale "The Hare and the Hedgehog," the hedgehog arranges for his wife to appear at the end of the racecourse, crying, "I am here already," thereby tricking the hare into thinking that the hedgehog finished first. The hare is so shocked by this that he demands that the race be run again, and he takes off back toward the beginning of the race, where the hedgehog still lurks. When he arrives, the hedgehog cries out, "I am here already," forcing the hare to run yet again towards the finish, where he is again met by the hedgehog's wife, fooling him a third time.

> So the hare ran seventy-three times more, and the hedgehog always held out against him, and every time the hare reached either the top or the bottom, either the hedgehog or his wife said, I am here already. At the seventy-fourth time, however, the hare could no longer reach the end. In the middle of the field he fell to the ground, blood streamed out of his mouth, and he lay dead on the spot. But the hedgehog took the louis-d'or which he had won and the bottle of brandy, called his wife out of the furrow, and both went home together in great delight, and if they are not dead, they are living there still.[40]

Other folk tales demonstrate the rabbit's arrogance in other ways. In the Grimm tale "The Hare and the Elephant," the arrogant hare zeroes in on size, rather than speed, by asking his friend, a young elephant, who is the bigger of the two. They decide to let the villagers determine the answer. When they reach the village, the people all exclaim at how small the young elephant is and how huge the hare is. When the hare gloats in his victory to the elephant, the elephant replies, "Get out of my way before a tiny elephant crushes a big hare like you!"

In other stories, the rabbit challenges a much stronger animal to a contest of strength, as in the Sioux tale "How Rabbit Lost Its Tail," in which he challenges a giant to a hammer-throwing contest. In the African "Tug of War," the hare challenges the hippopotamus and the elephant, each without the other's knowledge, to a tug of war contest, but sets it up so that the elephant and the hippo are on opposite ends of the rope. When the hare cuts the rope so that both competitors fall over, he claims his winnings. Finally, in many stories the rabbit or the hare is so arrogant that he challenges almost any animal to any kind of contest, such as in the Korean story "The Deer, the Rabbit and the Toad," in which the three animals argue about who is the oldest, with the toad winning the contest.

The Rabbit as Witch

Just as the myths and superstitions of ancient times held that the rabbit was a witch, many folk tales portray the rabbit as somehow affiliated with evil forces. This theme seems to be primarily found in European folk tales, such as the Irish tale "The Coming of Oscar." This story involves a rabbit who transforms into a man via magic, and is only discovered after the rabbit, whose tail was severed during a chase, turns into a man with a suspiciously bleeding backside. This motif (Motif No. D315.5) appears in quite a few other tales. In the German tale "Witch as Hare" (Aarne-Thompson type 3055), a hunter sees a hare in the forest and shoots at it; when his shots fail to kill the hare, the man assumes that the hare is magical, and loads his gun with consecrated powder and shoots again. But instead of killing a hare, the hunter finds a woman, shot dead in the breast. A related tale from England, "Witch and Hare," involves a witch who assumes the shape of a hare in order to trick a local hunter. Eventually, the witch is caught (bleeding and covered with wounds from an almost-successful hunt) and burned at the stake. Other European tales also echo this theme of hares transforming into humans (usually women) and ending up wounded—or dead—as punishment for their crimes. In "The Girl Who Transformed Herself into a Hare," for instance, a young witch is shot in the foot while in her guise as a hare. When she turns back into a woman, she endures a lame foot for the rest of her life.

The belief that witches could transform themselves into hares is also found in historical texts from the period. In *Daemonolgia: A Discourse on Witchcraft*, the seventeenth-century poet and translator Edward Fairfax discussed the appearance of just such a creature:

> On Thursday, the 4th of April 1621, my eldest son, William Fairfax, being in the field called Birkbanks aforesaid, started a hare out of bush and set a dog at her. Mr. Smithson, vicar of Fuystone, saw her also, and in like sort caused his dog to run at her; but they quickly lost the sight of her. That day, soon after, the child was in trance, and the strange woman did appear to her and told her that she was the hare which her brother and the vicar set their dogs at; and that she came over the water with her brother, William, and that he should see her again the next time he went to that place; which proved true. Also she affirmed that when she was in likeness of a hare, or of any such thing, she was then senseless.[41]

Fairfax's daughter then became bewitched, leading Fairfax to accuse the woman (and five others) of witchcraft. Ultimately, they were acquitted.

A similar account was recorded by a contemporary of Fairfax's, Sir William Scott, in his *Letters on Demonology and Witchcraft*:

> In the year 1663 an old dame, named Julian Coxe, was convicted chiefly on the evidence of a huntsman, who declared on his oath, that he laid his greyhounds on a hare, and coming up to the spot where he saw them mouth her, there he found, on the other side of a bush, Julian Coxe lying panting and breathless, in such a manner as to convince him that she had been the creature which afforded him the course. The unhappy woman was executed on this evidence.[42]

A number of Scandinavian tales focus on the "milk-hare," a spirit that witches use to steal their neighbors' milk from their cows.

Milk-hares were known throughout Sweden, Norway and Iceland, and the tradition dates back to at least the fifteenth century.[43] Tales involving the milk-hare are a variant of the English and Scottish tale "The Daughter of the Witch" (Aarne-Thompson type ML3035), about a girl who innocently displays her supernatural abilities by magically milking a neighbor's cow (motif D2083.1). In the Irish tale "The Old Hare," for example, an old woman rumored to be a witch lives in a cabin by herself. Nearly every week some of her neighbors' milk is gone. When a suspicious neighbor sees a hare come out of the old woman's cabin, he shoots the hare, hitting it in the shoulder. Upon entering the woman's cabin the next morning, the neighbor finds the old woman, her bloody shoulder wrapped in calico.[44]

The perceived association between witches and rabbits (or hares) may have had to do with the reputation both shared for being evil and lustful. Some of the association, too, may have been rooted in the very real context of rural people in medieval and Renaissance Europe, where women were the primary caretakers of rabbits and so were frequently seen tending, talking to and handling the animals. Still, the sheer number of stories and images in which women become rabbits, rabbits become women or creatures are half-rabbit, half-woman, is striking. As we've seen, the goddesses Ostara and Eostre were both frequently depicted as hares, and the Saxon goddess of the moon, in one illustration at least, appears in hare head gear. One Aztec sculpture from the fifteenth century also shows what appears to be a rabbit giving birth to a warrior's head, which is itself in an eagle helmet.

This close link between women, witchery, sexuality and rabbits would reach its nadir, of course, in the twentieth-century Playboy Bunny, but it manifested in a particularly bizarre manner even in the eighteenth century, when a woman was reported to have given birth to rabbit babies. Surgeon John Howard was called to the house of Mary Toft, of Godalming, England in 1726. Once there, he helped her give birth to nine dead rabbits and called in other prominent doctors to help investigate the mystery. Once they arrived, Toft gave birth to eight more dead rabbits and also claimed she had craved rabbit meat throughout her pregnancy, so much so that she had gone out to try to catch rabbits herself and even had dreams about rabbits in her lap.

The doctors, though amazed, decided to do some tests. They took a piece of one rabbit lung and put it in water; when it floated, they realized the rabbit must have inhaled air at some point, which meant it had not come from Toft's womb. The lack of placenta and umbilical cords was also suspicious. Despite the evidence, however, Dr. Nathanael St. Andre, a surgeon to King George I, decided the births had been real and actually published his findings. He was proven mistaken when several men admitted they had supplied Toft's husband with the rabbits. Toft soon confessed that she had put the dead rabbits in her womb. She was temporarily imprisoned, and the careers of John Howard and St. Andre were permanently ruined.[45]

Trickster Tales

Another common folktale theme is that of the trickster rabbit. In African, African-American, Native American and some Asian tales, the rabbit uses both cleverness and deceit to get out of scrapes. As in the tales discussed above, it is often the rabbit's arrogance or foolishness (or cowardice) that gets him into such predicaments in the first place. In the Korean tale "The Tiger and the Rabbit," the rabbit escapes a hungry tiger by repeatedly tricking him into thinking that there is something much better to eat than a rabbit—like burning hot rocks and twigs. Eventually, the rabbit convinces the tiger that he can catch tasty fish with his tail; the tiger ends up with his tail caught in a frozen river, while the rabbit goes free.

These trickster tales are derived from the satirical Northern European epic known as the *Roman de Renart*,[46] in which a stupid bear or wolf is duped by a clever fox. The fox is almost always the clever animal in European tales, but as these stories migrated from Europe to Africa (via traders and colonialists) and then to North America (often via slaves on slave ships), the clever fox gave way to other, indigenous species. Trickster animals are found among all Native American tribes, and include the spider, coyote and raven.

Tribes in the Plains and Great Lakes regions used the hare as their trickster animal; the Algonquin tribes' Great Hare Manabozho was a trickster rabbit. Africans in the Sudan and savannah country also see the hare as one of the most cunning animals, although the spider is the equivalent of the hare in the forest regions of Africa, probably because spiders are more common in forests than hares.

Trickster traits are both positive (e.g., brave and smart) and negative (e.g., greedy, mischievous and cruel). But in most trickster stories, the rabbit's wit and ability to squeeze out of dangerous situations derive from his prey status—his awareness that he could be killed. In the Hausa "King of Beasts" story from Nigeria, for example, the rabbit is supposed to be eaten by the lion. Instead, the rabbit tells him that he brought a pot of honey as a gift, but that another lion took it. When the lion demands who has taken it, the hare points to a well and says the thief is the lion in the well. The lion looks in the well, sees his reflection, becomes angry, curses the lion and eventually jumps in and drowns, leaving the hare to become King of the Beasts. In a version from Zambia, the hare becomes the King of the Beasts by tricking the lion into burning himself up.

In the Mexican story "The Smiling Rabbit," the rabbit tricks a very mighty predator: the jaguar. In this story, an old man and his wife own a rabbit and a jaguar. Because they are so poor, they decide to eat the rabbit and start heating a pot of water to cook him. The rabbit, realizing his fate, tells the jaguar that the couple is heating water to make hot chocolate, and that he should get into his cage so he can get the first cup. After locking the jaguar into the cage, the rabbit escapes, only to be later caught by the jaguar in a cave. To save himself, the rabbit tricks the jaguar into staying in the cave, holding up a wall that he says is falling down (reminiscent of "the end of the world" stories), while he escapes. Ultimately, the jaguar does catch the rabbit, and causes him to be shot into the air; the hare ultimately lands on the moon. The story ends as a just so tale, by telling us that this is why "on nights when the moon is full and red you can still see the rabbit bending over holding his stomach with laughter."[47]

Many trickster tales derive not from the rabbit's position as prey, but from his foolish tendency to get himself into sticky situations. In the myths of the Bushmen of South Africa, the rabbit was once a man who was turned into a rabbit through his stupidity (Aarne-Thompson motif D315.5). In versions of the tale "The Monkey's Heart" (Aarne-Thompson type 91), the rabbit must use his wits to get out of a situation in which another animal wants to eat one of his organs. For instance, the Korean tale "The Rabbit and the Turtle" involves a turtle tricking a rabbit into going down into the ocean with him so that his liver can be used to cure the queen of the fishes of an illness. Once the rabbit is in the sea and aware of his predicament, he assures his captors that he wants to help the queen by donating his liver, but that he left it on dry land, because he thought livers could not get wet. The turtle sends the rabbit back to get his liver, but of course the rabbit runs away.

In some tales, the rabbit acts as trickster for selfish reasons, such as wanting a girlfriend, or just wanting to dupe the stupid fox or wolf. In the Creek tale "How Rabbit Fooled Wolf" ("Rabbit Rides Fox A-Courting," Aarne-Thompson type 72), the rabbit fools the wolf into letting him ride him like a horse so that two pretty girls will think the wolf is just an old horse and will like Rabbit better. When wolf tries to get revenge, Rabbit keeps tricking him, such as by tying the wolf's tail to what looks like the tail of a dead pony ("Catching a Horse by its Tail," Aarne-Thomson type 47A). As it turns out the pony, who is very much alive, wakes up and drags the wolf away. In "The Rabbit and the Coyote," a Mayan tale, the rabbit deceives the coyote by telling him that the sky is falling, and that the coyote must lean against a big rock to hold up the sky. Later the rabbit tells the coyote that there is cheese at the bottom of the pond, and that if he drinks all the water, he will be able to get at the cheese. The coyote does so and ends up with a terrible stomach ache and a bad case of diarrhea.

Brer Rabbit

One of the most popular of all trickster rabbits is Brer Rabbit or Brother Rabbit. Joel Chandler Harris, a Georgian newspaperman, collected, probably expanded and published four volumes about the very tricky, very arrogant Brer Rabbit in the late 1800s and early 1900s. Told in the heavy dialect of Uncle Remus, a fictional, elderly plantation slave who is speaking to a young white boy, the stories center on Brer Rabbit, who was "born so little, so no matter whereabouts you put him he could cut capers and play pranks. What he couldn't do with his feet he could do with his head, and when his head got him in trouble, he put his dependence back on his feet, because that's where he kept his lippity-clip and his blickety-blick."[48] Harris's books not only popularized the stories of Brer Rabbit that he had heard as a child, but introduced white Americans to African-American speech patterns (what he called their "quaint dialect") and narrative styles.[49]

The Brer Rabbit books include *Uncle Remus: His Songs and His Stories* (1881), *Nights with Uncle Remus* (1883), *Uncle Remus and His Friends* (1892), and *Uncle Remus and the Little Boy* (1905). These stories draw on many of the themes found in earlier folk tales. Typical Brer Rabbit tales, narrated by Uncle Remus, involve Brer's cowardice, cleverness and ability to get himself into—and then out of—an extraordinary number of jams. For instance, in "Brother Rabbit Takes a Walk," from *Nights with Uncle Remus*, Brer Rabbit is afraid of the sharp teeth of Mr. Dog and suggests to the other animals that the dog have his mouth sewn shut. The other animals agree and suggest that the one who wants the sewing done do it himself, which is when Brer Rabbit decides that this is the exact time of day when he has to take a walk. In "Brother Rabbit's Riddle," from *Nights with Uncle Remus*, Brer Rabbit is about to be eaten by Brer Fox, but instead tricks him into sticking his head in a beehive. Not only was Brer Fox stung by bees, but he was caught by Brer Bear, who assumed that Brer Fox was robbing his beehive! In "Mr. Hawk and Brother Rabbit," from *Nights with Uncle Remus* (Aarne-Thompson type 122F; "Eat Me When I'm Fatter"), Brer Rabbit finds himself in the tight claws of Mr. Hawk. Brer Rabbit tries a number of ways to get Mr. Hawk to release him, telling him that he is too wild-tasting for him, and that he should wait till he gets tame—or that if he catches a couple of jay-birds to eat, Brer Rabbit will wait for him!

> Brer Rabbit, he said, "Well then, if that won't do, you had better wait and let me grow big, so I'll be a full meal of vittles."
>
> Mr. Hawk, he said, "Now you are talking sense!"
>
> Brer Rabbit, he said, "And I'll rush around among the bushes and drive out some partridges for you, and we'll have more fun than what you can shake a stick at."
>
> Mr. Hawk was sort of studying about this, and Brer Rabbit, he begged, and he explained, and the long and short of it was that Brer Rabbit got loose, and he did not get any bigger, and neither did he drive out any partridges for Mr. Hawk.[50]

Brer Rabbit is forever afraid that another animal—like Brer Wolf or Brer Fox—will catch him, or a member of his family, and eat them. (In the context of the tales, this has actually happened, yet Brer Rabbit and these predators often go fishing together, smoke pipes together and take walks together, which greatly expands the humor—and suspense—of these stories.) For instance, in "The Moon in the Millpond," Brer Rabbit convinces Brer Fox, Brer Wolf and Brer Bear to go fishing and have a "wang-dang-doodle all night long." The other animals take the bait. After a short time, Brer Rabbit shows them the moon's reflection in the water and convinces them that "Mr. Moon" has actually fallen in the water—and that if they don't get him out, "there won't be any fish caught tonight." Brer Terrapin joins in the act by saying that he's heard that anyone who gets the moon out of the water will get a big pot of money. The three predator animals, of course, insist on actually trying to net the moon and end up falling in the lake.

Brer Rabbit is in no mortal danger in this story—he just wants to have some fun. After his friends fall in the lake, "he went home and capered around in the grass one half of the night, and played

Figure 3.6. "Mr. Fox Is Again Victimized." In Joel Chandler Harris's Uncle Remus stories, the crafty rabbit outwits his predators again and again. Illustration by Arthur Burdette Frost from The Complete Tales of Uncle Remus by Joel Chandler Harris, compiled by Richard Chase (Boston: Houghton Mifflin, 2002).

with the lightning bugs the other half."[51] That trickster glee comes up in other stories, as well. In "Brer Rabbit Grossly Deceives Brer Fox," the hero tricks the fox into letting him ride him like a horse. At the end of the story, the two fight, and as Fox gets back up on his feet, "Brer Rabbit was running lickety-clickety, clickety-lickety off through the underbrush like a racehorse. He ran and ran, and after he'd been runnin' a mighty long time, he jumped up and cracked his heels together, and laughed fit to kill himself."[52] With such language, Harris captures the so-called "binky" with grace and humor, as well as the delight that the oppressed take in fooling their oppressors.

Many earlier trickster plot lines also appear in the Uncle Remus stories. In "Brother Fox Catches Mr. Horse," Brer Rabbit ties Brer Fox onto the tail of a sleeping horse, which results in Brer Fox getting kicked and harks back to "Catching a Horse By Its Tail." "Brother Rabbit Takes Some Exercise," from *Nights with Uncle Remus,* is an end-of-the-world story, as well as a trickster story. Uncle Remus tells how Brother Rabbit hears the sound of a man cutting down a tree ("kubber-lang-bang-blam!") and runs through the forest telling Brer Coon, "Mighty big fuss back there in the woods. Haven't got time to tarry!" Brer Coon becomes alarmed and takes off, encountering Brer Fox, and telling him, "Mighty big fuss back there in the woods. Haven't got time to tarry!" Brer Fox then takes off, meeting Brer Wolf, telling him exactly the same thing, and on and on through Brer Bear and all the other animals in the forest until the story reaches Brer Terrapin, who recommends that the other animals go back and confront Brer Rabbit himself. What makes "Brother Rabbit Takes Some Exercise" different from many other end of the world stories is that, according to Uncle Remus, Brer Rabbit was not himself scared. In fact, the whole episode is an exercise in making the other animals look like fools, and he is so good at it that Uncle Remus ends the story by simply saying, "Brer Rabbit was a mighty man in those days."[53]

There's even a story that echoes the Korean tale "The Rabbit and the Turtle" and other "monkey's heart" stories. In Harris's "Brother Rabbit and the Gizzard-Eater," Brother Rabbit finds himself trapped on Brer Alligator's back in the middle of a creek, because Brer Alligator thinks he has to eat a rabbit gizzard in order to cure himself of a disorder (that Brother Rabbit himself caused in an earlier story). Thinking quickly, Brer Rabbit responds that he's not only happy to help Brer Alligator, but that he is himself plagued with "double gizzard," and that he's been looking for a gizzard-eater to help him with his problem. Like the rabbit in "The Rabbit and the Turtle," Brer Rabbit then explains that, according to his doctor, gizzards cannot get wet, and that he left his double-gizzard in a hickory hollow. When Brer Alligator approaches the spot where Brer Rabbit says he hid his gizzard, Brer Rabbit jumps off his back, saying: "You poor old Gator, if you'd have known A from Izzard, you'd know mighty well that I'd keep my Gizzard."[54]

The Uncle Remus stories are clear proof that folk tales, like rabbits, crops and designer jeans, migrate from culture to culture via humans. This is most clearly evident in the so-called "tar baby" stories (Aarne-Thompson type 175), once again popularized by Joel Chandler Harris in "The Wonderful Tar-Baby Story," from *Uncle Remus: His Songs and His Stories*. Researchers think the tar baby story traveled via two routes from India to America: one by way of Africa, and the other via the Iberian Peninsula to America on another path.[55] In the course of this migration, the exact plot of the tale changed, but the essential elements remain the same: it is discovered that a mischievous rabbit has been stealing water (in the African versions) or food from a garden (in the American tales). In order to trap the rabbit in the act, the animals (or sometimes the farmer) who suspect the rabbit construct a "tar baby" out of pitch, rubber, tar or some other sticky substance. The rabbit tries to speak to the tar baby, and when it doesn't respond, he becomes frustrated, hitting it with his paws and getting caught on the sticky tar baby in the process. The animals finally confront the rabbit and debate amongst themselves the best way to punish him. The rabbit uses reverse psychology, begging his captors not to throw him into the briar patch. Convinced that he is truly terrified, the animals throw the rabbit into the briars, where, as a creature very familiar with and comfortable in such patches, he happily escapes (Aarne-Thompson type 1310).[56]

In Africa, the tar baby stories are known as "Rubber Girl." In these tales, oddly, the hare does not escape, and instead is beaten by the farmer (or other animals) and banished forever. The African tales take great delight in the hare getting the better of the authorities, but when he deceives his fellow animals (such as by stealing from them), he is punished.[57] In the Yoruba version of "Rubber Girl," during a time of drought, all of the animals cut the tips of their ears off to buy hoes to dig a well, except the hare, who simply steals their water. After being trapped with a rubber girl (made with bird feces), he is beaten and driven away to the grasslands where he has lived ever since, with the longest ears in the animal kingdom. In the Angolan version, after the hare is caught (on a wooden girl smeared with gum from a wild fig tree) and beaten, he is forced to sleep in a hole to keep away from his pursuers. Both of these stories are just so stories as well, since they explain the origin of the rabbit's long ears, and his penchant for sleeping underground. In the South African version, "The Dance for Water," the animals, again during a time of drought, agree to dance for water. The rabbit refuses to dance and again steals the water. To catch the rabbit, the tortoise creates a tar baby by smearing his own shell with bird feces. In this tale, however, once the rabbit is caught, it is agreed that he should be held by the tail and smashed into a rock. But when the lion swings him around to kill him, "The white skin slipped off from Rabbit, and there Lion stood with the white bit of skin and hair in his paw. Rabbit was free."[58]

An African-American version of the tale, probably borrowed from the Brer Rabbit tale, involves Rabbit and Fox. Rabbit drinks Fox's milk out of the spring, and in response, Fox throws Rabbit into the briar patch, where Rabbit exclaims, "Ah, this is just where I want to be, here where I was born and bred anyway."[59] The Brer Rabbit tar baby story, "The Wonderful Tar-Baby Story," has a completely different opening. Brother Fox creates the tar baby to catch Brer Rabbit, not because the rabbit stole from him, but simply to get him back for all the pain that he has caused him over the years. Brer Rabbit does not exactly escape at the end of this tale; Uncle Remus leaves the ending open to the listener's imagination. When the little boy asks if the Fox actually ate the rabbit, Uncle Remus replies: "Dat's all de fur de tale goes," replied the old man. "He mout, an den agin he moutent. Some say Judge B'ar come 'long en loosed 'im—some say he didn't. I hear Miss Sally callin'. You better run 'long."

◆   ◆   ◆

In all of the above tales, with the exception of those involving evil, the rabbit (or hare) is depicted in a manner that relates, to some extent, to the characteristics of real-life rabbits. Although anyone who has been bitten by a rabbit knows that they have sharp teeth, lagomorphs truly are prey animals and so can be timid, even alarmist. In order to survive, they must be swift. They can get them-selves in foolish, albeit comical, situations—jumping into buckets, for instance, or getting stuck behind refrigerators—but they also can exhibit great cleverness and naughtiness. And most of us have seen rabbits arrogantly take on creatures far larger than themselves, including humans, dogs and large birds.

That people around the world, in cultures as diverse as ancient Greece, sub-Saharan Africa, dynastic China and Native America have come up with stories and images about the rabbit that are so strikingly similar is remarkable in terms of what it says about the continuity between human cultures. It also demonstrates the strength of the rabbit as symbol. But why are rabbits mostly seen as timid prey in European (many of them Asian-derived) tales, and bold heroes in African, African-American and Native-American tales? Trickster rabbits, such as those immortalized in the folk traditions of the latter group, can probably trace their popularity to the fact that they represent, and appeal to, the ordinary man who is oppressed by more powerful beings, but often wins by his cleverness. African lis-teners loved to hear about how the clever rabbit escaped from his captors over and over[60]; African-Americans during the slave era clearly identified with Brer Rabbit's ability to get along in a white plantation culture through cleverness.[61] The Mayan trickster tales featuring the rabbit are said to be thinly disguised post-Conquest fables about dealing with the Spanish rulers.[62] Even Joel Chandler Harris, in his introduction to *Uncle Remus: His Songs and His Stories,* noted that the Rabbit is a "a fable thoroughly characteristic of the Negro; and it needs no scientific investigation to show why he selects as his hero the weakest and most harmless of all animals, and brings him out victorious in contests with the bear, the wolf and the fox. It is not virtue that triumphs, but helplessness; it is not malice, but mischievousness."[63]

This implies that Europeans (and perhaps Asians as well, since most of these tales originally came to Europe through Asia) identi-fy more with the more powerful fox, and are content to have the smaller, weaker animals remain as prey (or as magical familiars).

Whether or not we can make such a broad generalization, it is interesting to think that the folklore of a colonizing people might reflect this tendency to favor those seen as "superior," while the stories of those who were colonized might not romanticize or take pleasure in stories in which the docile, timid rabbit is vanquished by the powerful and threatening carnivore. Instead, the colonized people develop tales in which cunning, deceit and even humor can subvert power imbalances.

As we'll see in the next chapter, the representation of rabbits in contemporary culture, while echoing some of the themes found in older cultures, embodies a whole new set of paradoxes. While the rabbit (or hare) in ancient societies was both revered and feared for its sexuality, fertility, speed and cunning, the real rabbit was treated primarily as just game and pest. Today the rabbit plays a much more complex role in society: wild rabbits remain both game and pest, but domestic rabbits are also a raised as meat animals, fur producers, scientific tools and cherished pets. These varied uses make the rabbit's modern symbolic associations—whether in film, literature or collectibles—that much richer, and, at times, that much more disturbing.

Notes

1. In this chapter and the next, both rabbits and hares will be covered under the term "rabbit," although the rabbit was actually not known in many cultures in which the hare was known. For example, rabbits were unknown in classical lands before the time of Christ and were not introduced into Great Britain until the thirteenth century. Yet, once introduced, the rabbit came to take on much of the hare's symbolism. From Rowland, Beryl, *Animals with Human Faces: A Guide to Animal Symbolism* (Knoxville, TN: University of Tennessee Press, 1973), p. 92.
2. Rowland *op. cit.*, p. 90.
3. *Ibid.*
4. Aronson, Stanley, "The good and bad about bunnies," *Medicine and Health/Rhode Island*, the monthly publication of The Rhode Island Medical Society. Reprinted in *Providence Journal*, 2001.
5. Purchase, Barbara, *Rabbit Tales* (New York: Van Nostrand Reinhold, 1982), p. 112.
6. *Ibid.*, p. 108.
7. Cooper, J. C., *An Illustrated Encyclopaedia of Traditional Symbols* (London: Thames and Hudson, 1978), p. 79.
8. Rowland, *op. cit.*, p. 91.
9. Purchase, *op. cit.*, p. 106.
10. *Ibid.*, p. 110.

11. Parker, Derek and Julia, *The Compleat Astrologer* (New York: McGraw Hill Book Co, 1971).
12. Rowland, *op. cit.*, p. 89.
13. *Ibid.*, p. 64.
14. *Ibid.*, p. 21.
15. Cooper, *op. cit.*, p. 79.
16 Beal, Chandra, "The Magical Hare in the Moon," in *Llewellyn's 2000 Moon Sign Book* (St. Paul, MN: Lewellyn, 2000) and "Most Humble Hare," a birth story of Buddha, reprinted in *Rabbit Tales*, Purchase, pp. 42–44.
17. Ezpeleta *op. cit.*, p. 21.
18. Wicke, Charles R., "The Mesoamerican Rabbit in the Moon: An Influence from Han China?" *Archaeoastronomy*, Vol. 7, No. 46 (1984).
19. Rowland, *op. cit.*, p. 90.
20. Cooper, *op. cit.*, p. 80.
21. Rowland, *op. cit.*, p. 89.
22. Cooper, *op. cit.*, p. 80.
    Purchase, *op. cit.*, p. 188.
23. The Easter Bunny Page, http://www.holidays.net/easter/bunny1.htm.
24. Cooper, *op. cit.*, p. 60.
25. Catholic Encyclopedia, http://www.newadvent.org/cathen/05224d.htm.
26. Rowland even goes further, writing that the Queen Elizabeth, the Virgin Queen, was often called a hare by her enemies. Rowland, *op. cit.*, p. 91.
27. *Ibid.*, pp. 133–134.
28. *Ibid.*, p. 92.
29. Onions, C.T. (ed.), *The Oxford Dictionary of English Etymology* (Oxford: Oxford University Press, 1966), p. 235.
30. Rawson, Hugh, *Wicked Words: a Treasury of Curses, Insults, Put Downs, and Other Formerly Unprintable Terms from Anglo-Saxon Times to the Present* (New York: Crown Publishers, 1989), p. 94.
31. *Ibid.*
32. *Ibid.*, pp. 106–112.
33. Native American Lore Index Page, http://www.ilhawaii.net/~stony/loreindx.html.
34. *Ibid.*
35. *Ibid.*
36. Anti Aarne and Stith Thompson were folklorists who classified thousands of folk tales according to type and motif. We use their classification scheme in this chapter.
37. Cowell, E.B. (ed.), *The Jataka; or, Stories of the Buddha's Former Births* (Cambridge: Cambridge University Press, 1897), Vol. 3, No. 322.
38. Jacobs, Joseph, *The Fables of Aesop* (New York: Schocken Books, 1894), No. 68.
39. But in humorist James Thurber's version of "The Tortoise and the Hare," the tortoise, having read all the stories in which the tortoise bested the hare in a race, challenged the first hare he encountered to a race. They marked off a course 50 feet long, and when the hare crossed the finish line, the tortoise had barely gone eight inches. The moral of the story: "A new broom may sweep clean, but never trust an old saw." Reprinted from Purchase, *op. cit.*, p. 46.
40. *The Complete Grimm's Fairy Tales* (New York: Pantheon Books, 1944), pp. 760–764.
41. Quoted in Purchase, *op. cit.*, p. 120.
42. Scott, Sir Walter, "Letters on Demonology and Witchcraft," http://www.sacred-texts.com/pag/scott/lodw08.htm.
43. Lindow, John, *Swedish Folk Tales and Legends* (Berkeley, CA: University of California Press, 1978), pp. 171–172.
44. The term "milk-hare" is also connected to the moon in other traditions. For instance, many tribes of the northern and eastern United States gave names to each full moon. May full moon names include "flower," "milk" and "hare." The Old Farmer's Almanac, http://www.almanac.com/details/moondays.html.

45. Pickover, Clifford A., *The Girl Who Gave Birth to Rabbits: A True Medical Mystery* (New York: Prometheus Books, 2000).
46. Thompson, Stith, *The Folk Tale* (New York: The Dryden Press, 1951).
47. Mexican Myths Web page, http://www.elbalero.gob.mx/kids/about/html/myths.
48. Harris, Joel Chandler, "The Comeuppance of Brer Wolf," in Harris, *Jump!* Adapted by Parks, Van Dyke (New York: Harcourt Brace Jovanovich Publishers, 1986), p. 3.
49. The quotes from Chandler's books printed here have been updated to modern English.
50. Harris, Joel Chandler, *Nights with Uncle Remus* (Boston: James R. Osgood and Company, 1883), No. 65.
51. Harris, *Jump!*, pp. 36–38.
52. *Ibid.*, p. 32.
53. Harris, *Nights with Uncle Remus*, No. 20.
54. Harris, Joel Chandler, *The Complete Tales of Uncle Remus*, compiled by Richard Chase (Boston: Houghton Mifflin Company, 1955), pp. 701–708.
55. Thompson, *op. cit.*, 1951.
56. This tale is often told of the turtle or crayfish who begs his captors to not throw him into the water where he will drown, when of course turtles and crayfish live under the water.
57. Parrinder, Geoffrey, *African Mythology* (Middlesex: The Hamlyn Publishing Group, 1967), p. 130.
58. Honey, James A., *South African Folk Tales* (New York: AMS Press, 1978).
59. Afro-American Almanac Folk Tales, http://www.toptags.com/aama/tales/tales.htm.
60. Parrinder, *op. cit.*, p. 130.
61. Reesman, Jeanne Campbell (ed.), *Trickster Lives, Culture and Myth in American Fiction* (Atlanta: University of Georgia Press, 2001).
    Olorounto, Samuel B. "Studying African-American Literature in Its Global Context," *VCCA Journal*, Volume 7, Number 1, Summer 1992, pp. 4–12.
62. Giese, Paula, Maya Rabbit Stories, http://www.kstrom.net/isk/maya/rabbit.html.
63. Harris, Joel Chandler. Original Introduction to *Uncle Remus: His Songs and His Sayings,*" in *The Complete Tales of Uncle Remus*, pp. xxv.

4. "TRIX ARE FOR KIDS!"

The Rabbit as Contemporary Icon

———•••———

"She gave me a bright blue satin. It was so tight that the zipper caught my skin as she fastened the hook. . . . The bottom was cut up so high that it left my hip bones exposed as well as a good five inches of untanned derriere. . . . A blue satin band with matching Bunny ears attached was fitted around my head like an enlarged bicycle clip, and a grapefruit-sized hemisphere of white fluff was attached to hooks at the costume's rear-most point. . . . I looked in the mirror. The Bunny image looked back.

'Oh you look *sweet*,' Sheralee said. "Stand against the wall and smile pretty for the birdie."

Gloria Steinem, from "I Was A Playboy Bunny"[1]

IN A FAIRY-TALE neighborhood of Mediterranean cottages and leafy trees, nestled at the base of the San Gabriel Mountains, sits a pretty white stucco house, with a red tile roof, red flowers, green shrubs—and a twenty-foot tall "Roller Bunny" clutching an American flag.

Created for the 1998 Rose Bowl Parade, Roller Bunny, who has a pudgy body, a big round tail, and, yes, roller blades, was once a magnificent fellow. His white fur was made of pampas grass; his ears, eyes and nose were carnation petals; his pants and jacket were made of straw flower and his skates were covered with parsley. Four

Figure 4.1. "Roller Bunny." This giant rabbit was crafted by the Downey Rose Float Association for the 1998 Rose Parade. Courtesy the Bunny Museum.

years later, Roller Bunny's sheer size—especially on a suburban lawn—is still impressive. But his carefully cultivated features have all fallen (or been eaten) off and he's only half covered with creeping vines. As a result, he looks less like a happy-go-lucky rabbit than like a leering Disney-esque lagomorph rising from a bewitched bog.

Roller Bunny sits in front of the house of Candace Frazee and Steve Lubanski, both of whom have been collecting rabbit *stuff* since 1992, so much rabbit stuff, in fact, that they've turned their small home into the world's only Bunny Museum and now boast a 14,500-piece collection. There are bunny teacups, cookie jars, salt and pepper shakers and commemorative plates. There are bunny clocks, planters, wind chimes and hobby horses—or rather, hobby rabbits.

There are ceramic rabbits, clay rabbits, metal rabbits and even rabbits made of the feces of zoo animals and cows (that's "zoo doo" and "poo doo," according to Frazee). There are four other Rose Bowl Parade bunnies, in various stages of decay, plus a giant Tiki rabbit in the garage. There are bunnies dressed for Easter, bunnies dressed for Christmas and bunnies dressed for St. Patrick's Day, Halloween and even the Fourth of July. There's a whole bunch of representations of very famous rabbits, like the White Rabbit and March Hare from *Alice's Adventures in Wonderland*, Bugs Bunny, the NesQuik Bunny, Brer Rabbit, Roger Rabbit, the Trix Rabbit and Thumper (from *Bambi*). There are famous rabbit books (like those of Beatrix Potter and Howard Garis) and famous rabbit cartoons (like Bugs Bunny and Crusader Rabbit). There's even a small garden in which the broken rabbit figurines that Frazee and Lubanski couldn't bear to throw away are laid to rest.

It's hard to imagine that much rabbit paraphernalia all crammed into one place. But what's odd about walking into the Bunny Museum is not so much the sheer number of rabbit images that exist as how familiar most of those images are. Rabbit—or, more accurately, bunny—imagery has supersaturated this culture to the point where we hardly notice it anymore. That is, on close inspection, the bunny image is so visible it has nearly become *in*visible. As such, most people don't notice that many of these rabbit images are quite distorted, sometimes even disturbingly so. Most people also don't realize that the rabbit images they consume on a daily basis deeply inform their understanding—flawed as it is—of the rabbit itself. Whether it's a cherubic Hummel figure, a model in a gold lamé bunny suit or a monster rabbit rampaging the countryside, the contemporary images of rabbits this culture produces tell us much about the very ambivalent attitudes we still hold towards this mysterious creature.

Literary and Celluloid Bunnies
When we first started talking about this book we knew that some important rabbit characters inhabited the world of books and movies. Cultural icons, like Peter Rabbit, the Velveteen Rabbit and

Figure 4.2. Bunny magnets. Items for women and children are frequently decorated with or produced in the shape of juvenile rabbits. Courtesy The Bunny Museum. Photo by Margo DeMello.

the unnamed little rabbit in *Goodnight Moon* certainly sprang to mind, as did Thumper, Harvey and the inimitable Bugs Bunny. But when we took a closer look, the amount of material (famous and not so famous) that featured rabbits took us by surprise. In addition to beloved classic children's stories, rabbits inhabit hundreds, if not thousands, of other stories, videos and Web sites, from board books on counting and color to the "wild" rabbits that hop on the grass in Teletubbies and "Boinger the Cheerful Doll," a Christian, web-based character created to teach children about the Bible. Some of these rabbits are portrayed in ways that clearly draw on folklore and myths from earlier eras. Still others reveal the unique position that rabbits occupy in contemporary society.

Rabbits for Children, Rabbits as Children

Rabbits are among the most common animals in children's media. Sometimes the rabbits appear simply because they contribute something specific to the text, something that, say, a dog or a cat could

Figure 4.3. "When suddenly a White Rabbit with pink eyes ran close by her." The White Rabbit in Lewis Carroll's 1865 fantasy, *Alice's Adventures in Wonderland*, has the characteristics of both real and mythical rabbits.

not. The ever-late, always hurrying White Rabbit from Lewis Carroll's *Alice's Adventures in Wonderland* ("Oh dear! Oh dear! I shall be late!") was probably chosen because of the rabbit's well-known speed, timidity and prey status (as expressed in his fear of the Queen). The rabbit's tendency to scurry into holes at any sign of danger also works well in the book: the White Rabbit is the only character, besides Alice, who readily moves between the real world and the fantasy world, just as rabbits in ancient myths often mediated between the sacred and the profane, the netherworld and the human world, the heavenly realms and the earthly ones.

More often, rabbits in children's stories appear as substitutes for human children. In the very simplest depictions, the rabbits just look and act like children. The character of Thumper, who became the sidekick of the young fawn prince in Disney's 1942 classic *Bambi*, for instance, is almost a caricature of a bunny: he has huge ears, giant feet that drum at a comically spastic rate, a twitchy nose, buck teeth, a round tummy and an impossibly large cottontail. But he also has the big yawn and stuffed-up voice of a human child. Thumper is often brash and somewhat abashed—especially after his mother chastises him—but he's a fun-loving chap who introduces Bambi to flora, fauna and frolicking in the forest.

Rosemary Wells's bunny Max is likewise meant to evoke a simple character, in this case a toddler who is rather chubby, clothed, bestowed with big dopey-eyes, wears everything he eats and heartily resists his older sister's attempts to be in charge. This series is enormously popular with the younger set, and Wells has produced a number of other books featuring pudgy bunny characters, including the Bunny Planet trilogy, *Bunny Money, Bunny Cakes, Bunny Party, Emily's First Day of School* and *Shy Charles*.

More sophisticated children's literature uses rabbits to explore common emotional themes in childhood. Part of the astounding popularity of *The Tale of Peter Rabbit* stems from the fact that Potter so personified the little rabbit as to make him almost indistinguishable from a little boy. Peter is dressed in little people clothes, he still lives with his widowed mother and he constantly gets himself into trouble. The whole story, in fact, revolves around the consequences of his ignoring his mother's command to avoid Mr. McGregor's garden ("Your father had an accident there," she warns; "He was put in a pie by Mrs. McGregor"). Unlike his siblings, "who were good little bunnies," Peter, who is "very naughty," squeezes under the gate to Mr. McGregor's garden, eating his lettuce, beans, radishes and parsley until he is discovered. After rushing all over the garden, encountering a mouse and a cat and losing his jacket and both of his shoes among the vegetables, Peter finally manages to squeeze back under the gate to make it home safely—although he and the reader learn that naughty little bunnies are punished both by getting stomach aches and being put to bed early with chamomile tea (instead of the blackberries and bread his well-behaved siblings enjoyed).

In *The Tale of Benjamin Bunny*, published in 1904, Benjamin Bunny is likewise a rebellious boy who "did not very much want to

Figure 4.4. "Whatever is the matter, Cousin Benjamin?" Peter Rabbit and Benjamin Bunny, both modeled on Potter's own rabbits, appear in a number of Beatrix Potter stories. Illustration from *The Tale of Mr. Tod* by Beatrix Potter. © Frederick Warne & Co., 1912, 2002, reproduced by permission of Frederick Warne & Co.

see his Aunt," Mrs. Rabbit, and so goes around the back of her home to find his cousin, Peter Rabbit. Together, they decide to go get Peter's little coat and shoes, which still adorn a scarecrow in Farmer McGregor's garden. Once there, the two bunny boys charmingly fill a pocket handkerchief with onions (for Mrs. Rabbit), but then run smack into a cat. They hide under a basket and the cat sits on top "for *five hours*," Potter emphasizes. They escape only when Mr. Bunny, Benjamin's father, arrives (wearing a purple coat and smoking a pipe) and attacks the cat. Benjamin also pays the consequences of his naughtiness: Mr. Bunny whips his son with a switch. Mrs. Rabbit, however, forgives her son, "because she was so glad to see that he had found his shoes and coat."

One of the most famous childlike rabbits in children's literature appears in Margaret Brown's *Goodnight Moon*. This short, lyrical book focuses on the experience of a little rabbit in blue and white striped pajamas, who is getting ready to fall asleep in "the great green room." Brown's melodic litany contrasts the intimacy provided by familiar objects ("a comb and a brush and bowl full of mush") with the vast world beyond the windows ("good night stars, good night air, good night noises everywhere"), thus evoking both the comfort and the mystery a child experiences while falling asleep.

Clement Hurd, the illustrator, originally wanted to create human characters for the book, but both Brown and her editor insisted that the characters be rabbits, not because of any symbolic value, but because Hurd was better at drawing rabbits than he was at drawing children.[2] The emotional experience of this main character is so very human, so very childlike, however, that we almost don't realize it's a rabbit. Nor do we notice that the "quiet old lady" is a larger rabbit dressed up in old lady clothes. The fact that the rabbit is never personified with a name or a close-up view in Clement Hurd's wondrously simple illustrations also sustains the illusion that this is a little boy cuddled in his bed, not a pesky little rabbit.

Brown had thirty-seven rabbits as a child, which no doubt endeared the species to her. A number of her other books featured rabbits as well, including *My World* (a companion book to *Goodnight Moon* that further explores the rabbit-boy's life with his parents), *Bunny's Noisy Book*, *The Golden Egg*, *Home For A Bunny* and *I Like Stars*. *The Runaway Bunny*, one of her best-known rabbit books, also focuses on a common childhood psychology—the need to be both independent of the mother and assured that she'll never be far away. In this book, a young rabbit asks his mother how she would respond if he were to leave her—e.g., by running away, by becoming a sailboat, by turning into a flower. Each time, she lovingly replies that she would turn into whatever object it would take to keep him with her. This would be a teenager's worst nightmare, of course, but for very young children, who are struggling both to develop autonomy and to retain the maternal bond, the book provides the promise that the mother is able both to let the child explore and to protect him.

Sam McBratney's *Guess How Much I Love You*, winner of the 1996 Abby Award, features a personified lagomorph, too—but this

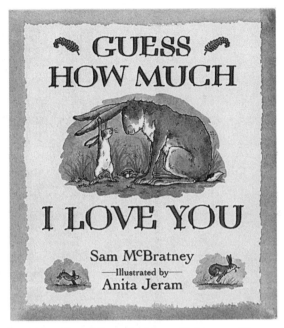

Figure 4.5. *Guess How Much I Love You?* has sold thirteen million copies since its original publication. Text © 1994 Sam McBratney; Illustrations © 1994 Anita Jeram. Reproduced by permission of the publisher, Candlewick Press Inc., Cambridge, MA, on behalf of Walker Books Ltd., London.

time it's a hare, not a rabbit. In Anita Jeram's lively illustrations, Little Nutbrown Hare and Big Nutbrown Hare have more of the qualities of a wild animal than do the characters in most bunny stories—these lepuses wear no clothing and display the proper white and brown coloring of a hare, as well as the huge ears, long back feet and telltale cottontails. On some pages, Little Nutbrown Hare also moves with the leaps, bounds and proper hopping gait of a true lagomorph. This is delightfully refreshing, considering all the roly-poly bunnies dressed in human clothes that walk upright through the pages of children's literature.

McBratney's story, too, plays on a common dynamic between child and parent—the game of exploring who loves the other more. Little Nutbrown Hare and Big Nutbrown Hare describe the boundaries of their love in very spatial terms—they declare they love each other as high as they can reach, to the tips of their toes, as high as they can hop, "down the lane as far as the river" and "across the river and over the hills." Each time, the father, who is bigger and stronger, loves more. In the end, however, a sleepy Nutbrown Hare declares, "I love you right up to the MOON," and his father kindly concedes, "Oh that's far. That is very, very far." But then as he snuggles his son into the shallow nest of dead leaves (another species-appropriate detail!), Big Nutbrown Hare smiles and has the last word: "I love you right up to the moon—and back."

The very close link between rabbit characters and childhood emotions is amply illustrated in Margery Williams' 1922 masterpiece, *The Velveteen Rabbit: Or How Toys Become Real*. The rabbit in this story is stuffed, but he is "really splendid," Williams writes. "He was fat and bunchy, as a rabbit should be; his coat spotted brown and white, he had real thread whiskers and his ears were lined with pink sateen." Still, this particular rabbit suffers from a common set of childhood emotions:

> He was naturally shy, and being only made of velveteen, some of the more expensive toys quite snubbed him. . . . [He] didn't know that real rabbits existed; he thought they were all stuffed with sawdust like himself, and he understood that sawdust was quite out-of-date and should never be mentioned in modern circles. . . . [T]he poor little Rabbit was made to feel himself very insignificant and commonplace . . . .[3]

This story focuses on the little toy's desire to become real, which as the Skin Horse explains, isn't about "'how you are made. . . . It's a thing that happens to you. When a child loves you for a long, long time, not just to play with, but REALLY loves you, then you become Real.'" In the course of this story, however, the velveteen rabbit actually is born into "realness" two times. The first birth occurs after months of being much loved by the little boy, when he tells his nanny that the bunny "'. . . isn't a toy. He's REAL!'"

When the little Rabbit heard that he was happy, for he knew that what the Skin Horse had said was true at last. The nursery magic had happened to him, and he was a toy no longer. He was Real. The Boy himself had said it.

That night he was almost too happy to sleep, and so much love stirred in his little sawdust heart that it almost burst. And into his boot-button eyes, that had long ago lost their polish, there came a look of wisdom and beauty . . .[4]

The second transformation comes after the cherished velveteen rabbit is thrown away, along with all the other toys, because the Boy has had scarlet fever. The rabbit is put into a sack and carried out into the garden to be burned. There he begins to reflect on his life in an epiphany that evokes a near-death experience:

He thought of those long sunlit hours in the garden—how happy they were—and a great sadness came over him. He seemed to see them all pass before him, each more beautiful than the other, the fairy huts in the flower-bed, the quiet evenings in the wood when he lay in the bracken and the little ants ran over his paws, the wonderful day when he first knew that he was Real. . . . And a tear, a real tear, trickled down his little shabby velvet nose and fell to the ground.[5]

From the rabbit's teardrop grows a flower out of which a fairy emerges and kisses him. She explains that she's the nursery magic Fairy who takes care "of all the playthings that the children have loved. When they are old and worn out and the children don't need them any more, then I come and take them away with me and turn them into real." The fairy flies with the little velveteen rabbit through the woods to where the "wild rabbits danced with their shadows on the velvet grass." He discovers he actually has hind legs and "the joy of using those hind legs was so great that he went springing about the turf, jumping sideways and whirling round as the others did. . . ."

Spring time

Figure 4.6. "Springtime." Illustration by William Nicholson. *The Velveteen Rabbit*, written by Margery Williams and originally published in 1922, plays on both Easter themes and childhood emotions.

The fact that the velveteen rabbit is first born into one kind of realness, and then re-born, or one might say resurrected, as a real rabbit in what appears to be wild rabbit heaven, makes *The Velveteen Rabbit* a clear analogy to the Easter story, long associated with rabbits. But what really makes the story resonate (on a more conscious level) with children and their parents is the fact that the bunny goes through periods of feeling alienated, inferior and unsure, and that he is "brought to life," twice, by the healing bonds of affection. Children know all too well the deep pain of being undervalued or misunderstood, and they also know the very immediate transformation that can occur with simple kindness and love.

Rabbit Hill, written in 1944 by American writer and illustrator Robert Lawson, was aimed at a slightly older children's market. This delightful tale is in part sheer fantasy—it centers on a family of rabbits that wear clothes, cook soup, sit in rocking chairs, sing songs, tell stories, put up preserves, sleep on pillows, build storerooms and get along quite amiably with foxes. The rabbit family lives in a burrow—which isn't accurate for the cottontails found in America. But much of what takes place in the book portrays the lives of rabbits quite realistically.

The story focuses on the excitement provoked by the news that "New Folks" are coming to the "Big House," and the fact that no one knows whether those New Folks will be nice people who put in good gardens or mean people who don't garden at all—or worse. Early in the tale, the mother rabbit recites a litany of the ways that wild rabbits can die, all of which are startlingly accurate:

> Down in the Rabbit burrow Mother was worrying harder than usual. . . . She had thought of every danger or unpleasantness which might accompany the arrival of New Folks and was now inventing new and unlikely ones. She had discussed the possibility of Dogs, Cats and Ferrets; of shotguns, rifles, and explosives; of traps and snares; of poisons and poison gases. There might even be *Boys*!
>
> She had repeated a horrid rumor which had circulated recently, concerning a man who had attached a hose to the exhaust pipe of his automobile and stuck it down folks' burrows. Several families were reported to have perished from this diabolical practice.[6]

Lawson's description of rabbit locomotion, especially, is dead on. At one point, Little Georgie reviews with his father "checks and doublings," or the best way to flee a pursuing dog. The young rabbit rattles off a charming—if exaggerated—account of a rabbit's zigzag flight pattern: "Sharp right and double left, double left and double right, dead stop and back flip, right jump, left jump, false trip, and briar dive."[7] Anyone who has chased a rabbit—whether out in the wild with the help of dogs or in a mad scramble through a house—can recognize the movements Lawson describes.

It turns out the New Folks are exceedingly kind—they don't believe in fencing the vegetable garden, or laying out poison or traps of any kind, much to the disbelief of the locals. They save Willie the mouse when he falls into a rain barrel and they put him in a little box lined with warm, soft cloth until he feels well enough to leave. They also save Little Georgie when he is hit by a car. In fact, at the end of the book, the New Folks put up a statue of Saint Francis, with a sign that reads, "There is enough for all," and spread out plenty of vegetables and nuts and seeds for all the little animals.

It's hard not to see *Rabbit Hill* as something of a morality tale, albeit a fanciful one, in which animals are kind to those humans who are also kind (in the manner of Victorian notions that all children should be taught to treat animals humanely). But all is not sweetness and light on *Rabbit Hill*, which gives this narrative considerable appeal. The animals on Rabbit Hill are perfectly capable of taking rather monstrous revenge when they think the New Folks have kidnapped—and are torturing—Little Georgie. Uncle Analdas (a rabbit) wants to cause an auto accident by skipping out into the road on a rainy night—a sport he enjoyed as a youngster. "'That'll wake 'em up!'" he says. "You'll see 'em slam on their brakes and go a-skiddin' and a-slitherin' and a-slidin' and a-crashin' into that there stone wall."[8] Other, "more violent" animals even suggest:

> that the rules of the Hill be thrown aside and that without waiting for Midsummer's Eve, they at once lay waste the gardens and lawns, the buckwheat field and the flower borders, that they ruthlessly slaughter every chick and duckling, every hen and rooster.[9]

But because the New Folks are kind, the animals don't raid their garden, don't cause an accident and don't eat the chicks and ducks. (Gray Fox even learns to love the fried chicken the cook leaves out for Phewie, the skunk, rather than eating the juvenile fowl.) Instead,

Red Buck, Phewie and Gray Fox *protect* the New Folks' property by patrolling for "wandering marauders" each night. The local handyman, of course, is boggled by the "beginner's luck" the New Folks have had and notes:

> I just can't understand it. Here's these new folks with their garden and not a sign of a fence around it, no traps, no poison, no nothing; and not a thing touched, not a thing. . . . Now me, I've got all them things, fences, traps, poisons; even sat up some nights with a shotgun—and what happens? All my carrots gone and half my beets, cabbages et into, tomatoes tromp down, lawn all tore up with moles. . . . I can't understand it.[10]

Why is it that rabbits are so frequently used as substitutes for children in children's literature? Many children's stories use talking and clothed animals as the main characters. In his classic work on children's fairy tales, *The Uses of Enchantment*, Bruno Bettelheim writes that the line between humans and animals is much less sharply drawn for children than adults, so the idea that animals can be children, or can turn into humans (think "Beauty and the Beast" or "The Frog King") seems quite possible.[11] In many fairy tales, Bettelheim adds, transformations between human and animal symbolize the process of personality integration, that is, of integrating the animalistic irrational parts of the personality with the more human, or rational parts.

On a more tangible level, rabbits' long ears, human-like eyes, silly big feet and fluffy tails delight young human minds, while their soft fur delights young hands. But animal behaviorists also maintain that the soft bodies, big eyes, stubby limbs and round faces of small animals appeal to humans because they recall the physical characteristics of infants[12] and so inspire children, especially girls, to "parent" their pets and toys. Dwarf rabbits, in particular, with their squashed-in faces, large eyes, short ears and diminutive bodies, appear to be perpetual babies. This is one reason, perhaps, that they are among the most popular pet breeds of rabbits.

The very fact that humans have for so long commingled and conflated images of humans and rabbits, however, leads to still another possible explanation: the physical and symbolic associations between rabbits and humans have become so great that rabbits have become a part of the human imagination in a way that, say, bears (who until the early twentieth century, when "teddy bears" were invented, were seen as predators rather than cuddly pets) have not. This is not a new association—people have been depicting rabbits as humans and humans (especially female humans) as rabbits for many centuries, and Dan Graur's DNA analyses hinted that rabbits are actually akin to humans (see Chapter One). But it's an idea that operates on a very unconscious level for most people. Take, for example, author Rosemary Wells's Web site (www.Rosemarywells.com), which includes a "Read to Your Bunny" inspirational message with an illustration of a Mommy rabbit reading to a baby rabbit. This image is so familiar, in a way so believable, that many people may not even realize they're looking at rabbits and not humans.

Rabbits as Tricksters

While children's literature seems to overflow with happy-go-lucky, cutely attired, apparently innocent rabbits masquerading as children, many other children's rabbit characters draw on trickster traditions.

The character of Rabbit in A.A. Milne's *Winnie the Pooh* books, for instance, displays the arrogant, busybody characteristics of rabbits in ancient trickster folktales. Take Chapter Five of *The House at Pooh Corner*, "In Which Rabbit Has a Busy Day, And We Learn What Christopher Robin Does in the Mornings." The chapter opens with a description of Rabbit's mood:

> It was going to be one of Rabbit's busy days. As soon as he woke up, he felt important, as if everything depended upon him. It was just the day for Organizing Something, or for Writing a Notice Signed Rabbit, or for seeing What

Everybody Else Thought About It. . . . It was a Captainish sort of day, when everybody said, "Yes Rabbit" and "No, Rabbit," and waited until he had told them.[13]

As Rabbit "trots" through the forest looking for an animal who is easy to boss around, he decides to go see Christopher Robin, because, the Rabbit tells himself, "Christopher Robin depends on Me. He's fond of Pooh and Piglet and Eeyore, and so am I, but they haven't any Brain. Not to notice." But at Christopher Robin's house (actually a tree), Rabbit discovers that the boy has gone out and left a somewhat incomprehensible note.

Rabbit takes it on himself to investigate the boy's whereabouts. He goes to Owl's house and tells him "You and I have brains. The others have fluff. If there is any thinking to be done in this Forest—and when I say thinking I mean *thinking*—you and I must do it."[14] Yet it is Eeyore—who in this case plays the tortoise to Rabbit's hare—who first figures out where the boy is; he says: "What does Christopher Robin do in the mornings? He learns. He becomes Educated. He instigorates—I *think* that is the word he mentioned, but I may be referring to something else—he instigorates Knowledge."

In *Song of the South*, Walt Disney's 1946 interpretation of the Uncle Remus stories, the character of Brer Rabbit is a wily trickster and, again, a stand-in for a boy. In the movie, the human boy, Johnny, is on his way to visit his grandmother. His mother is staying with the boy at the grandmother's mansion; his father is not. The source of the marital separation is not explained, but the tension, and the boy's resulting grief, is very clear. Johnny finds refuge in the paternal and kindly character of Uncle Remus, an older slave, who tells Brer Rabbit stories to coach the unhappy boy through a number of difficult situations: his wanting to run away to find his father, for instance, and his getting into trouble with some bullying neighbor boys.

The humans in *Song of the South* were live action, the Brer Rabbit stories were animated and the producers combined the two to gorgeous effect. Brer Rabbit himself has what were to become the classic rabbit characteristics of twentieth-century cartoons: big buck teeth, big feet, big cheeks, big ears and a big cottontail. He also has an exaggerated upright, boinging "hop" that resembles a rabbit on a pogo stick, or, perhaps, the locomotion of a flea. But his trickster character comes through plain and clear. As Uncle Remus puts it, "Brer Rabbit, he is the outdoingest, the most bodacious critter in the whole world."

Disney halted its fourth re-release of the movie in American theaters in 1986, after decades of charges that the film "sugar coated" slavery and depicted African Americans in a stereotypically happy-go-lucky way. (Videos and laser disks were available in Europe and other foreign countries until January 2002; the movie is now out of print worldwide.) One could perhaps argue that the African American characters actually come off better than the unhappy whites in the movie, and that the movie celebrates friendships that transcend class and race, as well as the healing power of love. More relevant to this work, however, is the way in which the character of Brer Rabbit and little Johnny are fused together so as to make them indistinguishable. The stories (as Uncle Remus tells them) put the trickster bunny in scrapes that closely parallel the emotional traumas Johnny suffers; at one point in the movie Johnny's face is even faded into the animated face of Brer Rabbit as Uncle Remus starts to spin a new tale. By the end of the film Johnny also adopts some trickster qualities, which lend him a personal strength he lacked before. As he tells his little slave friend Toby, "Being little and without much strength we're supposed to use our heads, not our foots"—which is exactly how Uncle Remus described Brer Rabbit's way of dealing with trouble.

Bugs Bunny, created by Warner Brothers only a few years after *Song of the South* was released, is the modern trickster descendent of Brer Rabbit: he is smart, quick and curious, and his glib, wisecracking, anarchistic and sometimes violent attitude was especially appealing to the war-weary American audiences that saw him in movie theaters in the 1940s. (Bugs started appearing on television in the

1960s.) His inquisitive nature gets him into some tight spots, but like a classic trickster he gets out of them through his wits.

Bugs Bunny (and the rest of the Looney Tunes characters created by Tex Avery) appealed to children. But many of Bugs Bunny episodes draw on some distinctly adult themes, including sex, racism, corporate greed and gender (Bugs, in fact, is forever dressing up like a woman). Like the fox or bear of the Brer Rabbit stories, Bugs' greatest opponent is a hunter, Elmer Fudd; a great many episodes follow Bugs as he outwits Fudd's clumsy attempts to kill him. In Elmer's first appearance in "Fresh Hare" in 1942, Elmer is a Mountie searching for Bugs, who is wanted dead or alive ("preferably dead"). Bugs ends up in front of a firing squad but escapes after getting everyone to sing "Camptown Races." As he leads the firing squad in the song, Bugs is in blackface, harking back to Joel Chandler Harris' equating of the Negro and the rabbit. (According to the Bugs Bunny Cartoon Database, the ending for this episode is no longer shown on television.) A few years later, in "The Big Snooze," Elmer becomes fed up with endlessly chasing (and never catching) Bugs; he quits chasing after him altogether, tearing up his contract with Warner Brothers (definitely a joke for the grownups), and retiring to go fishing.

Even before Elmer's appearance, Bugs spent a great deal of time battling (and beating) predators of various kinds who should have eaten him. His second appearance, in "Heckling Hare" (1941), involved his battles with a hunting dog who thinks he has killed Bugs and triumphantly brings flowers to his grave. Of course the dog is wrong and later meets his fate by falling off a cliff. Later opponents include Yosemite Sam, Porky Pig, Daffy Duck, the Tasmanian Devil and even historical figures like Adolf Hitler and Joseph Stalin—the latter being predators, obviously, not only of rabbits but humans.

In the more than 175 Bugs Bunny cartoons that have been made in the last sixty years, Bugs encounters many of the threats that real rabbits do: he's constantly in danger of being cooked, stuffed or used in some evil experiment or other. In "Easter Yeggs" (1947) the Easter Bunny even asks Bugs to stand in for him one year; Bugs agrees, but

Figure 4.7. The creators of Crusader Rabbit used references to rabbits' legendary reproductive powers to sell advertising on the show. Crusader Rabbit Press Book, courtesy Dan Goodsell, www.theimaginaryworld.com.

then gets so aggravated with the whole experience that he blows the Easter Bunny up. Still, the Bugs Bunny shows remain pure fantasy in that Bugs, like Brer Rabbit, is always the hero and always gets away.

While not as famous or long-lived as Bugs, Crusader Rabbit was a rabbit hero in the very early days of television. In 1948, Jay Ward, eventual creator of "Rocky and Bullwinkle," teamed up with animator Alex Anderson and created the first made-for-television cartoon series. Anderson's original intent wasn't to have a rabbit character; he just wanted to create a character whose personality clashed with its appearance. That character ended up being Crusader, a hot-tempered, aggressive hero in the body of a small rabbit. His sidekick became Ragland T. Tiger, who was something of a slow, dim bulb. True to his trickster roots, Crusader often got himself into trouble with villains like Bilious Green, Illregard Beauregard, and Simon LeGree; the pilot for the show even featured a trip Crusader and his partner took to Texas to battle hunters. Like all good trickster bunnies, however, Crusader always escaped.

Oswald the Lucky Rabbit, Walt Disney's very first animated animal star, was the father of all animated trickster rabbits. Oswald was not a highly developed character, having "lived" only from 1927 to 1928 and having lacked a voice, due to silent picture technology. But the series typically involved the rabbit getting into some kind of pickle from which he escaped by virtue of his wits. In "Trolley Troubles," Oswald is the driver of a trolley that must navigate ill-repaired tracks. He hits a cow (and bounces off) and then slides backwards down a hill. Oswald gets the trolley back up the hill by tricking a goat into pushing it back up, via a carrot on a stick. In "Oh What a Knight," Oswald has to rescue his girlfriend, who is being held captive in a castle by her father.

As a character, Oswald failed rather quickly, but his spirit lives on in Mickey Mouse, who was modeled on Oswald and shares his facial structure, clothing, and body shape. Oswald was also the first character from which Disney produced spin-off merchandise, in the form of a candy bar, a stencil set and a button—setting in motion a pattern that would reap the company billions of dollars over the next seventy-five years.

The Littlest Ministers

Rabbits have also been chosen as spiritual or moralistic mediators for children. The Uncle Wiggily stories, penned by Howard Garis, featured a kindly, pink-nosed, elderly rabbit gentleman, who carried a red, white and blue barber pole crutch and lived, quite platonically, with Nurse Jane Fuzzy Wuzzy, "a muskrat lady housekeeper." Uncle Wiggily Longears gets into mild trouble, or has a mild dilemma, in each of his very short stories, but he always finds a way to help out a neighbor, child or relative. In "Uncle Wiggily and the Apple Dumpling," for instance, he ends up giving a homemade apple dumpling to a starving squirrel family. In "Uncle Wiggily and the Wagon Sleds," the "nice old rabbit gentleman" helps Jackie and Peetie Bow Wow, the puppy dog boys, shake a snow-bound bad mood when he turns their wagons into sleds.

Boinger Bunny, the Web-based Christian character, is an altogether different creature. According to the Web site, Boinger is a "funny lovable Doll that lives in Heaven and was named Boinger *because* each time Boinger hops—his legs make a cheerful happy BOING sound." Boinger came into being because "On earth a little 4 year old orphan boy named Jimmy is so sad that he cries almost all day long because Jimmy feels as if no one in the world loves him. So our Loving Heavenly Father, because he loves Jimmy, God asks cheerful happy Boinger to go to earth to be Jimmy's new pal."

Boinger befriends Jimmy and takes him back in time so that he can witness the Bible stories—including that of Noah's Ark, David and Goliath, and Jonah and the Fish—unfolding in real life. Boinger clearly isn't bound for the same classic status as the characters discussed above, but he nevertheless exemplifies certain key aspects of our culture's idea of the rabbit. The producers of Boinger no doubt chose a rabbit because of its associations with the Easter Bunny and the Easter story, as well as the species' universal appeal to children. A spokesperson for the "Boinger the Cheerful Doll Company," which makes the Boinger doll, said only that the founders of the site chose the doll because "Rabbits are warm friendly animals."

Grown-Ups as Rabbits

While rabbits in books, television shows and movies for children are generally lovable, adorable and childlike, adult rabbit tales feature more mature themes, including sexuality, death and transcendence. Certain rabbit characteristics—most notably the trickster, as embodied in Bugs Bunny—appeal to both children and grown-ups. But the symbolism of the rabbit tends to evolve significantly from children's media to that of adults. Rabbits featured in adult films or literature are entirely different from the adorable, naughty, childish creatures found in works for children. Instead, rabbits for grown-ups are more akin to the witchy, sexy rabbits of earlier eras.

In the 1937 John Steinbeck novel *Of Mice and Men*, for instance, rabbits are associated with childishness, but also with class tensions, adultery and murder. Lennie, a mentally retarded migrant worker, dreams of owning land with his friend George one day and of raising rabbits there. Throughout the book, Lennie repeatedly asks George to tell him "about the rabbits," as a way of asking George to daydream aloud about living off of the land and being self-sufficient:

> "An' rabbits," Lennie said eagerly. "An' I'd take care of 'em. Tell how I'd do that, George."
>
> "Sure, you'd go out in the alfalfa patch an' you'd have a sack. You'd fill up the sack and bring it in an' put it in the rabbit cages."
>
> "They'd nibble an' they'd nibble," said Lennie, "the way they do. I see em.
>
> "Ever six weeks or so, " George continued, "them does would throw a litter so we'd have plenty of rabbits to eat an' to sell. . . ."[15]

But the rabbits also represent something else to the slow-witted Lennie: something soft to stroke and nurture, something innocent and childish he himself can parent. When the wife of another worker asks him, "What makes you so nuts about rabbits?" he responds, "I like to pet nice things. Once at a fair I seen some of them long-hair rabbits. An' they was nice, you bet." Unfortunately, the wife, who is setting off lust and competition among the men, invites Lennie to pat her own long hair—thereby symbolically making herself into a rabbit, or prey. She grows angry when he gets rough, struggles to get free, and he inadvertently breaks her neck, a common technique, by the way, for killing rabbits grown for meat or fur.

Lennie flees to a riverside, where "from out of his head," Steinbeck writes, "came a gigantic rabbit. It sat on its haunches in front of him and it waggled its ears and crinkled its nose at him. And it spoke in Lennie's voice, too." This rabbit isn't friendly; it's both a prophet (harking back to the fortune-telling reputation of ancient rabbits) and a monster (conjuring those frightening hares that bounded through the medieval imagination). The rabbit tells Lennie that he couldn't possibly care for rabbits in real life and that George is going to first "beat hell outa you with a stick" and then "go away and leave you," thus destroying Lennie's dream. When George, who has joined a group of men looking to avenge the woman's death, emerges from the bushes, the rabbit, Steinbeck writes, "scuttled back into Lennie's brain." As the two men talk, Lennie again begs George to tell him about the rabbits. George complies, but then shoots Lennie as he stares dreamily off across the river.

The rabbit in the 1987 film *Fatal Attraction*[16] is also associated with innocence—and eventually, innocence lost. After a one-night stand with Dan (played by Michael Douglas), Alex (played by Glenn Close) cannot accept his rejection of her and turns to stalk him. In one scene, she kills his daughter's pet rabbit and then leaves it boiling in a soup pot on the kitchen stove for the family to find. The purchase and surprise gift of the white bunny from Dan to his daughter are played up in the film to symbolize Dan's love for his family. But with the affair, he destroyed the sanctity of his marital bond. When he tries to break off ties with Alex, she takes revenge by targeting the symbol of his fatherly love, the rabbit. In so doing, she also destroys childhood innocence—symbolized by the rabbit's whiteness.

The rabbit also becomes a surrogate for Alex's ultimate targets, Dan and his wife. Animal and child welfare experts now know that violence against pets often precedes the abuse of children, spouses, or other people. Many serial killers, in fact, start out by torturing animals. Alex, who could be said to be "mad as a March hare" due to her surfeit of sexual feelings, does indeed end up in a murderous rage over her thwarted love. In fact, much of the tension in the final third of the film, which admittedly goes a bit over the top, swirls around her intent to kill Dan and his wife.

In *Who Framed Roger Rabbit,* a delightful combination of animation and real action that won four Academy Awards in 1988, Roger Rabbit is no doubt a childish character. He looks a bit like

Bugs Bunny, but with exaggerated features, an effeminate voice and silly clothes—and without any of Bugs's trickster qualities. Roger Rabbit, in fact, is a cowardly idiot (or, as the villain calls him, a "bucked-tooth fool") who can make humans laugh and can pull great stunts, but seems incapable of saving his own skin, never mind anyone else's. His wife, however, a cartoon human named Jessica Rabbit, is a sexy broad with huge breasts, a wasp waist, a sultry voice and swelling hips. This film isn't about happy little bunnies frolicking like young children (although children might enjoy the crazy antics of Roger Rabbit). It's about murder, adultery, jealousy, politics, career slumps, corporate greed and mass transit.

The rabbit character in *Harvey*, a film released by Universal Studios in 1950 (and based on the Pulitzer Prize-winning play by Mary Chase), is initially associated with childishness but becomes much more complex through the course of the movie. The rabbit itself is an adult—actually a 6' 3" adult white rabbit with a bow tie. But this "Harvey" is the imaginary friend of Elwood P. Dowd, who, as played by Jimmy Stewart, is himself a merry, innocent, flower-loving and curious character. Moreover, like many children, he inhabits a world of women. Since his own mother died, Elwood has been living with his somewhat matriarchal sister, Vita (who, he notes, takes care of all the "signing and managing of papers," and who still refers to him as her "baby brother") and her niece. He has also stopped visiting the Yale Alumni Club, a male bastion. Instead, he has started hanging out with his imaginary bunny friend Harvey, which makes him seem both childish and, well, insane.

Harvey's rabbit-like functions in the story are not limited to his appearance and his association with childhood. His existence catalyzes a whole series of flirtations and couplings among the characters, which again reinforces our association between rabbits and lust. And Elwood claims that Harvey is actually a "pooka," or a fairy spirit in animal form, which conjures the association between rabbits and magic. Harvey, according to Elwood, can foresee who will be dropping by, stop clocks, grant his friends their wildest fantasies and then restore order.

The primary tension in the movie revolves around whether or not Elwood—and his sister—will end up in the psych ward. A subtler tension revolves around the issue of whether or not Harvey is real. Vita on several occasions admits that she has seen Harvey, and towards the end of the movie we, as viewers, begin to see mysterious things like doors opening and closing, wallets mysteriously disappearing, a swing swinging on its own and a hat with two holes cut out in the top, as if for a rabbit's ears. Even Dr. Chumley, the head psychiatrist, ends up believing in the rabbit. As such, within the film, the imaginary rabbit friend of a childlike character becomes accepted by the very man who most symbolizes scientific—or rational—thinking. Outside of film, this invisible rabbit became one of the most cherished characters in Hollywood history.

Both the book and film versions of *Watership Down*, written by Richard Adams, differ from most rabbit tales in that they are the only popular works that attempt to portray rabbits realistically (aside from the necessary convenience of having them speak English). The book, which was based on Ronald Lockley's *The Private Life of Rabbits*, hits on key points of rabbit habits and social relations, including the "satellite" young males who often wander in search of other warrens, does who resorb their litters when warrens are too crowded, domestic rabbits who have no idea how to survive in the wild, the impressive fighting and coping skills of these prey animals and their daily rhythms of feeding, resting and playing. But the book is also quite explicit about the ways that rabbits die in human hands—including being shot, gassed inside the warrens and caught in snares.

Watership Down is unique because, unlike other contemporary rabbit stories (or ancient myths or folk tales), its rabbits aren't used as a symbol of anything else, although Adams, who obviously did his homework, includes rabbits who can foretell the future and rabbits who are cunning, and the character of El-ahrairah (or the Prince with a Thousand Enemies) is obviously akin to the trickster rabbit of Africa and Native America. In this book's cosmology, Frith, the rabbit god, created the world, the animals and the birds, and El-ahrairah was the first rabbit created. The book's mythology describes how El-ahrairah is blessed by Frith with a cunning mind and lightning speed; he remains a folk hero for all rabbits who come after him, including the "real" rabbits of *Watership Down* who tell the story to their young:

> All the world will be your enemy, Prince with a Thousand Enemies, and whenever they catch you, they will kill you. But first they must catch you, digger, listener, runner, prince with the swift warning. Be cunning and full of tricks and your people shall never be destroyed.[17]

The fables told by and for rabbits in *Watership Down* operate in much the same way that many human folk tales do: the stories of El-ahrairah, like the Wabanaki stories of Ableegumooch or many of the Tar Baby stories from Africa, both teach the rabbits why things are the way they are (e.g., why rabbits have strong hind legs) and entertain them with tales of heroism, wit and wonder.

Perhaps the most striking aspect of *Watership Down* is its enormous success—the book was a bestseller, was made into a movie in 1978 and is now the subject of a plethora of Web sites and listserves (including some with "fan fiction" sequels and some with interactive games)—despite the fact that it was a book about rabbits. Ironically, Richard Adams himself wasn't any big rabbit advocate. He told *The Ottawa Citizen* in 1998 that he supported a massive cyanide "cull" of wild rabbits in England because it was a "regrettable necessity." The *Citizen* noted that Mr. Adams also told a London newspaper, "I've never been one of these sentimentalists. I'm not a fluffy bunny sort of person at all. If I saw a rabbit in my garden, I'd shoot it."[18]

Rabbits as Monsters
The idea that rabbits can be monsters is an old one, of course, but it seems alive and well in the contemporary imagination, at least judging by movies that have used the same theme. In the 1972 camp classic *Night of the Lepus* (based on the novel *The Year of the Angry*

Figure 4.8. "She found it rather trying to her nerves at first, to meet with rabbits as big as horses." This drawing by Reginald Bathurst Birch appeared in *The Admiral's Caravan* (1892) by Charles E. Carryl, an American poet who specialized in writing fantasies for children. *The Night of the Lepus* drew on similarly eerie images of giant rabbits. Library of Congress, Prints and Photographs Division. [Reproduction number LC-USZ62-100500]

Rabbit, by Russell Braddon), a colony of mutated rabbits terrorizes an Arizona town. The movie was part of a whole flock of 1970s horror flicks that focused on the dangers of either mutated or really pissed-off animals (e.g., *Kingdom of the Spiders, The Food of the Gods, Killer Bees, Empire of the Ants, Jaws* and *Day of the Animal*). In *Lepus* the premise is alarmingly realistic: a biologist intending to reduce the rabbit population on an Arizona ranch by injecting them with substances actually injects them with a serum he doesn't entirely understand. The scheme backfires (Australians take note!) and one injected rabbit becomes monstrously prolific, creating hundreds of giant-sized bunnies with a taste for human flesh.

Starring *Star Trek's* DeForest Kelley and Janet Leigh (in what very well may be one of their worst career moves), the movie's special effects are notoriously badly done. Close-ups of live, domestic rabbits with ketchup on their faces, as well as humans dressed in bunny costumes (and sometimes walking upright), are supposed to convey the horror of these mutated creatures. This makes for quite an entertaining romp, especially given the sound of the rabbits "roaring" while attacking, and lines like "Attention: There's a horde of killer rabbits headed this way," spoken by a sheriff's deputy. But the movie ends with the rabbits being killed (after a failed attempt with dynamite), unwitting victims, again, of human attempts to control nature.

A better-known (and better done) movie featuring killer rabbits is *Monty Python and the Holy Grail.* Here a small white rabbit is the fearsome guard of the Cave of Caerbannog. Upon approaching the cave and seeing the rabbit, King Arthur and his men cannot understand why everyone is afraid. Arthur asks if there is something behind the rabbit; his knight responds that the problem *is* the rabbit:

ARTHUR:
You silly sod!
TIM:
What?
ARTHUR:
You got us all worked up!
TIM:
Well, that's no ordinary rabbit!
ARTHUR:
Ohh.
TIM:
That's the most foul, cruel, and bad-tempered rodent you ever set eyes on!

After losing three men to this fierce "rodent," and uttering the famous cry, "Run away! Run away!" the knights finally kill the monster bunny with the Holy Hand Grenade of Antioch.

At its surface value, the impact of these films seems to derive from the ludicrousness of the situation (rabbits are supposed to be snuggly pets, after all). But the rabbit-as-monster motif is actually tied to very deep-rooted beliefs that rabbits are monsters, that they have supernatural or very witchlike powers—that they are something to be feared, even if only for their destructive tendencies when it comes to vegetation. This theme even continues today in the television show "Buffy the Vampire Slayer, " in which Anya, a vengeance demon with fierce powers, is deathly afraid of rabbits.

Other contemporary films use the rabbit as a thematic element. For instance, *Rabbit Proof Fence*, an independent Australian film released in 2002, deals with the true story of three Australian Aboriginal girls who were taken from their home by the Australian government to be raised as servants for white families. After escaping from their captors, the girls begin a 1,500-mile walk across Australia to their homes. The movie's title refers to the path that they follow: the 1,500-mile-long "rabbit proof fence" built by the government in 1901 to keep rabbits off the farmland that they were destroying. In the movie, then, the tradition of forcibly removing Aboriginal children from their homes—and from their mothers—to work as servants for white people parallels the government's various attempts at controlling and killing the rabbits that white people themselves introduced to Australia.

The rabbit is also used to subtle effect in the *Rabbit in the Moon*, a 1999 documentary by Japanese-American cinematographer Emiko Omori on the internment camps used by the United States to imprison Japanese Americans between 1942 and 1945. The title comes from the difference in the way that Westerners and Easterners look at the moon. In the West, we see a man in the moon. Some eastern cultures, including the Japanese, claim to see a rabbit in the moon. Metaphorically, the title refers to the way that the filmmaker's family had to disengage from their own culture as they were forced into camps run by the dominant American culture.

Rabbit, Run

Perhaps no other popular work combines the many conflicting images of rabbits in our culture more effectively than John Updike's *Rabbit* tetralogy, which follows the life of Harry "Rabbit"

Angstrom, a blue collar worker in Pennsylvania, from the 1950s until the 1990s. Updike's "Rabbit" character is one of the least likeable characters in modern fiction; during his decades-long transformation from a self-absorbed frustrated, rebellious young man to a pot-bellied, arteriosclerosis-ridden middle-aged man, Rabbit remains selfish, racist, greedy, misogynistic, domineering, unfaithful, not particularly bright and rather immature. But he is not without his virtues. Although Rabbit is both shaped by and resentful of the norms of his culture, he is continually striving for something else, a "grace" as he sometimes calls it, a sense of transcendence or spirituality that goes far beyond the Judeo-Christian norms of his culture. And although he can appear and act incredibly hardhearted, his heart is not immovable. Small things—like the slant of light in his garden, mist on a lake, or the freckles on his granddaughter's nose— touch him profoundly.

That Updike named his central character "Rabbit" is not a coincidence. In the beginning of *Rabbit, Run*, the narrator explains that Harry Angstrom was nicknamed "Rabbit" as a boy because of the "breadth of white face, the pallor of his blue irises, and a nervous flutter under his brief nose."[19] (John Updike also was nicknamed "Rabbit" as a boy,[20] although no one could say that these books are strictly autobiographical.) In addition, Updike has described the structure of the novel as being "darting, fragmentary, zigzagging,"[21] the very same pattern, one might add, that a rabbit takes when fleeing predators. Similarly, in the Franklin Library edition of *Rabbit, Run* (1977), Updike notes how the use of the present tense—considered very revolutionary at the time—helped him "emphasize how thoroughly the zigzagging character live(s) in the present."[22]

Harry is also a "Rabbit" because, as the first book's title clearly states, he runs, both physically and emotionally, from what most frightens him. In his twenties, Rabbit runs from the oppressiveness of a dead-end job (he works as a kitchen gadget salesman) and from domestic life with a wife who is pregnant, slovenly, alcoholic and a "dumb mutt," as Rabbit repeatedly calls her. More generally, he is also fleeing the oppressive strictures of the Eisenhower years of the 1950s, with that period's emphasis on conformity and respectability.

The first book is also littered with images that evoke both a domestic rabbit's experience and a wild rabbit's way of moving and sensing the world. Harry enters his parents' yard to pick up his son, Nelson, much like a rabbit trespassing into a garden; Updike writes: "Rabbit stealthily approaches his old home on the grass, hopping the little barberry hedge and the wire. . . ."[23] When he doesn't fetch his son, and decides to run away instead, he sneaks over to his wife's parents' house, to get his car. When it stalls, "Rabbit's heart rises and a taste of straw comes into his mouth,"[24] as if he were a hutch rabbit.

Once on the road, Rabbit gasses up in a smaller, more rural town and realizes, ". . . this was another world. It smells differently, smells older, of nooks and pockets in the ground that nobody's poked into yet,"[25] an allusion, perhaps, to a wild rabbit's searching for a burrow. Later, Updike again refers to the rabbit's gait to describe Rabbit's flight from domesticity: "Hopping onto the highway, he turns instinctively right, north."[26]

Rabbit, Run also uses imagery of nets, traps and holes to denote both the safety and suffocation of "home." When Rabbit enters the small, disheveled apartment he shares with his pregnant wife, the mess "clings to his back like a tightening net,"[27] much as a net might ensnare a wild rabbit. When his wife asks him to pick up a pack of cigarettes for her, he "freezes" and stands, "looking at his faint yellow shadow on the white door that leads to the hall, and senses he is in a trap. It seems certain."[28] Moments later, the very traffic in his city "begins to feel like a part of the same trap." During a game of golf with the Reverend Eccles, who is trying to get him to go home again, Rabbit thinks to himself, "*Oh you moron go home.* Home is the hole. . . ."[29]

Throughout his flight, Rabbit sees more nets—in tree twigs illuminated by his headlights[30] and in the red and blue lines on a confusing map—which he then "claws" and "tears" at.[31] But sometimes the image of a hole also symbolizes safety; when Harry takes refuge with his old basketball coach, Marty Tothero, for instance, he lies down on the coach's bed. Updike writes, "Though the idea is distasteful, getting into the old man's hollow, the sensations are good, being able to stretch out at last and feeling the solid cool wall close to him and hearing cars moving maybe hunting him far below."[32] Yet again a hole denotes the suffocating net of domesticity. As he flees, panic-stricken, through the woods after his newborn daughter's funeral, Rabbit is aware of a "hollow" and "brown tunnels"(an allusion to warrens); he even tears off his blue coat, much as Peter Rabbit loses his blue coat as he flees Farmer McGregor.

In the following books, as Rabbit ages into a 230-pound retiree living in a Florida condominium, he stops running physically and emotionally, although he keeps commenting on the banality of his life. The rich rabbit imagery eases up in the following books; by the third book, *Rabbit is Rich*, Harry isn't even called Rabbit anymore; he's simply called Harry. That's not to say the rabbit imagery is gone; allusions to caverns beneath the earth's surface (like warrens) come up in *Rabbit is Rich,* as do images of nets and traps. As he tries to counsel his son against marrying Pru, the woman he has impregnated, Harry says, "I just don't like to see you caught, you're too much like me." Nelson protests, "I'm not you! I'm not caught!" and his father responds, "They've got you and you didn't even squeak."[33]

Although the very direct rabbit imagery eases in the last three books of the tetralogy, two more subtle associations with rabbits are reinforced: Harry's sexual appetite and his almost paganistic spiritual quest.

That this fictional Rabbit, like real rabbits, is a lusty fellow cannot be disputed. In the course of the tetralogy Rabbit has adulterous sex with five women, including Pru, his daughter-in-law. He lusts after far more women, including a reverend's wife, a friend's tantalizing wife, waitresses and even the nurses who care for him after his first heart attack in *Rabbit at Rest*. As Nelson, who is tangled in an excruciating Oedipal complex with his father, cries, "Dad, when are you going to get your mind off boffing? You're what, fifty-seven? . . . and you're so damn adolescent. There's more things in the world than who's boffing who."[34]

For Rabbit, the only other thing beside boffing (and eating—as his wife notes, "Harry has his little vegetable garden . . . all he grows is lettuce and carrots and kohlrabi, he does love to nibble")[35] is a mystical something to fulfill his life. This quest, which evokes associations between rabbits and divinity, is not a Christian one; three of the books, in fact, include Christian "leaders" who are weak, if not foolish. Instead he looks for transcendence—what he calls, in *Rabbit, Run*, "this thing that wasn't there"—more polytheistically in ordinary life, especially in the game of golf (which, of course, centers on little holes in the ground). "Golf is the game wherein the wall between us and the mystical is rubbed thinnest," Rabbit thinks in *Rabbit, Run*. At one point, he even sees redemption in the arc of a golf ball, which is described much like the flight of a wounded rabbit:

> Stricken; sphere, star, speck. It hesitates, and Rabbit thinks it will die, but he's fooled, for the ball makes his hesitation the ground of a final leap: with a kind of visible sob takes a last bite of space before vanishing in falling. "That's *it!*" he cries and, turning to Eccles with a smile of aggrandizement, repeats, "That's it."[36]

Throughout the tetralogy Rabbit is frequently compared to religious figures; people refer to him—and he refers to himself—as a saint, Jesus Christ, an apprentice angel and the Dalai Lama. "I'm a mystic. I give people faith," he tells his prostitute girlfriend Ruth in *Rabbit, Run* when she wonders aloud why people love him. The morning of his daughter's funeral, he even has a vivid dream in which the moon "swallows up" the sun during an eclipse—evoking ancient associations of rabbits and the moon. Then, "Intensely relieved and excited, he realizes he must go forth from this field" (as if, again, he is a wild rabbit) "and found a new religion."[37]

More poignantly, even at the end of *Rabbit, Run*, as he runs through the streets of Brewer, Pennsylvania, he undergoes a spiritual transformation that evokes images of rabbits fleeing entrapment:

He feels his inside as very real suddenly, a pure blank space in the middle of a dense net. . . . I don't know, he kept telling Ruth; he doesn't know, what to do, where to go, what will happen, the thought that he doesn't know seems to make him infinitesimally small and impossible to capture.[38]

Moreover, at repeated intervals, Rabbit is associated with renewed life, fertility and springtime, seasonal events long associated with rabbits. To introduce his main character in the first pages of *Rabbit, Run*, Updike writes, "The month is March. Love makes the air light. Things start anew; Rabbit tastes through sour aftersmoke the fresh chance of air. . . . His upper lip nibbles back from the teeth in self pleasure. His big suede shoes skim in thumps above the skittering litter of alley gravel."[39] The image of a rabbit in shoes traveling in "thumps" across a landscape, of course, conjures images not only of big rabbit feet, but even of the Easter Bunny, long a symbol of fertility and often depicted in clothing.

Equally important, Rabbit comes to be seen as a symbol of fertility and renewal even to others. After he has been hired to help Mrs. Smith tend her garden, the old lady tells him: "You kept me alive, Harry; it's the truth; you did. All winter I was fighting the grave and then in April I looked out the window and here was a tall young man burning my old stalks and I knew life hadn't left me. That's what you have, Harry: life."[40] And in *Rabbit at Rest*, Harry saves his granddaughter, Judy, when she appears to be drowning. This is a clear symbolic replacement for the drowning of his own infant daughter, Rebecca June, which occurs in *Rabbit, Run*.

More commonly, though, Rabbit finds transcendence through sex, which gives him a sense of connection and purity. This is especially true in one scene with Thelma, where Rabbit first experiences anal sex and finds it feels like "a void, a pure black box, a casket of perfect nothingness. . . . He can't take his mind from what he's discovered, that nothingness seen by his single eye." These references are more akin to the spiritual quest for "emptiness" of Buddhism than to the quest of Christianity, but they recall the way in which sexuality and religion have been associated with rabbits throughout history.

That Rabbit is also strongly associated with bad luck is also unmistakable. Throughout the book, the narrator refers to the deep, dark secret he and his wife share: that they were complicit in the death of their daughter. Nelson also frequently blames Harry for the death of Jill, a young hippie girl who lived in their house in the second book, *Rabbit, Redux*, but who died in a fire there. Ruth, in the first book, also openly calls him "Mr. Death" in the scene where she tells him she's pregnant.

The fact that Rabbit is imbued with the behavior and sensibilities of a wild rabbit and that he symbolizes so many of the characteristics that the ancients associated with rabbits is testimony not only to Updike's genius but also to the many contradictory and unconscious roles rabbits play in our culture. From bumbling childish bunnies to sex-crazed, yearning middle-aged men, the fine line between humans and rabbits—even at times the equating of the two—seems to signal our deep affinity for the rabbit's nature, even in its most negative connotations.

Bunny Slippers, Teapots and Jammies
Bunny Collectibles
Pasadena's Bunny Museum seems like an altar to a whole different image of rabbits—the cute, sweet, cuddly, childish bunnies that we all know and love. In fact, the collection started on Valentine's Day in 1992, when Steve Lubanski gave Candace Frazee a white plush bunny with a red heart, partly because they each called each other "Honey Bunny." In return, Candace gave Steve a white porcelain bunny that Easter, thus starting a tradition of bunny exchanges that continues to this day, with the couple giving each other a new bunny item every single day.

The Frazees' habit is reminiscent of the ancient Romans, who gave rabbits as signs of love. The couple has gone to even further extremes: they contacted the parents of the first baby born at a local hospital in the Year of the Rabbit, 1999, to ask to become his god-

Figure 4.9. Bunny Slippers. Photo by Susan Davis.

parents (the parents agreed) and Candace and Steve plan to stuff their own, real rabbits after they die. But the fact that Candace and Steve are able to exchange presents daily says as much about the sheer plethora of rabbit stuff available as about their devotion to each other. While the Bunny Museum can be seen as the culmination of one couple's commitment to each other and to rabbits, it also embodies the very broad iconic spectrum of the rabbit in this culture.

One key part of that spectrum is the world of bunny collectibles, or what could be called "bunny kitsch": the countless items in the shape of—or inscribed with the image of—rabbits. These kitschy items include bunny slippers, plush rabbits, baby clothes and toys, rabbit wind socks, rabbit weather vanes, rabbit lawn ornaments, rabbit cream pitchers, rabbit book ends, rabbit clocks, rabbit wind chimes, rabbit musical figurines, rabbit oven mitts, rabbit sweatshirts, rabbit aprons, rabbit earrings, rabbit dolls, rabbit stationery and even rabbit boxer shorts.

Like other representations of rabbits, rabbit collectibles are symbolically potent and bring up a number of questions: What do they mean? Why is the demand for these items so great that it supports an entire cottage industry, and even an entire museum? And what clues do their popularity offer to understanding the rabbit's awkward position in American culture today?

Rabbit toys and collectibles are as old as other forms of art, myth and symbol. Historians have found rabbits on tunics from the sixth century, ceramic plates from the fourteenth century, decorative platters from the fifteenth century, floor tiles from the seventeenth century and game pie dishes (used to cook, presumably, rabbits) from the eighteenth century. There are toys from the nineteenth century, and jewelry decorated with rabbits has been found from all periods of European history. (Rabbit rings were often exchanged by newly wedded couples in the Middle Ages to increase their fertility, and the Hopi continue to wear rabbit rings today to bring fertility to crops and humans alike.) Rabbits have decorated coins and paper money from ancient times and are found on stamps from around the world. Most of these early items were decorated with rabbits no doubt because rabbits are pleasing to look at, or because they made a logical addition to the pastoral or hunting scene being rendered. Some items clearly had a symbolic significance, such as sculpted figures showing a rabbit with the moon or in the company of a god or (more commonly) a goddess, or those items decorated with images of rabbits in flight, emphasizing swiftness. Other objects, such as the popular Hummel figurines from the 1930s, depict rabbits in the company of children, evidence of that burgeoning relationship and of a growing belief that rabbits were sweet, innocent and childlike.

That's not an unusual depiction. Early rabbit collectibles, as well as the myths and symbols of ancient peoples, reflected some of the negative connotations of rabbits. Those associations are missing, or are largely masked, in contemporary collectibles, which most often show the rabbit as it appears in children's film and literature: soft, round, cute and cuddly creatures, the ultimate childlike, non-threatening animal. To further distance this image from real rabbits (and to further cement the similarity between rabbits and humans), the producers of these images often clothe the animals, either in childlike garments or in colorful, homespun fabrics. Images of rabbits found on aprons or bookends, or in bunny statues, are rarely represented as sexualized animals and never depicted as prey. They are not presented as tricksters, and are never seen as harbingers of bad luck or black magic.

Rabbits are sometimes associated with a more benign form of magic, however—the magician's show. Today the association between rabbits and magicians is so strong that it's difficult to find a book, magazine, Web site or artifact associated with magic that doesn't have a rabbit's image—and, in particular, a rabbit in a hat— somewhere. This link with magic acts is fairly recent, starting in the early twentieth century; the first magician to pull a rabbit out of the hat was Harry Blackstone, Sr. (Leroy Boughton). According to magician Neil Alexander, at the end of his shows Blackstone would produce a live rabbit from a hat, then put the rabbit in a box and give it to a child. "When the child opened the box later at home," Alexander says, "he would discover, no doubt to his parents' great relief, that the rabbit had been transformed into a box of candy." This trick, later formalized as the "nest of boxes," became extremely popular and even inspired a whole host of other rabbit tricks, like "Hippety Hop Rabbits," "Multiplying Rabbits," "Fraidy Cat Rabbit" and "Rabbit Wrangler." Magicians Edwin Schmitt and Mike Mann also recall other Blackstone rabbit tricks, including pulling a rabbit from a cake, and then, in front of the crowd, turning him into two rabbits—a great trick for people who remain puzzled by the rabbit's reproductive powers! Mann notes that Blackstone always carried a rabbit hidden in his coat in case he "was called upon to perform a 'miracle.' "

Many magicians do use other animals (like the white dove), and others have now turned to fake rabbits. But rabbits continue to be the iconic animal for magic acts. Magicians, in fact, can purchase a whole book on rabbit acts (*The Bunny Book for Magicians*, by Frances Marshall), which includes more than one hundred tricks involving rabbits, as well as basic rabbit care and information on purchasing equipment. Magicians can also buy countless varieties of fake rabbits (made of sponge, paper, cardboard or cloth), and anyone can buy clothing, pins, jewelry and toys featuring rabbits emerging from hats or with wands.

This is not always a cheerful association. Alexander the magician notes that during the nineteenth century, magic acts were promoted on posters and handbills decorated with Faustian images of devils and imps, emphasizing the demonic roots of magic. That this imagery has been replaced by rabbits is indicative of the twentieth-century transformation of magic to something wholesome, rather than evil. It's also indicative of the rabbit's shift in the popular mind from a supernatural creature to a childish one.

Children's Items

Baby toys and accessories, as well as representations of rabbits with small children, show this link between youthful innocence and rabbits most clearly. Today, it's impossible to walk into a baby's room or a store selling baby goods without running into myriad cuddly bunny images: on pajamas, sweaters and hats, in the form of stuffed animals, rattles and teething toys, and on swaddling blankets, crib bumpers, lamps, wall hangings and quilts. Some of these rabbit items and images are generic; many are spin-offs of popular characters in children's books, like Max, the *Pat the Bunny* rabbit and the little rabbit in *Goodnight Moon*. The number of products for babies and small children that feature Peter Rabbit are almost too numerous to list. In her book, *The Case of Peter Rabbit: Changing Conditions of Literature for Children*, Margaret Mackey, an associate professor of library science at the University of Alberta, lists hundreds of products based on *The Tale of Peter Rabbit*, including stuffed animals, crib toys, mobiles, puppets, board games, baby clothes, baby dishes, ready-made children's clothes, bolts of cotton fabric, soap, toothbrushes, stencils, a daybook for the baby's first year, a "baby sleeping" sign, christening mugs, cloth books, cloth rattles, hooded towel sets, pacifiers, plastic bath books, cups, coloring books and activity books, software and music boxes.[41] (She also lists the many "adaptations" of the *The Tale of Peter Rabbit*, including pop-up books, books with modified language, illustra-

Figure 4.10. Peter Rabbit now adorns items ranging from baby blankets to teapots and dishtowels. Courtesy The Bunny Museum. Photo by Margo DeMello.

Figure 4.11. "Plush" rabbits are a favorite gift for young children. From the collection of Phoebe Brand. Photo by Susan Davis.

tions and page breaks, and a video that turns Peter Rabbit into a Christian preacher who sings songs about God and Jesus—along with singing animated vegetables.)

Even a quick walk through a store devoted to babies and children shows that, with the possible exception of teddy bears, rabbits are by far the most popular animal for goods manufactured for young humans. All of these items depict rabbits as chubby, sweet and childlike, and are obviously created to appeal not just to babies and children, but to grown-ups, and especially women, who are often the primary decision-makers about their young children's room decorations and toys. As such, these animal images are both feminized (in that they appear gentle, sweet and quiet) and domesticated (in that they are clothed or otherwise made to look like human babies), thus obscuring the real nature of both domestic and wild rabbits.

Feminine Collectibles

Women may be drawn to rabbit items for their young children, but they are also drawn to a whole category of adult rabbit items for themselves: so-called "feminine collectibles." A number of lines of china figurines, for instance, feature little bunnies. Hummel figurines often depict chubby little rabbits (both wild and domestic) in the company of small children. One example is "Good Hunting," manufactured around 1955, which features a little boy with a rifle and binoculars, clearly looking for something to kill, with a little wild rabbit sitting up on his haunches, staring up at the boy. This figurine manages to romanticize—even to make adorable—the image of a boy pondering the shooting of a wild rabbit. The "Sensitive Hunter" also features a young boy—again with a rifle—charmingly confronting a little wild rabbit with cartoonishly oversized ears, who, again, is sitting up to look at him. Yet Hummel also has manufactured a "My Best Friend" figurine that features a little boy holding a domestic rabbit.

To its credit, Hummel has manufactured some figurines that actually look like real rabbits—including one of a jackrabbit, with the proper lean body shape and coloring, and one of a mother rabbit and baby, which likewise has the appropriate coloring and body type for what looks like a wild European rabbit. And most of the company's domestic rabbits remain blessedly free of clothes. Three other popular collectible brands, however (Blushing Bunnies, Pendelfin and Patchville Bunnies), brazenly market babyish rabbits in human attire. These are rabbits as children, sleeping in little beds with little blankies, and picnicking, cooking, painting or doing any number of other domestic chores, all within the traditionally female realm. Some of these rabbits do engage in male activities—like riding Harleys or going fishing (both by Pendelfin)—but even these bunnies have the round cheeks, doe eyes and pudgy tummies that are so reminiscent of human infants and toddlers.

Similarly, kitchen items decorated with roly-poly little bunnies, such as potholders, salt and pepper shakers, tea pots, cookie jars, bowls, baking dishes, teacups, bread boxes and cake pans are primarily used (and bought) by women, as are decorative garden items like wind chimes, wind socks and weathervanes. Most bunny clothing—including sweaters, tee shirts, sweatshirts, and aprons—is worn by women. One does not find a parallel association between men's items and rabbits; there are no rabbit hammers, rabbit table saws, rabbit belt grinders or rabbit drills. Nor are there rabbit golf clubs, rabbit fishing poles, rabbit weight sets or rabbit running shoes—unless they're decorated with the Playboy logo.

Contemporary, grown-up rabbit kitsch also embodies a feminine theme we don't find in ancient collectibles: country simplicity. In fact, rabbits are part of a whole genre of "country critters" that decorate household items like weather vanes, oven mitts, wind socks, salt and pepper shakers, creamers, wall hangings and lawn ornaments, all manufactured in the shape—or bedecked with images—of farm animals, including cows, pigs, chickens, ducks, rabbits, sheep, lambs and chicks. Bunny-themed items comprise a large share of these goods; the Peter Rabbit theme is the mother of them all. In *The Case of Peter Rabbit*, Mackey lists dozens of Peter Rabbit items that are made for adults, rather than children, including paper towels, clocks, knitting patterns, place mats, wastebaskets, teas, jams, aprons, coasters, photo albums, notebooks and musical tea pots; all of these would appeal primarily to women. The Web site for "The Bunny Store" (www.thebunnystore.com) sells dressed stuffed bunnies with matching accessories, plaques that say "Welcome" and feature bunnies with red hearts, garden tools with "happy bunnies"—

Figure 4.12. Ornaments like this one make rabbits seem like an asset to gardens, rather than a liability. Photo by Susan Davis.

yes, dressed in human clothes—on the handles, wooden planter boxes with rabbits carved into them, even miniature bunny Adirondack chairs.

Of course, having little bunny statues and plaques in a garden is odd, given the fact that most gardeners consider real rabbits to be pests. But all of these images, with their folksy esthetic, are meant to offer comfort to a largely urbanized population that has had no real contact with real rabbits, cows or pigs. The purchaser of such items may live in a big-city high-rise or a brand-new surburban development, she may surf the Internet to keep track of her stocks, and she may have a minivan rather than a pick-up truck in her garage. She may, in fact, never have milked a cow, touched a tractor engine, slogged through rain-soaked pastures or treated a rabbit for ear mites. But if she can hang a painted wooden bunny on her kitchen wall and use dishtowels with a cow motif, she may feel she is part of a more rural (and hence simpler and more authentic) lifestyle.

This powerful movement toward "country critters" is very much rooted in the historical context of the twentieth century and some rather chilling psychological reactions to the changes it has witnessed. As Laurie Winn Carlson writes in her history of the cow,

With the onset of industry, people began to view animals as "machines," suitable for use and then abandonment. Urbanization distanced people from agricultural and pastoral life. As animals became badly treated, a backlash set in. A romantic vision of animals that were adored for their "loveableness"—such as Black Beauty, Lassie, even Elsie, the Borden milk cow—captured popular imagination.[42]

Bunny kitsch likewise serves to distance us from the reality of the lives of both wild and domestic rabbits. That can seem like an overstatement, of course; we're only talking about rabbit figurines and little signs that say "Bunnies Crossing," after all. But when humans' only contact with a species is with its *representations*, those images become the only source of knowledge about that species, which means that our knowledge base can be very shaky. In *Picturing the Beast*, Stephen Baker notes:

> [M]uch of our understanding of human identity and our thinking about the living animal reflects—and may even be the rather direct result of—the diverse uses to which the concept of the animal is put in popular culture, regardless of how bizarre or banal some of these uses seem. Any understanding of the animal, and of what the animal means to us, will be informed by and inseparable from our knowledge of its cultural representation. Culture shapes our reading of animals just as much as animals shape our reading of culture.[43]

In the case of rabbits, the dominant images produced by the collectibles culture are those associated with women and children. That is, the cute beings depicted in bunny collectibles belong in an idealized, female, domestic realm, in which women, rabbits and children are innocent, sweet, passive and forever frozen in a juvenile state.

The Playboy Years

Outside of the collectibles realm, the strongest—and most bizarre—contemporary association between women and rabbits is found in the Playboy Bunny, a spin-off of Hugh Hefner's fabulously successful magazine *Playboy*. Hefner's original idea had been to start a magazine, aimed at hip, urban men, called "Stag Party," with a buck as its logo. But when he discovered that a magazine called "Stag" already existed, someone suggested "Playboy." The magazine's art director proposed a rabbit logo, playing up on the idea that rabbits like sex. Hefner has since said that he chose the rabbit

> . . . because of the humorous sexual connotation, and because he offered an image that was frisky and playful. I put him in a tuxedo to add the idea of sophistication. There was another editorial consideration, too. Since both *The New Yorker* and *Esquire* use men as their symbols, I felt the rabbit would be distinctive; and the notion of a rabbit dressed up in formal evening attire struck me as charming, amusing and right.[44]

The art director took about half an hour to come up with his design. But what he created was one of the very few "bunny" images aimed at the male psyche and one that resonated deeply with an American male public ready to become more sexy and more urbane.

The logo became so famous so fast that by 1959 a letter with only the rabbit head for an address actually arrived at Playboy's offices. Today that logo bedecks everything from navel studs to luggage, and from lingerie (including Playboy days-of-the-week panties and Playboy G-strings) to martini sets (complete with rabbit-head olive picks), pajamas, lighters, purses, socks, ashtrays, cell phone cases and laptop briefcases. The Playboy rabbit air fresheners, alas, are no longer available.

The Playboy Bunny, however, which was developed as Hefner was getting ready to staff the original Playboy Club in Chicago in 1960, was a distinctly female symbol. Hefner's club was modeled

Figure 4.13. Playboy Bunny. Although the Playboy Bunny seems to be a product of the mid-twentieth-century male imagination, images of women dressed as rabbits date back to ancient times. Reproduced by special permission of *Playboy* magazine. Copyright 1965, 1993. Photo by Pompeo Posar.

after the Gaslight Club, also in Chicago, which had women in Gay Nineties costumes serving drinks. Hefner and his staff originally thought that dressing the women up as Playmates—i.e., in short nightgowns—would work well. Then Ilsa Taurins, who was dating Playboy's promotions director, suggested dressing them up as rabbits. Hefner at first resisted, saying that rabbits were too masculine. But after fiddling with the costume, Taurins came up with something undeniably feminine: a satin bustier with a fluffy tail, high heels, and rabbit ears. The costume draws, remarkably, on ancient hare-women figures like the Saxon moon goddess, the Teutonic moon goddess (Ostara) and the Anglo Saxon moon goddess (Eostre), all of whom were depicted as hares or with hare heads. Yet it also draws on a long line of ancient stories about witches who could transform themselves into hares and rabbits. In all of those stories, of course, the witch is eventually wounded or killed as a result of her crimes, which is to say, man the hunter conquers her.

Two years later, the Playboy costume was perfected by Renee Blot to include a bow tie, shirt cuffs and D-cups made of foam rubber.[45] This couldn't have been a more perfect symbol of a magazine and lifestyle aimed at fulfilling men's fantasies—or of the confused conception of womanhood in the mid-to-late twentieth century. The twenty-five thousand women who became Playboy Bunnies after 1960 were working girls, after all, young women focused on establishing careers. As a step toward that career, they dressed up (or half dressed up) as a creature that was part rabbit and part woman, a creature with an uplifted tail (a sign of sexual excitement in a rabbit), a creature, moreover, that men all over the world found unbearably sexy, no doubt because of its very deeply embedded associations with prey, childish innocence, lust and fertility.

This distorted form of sex appeal often appealed to women as well. Plenty of Playboy Bunnies were proud of themselves and their accomplishments. And plenty of women wanted to be Bunnies even after charges of sexism and exploitation began to arise. After *Show* magazine published Gloria Steinem's account of her undercover stint as a Playboy Bunny, *more* women applied for the Playboy Bunny jobs; when Barbara Walters donned the costume for a "Today" show feature, she told Hugh Downs, on air, that she was secretly pleased the doorman thought she was a real Bunny. This woman-rabbit image, then, had a kind of talismanic appeal that struck a chord even in "modern-day" America.

The last Playboy club closed in 1991. Some Playmates still wear Bunny costumes at special occasions (the first-ever gold lamé bunny costume was created in 1999 for Playmate of the Year Heather Kozar). But in general, the bunny remains a relic of the 1960s, '70s and '80s, when both the sexual revolution and archaic notions of female sexuality (that is, both animalistic and childish, both conquest and trophy) were still in full swing. Candace and Stephen of the Bunny Museum, by the way, don't include any Playboy bunny memorabilia in their collection—it's "outside the bounds of our marriage," Candace says. "And we only collect what's cute."

Deceptive Depictions

In *The Private Life of Rabbits*, Ronald Lockley waxed enthusiastic—even erotic—as he tried to explain just what it was that made rabbits so appealing to humans:

> Some students of human psychology have suggested that the preference for the round baby-like head and fear of the long, pointed mature one with thrusting nose can be traced to an old deep-seated primitive instinct in man. We accept roundness because it is a feminine shape, seductive, receptive, protective, suggestive of the welcoming shelter of the stone-age cave, the open door, the warmth of the womb and the round vaginal entrance through which the child has been expelled into this world of pain, coldness, and fear, and to which it subconsciously longs to return. The long face of lean, hungry man, of savage wold and dog, fox and ferret, is a masculine shape, destructive, often bringing terror and death, as does the pointed head of the long, forward-sliding snake; it may also have a phallic significance in the primitive subconscious, symbolic of the terrifying erotic power of the thrusting male organ, a seed-sower and sword ruling man's future.[46]

That may be one of the more suggestive descriptions written of why humans like the morphology of rabbits. Lockley also describes the female rabbit as "woman" in many places in the book, although he rarely calls the male "man," and he refers to these "women" in almost erotic terms: he notes they can have "sexual satisfaction" and refers to one young doe as "young, ripening Miriam."

Where did he get these ideas? Lockley may have been unconsciously influenced by the long history of associations between women and rabbits—most of which, unfortunately, are negative. Consider this: terms like "dumb bunny," "bunny slope," "snow bunnies" and "ski bunnies" paint both women and rabbits as being dumb and childish. In fact, the term "bunny" is a diminutive of the word "bun," which means "rabbit's tail" and was recorded as another term for "prostitute" as late as 1934 (something Playboy Bunnies in later decades may not have realized).[47] Today "bunny" shows up in the name of Nevada whorehouses almost as frequently as "pussy."

These aren't just coincidental associations. Joan Dunayer, author of *Animal Equality: Language and Liberation*, notes that animal pejoratives typically denigrate the animal used in the expression and the person (usually a woman) to whom it refers.[48] With a few exceptions, all of the above terms refer to women and girls only and imply a number of negative traits, like stupidity, passivity, childishness, shallowness and (passive) sexuality, all of which are also associated with rabbits. In other words, the huge number of expressions linking negative traits in women with a degraded and misunderstood animal—the rabbit—demonstrates not just the disdain for the rabbit, but for the woman as well. Germaine Greer once wrote, in reference to a word that itself links women, their genitals and rabbits, "Part of the modesty about the female genitalia stems from actual distaste. The worst name anyone can be called is cunt."[49]

Anthropologist Edmund Leach suggested that by creating pejoratives from the names of animals (e.g., sow, cow, bitch, dog and chick) humans establish distance between themselves and the animals they regularly abuse.[50] Rabbit phraseology is no exception. The word "bunny" has without question been used as a term of endearment for women and children for centuries; as early as 1606, William Hazlitt wrote "Sweet Peg . . . my honey, my bunny, my duck, my dear."[51] But most terms associated with rabbits are derogatory, including "harebrained" (meaning frivolous or stupid), "rabbity," (meaning small, cowardly or rabbit-like), and "rabbit shouldered" (meaning slumped in the shoulders). The term "rabbit sucker," now obsolete, once had three meanings: a suckling rabbit, a greedy person or a pawnbroker. The verb "to rabbit" means to hunt rabbits, but it also means to crowd together, as in "The common people . . . rabbit together in miserable warrens," noted by the *Sunday Magazine* in 1892. Even the word "rabbit" itself was at one time used as a general expression of contempt; recall William Shakespeare's "Away you whorson upright rabbit, away!"[52]

In her analysis of the history and mythology of the turkey, Karen Davis[53] makes the same claim: when we're determined to do violence to an animal, we must first turn the victim into a despicable "thing" that deserves such treatment (i.e., the animal is stupid or otherwise revolting). In other words, the term "dumb bunny" or, for that matter, "cunt" may, on one level, be a comment about a woman. On a deeper level, it's a comment on a whole species. The result of such slang expressions, however, is a cultural space in which both women and rabbits are belittled, objectified and commodified, and in which rabbits are reduced either to icons of childhood or a very sexual, stupid and derogatory vision of womanhood.

"Going and going and going"

Oddly, despite their many negative associations, rabbits' very broad appeal has made them a popular icon for selling products. Over the past one hundred years, rabbits have been used to advertise a wide range of products, including carrots (Bunny Luv), sweet potatoes (Jack Rabbit), bread (Bunny Bread), macaroni and cheese (Annie's), fertilizer (Rabbit Furtilizer), children's cereal (Trix), chocolate and strawberry milk (NesQuik), Energizer batteries (alleged to keep "going and going and going") and children's software—e.g., Reader Rabbit's advertisements in autumn 2002 featured children in bunny ears and the headline "All thinking caps should come with rabbits' ears." The Nature Company has a rabbit as its logo, as do the Coalition for Consumer Information on Cosmetics and PETA. In 1975, Volkswagon released its "Rabbit"—to replace the poorly selling Beetle. Speed is good in a car, of course, but "rabbit" seemed an

Figure 4.14. Rabbit imagery has long been used to sell a variety of foods for both children and adults. Courtesy the Bunny Museum. Trix Rabbit courtesy of General Mills, Inc. Photo by Margo DeMello.

Figure 4.15. During WWII, the government used rabbit imagery as part of its campaign to stop sexually transmitted diseases among the armed forces. The "Pro Station" shown on this sign was a place where sailors could procure condoms before going "on liberty" in foreign or domestic ports "Dumb bunny" in the text referred to a man who was looking for sex. Library of Congress, Prints and Photographs Division. [Reproduction number LC-USZC4-4256]

odd name, given the very masculine, usually predatory animal names given to most cars in that era, like the Mustang, Jaguar, Barracuda, Cougar, Bronco, Stingray and Falcon.

In June 2002, Subaru also tried to use a rabbit theme to sell its Forester sport utility vehicle, but the advertisement backfired badly. The advertisement, entitled "Out of the Box," featured a mother and daughter "rescuing" a classroom rabbit and liberating it in a forest, the implication being that people who love nature and think independently would like a Forester SUV. Rabbit lovers across the country, however, immediately recognized the rabbit as a domestic breed and jumped on Subaru for promoting the "dumping" of domestic

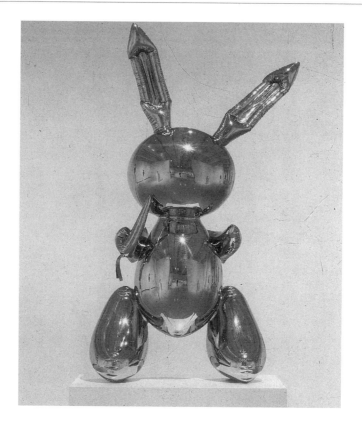

Figure 4.16. "Rabbit," Jeff Koons, 1986. Stainless steel, 41 x 19 x 12 inches. Courtesy The Eli and Edythe L. Broad Collection, Photograph © Douglas M. Parker Studio.

animals in the wild. In what became a comedy of errors, Subaru then claimed that the rabbit had actually been a wild rabbit, even though the likelihood of a classroom having a wild lagomorph is quite low and the rabbit *looked* domestic. In the face of further criticism, Subaru pulled its ad within a week.

◆　◆　◆

But what of the real rabbit? Cultural "texts," whether they are religious beliefs or folktales, children's stories or adult entertainment, reinforce a particular understanding of the rabbit. This, in turn, influences a particular form of treatment. Commercially available rabbity items reflect a worldview that sees rabbits as simple, innocent creatures fit for a child—or lustful, sexy breeding machines. Neither view accurately portrays the real behaviors or lives of real rabbits.

Perhaps the artist Jeff Koons, who has long used everyday objects to comment on popular culture, best summarized the odd position of the rabbit in our culture when he created "Rabbit," an inflatable Easter Bunny cast in stainless steel. The round head and body and stubby limbs make the rabbit look endearing, comforting, familiar and baby-like. The cool steel makes it look mechanical, even robotic. Yet the figure has neither rabbit nor human nor robot features. Instead, the smooth stainless steel simply acts as a mirror, reflecting the viewer and viewer's context from every angle. One person may see "Rabbit" as a cute baby bunny akin to Thumper. Another may see it as a sexual machine. Most people will have no idea how such a figure masks the real nature of real, living rabbits.

Notes

1. Steinem, Gloria, *Outrageous Acts and Everyday Rebellions* (New York: Henry Holt, 1983), p. 39.
2. Marcus, Leonard, in Brown, Margaret Wise, *Goodnight Moon*, with a 50th Anniversary Retrospective (New York: HarperCollins, 1947).
3. Williams, Margery, *The Velveteen Rabbit* (Philadelphia: Running Press, 1981), pp. 10–12.
4. *Ibid.,* p. 24.
5. *Ibid.,* pp. 39–40.
6. Lawson, Robert, *Rabbit Hill* (New York: the Viking Press, 1944), pp. 27–28.
7. *Ibid.,* p. 37.
8. *Ibid.,* p. 107.
9. *Ibid.,* pp. 115–16.
10. *Ibid.,* p. 128.
11. Bettelheim, Bruno, *The Uses of Enchantment: The Meaning and Importance of Fairy Tales* (New York: Vintage, 1989), p. 47.
12. Morris, Desmond, *Dogwatching* (New York: Crown Books, 1986).
13. Milne, A.A., *The House at Pooh Corner* (New York: E.P. Dutton, 1928), p. 73.
14. *Ibid.,* p. 77.
15. Steinbeck, John, *Of Mice and Men* (New York: Penguin, 1993), p. 840.
16. Paramount Studios, 1987.
17. Adams, Richard, *Watership Down* (New York: Avon, 1989), p. 274.
18. *Ottawa Citizen,* August 14, 1998.
19. Updike, John, *Rabbit Run* (Franklin Center, PA: Franklin Library, 1977), p. 3.
20. Pinsker, Sanford, "Restlessness in the 1950s: What Made Rabbit Run?" in Trachtenberg, Stanley (ed.), *New Essays on Rabbit, Run* (New York: Cambridge University Press, 1993).
21. Campbell, Jeff, "John Updike Talks About the Shapes and Subjects of His Fiction," in *Updike's Novels: Thorn Spells a Word* (Wichita Falls, TX: Midwestern State

University Press, 1987), as quoted in Boswell, *John Updike's Rabbit Tetralogy: Mastered Irony in Motion* (Columbia, MO: University of Missouri Press, 2001), p. 279.

22. Updike, *op. cit.*
23. *Ibid.,* p. 19
24. *Ibid.,* p. 27.
25. *Ibid.,* p. 30.
26. *Ibid.,* p. 40.
27. *Ibid.,* p. 19.
28. *Ibid.,* pp. 19–20.
29. *Ibid.,* p. 124.
30. *Ibid.,* p. 37.
31. *Ibid.,* p. 39.
32. *Ibid.,* p. 47.
33. *Ibid.,* 194.
34. Updike, John, *Rabbit at Rest* (New York: Knopf, 1990), p. 257.
35. Updike, *Rabbit At Rest,* p. 309.
36. Updike, *Rabbit, Run,* p. 126.
37. *Ibid.,* p. 260.
38. *Ibid.,* p. 308.
39. *Ibid.,* pp. 11–12.
40. *Ibid.,* p. 207.
41. Mackey, Margaret, *The Case of Peter Rabbit: Changing Conditions of Literature for Children* (New York: Garland Publishing, 1998), pp. xxii and Appendix.
42. Carlson, Laurie Winn, *Cattle: An Informal Social History* (Chicago: Ivan R. Dee Inc., 2001), pp. 28–29.
43. Baker, Stephen, *Picturing the Beast: Animals, Identity and Representation* (Chicago: University of Illinois Press, 2001) p. 4.
44. FAQ on the Playboy logo, http://www.designboom.com/portrait/playboy.html.
45. Playboy.com.
46. Lockley R.M., *The Private Life of Rabbits* (London: Corgi Books, 1954), p. 14.
47. Rowland, Beryl, *Animals with Human Faces: A Guide to Animal Symbolism* (Knoxville: University of Tennessee Press, 1973), p. 134.
48. Dunayer, Joan. "Sexist Words, Speciesist Roots," in Adams, Carol and Josephine Donovan (eds.), *Animals and Women: Feminist Theoretical Explorations* (Durham: Duke University Press, 1995), p. 12.
49. Greer, Germaine, *The Female Eunuch* (New York: Farrar, Straus & Giroux, 1981), p. 39.
50. Leach, Edmund, "Anthropological Aspects of Language: Animal Categories and Verbal Abuse," in Lenneberg, Eric (ed.), *New Directions in the Study of Languages* (Cambridge, MA: MIT Press, 1964).
51. From *Wily Beguilde, a pleasant comedie called 1606,* in Oxford English Dictionary.
52. William Shakespeare, *Henry IV, Part II,* 1596–97.
53. Davis, Karen, *More than a Meal: The Turkey in History, Myth, Ritual and Reality* (New York: Lantern Books, 2001).

Part Three

Hopping Dollars

Rabbits as Revenue

MOST AMERICANS ASSOCIATE rabbits with pet stores, Easter, cute collectibles, children's stories and the Playboy Bunny. But the majority of the world's rabbits are raised for less sentimental reasons—to provide meat for humans and animals, to create soft pelts for clothing, blankets and toys, and to produce scientific data on the safety of drugs, cosmetics and household products, as well as medical information required by researchers.

Regulatory quirks make statistics on rabbit industries notoriously hard to gather, but according to the USDA some 800 million rabbits were slaughtered worldwide for meat in 1998. At least 500,000 were probably killed in the course of scientific research (U.S. researchers alone used 300,000), and another two million were killed by the fur industry worldwide. By contrast, only about five million rabbits were kept as pets.

Put another way, the USDA estimates that the commercial rabbit industry (the industry devoted to using rabbits for meat, fur and experiments) is worth about $25 million, of which $15 million comes from laboratory uses.[1] The pet rabbit industry is more difficult to quantify, largely because of its unregulated nature.

That we see rabbits as both pets and products is unusual, because the species we use as commodities generally are not the same species we keep as companions. In this culture at least, we don't eat pet species like cats, dogs, horses or guinea pigs. The fish that we eat (e.g., cod and salmon) are not the same species that we keep in home aquariums; the birds that we eat (e.g., turkeys and chickens) aren't the same species that we keep in our living rooms. Conversely, most people keep neither the species commonly eaten—like cattle, sheep or hogs—nor common fur-bearing species—like mink, fox and beaver—in the backyard as pets.

We also don't generally sustain deep bonds with the species used in laboratories, although the division here gets murkier. While some laboratories do use cats and dogs in their experiments (about 100,000 annually), the idea of this makes most people uncomfortable, and these numbers have declined by about sixty percent over the last twenty-five years. And while mice and rats—who are involved in about ninety-five percent of all experiments today—are common household pets, they're neither as common nor as cherished as rabbits. In fact, despite the popularity of literary and celluloid mice like Stuart Little and Mickey Mouse, most people are either scared of or disgusted by real mice and rats.

That means that rabbits are the only animals in this culture that we both fancy as pets and kill for a multitude of other purposes. Or, as one writer for *Life* magazine jubilantly (if not tactfully) exclaimed in 1943, "Domestic rabbits are one of the few pets which can be enjoyed dead or alive."[2]

It's hard to imagine the American Kennel Club announcing that puppies are both good to eat and nice companions for children, but such comments remain astoundingly common in the rabbit world. (In its introduction to its *Official Guidebook*, for instance, the American Rabbit Breeders Association claims, "Above all, the domestic rabbit produced commercially in this country is very good and healthful to eat. Rabbits also teach children animal husbandry, and delight them as cuddly pets."[3]) This cultural blurring may be partly due to the fact that so many breeders have to raise rabbits for many different markets in order to make any profit. According to one 1998 ARBA survey, 66.5 percent of all rabbit breeders raise rabbits for the pet market and 86.5 percent of breeders raise rabbits for meat, suggesting a degree of overlap that just can't be found in any other breeding industry.

As such, a considerable gap exists between, on the one hand, our understanding of rabbits as pets or pop culture icons, and, on the other hand, our understanding of the world that uses rabbits as products. This is partly because few government agencies and private animal welfare organizations have paid much attention to how commercial rabbits are treated—with the exception of those animal rights groups that have addressed the plight of lab rabbits. It's also because most people who like rabbits generally don't like to hear— or think—about what happens to them in processing plants, laboratories or even pet stores. This is an understandable reaction. Most people cringe at the details of how pigs and cattle are slaughtered or how mice fare in experiments—and those species aren't nearly as beloved as rabbits. The result of this widespread ignorance, however, is that rabbits are treated in ways that most people, oddly enough, would find unacceptable in most other species, even species with whom we have a much more utilitarian relationship. Indeed, how rabbits live and how rabbits die in commercial industries is shocking, sad, and badly in need of reform.

Notes

1. United States Department of Agriculture, "Rabbit Calicivirus Disease, Iowa, April 2000 Impact Worksheet," http://www.aphis.usda.gov/vs/ceah/cei/rabbitcal.htm.
2. "Rabbits: Raising Them for Meat Is Now Helpful Patriotic Hobby," *Life*, January 4, 1943.
3. American Rabbit Breeder's Association Official Guidebook.

5. "Why Not Rabbit For Dinner?"[1]

The Rabbit Meat Industry

———•-•-•———

I hear a sudden cry of pain!
There is a rabbit in a snare:
Now I hear the cry again,
But I cannot tell from where . . .
Little one! Oh, little one!
I am searching everywhere.

James Stephens, from "The Snare"

A FEW HUNDRED feet from Clyde Marsh's trailer in Hollister, California, three hundred rabbits are bunched together under an open-sided shed. The rabbits live—temporarily—in four rows of hanging, rusty metal cages. Eight to ten rabbits are crowded in each cage; the tops of one row are covered with rabbit pelts, plus empty feed bags, white plastic buckets and other tools and debris.

The rabbits are mostly New Zealand Whites, nine to ten weeks old and about four to six pounds in weight—the perfect size for being slaughtered and sold as "fryers." From across the yard, this crowd of youngsters looks like one big mass of wriggling young rabbit activity. Upright ears flap back and forth as the rabbits take in the sounds of their surroundings; delicate heads poke up into the air with curiosity; bright pink eyes dart back and forth and slender legs dance as the rabbits, just in from a local breeder, explore their new (albeit cramped) quarters. But look at this crowd more closely and

229

the individual rabbits come into focus. One hops about the cage, nudging his mates, as if he wants to play. One sits up on his back legs to look at passersby—ears cocked forward as if to say, "Who are you and what have you got for me?" Another sits hunched in a corner, clearly ill, frightened or depressed. Still another looks out at visitors with a squinted, leery eye, the expression—for those who know rabbits, or any animal for that matter—of a being that is expecting the worst.

Marsh's establishment is the second-largest rabbit meat processing facility in California, where more rabbit meat is produced than in any other state in this country. As such, you might expect something fairly sizeable or modern. In fact, although he slaughters about 1,200 rabbits a week, Marsh's facility is small and rather ramshackle. No sign advertises the business out front; the only feature by which visitors can identify the place is the upended garbage cans marked "inedible" by the dirt driveway in front. The large backyard is littered with objects: several large, open carts for transporting the rabbits from the shed into the slaughter room, an old boom box, a broken-down bicycle, some cast-off tires. An abandoned chicken coop sits off to one side. On the cold, rainy spring day when Susan visited in 2002, the whole property seemed slipshod, neglected and depressing.

The slaughter room itself measures only about fifteen feet by twenty feet and lies on the first floor of a two-story stucco house owned by Marsh's landlord. (Marsh himself lives in a dirty trailer in the back yard.) The slaughter room, with its cement floors, stainless steel counter, gambrel hooks and giant, stainless steel "kill tank" (where the dead rabbits are thrown into cold water before being eviscerated), feels ruthlessly cold and clean; the unmistakable smell of raw meat stains the atmosphere.

Marsh has been in the rabbit slaughtering business for almost fifty years, since the days when California was the center of the industry and huge rabbitries and processing plants could be found all over the state. Today the rabbit meat industry is surviving, but hardly thriving, and Marsh's establishment, though somewhat dilapidated, is representative of many rabbit meat processors in this country. That is, it's small, it's in a rural location and it's a one-man, or sometimes a few-men, operation. Most rabbit breeders—or "rabbit growers," as the industry calls them—are also small-scale operations, with fewer than one hundred breeding females, called does, in their barns. Both groups tend to go in and out of business at a rapid rate; one common refrain in the rabbit industry is that at any given time, "one-third of the people are getting into the business, one-third are in it and one-third are getting out." Nor are the rabbit growers and processors well organized, in part because they are so far flung. The American Rabbit Breeders Association (ARBA) primarily represents show and pet breeders today; Pat Lamar, founder of a fledgling organization called the Professional Rabbit Meat Association (PRMA), readily admits that her group represents only a handful of the country's growers and processors.

As such, exact statistics on the growth or current status of the rabbit meat industry are hard to find. According to the USDA, federally inspected U.S. rabbit farmers—just a fraction of the total rabbit farmers in this country—sell about 300,000 rabbits for meat annually. The Office of International Affairs of the National Academies (this office is now called the Policy and Global Affairs Division of the NA) reports that 8.5 million rabbits are raised and slaughtered each year in the United States for meat.[2] Other sources note that the United States produced about 35,000 metric tons of rabbit meat in 1990 and 1999.[3] These figures sound high, but the United States plays a relatively minor role in the international rabbit meat scene. The USDA estimates that some 800 million rabbits were slaughtered worldwide in 1998, producing about 1 million metric tons of rabbit meat. Of that total, China and some European countries, especially Italy and France, contributed the bulk of the rabbit meat, with China producing about thirty-one percent of the world total.[4] (For 1990, the United Nations Food and Agriculture Organization [FAO] estimates that Italy produced 300,000 tons of rabbit meat, France produced 50,000 tons and China produced 120,000 tons.)

Current production figures in the United States also pale in comparison to those of earlier days. Americans had been eating wild rabbit since colonial days, but the idea of raising domestic rabbits for meat didn't become popular until the early twentieth century, with the so-called "Belgian Hare boom"—which ended rather abruptly in the early years of the century, as a market for domestic rabbit meat was not yet firmly established and the buy-back schemes fell apart.

This "boom and bust" cycle has characterized the rabbit meat industry ever since. Time after time, rabbit breeders have claimed that rabbits, and especially certain breeds of rabbits, would bring riches to whoever bred them for meat, for four primary reasons. First, the meat is high in protein and low in fat, and, according to some, tastes good. Second, establishing a small rabbitry takes relatively little money and relatively little space. Third, because the United States Department of Agriculture classifies rabbits as "multi-use animals" rather than "livestock," a backyard grower is less likely to be restricted by the kind of zoning regulations that forbid chickens, sheep or, say, beef cattle in suburban or urban backyards. And fourth, because rabbits multiply and grow so quickly, an investment in several bucks and does can bring profits—albeit modest profits—relatively quickly. Rabbit breeders typically estimate that a ten-pound doe can produce ten to thirty times her weight in meat in just one year, depending on how many litters she has. That is, as induced ovulators with short gestations, female rabbits can be bred at almost any time, and can create up to forty kits per year, all of whom will be ready to be slaughtered in just nine or ten weeks.

The next wave of interest in rabbit meat began during and just after World War I, when the government urged citizens to grow their own vegetables and raise their own meat.[5] A number of rabbit breeders came out with books during this time, all of which advocated rabbit raising as a backyard industry and described both the breeds available and the husbandry required for a successful business. F.L. Washburn, author of the 1920 *The Rabbit Book*, actually ridiculed the Belgian Hare craze, but went on to promise rabbit growers a doubling, tripling or even quadrupling of their investment if they raised other breeds at home and then sold the meat. He promised readers that they would earn five times their initial investment if they went on to sell breeding stock.[6] "The fecundity of both wild and domestic varieties is almost incredible," he wrote. "The author has obtained from a Gray Flemish doe forty-nine pounds of meat (young rabbits) in six months; and the claim is made that 200 pounds of meat a year may be obtained from the progeny of one animal."[7]

Only four years later, Marcellus Meek, a prominent rabbit breeder and very prolific rabbit book writer (he produced at least ten books on rabbit production and cooking in the first half of the century) claimed that demand could more than meet this potential for supply. "It is estimated that the market trade of Los Angeles and adjacent cities consumes about 13,000 rabbit 'fryers,' 3 to 4 pounds in weight, weekly during the summer months and perhaps a third more in winter," he wrote. "In the vicinity of Pomona, Cal., some 5,000 rabbit fryers are marketed weekly." Total consumption of "fryers" in the Los Angeles area alone, he claimed, had risen from 200,000 in 1918 to more than one million in 1923. "Rabbit raising, or more properly, rabbit 'farming,' is fast coming to the front as one of the dependable money crops to small ranchers in the West and particularly in the Los Angeles district of Southern California," he continued. "No other farm animal produces nutritious, palatable meat so cheaply as the domesticated rabbit."[8]

The rabbit market truly peaked during World War II, when beef shortages sent many consumers scurrying in search of other forms of protein. Numerous magazine articles encouraged their readers to start backyard rabbitries; in 1943, *Life* magazine exhorted its readers to breed these "friendly and decorative" creatures, because "With the U.S. meat supply for home consumption dwindling, rabbit-raising now becomes a patriotic hobby."[9] Many rabbit processors began selling meat to the U.S. Army for military rations overseas. The U.S. government's Food for Freedom campaign, which was part of the 4-H program, even urged children to begin backyard rabbitries because commercial rabbitries couldn't keep up with the civilian or military demand for rabbit meat.

Figure 5.1. The U.S. government exhorted citizens to raise rabbits to bolster meat supplies during WWII. Wildlife Leaflet #218, Fish & Wildlife Services, Courtesy USDA National Wildlife Research Center.

The National Academy of Sciences estimates that 24 million rabbits were slaughtered for meat in 1944 (versus about 8.5 million annually now).[10] Much of that industry, again, was centered in Southern California, as the climate there is so well suited to raising rabbits. Writing in 1947, Meek boasted that between 1940 and 1944, the rabbit meat industry in Los Angeles County alone grew from a $1,308,750 business to a $5,898,224 business, bringing its revenues surprisingly close to the $7,681,562 poultry industry that year. Meek was so sure of the potential profits in rabbit meat that he suggested that "depression-shy" heads of families start backyard rabbitries to provide both food for the home table and extra income for the house-

RECIPES FOR COOKING
DOMESTIC
RABBIT
MEAT

WILDLIFE LEAFLET 240
FISH AND WILDLIFE SERVICE
U.S. DEPARTMENT OF THE INTERIOR

Figure 5.2. This booklet positioned rabbit meat as being central to the American dinner table and family during WWII. Wildlife Leaflet #240, Fish & Wildlife Services, Courtesy USDA National Wildlife Research Center.

hold. "Since Bunny can help mightily to buy the bungalow in the country later on," he wrote, "[the rabbit business] is a good start toward that economic independence of which Henry Ford has said, 'no unemployment insurance can be compared with an alliance between a man and piece of land.' "[11] (This theme is picked up in Steinbeck's *Of Mice and Men,* as Lennie and George's dream of self-sufficiency revolves, in part, around raising meat rabbits.)

Throughout the 1950s and '60s, rabbit meat production declined again, as other meat sources became available (although during this period Pel-Freez, currently the largest rabbit meat producer in the country, became the first company to sell frozen rabbit meat). European production of rabbit meat had always outstripped

Figure 5.3. Sugar is a Californian, which is a common meat breed. Photo by Ken Mark.

American production, as Europeans are more accustomed to this meat, perhaps due to their longer history of hunting and raising the animals. But during the 1960s and '70s, European production rose still further, as some rabbit growers began experimenting with "intensive production" systems, which were much like the nascent "factory farms" for cows, chickens and pigs here in the United States, with their emphasis on producing more meat in less space and with lower labor costs.

Under the European system, breeders experimented with housing thousands of rabbits together (sometimes as many as ten thousand does, as is currently done in Hungary), artificially inseminating them to obtain more pregnancies, using light and hormone treatments to increase fertilization and sperm production and weaning the kits early so that does could be bred more times in one year. While many rabbitries throughout Europe continued to use fairly traditional rabbit-raising techniques, the new system boosted production rates by nearly one hundred percent in some cases. Today, some European producers are now getting fifty to sixty "fryers" per doe per year versus the thirty to thirty-five "fryers" American does produce.[12]

Such techniques have never really taken off in the States, in part because "it requires so much more labor to tend establishments with 1,000 or 2,000 does," says Dr. James McNitt, a rabbit production specialist in the Small Farm Family Resource Development Center of Southern University in Baton Rouge. Instead, most rabbit growers in this country are fairly small operations, with less than a hundred does and just a few workers—often family members—who tend the animals. Still, modern breeding philosophies and techniques do come into play. Most growers raise New Zealand Whites—the large, white breed with pink eyes—because that particular breed produces so much meat, although Californians, and, less commonly, Satins, Rexes and Flemish Giants, are also bred for meat. Most growers also breed very carefully to create meat rabbits that "throw" big litters, nurture them well or create offspring that produce large, meaty carcasses. A number of breeders have also experimented with new strains, like the "B-10" (a cross between a Giant Chinchilla and a New Zealand White) and the "Altex" (a cross between a Flemish Giant, Champagne d'argent and Californian).

"Buy-back schemes" such as those that characterized the Belgian Hare period still seem to run rampant—even in the fall of 2002, breeders on one rabbit meat email list were complaining about companies that offered to sell them foundation stock at high prices and "buy back" the young, but never shipped the rabbits or never actually bought back the "fryers." As one breeder noted,

> You have got to be very careful about deals like this. I cant [sic] tell you how many people call here and have been scammed. They buy the breeding stock (and most the time they are not what they are suppose to be). Then they start producing babies and the person is looooong gone. Then they are stuck sitting on hundreds of fryers with no place to go. I am not trying to say anything bad about whoever is

selling these, but just be careful. Most of these growers have contracts and still get stuck with the animals.[13]

Today, the market for rabbit meat is holding steady at a not-great rate. Ironically, much of the domestic consumption of rabbit meat occurs in high-end restaurants, including such prestigious establishments as the French Laundry in Yountville, California, the Brasserie in San Francisco and the Rainbow Room and the Gramercy Tavern in New York City. Rabbit meat, in other words, has gone from being a food the masses eat when times are tough to a food of the elite that costs three times as much as chicken on some menus.[14] Some demand also is coming from ethnic communities, especially in urban areas.

There are a number of reasons why the market in the United States hasn't taken off the way rabbit meat proponents want it to. The first reason is what chefs and breeders call, with disparagement, the "Easter Bunny syndrome" or the "Peter Rabbit syndrome." That is, most people in this country are so fond of rabbits (or the idea of them) that they don't want to eat them, especially as a "slab on a plate," Chef Paul Bertolli, formerly of Chez Panisse in Berkeley, told the *Wall Street Journal* in 1996.[15] To get around that, some chefs have begun disguising rabbit meat in other dishes, including ravioli, stews, lasagna, pot pies, corn enchiladas and sausages. One New York establishment even came up with an ingenious meal of tiny carrot gnocchi in a rabbit sauce.[16] Still, Jacques Pepin, who likes to cook with rabbit, declared in that same *Wall Street Journal* article that he'd never *skin* a rabbit on his show because "I would go to jail or be assassinated by some league or another."[17] Presumably, his audience wouldn't much want to watch him skin a hog, cow or lamb on his show either, but they wouldn't be considered overly sentimental for feeling that way.

There may also be a problem with nomenclature, in that rabbit meat is still called "rabbit meat," unlike cow meat ("beef"), pig meat ("pork"), calf meat ("veal") and even deer meat ("venison"). "People don't look at rabbits as food," notes Richard Parsons, of the USDA/AMS Poultry Market News Branch. "They look at them as sort of bunnies. The fact that they have the same name as the live animal is a major stumbling block that hasn't been addressed by the industry." Marketing the rabbit whole—rather than cut up—may also be a detriment to sales, as consumers cringe at the sight of a rabbit carcass in the case. This is nothing new. As early as 1826, William Hazlitt claimed that "we should . . . not leave the form (of food animals) standing to reproach us with our gluttony and cruelty. I hate to see a rabbit trussed, or a hare brought to the table in the form which it occupied while living."[18] Nearly 100 years later, in 1919, Farrington noted, "The appearance of a dressed rabbit sometimes prejudices people against it when they see it for the first time. . . . [I]t often pays to cut the rabbit into smaller pieces before delivering it to customers."[19] As recently as the summer of 2002, James McNitt also told us that "People just don't buy whole rabbits. But de-boning increases the labor costs at the plant."

The fact that USDA inspection is only voluntary in the rabbit meat industry has also been a detriment to its sales. Although all commercial processors are subject to state laws and inspections, USDA certification is currently on a volunteer basis. For most rabbit processors, the cost of a voluntary inspection is too high to be profitable (although other processors have noted that if the cost of being inspected several times a year is spread out over a year's worth of slaughtered rabbits, it can amount to only a few cents per carcass). Several efforts to pass legislation requiring government-paid USDA inspections (as are required in all other meat industries) have failed. Some processors have noted that a seal of USDA approval might make rabbit meat in general more marketable, because the product would be deemed safer. Other processors have claimed they'd go out of business if they had to re-tool their facilities to meet the standards. Still another hurdle has been the United States' need to maintain good trade relations with China, which exports massive amounts of rabbit meat to this country, and mandatory U.S. inspections would prohibit Chinese imports.

Some American rabbit meat advocates wouldn't mind if Chinese rabbit was banned, since it's cheap and threatens the domestic trade.

"If you look at the product, though, it's a disgrace," says Jennifer Thorn, a nutritionist with the University of Maryland Cooperative Extension Service, who worked on rabbit marketing issues in the 1990s. "The Chinese are selling frozen, whole rabbits, with a high proportion of bone to muscle. It's disgusting. It's not even wrapped in standard meat packaging; it's just in plastic cling wrap." The European Union banned the import of Chinese rabbit meat in February 2002, because the country had instituted no controls on the use of veterinary drugs and other contaminants. Some people also worry that Chinese rabbit meat was the original source of rabbit hemorrhagic disease (RHD) in the United States and that continuing to import it threatens all domestic rabbits here.

Thorn helped a cooperative of rabbit growers produce a USDA-inspected product during the 1990s. She says that one of the biggest problems is maintaining a supply of rabbit meat that is steady enough to meet the demand. (Traditionally, rabbit supplies drop off during the summer, because heat affects rabbits' ability to conceive.) "We were distributing to five major supermarket chains here in the Southeast," she says, "and we were distributing a high-quality, fresh, vacuum-packed product. But it was really hard to get a supply of live rabbits to meet the demands. It's easier if you're doing frozen, because you can stockpile against supply shortages and still meet your customers' demands."

At the time we were writing this book, a new cooperative of some 1,500 rabbit growers was just about to launch. Called the United Rabbit Growers, the cooperative, led by Eugene Sadler, who runs a large rabbitry (three thousand does) in Arkansas, planned to buy and run a processing plant that would sell whole and cut-up rabbit meat, as well as rabbit meat hot dogs, deli meats, hamburgers and microwaveable dinners. "I'm hoping this operation will let growers get a halfway decent price for their rabbits," Sandler said, "that they'll get $7.00 or $15.00 per head, instead of the $4.00 or $5.00 they currently get."

One way that growers and processors ensure a more steady income is by also selling live or frozen rabbits to zoos and to people who keep reptiles. "I sell them any way I can," says Bobby Martin, a processor in Mississippi, "live or dead, fresh or frozen." One processor in Florida sells as many three hundred rabbits to the "reptile/cat/alligators" market per week, and because she sells them frozen and whole, she said on one recent PRMA online chat, "It's less work." (Some zoos also take donations of live rabbits from breeders who have too many or from laboratories ready to "retire" their lab rabbits.) Many processors sell rabbit by-products, including blood, brains, spleens, bladders, aortas, lungs, ovaries and testicles for use in medical products and procedures. (Pel-Freez, the country's largest rabbit meat producer, is also a major supplier of rabbit-derived medical products.) Rabbit eyes can be sold to medical schools, because rabbit eyes and human eyes are so similar, and some processors still sell rabbit feet as lucky charms, as well. Others sell rabbits to people who feed their dogs the BARF (or "bones and raw food") diet instead of commercial dog food. Some meat breeders sell excess rabbits as pets. In 1990, a slaughterhouse scheduled to open in Clinton, Oklahoma even planned to sell recordings "made of squeals emitted by the rabbits as they are slaughtered" to hunters, so as to better attract predator animals.[20] The Federal Bureau of Investigation also used the screams of rabbits being slaughtered to unnerve both Panamanian dictator Manuel Noriega and the Branch Davidians at Waco.[21]

In earlier decades, many Americans—especially rural Americans—understood how rabbits were raised and slaughtered, because many more Americans were eating rabbit. Today, however, the workings of the rabbit meat industry are hidden from public consciousness, in part because the industry is small here in the United States and in part because no animal welfare group has ever investigated—much less publicized—the conditions under which rabbits are raised and slaughtered for meat. Our own year-long investigation into the modern rabbit meat industry found that it combines some of the worst aspects of both intensive production (i.e., an emphasis on production at the expense of animal welfare) and small farming (i.e., a lack of legislative or public oversight).

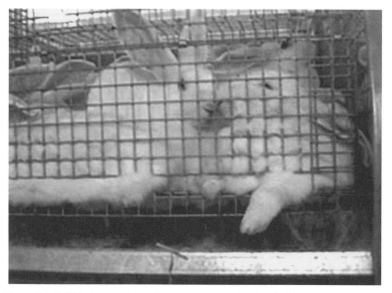

Figure 5.4. Rabbits in a cage in a German meat production facility. Courtesy Alexander Farkas.

Growing Conditions

The life of a meat rabbit, though short, is not easy. Baby rabbits, also called kits, are often weaned early (at four weeks, rather than the six, eight or even more weeks that are standard without forced weaning), so that their mother can be bred again quickly. At that point, the kits are considered "fryers" (or rabbits that, within a few weeks, will be slaughtered and sold as "fryers"). Rabbit breeders readily admit that such forced early weaning can create "weaning shock," a condition marked by a failure to gain weight, or even loss of weight. The "weaning process can be quite stressful for the 'fryers,'" the Web site for the Cornell Bunny Barn in Saskatchewan notes, "and can result in conditions like enteritis and pneumonia if the animals aren't monitored."[22]

Typically, American breeders keep half a dozen of these young rabbits together in a cage that is about twenty-four inches by thirty inches, a size that seems impossibly small, given the very high activity levels of young rabbits. Does with babies are also kept in cages of this size. Some rabbits, however, are kept in much smaller cages, especially in Europe. Photos of meat rabbits from one German facility show rabbits crammed so tightly into cages that their legs are hanging out through the wires. In intensive rabbit production facilities in France, a female breeder may be put in a cage that's only twelve inches wide by twenty inches long and twelve inches high. A buck may be in a cage that is only slightly wider.

The FAO notes that females without young can be kept together as long as they have half a square meter of space each. Oddly, this amount of space equals that of the *litter box* or *nesting box* (a box in which a female keeps her young) recommended for hutches in a 1920 text on rabbit keeping.[23] The actual hutch recommended for each rabbit in that text was six feet by two feet, or even a small yard or courtyard—measurements that seem huge by today's standards but clearly give the rabbits room to engage in some natural behaviors, like hopping or stretching out. Even as late as 1968, George Templeton, a very prominent breeder and rabbit meat expert, recommended hutches as long as six feet for some of the giant breeds. Yet in the 1997 book *Rabbit Production* (which is a later edition of Templeton's original *Domestic Rabbit Production*), McNitt recommends that rabbits be housed in a cage that is at most thirty inches deep and thirty-six inches wide.[24]

Breeding females and breeding males live in solitary cages. This is practical, as unaltered rabbits can fight viciously when they feel their space is being invaded, and breeders want to be able to control with whom each rabbit mates and when. But it's hardly natural. European rabbits, as we have seen, are highly social animals and prefer the company of other rabbits for comfort, keeping watch and mutual grooming. Research on stress in meat rabbits is scarce. However, the problems of bored or frustrated rabbits gnawing on cage wires, pulling out their fur and biting other rabbits' tails and ears is frequently mentioned in literature on laboratory rabbits, who live in similarly confined conditions.

Caging rabbits has been shown to create other health problems, as well. The cramped quarters can cause mobility problems, even spine deformation. Crowding too many rabbits into a small area (as occurs in intensive production systems), facilitates the spread of disease; in other farmed species, such crowding has been associated with the contamination of meat and illness in consumers. The wire mesh on which most commercial rabbits are kept is also notorious for causing "sore hocks," a condition marked by chafed or infected hind legs, and breaking nails, which can lead to infections.

Daniel Rolke, who did an undercover investigation of the rabbit farming industry in Sweden, says that the Swedish rabbit farmers he interviewed readily told him that their animals often broke their legs in their cages and were simply left injured until they were slaughtered. "What we found was horrible," Rolke says, "animals with lots of bite injuries, large numbers of animals put together in small areas just before slaughter that were in really bad condition." Marion Selig, who works with People for Animal Rights in Germany, notes that in commercial breeding establishments, rabbits are kept in barns "not unlike the battery cages of laying hens," and that "[T]here are a lot of health problems at the rabbit farms: damage of paws because of the metal or plastic grating. . . . Because of the lack of space, they get damage of the spine. Also cannibalism is a problem. A high percentage dies of infectious diseases." One former USDA inspector (now an investigator with In Defense of Animals) also told us that on one of his visits to a breeding facility in Missouri he found:

> . . . hundreds of rabbits in cages with no food or water and beneath a tin shelter. When I confronted [the owner] about that situation, he explained that those were slaughter rabbits. I advised that the Animal Welfare Act did not allow for such a distinction and that all rabbits needed to have minimum requirements as specified in the regulations. To make matters worse for the rabbits there were several large dogs that were wandering around near the cages and the poor rabbits were terrified especially when the dogs started sniffing around the cages. On my second visit to the facility the owner got so irritated at me that he pulled a rifle on me and told me to get off of his property.

Figure 5.5. This German rabbitry practices intensive production by keeping the animals crowded together in small cages. Courtesy Alexander Farkas.

It's not just animal rights activists who have noted the problems with the rabbit meat industry. The Food and Agriculture Organization, which advocates rabbit as a food source, notes that the stress of cramped quarters, especially in warehouse situations where hundreds or thousands of cages full of rabbits are found, can contribute to ill health, including diarrhea and respiratory illnesses. "The mere fact of raising five or six rabbits together in a cage one-third of a square meter in a room with 100 or 1,000 other cages acts as a sort of sound board to amplify (other stressors that affect rabbit health)," the organization notes in its handbook to rabbit meat production.[25] Those stressors, the FAO writes, can include transportation ("especially during the postweaning period"), being put in a cage (as happens when the babies are weaned) and unfamiliar noises.[26]

The very nature of the rabbit meat industry means that the animals will be exposed to all those stressors. Because of the paucity of rabbit slaughtering plants in this country (as of 2002 there were only about fifty-five in the entire country), most growers have to ship their rabbits, via truck, long distances to have them processed. Most rabbits don't like traveling in vehicles; they tremble, breathe rapidly and "freeze" even on short rides in relatively quiet cars. But many young rabbits end up traveling many hundreds of miles before they're slaughtered. Marsh's rabbits, for instance, come from all over California and Oregon, a small processor in Arizona brings in rabbits from New Mexico and Colorado and Pel-Freez gets them from all over the country. Often those rabbits travel in crates that are only six inches high (which isn't even enough room for a young New Zealander to stand on all fours) or eleven inches high (which isn't enough for a rabbit to keep its head up) and that are first packed with as many as eight other rabbits, and then stacked on the bed of a pickup truck or inside a tractor trailer truck with hundreds of other crates, also filled with young, frightened rabbits.

The problem of rabbits either dying from stress and injury or experiencing "shrinkage" (a reduction in live weight due to loss of fluid) is well known in the industry—as it is also known in the cattle and hog industries. But the problem is compounded with rabbits because even the breeders note that they tend to "pile up" in the crates, which can cause a catastrophic buildup of heat in hot weather. One way that some "runners" deal with this situation is to squirt water all over the animals with a garden hose—a tactic that no doubt brings down their body temperature, but probably also terrifies them, as most rabbits don't like to get wet. As one "runner" noted in an online chat of the Professional Rabbit Meat Association, "We try not to pack as tightly in the summer. But need [sic] to make the runs pay. There is not a lot of profits in small loads."[27]

Just what the young rabbits do all day—before they're crammed onto trucks, that is—is something of a mystery. Rabbits play by running and hurling themselves through the air or by picking up small objects and tossing them about. Clearly, cage-restrained meat rabbits don't move around much. Nor do they get many toys with which to stave off boredom. When one breeder on the meatrabbits@yahoogroups.com listserve noted that she sometimes gives her bunnies toilet paper rolls to play with, others expressed great shock at the idea that rabbits played at all and worried that the rabbits might eat the cardboard. Still others on the list were surprised to learn that rabbits enjoy chewing on and flinging pinecones and twigs.[28] Yet people who live with house rabbits have known that bunnies like to play with tubes, twigs, and pinecones—and that this is safe—for more than fifteen years.

Giving rabbits these sorts of toys is a simple gesture that can relieve the boredom and stress inherent in living in difficult conditions. But the topic was not raised again over the course of the twelve months we monitored this listserve. Other topics regarding rabbit welfare were also dispensed with in short order. In January, 2003, for instance, several members started joking around about the number of scratches they had gotten on their hands and arms from struggling rabbits. No one suggested the rabbits might be struggling for a reason (or even that the rabbits' nails might be too long). Similarly, when one member asked for advice on dealing with a "nasty"—i.e., biting—rabbit, one breeder suggested, "FRYING PAN POSITIVE CURE!!!!!!!!!!!!!!!!!"[29] Another said she bangs her biting rabbits' noses with a piece of plastic pipe. No one suggested that a biting meat rabbit might simply be protesting the short miserable life created for him.

Group Living

A few breeders, especially in Europe, have experimented with what is known as "colony" breeding," in which bucks and does are allowed to live in a large pen together. But many breeders are adamantly against such practices, noting that the does may eat the other does' young, that the bucks may kill the young, that the does may castrate the bucks and that disease—especially coccidiosis—may sweep through a colonized herd faster than it would through a barn full of individual cages.[30] "It's also impossible to keep any records on your breeding lines," Eugene Sadler explained "You have no way of knowing which bucks are throwing which litters and which does are producing in what way."

Other breeders have experimented with just letting the "fryers" live in a large pen rather than a traditional cage. A handful of studies have been done on this alternative, with conflicting results. One found that the "production performance" of rabbits was similar whether the animals are raised in cages or in a "stock pen." Another found that the penned rabbits showed slower growth (which results in a later slaughter time, which means the grower spends more money raising the rabbit) and produced less meat, presumably because they were more active in the pen.[31] Because of this risk, McNitt recommends that "fryers" in a group cage be kept at "a fairly high stocking density" (i.e., several hundred rabbits per "feedlot cage") to keep the animals "from running and playing, which increases energy expenditure and feed requirements."[32]

However, anecdotal evidence suggests that in some instances, especially for home production, group living can work. One writer on the meatrabbits@yahoogroups.com listserve noted that he lets his entire herd "romp" around on an eighty-by-sixty-foot floor, and that "when the dominating male or female is in a terror (the others) just hide out and wait."[33] Another said he groups together adult rabbits that "are long past their prime as breeders, but have been too good and been with me too long for me to be able to eat." He wrote that the rabbits enjoy lying in the sun together, and that they dig very large tunnels, but that not many of their young survive, in part because the openings in the wire around the pen are so large that predators can get at them.

The idea of "retired" rabbits digging and playing and lolling about is appealing; the idea that the "kits" die because of inadequate fencing—which the breeder doesn't seem especially interested in fixing—is not so attractive. Nor is the realization that even in the most "progressive" factory farm conditions, the rabbits are so closely crowded together that they can't get the play and exercise that all young animals need and enjoy, that the requirements of efficient production, in short, are more important than the moral call for treating animals with care and respect.

Slaughtering Methods

Once at the processor, the rabbits live for a few days to a week—often in an open shed like the one at Marsh's establishment, other times in warehouses—before they are slaughtered. The issue of how best to slaughter rabbits is a subject of much informal debate within the rabbit industry itself; the topic comes up over and over on various Internet chats and lists dedicated to meat rabbits. According to the USDA's Humane Slaughter Act, most animals that we eat, including cows, horses, sheep and pigs, have to be stunned—either by gunshot or a blow to the head—before being slaughtered, so as to render them insensitive to pain. Pigs, sheep, horses and cows are generally stunned with an electric shock to the forehead; chickens are shocked in an electrical bath. Because the USDA doesn't classify rabbits as "livestock," they don't fall under the protection of the Humane Slaughter Act. Still, many processors do try to stun the animals before hanging them up and cutting them to drain the blood. Many stun the animals through "cervical dislocation"—or breaking the neck by pulling down on the rabbit's head while simultaneously pulling back on its hindquarters. Most processors who use this technique pride themselves on being able to slaughter one hundred rabbits an hour; one writer claims that stunning rabbits via cervical dislocation is such a "cinch" that a ten-year old boy can do it.[34] Yet according to the American Veterinary Medical Association's Panel on Euthanasia, cervical dislocation is only a humane method of killing (or stunning) for rabbits that are less than one kilogram (2.2 pounds) in weight, because in larger animals the muscles are much thicker, making proper cervical dislocation difficult to do correctly. Rabbits that are sold as "fryers," which is the smallest rabbit available for meat, are typically four and a half to five and a half pounds; "stewers" are six pounds and up and a "roaster" can be more than eight pounds, or four times the weight that the AVMA recommends for cervical dislocation.

"The concept of humane death centers on the idea that an animal shouldn't be in a situation where it is conscious and feeling fear or pain without being able to respond," notes Dr. Bonnie Beaver, a professor in the College of Medicine at Texas A&M University and chair of the AVMA panel. "If a rabbit is larger than one kilogram, it may be strong enough to make it hard to break the neck in the right place. If the neck is broken too low the rabbit will be paralyzed, but very conscious of what's happening." One other complicating factor is the fact that rabbits will sometimes become immobile, or "play dead," when terrified, the report notes, which can be interpreted as loss of consciousness when in fact the animal remains fully awake and conscious. The AVMA report also notes that even when dislocation is performed correctly, the rabbits will remain conscious for about thirteen seconds after the neck is broken—and "rapid exsanguination" (or "bleeding them out")—does not hasten loss of consciousness. Unfortunately, many processors hang the rabbits upside down (by putting large metal hooks through their back legs) and cut the animals' throats (to bleed them out) during that time frame—which means the rabbits may be conscious of those procedures.

Some processors agree that cervical dislocation is inhumane. Dean Goforth, owner of the Blue Chip Farms rabbit processing plant in Fountain Inn, South Carolina, believes that "cervical dislocation is the very most inhumane method of stunning rabbits, because they are often still conscious when you put them up on the chain. You'll have a whole lot of misery in a plant that uses cervical dislocation, because the rabbits will be kicking and screaming while they're hanging on the hooks." Goforth, who raises his own rabbits for slaughter and has one of the largest processing plants in the country, prefers to knock the animals out with piece of iron pipe and then quickly decapitate them.

"I've been processing rabbits for twenty-one years and of the millions of animals I've slaughtered here, I haven't even had a half dozen that didn't stay unconscious," he says. Stunning rabbits by hitting their heads is humane, according to the AVMA, "for neonatal animals with thin craniums," as long as the people administering the blows are properly trained and "aware of its aesthetic implications," which can include (according to processor accounts) gushing blood and eyeballs popping out of the skull. (The meat along the shoulders

A, Steps in skinning rabbits. (From right to left.)

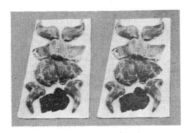

B, Cuts of a rabbit carcass and methods of display for market.

C, Pelts properly placed on shapers, both front legs on one side.

Figure 5.6. Rabbit processors today use the same methods processors used sixty years ago, shown here in a "Food for Freedom" brochure. Wildlife Leaflet #218, Fish & Wildlife Services, Courtesy USDA National Wildlife Research Center.

may also get bruised, which makes it less marketable.) Whether or not ten-week-old New Zealand Whites have thin craniums is "uncertain," Dr. Beaver said. But video footage from Sweden shows a rabbit that was hit over the head still kicking wildly—as opposed to twitching reflexively, which is common—while it is being "bled out."

Other processors use other techniques, including stunning the animals with a non-penetrating captive bolt before hanging them "on the line" to be bled out—a technique that is not accepted as humane by the AVMA—and decapitating the animals, which is the method of choice for Stephen Edwards of Aspen Hill Farms in Michigan. Edwards slaughters about one thousand "B-10" rabbits annually for the local high-end restaurant market in northern Minnesota. He prefers to decapitate his rabbits with a "razor-sharp knife," because it's the fastest and most humane way of doing it.

"Frankly, I hate even doing it that way," he admitted in a rare show of remorse among processors. "But knocking them over the head made me sick to the stomach." He continues to do the processing himself, because it saves him money and saves the rabbits the stress of being transported. The AVMA considers decapitation "conditionally acceptable" for euthanasia, as long as the rabbit is adequately restrained, the blade is very sharp and the person doing the cutting is well trained. The panel notes, however, that the "handling and restraint required to perform this technique may be distressful to animals."

Not all rabbits are slaughtered in processing plants. Plenty of growers butcher their own rabbits for their families and friends, to sell as "custom butchered" meat for human consumption, or as food for snakes and other reptiles—even to feed to their own cats and dogs. Rabbits slaughtered at home can't be sold through the retail market, and such slaughter isn't regulated. As with the professional processors, the slaughtering method of choice among hobbyists varies from breeder to breeder. Some backyard producers shoot their rabbits with pellet guns (or .22s), decapitate them or use "the broom handle method," in which the human puts a broom handle across the rabbit's neck, steps on both ends of the handle, then pulls on the rabbit's flanks, again to break the neck. "You should feel the neck give," one breeder wrote in September 2002, "and yes, overenthusiasm is better than too little, although if the head comes all the way OFF, it solves the throat cutting problem." Despite the gallows humor, however, one new member of the listserve provoked cries of outrage from the veterans when he wrote that he hangs the live rabbits upside down by their feet and then slowly pulls on their heads to break their necks. "If you have ever heard of a machine from the Middle Ages called the 'rack,' that's essentially what you are doing to your hung-up rabbit," protested the same woman who had joked about her broom handle method, "just so you know what's happening on a physiological basis. Add to that the fears engendered by hanging the live rabbit by the feet while conscious and you get what I personally, and many scientifically-inclined articles, would call 'cruelty' for the prolonged fear and pain before death occurs."

Indeed, it would be unfair to portray all breeders as merciless or cruel. A number have posted on various chats and listserves that they "don't have the heart" to knock a rabbit over its head or break its neck—and that they've been heartbroken when a slaughter has gone awry. One man noted that when his neighbor showed him how to hit rabbits over the head while holding them up by their rear legs, "It was terrible. I've never heard such pathetic squealing in all my life. (Didn't seem to bother my neighbor at all, but my wife who was inside the house having no part of the butchering was in tears when I came inside)." That man now uses a .22 rifle, which almost all growers agree makes for a short, merciful death. Another man described what happened when he tried to use a stun gun on a rabbit: "It did not work. The rabbit screamed bloody murder and jumped out of my control and into my arms so I could protect it from whatever that was that attacked it. It was funny kind of because she turned to me for protection, but I will never try it again because of the scream." That man now bonks rabbits over the head with a hatchet.

Still another member expressed dismay at the way hitting a rabbit over the head had failed the first time she tried, using a sawed-off wooden baseball bat. She noted that "blood immediately poured from its ears and mouth, but it was still kicking! It looked like it was still breathing, so I hit it hard again . . . and again . . . and . . . and it was STILL kicking and blowing blood bubbles, making little gurgling and gasping sounds, until I cut the head off."[35] We think it's pretty safe to assume those sounds and movements were not mere "reflexes."

These are gruesome stories and the fact that they come up over and over on this meat rabbit listserve is surely a sign that something is seriously wrong here. Whether they're doing it in their backyards or in a processing plant, many, many people are slaughtering their rabbits in ways that are inhumane and no doubt create suffering. In one particularly horrific 2003 case, a Long Island family was seen on videotape letting their dog attack one live meat rabbit and skinning another one, which was also still alive and screaming in pain. (That rabbit had regained consciousness after being stunned by a blow to the head.) Throughout the video, the family is seen laughing and bantering. The case was difficult to prosecute because rabbit cruelty is not covered by felony cruelty laws (which apply to companion animals, not "meat" animals) or, as we have mentioned, the Humane Slaughter Act. At the time of this writing, authorities were considering charging the family with felony animal fighting.

Life as a Breeder

Female rabbits who are kept as breeders get to live longer than "fryers"—generally about two years—before being killed for home consumption or other meat markets. (On occasion a favorite doe or buck will be kept on as a pet.) But their lives can be just as stressful as those of meat rabbits. Rabbits become fertile at a relatively young age—just four months, on average—and breeding does are usually bred for the first time around that age, although a good twenty-five to thirty percent of does die of pneumonia or other causes after their first or second litter. Those who live are generally "bred back" (i.e., re-bred) anywhere from one to forty days after giving birth, which means they produce six to twelve litters a year.

The optimal period of rest between breedings is a topic of some debate among breeders. In earlier periods, does were allowed to rest at least until after they had naturally "weaned" their young, which meant about eight weeks, or sometimes even later in cold weather.[36] In 1920, Washburn cautioned that six litters a year would be "an exhausting experience" for a doe and that three breedings, or at most four, would be more appropriate.[37] Edward Stahl, who wrote *Chinchilla Rabbits* in 1926, gave the same advice, and recommended weaning at six to eight weeks (versus the current four), as well.[38]

As late as 1968, George Templeton, who ran the USDA's Rabbit Experiment Station in California, noted that four litters a year would create:

> . . . an extremely hard-worked animal, as may be seen by comparing her yearly production with that of other animals. (That is, a 400-pound sow who had two litters of eight pigs would produce 400 pounds of meat, or 100 percent of her weight, while a 1,000-pound cow generally only produces a 400-pound calf in a year, which is just 40 percent of her live weight. But an 11-pound rabbit who weaned 30 four-pound fryers would create 120 pounds of meat, or 1,000 percent of her live weight.)[39]

In the late 1960s, however, researchers began putting their does through ever more intensive breeding schedules. Some re-bred the does as soon as twenty-four hours after they had given birth to a litter. Others chose to breed again seven or fourteen days after birth. In a recent article on welfare considerations in the rabbit meat industry, McNitt claimed that post-partum breeding isn't stressful for the doe because European rabbits in the wild are capable of breeding that often. Yet studies of laboratory rabbits—which, like meat rabbits, are also often New Zealand Whites—have found that the does may be receptive twenty-four hours after giving birth, but become increasingly less receptive after that, until fifty days after birth. Similarly, rabbits in the wild have very distinct breeding seasons. That means that a rabbit giving birth twelve times a year isn't reproducing normally at all.

A number of researchers and organizations have begun to look at the welfare of other species of animals that are slaughtered for meat, and to protest the "factory farm" conditions now endemic to the cow, chicken, sheep and pig industries as being inhumane. Those conditions include quarters so cramped the animals can barely move, very early weaning of young from mothers, force feeding, a lack of social interaction with other species members, mutilations (like de-beaking chickens), an inability to engage in natural behaviors (like rooting in pigs and pecking in chickens), inappropriate use of antibiotics and hormones, and slaughter methods in which the animals are not entirely unconscious before being butchered or boiled. This concern about animal welfare—that is, how the animal fares during raising and processing—has prompted a number of books, articles and investigations into the treatment of the animals, the environmental degradation associated with meat production and the health risks of both unsanitary conditions and drugs, including antibiotics and hormones.

This isn't just bleeding-heart stuff—the suffering of the animals has been evaluated by looking at both behavioral symptoms of stress (like chewing on bars and rocking back and forth) and biochemical measures, including levels of stress hormones and amounts of ammonia in the muscles, as well as changes in brain activity, heart rate and body temperature. These studies have shown that animals who are raised in close quarters and who are unable to exhibit natural behaviors show greater levels of stress than animals who are allowed to live more "natural" lives, and that certain kinds of slaughtering techniques create more stress than other kinds. Temple Grandin, a professor of animal behavior at Colorado State University, has ardently and effectively advocated creating handling equipment and holding conditions that reduce anxiety in animals about to be slaughtered. Her work is so well respected by both animal welfare activists and the beef industry that the National Council of Chain Restaurants and the Food Marketing Institute incorporated her recommendations for humane growing and processing conditions in its Food Industry Animal Welfare Report (FIAWR), released in June 2002. Safeway, Albertson's and Kroger are all adopting the recommendations; McDonald's and Burger King instituted their own humane guidelines, based on Grandin's work, even before the FIAWR came out.

Rabbit meat growers and processors tell anecdotes of animal rights activists burning down barns or "liberating" rabbits into the wild. Yet major animal protection groups, like People for the Ethical Treatment of Animals, the Humane Farming Association and

Compassion in World Farming, have never undertaken organized campaigns against the industry. In fact, despite this culture's adoration of the "bunny," only two animal rights groups have addressed the rabbit meat industry. In the 1980s, Humans Against Rabbit Exploitation (HARE), an offshoot of Trans-Species Unlimited, Inc. (TSU), tried to bring public attention to the plight of meat rabbits. The organization mostly staged protests and did public education; it disintegrated in 1993 after a change in leadership in TSU. In the summer of 2002, a national grocery chain also contacted the Animal Welfare Institute to ask them to develop standards for the "humane farming" of rabbits. Those standards, which included less crowding, having bedding in the cages, and opportunities for natural behaviors, were released the following year.

House Rabbit Society members do sometimes write letters to local restaurants or grocery stores selling rabbit meat, but the organization hasn't advocated for the welfare of such animals while still alive—primarily because many HRS members disapprove of eating rabbit meat entirely, and many others are vegetarian and so oppose the eating of all animals. This issue remains a bone of contention among the leadership. The broader lack of public interest in the rabbit meat industry is more of a puzzle. It may be partly due to the fact that most rabbit growers and rabbit processors run fairly small establishments. Pel-Freez, the largest rabbit processor in the country, slaughtered about 227,000 rabbits in 1998; more typical processors slaughter several thousand a year. Put another way, the total of 8.5 million rabbits slaughtered each year here is fairly dwarfed by the 5 billion other animals (including cows, calves, chickens and pigs) killed for meat annually. So too is the 20 million pounds of rabbit (about 10 million pounds each produced by conventional and backyard processors) versus the 45 *billion* pounds of other species.[40]

Unlike chicken, cattle and sheep growers—who often raise many hundreds or thousands of animals in "intensive confinement" or "factory farms"—most rabbit growers have backyard operations that are typically hidden from the view of the public. Since rabbit meat consumption in this country is also minuscule (the annual per capita consumption of rabbit meat in this country is only .14 of 1 kilogram, versus 8.89 kg in Malta, 5.71 kg in Italy and 2.76 kg in France), most people aren't even aware that a rabbit meat industry exists. In addition, people who really love rabbits as pets generally don't eat them (just as most cat and dog lovers don't eat cats and dogs) and so tend not to be focused on this issue.

The lack of attention to the rabbit meat industry may also be due to the fact that the culture at large doesn't know enough about rabbits to take action. Without understanding that rabbits are intelligent, social and sensitive, consumers may not care that the animals are stressed from living in cramped, crowded (or isolated) conditions—or from being held down to be slammed over the head with a hammer, or having their necks "twisted and crunched" (as breeders say) or from hearing the screams of other rabbits being so dispatched. In 1997, the *Washington Post* quoted a breeder telling chefs that the way to get over their squeamishness about killing baby bunnies was to "remember that they really have no more brains than a chicken. They just have more charisma."[41] While we don't cherish our cattle and chickens for their intelligence, either, significant moves are afoot to spare their suffering in the course of being raised or slaughtered.

"Rabbit Meat Will Feed the World!"[42]

Perhaps the greatest market for rabbit meat now lies in the Third World, where development specialists are seeking small, inexpensive projects that can help villagers become self-sufficient. A number of organizations, including the non-profit Heifer Project, The Peace Corps, CARE and the United Nations, advocate and help set up backyard rabbitries. Those organizations choose the rabbit specifically because it's prolific, has limited space requirements, is able to live in difficult environments and can convert a broad range of foods into high-protein meat. Programs have been started in Mexico, Kenya, Tanzania, the Philippines, Indonesia, Vietnam, Costa Rica and El Salvador, among other countries. In Ghana, the name of the program is "Operation Feed Yourself," and at various times its radio

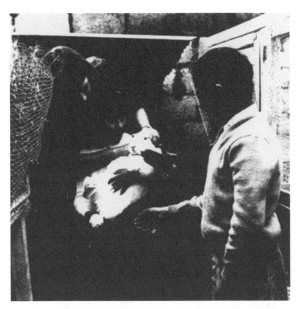

Figure 5.7. Several aid organizations have set up rabbit-growing projects in the Third World, like this Peace Corps venture in the Eucadorian highlands. Reprinted with permission from *Microlivestock: Little-Known Small Animals with a Promising Economic Future*, © 1991 by the National Academy of Sciences. Courtesy of the National Academies Press, Washington, D.C.

jingles have included "Get the bunny money!" and "Grow rabbits, grow children."

Such programs upset rabbit advocates who prefer that no rabbits be eaten at all. Yet as Dr. Susan Smith, a professor of nutrition at the University of Wisconsin-Madison (and an educator with House Rabbit Society) notes, poor people the world over need help feeding themselves. "One challenge faced by lovers of companion rabbits is understanding that we are a fortunate minority," Dr. Smith says. "Those of us living in developed nations have ready access to inexpensive and nutritious foods. Our high income gives us the ability to view an animal as friend instead of food. Like it or not, rabbits have been an ideal solution for those living in resource-poor locations. Rabbits are prolific and grow quickly. They can eat local plants and forage that people can't eat, and convert it into a protein form that malnourished people desperately need."

Figure 5.8. This Heifer Project advertisement features two rabbits with Tanzanian children. Advertisements such as these lure people who otherwise might feel uncomfortable with the idea of killing rabbits for their meat. Courtesy Heifer International, 800-422-0474.

In keeping with the centuries-old associations between women and rabbits, many of those programs are aimed at women. In a UNESCO report on a development program to improve the lives of destitute women in Kenya, rabbit breeding (as well as beekeeping, milk-goat farming and fish breeding) were recommended as suitable occupations for women, due to the "women's poor physical and mental condition."[43] The FAO is also promoting a program to set up rabbit breeding for food security in Mediterranean countries, again focusing on women.[44] According to FAO expert René Branckaert, "Rabbits fit well in household production and can be looked after by women farmers."[45] Similar government or NGO programs specifically targeting women as rabbit producers can be found in Egypt, Papua New Guinea, Uganda and the Himalayas.

While the programs may benefit Third World families, their advertising campaigns exploit First World sentiments with abandon.

Take the 2002 Christmas brochure for Heifer International, which blurs the idea of rabbit-as-pet and rabbit-as-product in an almost mind-boggling way. The headline for the rabbit section reads "Wrapping Paper, Ribbons . . . and Rabbits"—clearly evoking the image of rabbits popping out of a Christmas package. The introductory copy reads, "Your granddaughter is celebrating her very first Christmas. What better way to share the joy you see in the eyes of such a healthy, happy little girl than to give a trio of bunny rabbits to a struggling family in her name?" This sounds like the little girl is giving adorable *pets* to the family, but in fact she would be giving a "low-cost, high-yield gift" that would increase the "protein intake and income" of an impoverished family. The association between children and rabbits effectively disguises the fact that these rabbits are to be killed and eaten.

Even with seductive campaigns like that one, attempts to promote rabbit meat production in the Third World could run into one pretty sizable problem: people's reluctance to eat rabbits. In one FAO study of sixty-four developing countries, thirty percent of the people surveyed said that they could not support rabbit meat production, for social, religious or other reasons.[46] In countries where such taboos are less strong, developing rabbitries could also create a whole different kind of problem: that of feral rabbits. If the historical experience of Europe or Australia anything to teach us, it's that domestic rabbits can easily escape their keepers, overrun the countryside and create whole other categories of problems for their governments.

Most people who love rabbits do not also eat them. Many rabbit lovers believe no one should eat rabbits. Still others believe it is inevitable that humans will eat rabbits—but that the rabbits need to be treated more humanely before they die, just as cows, pigs, sheep and chickens should be treated more humanely. Navigating through the many positions in the animal welfare and animal rights movements to decide how one feels about eating any one species—or any species at all—is a personal journey, one that has confused people who care about animals for hundreds of years, and one that is beyond the scope of this book. But the question of eating rabbits can, at the very least, inspire us to examine our attitudes toward eating any animals. That is, how do we decide which species are all right to eat and which are not? How do we decide that eating cows, sheep and chickens is acceptable (in this culture, at least), but eating dogs, cats and horses is not? How do we decide which animals deserve merciful slaughter and which can be killed any which way?

One might argue that these decisions are based on the animal's intelligence—that cattle, sheep, chickens and rabbits are "dumb," while cats and dogs are not. But the question of whether we have the tools and the understanding to accurately measure nonhuman intelligence, let alone determine which if any animals can safely be considered "dumb," is open to debate. Our decisions could also be based on taste (cows, pigs and rabbits taste good to some, while cats and dogs do not). But taste is culturally defined. We may decide whom to eat based on which animals live outdoors, as livestock (e.g., cattle, sheep and, traditionally, rabbits) and which live indoors, as pets (e.g., cats and dogs). But that's where the categories break down, because rabbits have lived as both pets and livestock, both indoors and outdoors, for many years. To look at it another way, the very page-turning tension in *The Tale of Peter Rabbit* stems from the fact that Peter, like his father, may be caught and turned into a rabbit pie. As readers, we powerfully identify with the bunny and hope he'll escape Farmer McGregor's garden and go safely home. Yet as a culture at large, we seem to believe that it's okay for people not only to eat rabbits, but to treat them inhumanely in the course of being "grown and slaughtered." A handful of people have stood up for the rights of chickens, pigs and cows—none of which are particularly cherished. No one has stood up for the rabbit, despite the fact that the species serves as a storybook hero, a cultural icon and a beloved pet.

Perhaps Beth Seely, a rabbit grower and processor in Florida, best summarized the way this culture splits off the "meat" rabbit from all the other rabbit images in our culture. After noting that some rabbit lovers complain that processors "kill their pets" she said simply, "We don't kill their pets. The rabbits we breed for meat are very different animals than the ones bred for pets." But the truth is, plenty of breeders sell the rabbits they cull from meat herds as pets. Plenty of breeders slaughter the rabbits they cull from pet herds for meat. The rabbits are the same in either case. It's the way that people look at them that varies so wildly. Pamela Alley, a breeder in Oroville, California, admitted that she sometimes "falls in love" with some of her rabbits, even cherishes them as pets and "bawls like a baby" when her pet rabbits die. To keep herself from getting that attached to the rabbits she raises for meat, she said, "I just don't handle them as much. I make it a point to avoid working with them, to avoid getting to know them, so I'm not bothered by killing them." The human heart, it seems, has an amazing capacity for hardness.

Notes

1. "Why Not Rabbit for Dinner?" *Good Housekeeping* 118: 88–89, February 1944.
2. Office of International Affairs, *Microlivestock: Little-Known Small Animals with a Promising Economic Future* (National Academy Press, 2000), p. 179.
3. Food and Agriculture Organization of the United Nations (FAO), *The Rabbit: Husbandry, Health, and Production* (Rome: 1997) p. 5. Also see McNitt, James, et al., *Rabbit Production*, 8th edition (Danville, IL: Interstate Printers and Publishers, Inc., 1996), p. 20.
4. United States Department of Agriculture, "Rabbit Calicivirus Disease, Iowa, April 2000 Impact Worksheet," http://www.aphis.usda.gov/vs/ceah/cei/rabbitcal.htm.
5. Washburn, F.L., *The Rabbit Book: A Practical Manual on the Care of Belgian Hares, Flemish Giants and Other Meat and Fur Producing Rabbits* (Philadelphia: Lippincott Company, 1920), p. 5.
6. *Ibid.,* p. 8.
7. *Ibid.,* p. 27.
8. Meek, Marcellus, *Fur Rabbits* (Arcadia, CA, 1924), p. 10.
9. "Rabbits: Raising Them For Meat Is Now Helpful Patriotic Hobby," *Life*, January 4, 1943.
10. Office of International Affairs, *op. cit.*, p. 179.
11. Meek, Marcellus, *Rabbit Raising for Profit* (New York: Greenberg, 1947), pp. 3–8.
12. McNitt, *op. cit.*, p. 457.
13. Posted on meatrabbits@yahoogroups.com, October 2, 2002.
14. Ruggless, Ron, "It's rabbit season: Hares make the hop toward haute cuisine," *Nation's Restaurant News*, Nov 18, 1996, 30(45): 35.
15. Pollock, Ellen Joan, "Rabbit, Run or Else You May Wind Up as The Main Course," *Wall Street Journal*, December 5, 1996.
16. Fabricant, Florence, "Here comes Peter Cottontail and guess what? He tastes like chicken," *Nation's Restaurant News*, May 29, 1995, 29(22): 35. Ruggless, *op. cit.*
17. Pollock, *op. cit.*

18. Hazlitt, William, *The Plain Speaker*, Quoted in Adams, Carol, *The Sexual Politics of Meat* (New York: The Continuum Publishing Company, 1991), p. 48.
19. Farrington, *op. cit.,* p. 129.
20. Green, Gerald, "Rabbit Processing Plant Coming to Clinton," *Oklahoma Daily News*, July 11, 1990.
21. Kopel, David B., and Paul H. Blackman, "Waco Lessons for War," *National Review*, November 6, 2001.
22. Cornell Bunny Barn Web site, http://www3.sk.sympatico.ca/comllc/rabbits.htm
23. Farrington, Edward, *Practical Rabbit Keeping* (New York: Robert McBride & Company, 1919), p. 63.
24. McNitt, *op. cit.,* p. 66.
25. FAO, *op. cit.,* p. 104.
26. FAO, *op. cit.,* p. 98.
27. "Hauling Rabbits in Summer Heat" with guest speaker Gwen Weidner, PRMA Director of Runners, PRMA chat, June 29, 2000.
28. These postings all took place between September 10 and October 3, 2002.
29. Posted to meatrabbits@yahoogroups.com on January 15, 2003.
30. Rudolph's Rabbit Ranch Web page, http://www.qsl.net/ki0dz/rrr.htm.
31. Van der Horst, F. et al., "Growth and slaughter performance of Normand rabbits raised in wire mesh cages or in pens," in the English and French Abstracts from the 8th French Rabbit Days (8èmes Journées de la Recherche Cunicole), Paris, June 9–10, 1999, *World Rabbit Science* (special issue), 1999.
32. McNitt, *op. cit.,* p. 67.
33. Posted to meatrabbits@yahoo.com on September 18, 2002.
34. Belanger, Jerome, *Raising Small Livestock* (Emmaus, PA: Rodale Press, Inc. 1974), p. 13.
35. Posted on meatrabbits@yahoogroups.com November 15, 2002.
36. Farrington, *op. cit.,* p. 110.
37. Washburn, *op. cit.,* p. 27.
38. Stahl, Edward, *Chinchilla Rabbits: The Fur Rabbit De Luxe* (Holmes Park, MO: Stahl's Outdoor Enterprise Company, 1926), p. 74.
39. Templeton, George, *Domestic Rabbit Production* (Danville, IL: Interstate Printers and Publishers, Inc., 1968), p. 119.
40. Patton, Nephi M., "Colony Husbandry," in Manning, Patrick, et al (eds.), *The Biology of the Laboratory Rabbit* (New York: Academic Press, 1994), p. 27.
    Food, Safety, and Inspection Service of the USDA, Animal Disposition Reporting System, http://www.fsis.usda.gov/OPHS/adrsdata/2001/01crm1.htm.
41. Sagon, Candy, "Rabbit on the Rise," *Washington Post Food Section*, January 15, 1997.
42. Ardeng Web site, www.ardengrabbit.com/facts.html. Accessed Aptil 8, 2002.
43. Tilly Louise A. and Joan W. Scott, *Women, Work & Family* (New York: Methuen, 1987), pp. 44–50.
44. UNESCO, http://www.unesco.org/most/africa4.htm.
45. FAO, http://www.fao.org/waicent/ois/press_ne/presseng/1999/pren9913.htm.
46. FAO, *The Rabbit*, online version, http://www.fao.org/docrep/t1690E/t1690e03.htm#worldproduction.

6. "Ermine From Your Own Backyard!"[1]

The Rabbit Fur Industry

—————

Bye bye baby bunting
Daddy's gone a-hunting,
Gone to get a rabbit skin
To wrap the baby bunting in.

Nursery Rhyme

RABBIT FUR HAS never been as valued—or as valuable—as more luxurious furs, like lynx, sable or beaver. Yet the American rabbit fur industry, like the meat industry, has gone through repeated boom and bust cycles over the last century. Furriers and consumers alike have periodically turned to these "pleb" pelts as a substitute for more expensive furs. At the same time, passionate advocates of rabbit fur, as well as old-fashioned scam artists, have been pushing backyard fur production as a get-rich scheme for decades.

The general American fur industry took off in the early colonial years, with Europeans killing so many beaver and otter (or paying Native Americans nominal amounts to do the dirty work) in the Northeast that these species began to disappear by the mid-eighteenth century. By the late nineteenth century, eastern species of elk and bison had been nearly or altogether wiped out (slaughtered for their hides and their meat), as had the "sea mink" of coastal Maine, Nova Scotia and New Brunswick, the bison, pronghorn antelope, wolf and grizzly bear of the Great Plains and the wolf, pine marten, fisher and wolverine of the Far West.

The invention of the fur-sewing machine in 1895 made it possible to churn out many more fur garments than in the days of hand sewing. Wartime affluence in the late teens and early twenties also increased the demand for wild fur, with more than 125 species being trapped to create some fifty million pelts between 1919 and 1921. The fact that many of the wild fur-bearing animals were already extinct, or nearly so, led to the establishment of the first fox and mink "farms" in North America. It also created more demand for low-end pelts, like those from rabbits, squirrels, moles and opossum.[2] It would be another fifty years before public outcry against the sheer number of animals consumed—and the manner in which they were trapped, or raised and slaughtered—would make any dent on the human appetite for fur.

Making Rabbits Pay

Rabbit fur generally doesn't wear as well as higher-end furs (and wild rabbit fur is of even lower quality than domestic rabbit fur). But by the 1920s, rabbit fur was being used for everything from fur coats and wraps (using the pelts of thirty to forty rabbits per coat) to jacquettes, chokers, capes, collars, auto robes, baby blankets, hats, mittens, pillow trim and cuffs. American rabbit fur, which was usually of lesser quality than the European imports, was also the primary ingredient in the felt of felt hats. In 1927 the American hat trade used seventy-five million rabbit skins for felt hats alone—with three pelts going to each hat.[3] The felt was also used on the sounding hammers of pianos, and on toys, slippers, millinery and novelty items.

The rabbit market seemed so hot in the 1920s that Marcellus Meek, always a rabbit enthusiast, claimed that rabbit skin "was destined to take a position with respect to the breeding industry, not far dissimilar to that which gasoline took in the oil business."[4] Indeed, he noted, by 1924 rabbit fur comprised more than one-half of the American fur trade, and fifteen of the one hundred fur dressing and

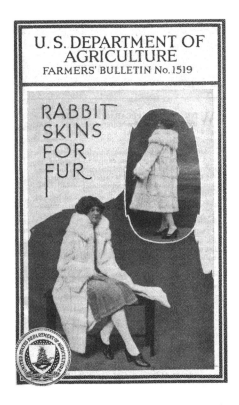

Figure 6.1. This USDA publication explained why raising rabbits for fur could be lucrative, and told readers how best to grow, slaughter and process the rabbits. USDA Farmers' Bulletin #1519, "Rabbit Skins for Fur." Courtesy USDA National Wildlife Research Center.

dyeing plants in New York City worked exclusively with rabbit fur. A writer for the *Fur Trade Review* expressed similar admiration for the rise of the lowly rabbit pelt:

> The part played by the rabbit in the fur trade throughout the world has grown almost beyond the belief and expectation of the members of the fur industry. At one time the pelt of a bunny was considered a "pleb" among the many furs that are available today, and a dealer that handled them was not considered a fur dealer in any sense of the word. Today, the same dealers rank among the largest in the world and there

are few dealers who do not in some way or other handle the once spurned pelt.[5]

Only three years later, the USDA's *Farmer's Bulletin* declared "Rabbit fur is used more extensively by the fur trade than any other kind, with more than 100,000,000 being used annually."[6]

Part of the attraction of rabbit fur was that it was dense, lustrous and soft, yet much cheaper than the furs of wild animals; thus it brought the touch of luxury into the hands of the masses. As Meek noted, probably with some exaggeration, "[W]here one sealskin coat graced Milady of Fifth Avenue in 1900, a hundred thousand fur coats of rabbit-seal are turned out on Sixth Avenue during the fur season for the Misses of Main Street all over America."[7] But rabbit fur was also attractive because it could be plucked, sheared and dyed to look like other types of fur, including ermine, beaver and leopard. Much as "Hudson Seal" was actually sheared and dyed muskrat skins, the names given to modified rabbit furs often disguised their humble origins. "Minkony," for instance, was mink-dyed rabbit, while "Near Seal," "Roman Seal" and "Northern Seal" all referred to rabbit fur that was sheared and dyed a seal color. Both "Ermiline" and "Ermilinette" were white rabbit furs, while "Fox Hair" was wild hare fur dyed to look like a fox. Using the same play on words, "Sable Hair" referred to sable-dyed hare, and both "French Leopard" and "Russian Leopard" referred to hare pelts dyed and marked to resemble a leopard. This was a great marketing technique, but in 1938 the Federal Trade Commission ruled that the practice was just deceptive enough to be illegal. Instead, the commission stipulated that the name of the animal used had to be marked on the label along with the name of the fur imitated, e.g., "seal-dyed coney" or "beaver-dyed rabbit."

During this time a huge demand existed for white pelts, especially (such as those from New Zealand White rabbits), because they could be easily dyed. The pelts were also desirable because, when left undyed, they looked remarkably like ermine, a far more expensive product. The furs of other rabbit breeds, including the French Silver,

Figure 6.2. Rabbit fur was popular because it could be dyed to look like other more exotic and expensive furs. From USDA Farmers' Bulletin #1519, "Rabbit Skins for Fur." Courtesy USDA National Wildlife Research Center.

Havana, Lilac, American Blue, Himalayan, Checkered Giant and Silver, could also be used without dyeing. The fur was so remarkably useful, the USDA's *Farmer's Bulletin* declared in 1924, that it "may be prepared for market with less trouble than is required to bury it,"[8] an inducement if there ever was one.

The pelts of Chinchilla rabbits were even more valuable, as they so closely resembled the fur of the real chinchilla, a small South American rodent that was going extinct at the time due to over-hunting for its incredibly soft pelt. (After World War II, little chinchillas were in such high demand—and scarce supply—that the Chilean, Peruvian and Bolivian governments prohibited any more exports of the animals.) Chinchilla rabbit fur had the same slate blue, gray and black hues as the chinchilla rodent, and the size of a pelt from a baby Chinchilla rabbit was also the exact size of a pelt from a real chinchilla, about seven by ten inches.

Edward Stahl, a Chinchilla rabbit breeder, was one of the most enthusiastic of a whole herd of very enthusiastic rabbit fur proponents in the 1920s. Stahl's motto was "The Chinchilla Way Makes Rabbits Pay" (something no rabbit could argue with) and in his 1926 treatise on the breed, entitled *Chinchilla Rabbits: The Fur Rabbit de Luxe*, he claimed the species was the "most marvelous fur discovery in the history of fur farming."[9] In addition to the "big return on your money," he wrote, "you have an endless amount of pleasure in raising your beauties. You have an opportunity to be out of doors, and the health and happiness derived from the raising of Chinchillas, are in many cases more than you can figure in dollars and cents. When you take into consideration that you are raising something for the adornment of the ladies, you are creating something for which there is an everlasting and never ending demand."[10] In fact, Stahl was so impassioned about all things Chinchilla he used a poem to dedicate his book to potential breeders:

> C—is for CHINCHILLA, the Rabbit Supreme,
> H—is for HER HIGHNESS, the Chinchilla Queen,
> I—is for INVESTMENT, which you will not lose,
> N—is for NONE BETTER, if Chinchillas you choose,
> C—is for CHAMPION, the Peer of the Lot,
> H—is for HARDINESS, which Chinchillas have got,
> I—is for INSPIRATION, for young and for old,
> L—is for LOVE'S LABOR, that never grows cold,
> L—is for LANIGERA, the source of Chinchilla's name,
> A—is for ASSOCIATION, that's bringing them fame![11]

Foreign Competition

Yet even in the early decades, the U.S. market for rabbit fur was bedeviled by foreign imports. According to Meek, the United States imported more than fifty-two million undressed hare, coney and rabbit skins in the first seven months of 1924.[12] Three years later, the USDA claimed that fully ninety-eight percent of the rabbit skins used in the United States were imported from other countries,[13] including China, Japan, New Zealand, Australia and European countries. "Cannot a small portion of this tremendous market be supplied by rabbit breeders?" Meek implored and then went on to quote C.A. House, a prominent British rabbit breeder, judge and author, who called for "mass production" in the rabbit business:

> In the poultry industry this has been realized. The man who keeps only a few hens in his back yard cannot make them a successful commercial proposition, but the poultry farmer with his 5,000 to 10,000 hens can, and does do it. . . . The need of the moment is men and women of vision. . . .[14]

Despite this "vision" of large-scale pelt production, Meek and others mostly pushed backyard breeding as a profitable hobby—for just about anyone. "To be successful one needs no special qualifications," Meek wrote. "The dullard has an equal chance with the scholar, the weak with the strong, the cripple with the athlete. Common sense, perseverance, and a true sense of sportsmanship will carry one a long way."[15] Stahl even went so far as to advocate rabbit breeding for women, whom he apparently believed to be incapable of handling other, presumably more complex, kinds of animal husbandry. "It is an enterprise that can be successfully managed by either sex," he wrote. "In fact, I might say it is a vocation highly adaptable to women as there is nothing complicated about the management of rabbits."[16]

The American fur industry in general went through something of a roller coaster ride between the 1930s and the 1990s. More and more pelts came from fox and mink raised on fur farms, but the numbers of fur garments sold fluctuated wildly, with dips occurring in the 1950s (due to hunting restrictions and extinctions), the early 1970s (due to public opposition to fur farming and trapping) and the 1990s (due to still more intense public distaste with the fur industry).

Each time the overall fur market has dipped, the fur industry has pushed rabbit as a cheap, "fun fur" that is within the reach of less affluent, often younger, fashion-conscious consumers. During the 1950s, for instance, the Fur Information and Fashion Council promoted "fun" rabbit fur so strongly that it actually helped lift the market from its doldrums. In the 1970s, the industry again pushed both "glamour furs" (like those from the lynx, wolf and bobcat) and "fun" furs, like those made from rabbit skins.

A number of companies in the 1970s started pushing Rex rabbit pelt production as a way to get rich. Just as some companies promoted "buy-back" schemes for rabbit meat, these companies told would-be breeders that if they bought the company's foundation stock, they'd get paid for all the "non-mink mink" pelts they could produce. These schemes, too, turned out to be scams, as the companies often didn't buy back any foundation stock at all. And the experience left a bitter taste among breeders for decades to come. "These outfits used to promise a zillion dollars in profits," says Pamela Alley, who has been breeding Rex rabbits in Oroville, California, since 1982. "They'd sell you breeding stock for $50 or $200 a head and promise to buy back the pelts for $20 or $50 apiece. If you were lucky, they'd buy back from you for one or two cycles. But then the outfit would just disappear, leaving the breeder with what was usually substandard stock, no market for the pelts, and no clue as to where to go."

Such get-rich schemes still rear their ugly heads from time to time. In 2001, a woman on the "Kountrylife" Web site ("Country Skills, Country Crafts, Country Living") wrote that she had received a brochure from a "National Marketing Service" claiming great profits on Rex rabbit breeding:

> They are claiming to have a solid buyers market and need people to raise these rabbits for the buyers. Supposedly, their hair is shedless, smooth and shiny like a mink. There are 20 different color combinations, and depending on the size and color, you get $25.00–$100.00 per 2–3 month old rabbit.

The brochure says they guarantee $25.00. The start-up cost is less than most animals, but is still substantial, at least for us. We own 120 acres and have 6 kids. We are trying to keep me home with the kids. Most of our land is woods, 2 creeks, and 1 swamp. We have 12 sows and 4 cows, but do not have enough pasture for much more cattle and to increase the hogs would take a new building. We are farrowing in a 3-sided barn now as it is for half of the sows. We were hoping that this would be a good way to make $500–$1000 per month with minimal outlay. Anyone have any first hand knowledge of this?[17]

Other people on the site immediately wrote back discouraging her, noting that the most anyone ever gets for a whole Rex is about $30 and that Rexes actually do shed. One participant on the chat best summarized the nature of the deal with the age-old adage, "If it sounds too good to be true it probably isn't true."

Retro Looks, Retro Furs
In the late 1990s and early 2000s, the fur industry once again started pushing rabbit fur as a cheap but hip alternative to trendy, high-end furs. In 2002 more than 170 designers, including Oscar de la Renta, Dolce & Gabbana, Fendi, Gianfranco Ferré, Gucci, Michael Kors, Karl Lagerfeld, Yves St Laurent, Valentino and Versace used fur in their runway fashions.[18] Some of them used rabbit fur, because it appeals to the "younger demographic, which doesn't have as much money to spend on luxury furs," says Kevin Fagan, executive director of the International Fur Trade Federation. "And with this whole trend toward '70s fashion, we're seeing a lot of rabbit fur again, because it was so popular back then."

Still, the number of rabbit pelts sold annually pales in comparison to the number of mink or fox pelts sold. The Copenhagen Fur Centre—the only fur auction house in the world that deals with rabbits—sells about 20,000 Rex rabbit pelts per year, compared to 13,000,000 mink skins per year. (Stig Reinhold, a sales manager and

Figure 6.3. "Young rabbits being kept together until ready for marketing." USDA Farmers' Bulletin #1730, "Rabbit Production." Courtesy USDA National Wildlife Research Center.

auctioneer at the CFC, said there is almost no market for any other kind of rabbit fur.) Most of those pelts come from Europe and China. According to the USDA, the U.S. did import 657,000 hare and rabbit skins in 1999, primarily from Spain, Argentina, France, Belgium and Chile.[19] But almost no one in this country is selling rabbit pelts, as the price paid for the pelt—about $12.00 for a Rex—doesn't cover the cost of tanning and shipping. "Sometimes I'll tan one myself, just for fun," rabbit meat processor Clyde Marsh told Susan, as he gestured to the pelts draped across the top of his rabbit cages. "But it's generally not worth the trouble or the money." Even the market for furs for felt has dried up, because scraping the fat off the skin of a rabbit is so labor-intensive that felt is now mostly made from synthetic materials.

Many rabbit breeders in the United States do skin their rabbits and tan the pelts themselves, however, to make small toys, pillows, mittens, earmuffs and decorations. Some also sell pelts to fishing supply stores, which use the rabbit hair to make flies; some trappers provide wild hare heads and feet for the same purpose.

The number of rabbits raised worldwide for fur is currently unknown, as are the exact conditions under which those rabbits are raised. Most major anti-fur groups focus on mink and fox ranching, which produce by far the most pelts for the fur industry (about thirty million pelts in the year 2000). The fact that some rabbit fur farmers claim the fur is just a by-product of meat production has also obfuscated the issue. In fact, although the pelts from "fryers" can be used to make trim or decorations, they're not nearly as durable as the pelts from "mature" rabbits, over the age of six months, whose fur is in prime condition. Still, it is safe to assume that rabbits raised for fur production are not kept—or slaughtered—in conditions that are any more humane than in the rabbit meat industry or in other fur farming operations.

Several European countries have outlawed keeping animals to slaughter solely for fur in the last few years, including England, Wales, Scotland and Sweden, and other European countries are also debating full or partial bans on fur farms. This could certainly slow the rabbit fur industry down. But truly stopping the rabbit fur trade may be even harder than stopping the trade in furs of more endangered animals. That is, it's relatively easy to convince people that fur is wrong when the animal is endangered (like the leopard or tiger), or when wild animals are being caught in leg-hold traps or captive bred in abysmal conditions (like fox and mink). It's a lot harder when the animal is considered neither rare nor noble and when no one is publicizing the conditions under which the animal is raised or slaughtered. In this country, that lack of publicity may be due to the fact that most commercial rabbit fur production takes place overseas. Yet in recent years many animal advocacy organizations have been campaigning against the annual global slaughter of some two million cats and dogs for their fur. Far more than two million domestic rabbits are slaughtered annually for their fur, too, but getting any solid information on the international trade in rabbit fur has been next to impossible, as no groups have addressed the issue.

Unfortunately, our myopic view of rabbits as pure cuteness and fluff allows us to ignore what happens to real rabbits in real production situations. Since our culture promotes the cuddly aspect of soft rabbit fur in books like *Pat The Bunny* or touch-and-feel books about baby animals, one might think we'd recoil from wearing the pelts of equally cute *real* bunnies, just as most of us recoil from the idea of wearing coats made from cats and dogs. But rabbits are different. Rabbits may be pets, but they are cheap, and that makes them "expendable." They don't engage with humans—or so people think—the way that cats and dogs do, and that makes them "dumb." In the public mind, rabbits don't suffer, which justifies killing them for their soft fur. A post on meatrabbits@yahoogroups.com in 2002 perhaps best summarizes the culture's ambivalent feelings toward "bunny" fur:

> Just starting out I was a little worried that I might not be able to go through with butchering and want to KEEP all the bunnies. Well today I was out with the rabbits and was petting a non-fertile buck admiring his coat and thinking how sad that he was a horney boy but couldn't do anything about it. Then I *really* looked at his coat and thought, "Gee, what a beautiful pelt. If I put him in the freezer I could make a great pair of baby slippers!" Then I was sad that I'd promised the kids we wouldn't kill any rabbit we named. I'm going to have to figure out how to explain culls to them and get around that. I think that answers that! I look into the sweet, brown eyes of an adorable bunny and think SLIPPERS!

Notes
1. "Ermine From Your Own Backyard," *Popular Science*, 118, January 1931: 23–4.
2. Animal Welfare Institute, *Facts about Furs* (Washington, D.C.: Animal Welfare Institute, 1980).

3. "Hare-Raising Hazards," *Saturday Evening Post*, April 27, 1929, p. 43.
4. Meek, Marcellus, *Fur Rabbits* (Arcadia, CA, 1924), p. 11.
5. *Ibid.*, p. 14.
6. United States Department of Agriculture (USDA), "Rabbit Skins for Fur," *Farmer's Bulletin* (Washington D.C., No. 1519, 1927): 1.
7. Meek, *op. cit.*, p. 14.
8. USDA, "Rabbit Skins for Fur," *Farmer's Bulletin* (Washington D.C., No. 1090, 1924): 1.
9. Stahl, Edward, *Chinchilla Rabbits: The Fur Rabbit De Luxe* (Holmes Park, MO: Stahl's Outdoor Enterprise Company, 1926), p. 43.
10. *Ibid.*
11. *Ibid.*
12. Meek, *op. cit.*, p. 7.
13. USDA, "Rabbit Skins for Fur," *Farmer's Bulletin* (Washington D.C., No. 1519, 1927): 1.
14. Meek, *op. cit*, p. 7.
15. *Ibid.*, p. 9.
16. Stahl, *op. cit.*, p. 8.
17. Country Living, Country Skills, Country People Web site, http://www.kountrylife.com/forum/messages/19381.html.
18. International Fur Trade Today Web site, www.iftf.com/today.html.
19. USDA, "Rabbit Calicivirus Disease, Iowa, April 2000 Impact Worksheet," http://www.aphis.usda.gov/vs/ceah/cei/rabbitcal.htm.
20. Posted on meatrabbits@yahoogroups.com September 25, 2002.

7. "40 Smoking Rabbits"

The Vivisection Industry

"Forty rabbits are each smoking a pack of cigarettes per day and enjoying it."

From "40 Smoking Rabbits Aid Lung Cancer Research"
In *Science News Letter,* June 22, 1957

LATE IN THE summer of 1991, Margo received a call from a local humane society. Officers for the society had found six male New Zealand White rabbits in the basement of a local government laboratory in a routine visit; one officer was so horrified at their living conditions that she charged the lab with animal cruelty. After a year of experimenting on these rabbits, the researchers had switched to cats. But rather than euthanize the rabbits, as is the usual practice at the end of an experiment, the researchers decided to keep the animals indefinitely, just in case they were needed again. The rabbits continued to live at the lab for five additional years.

According to the animal control officer, who was in tears when she called Margo, all six rabbits were living in individual steel metal boxes in a completely dark room. They had no contact with other animals or humans, except when they were fed. Margo ended up with the three of the rabbits, one of whom—Stimpy—lived with her for four years. When this big white rabbit first arrived at Margo's house he was curiously stooped, his head hanging somewhat lower than normal on his body, and he moved by walking, rather than hopping. Throughout his four years with Margo, he suffered from conjunctivitis and battled countless infections; perhaps because he went from a sterile environment to a normal, less-than-sterile home. But Stimpy was neutered (at six years of age), learned to hop again and enjoyed the company of rabbits, the joys of toys and the delight of stretching his limbs for a few good years at Margo's house.

Stimpy's is not an unusual case. Each year, hundreds of thousands of rabbits live their lives and experience their deaths in laboratory settings. Not all of those rabbits fare as badly as Stimpy and the other rabbits in the laboratory basement; a lucky few live fairly comfortable lives in large quarters with loving handlers. But even a cursory look at the history and current status of research rabbits shows both the abuses to which they've been subject and the very viable alternatives that are being developed.

Why the Rabbit?

Animals have been used in medical research and experiments since the Greeks first started studying anatomy and physiology. Animal experimentation became a standard part of medical research in the late eighteenth century, with primarily wild animals, domestic livestock, cats and dogs being used as the research animals. Rabbits were first used in the mid-nineteenth century but were not bred for the purpose until the twentieth century.[1]

Rabbits worked well in laboratory settings for a number of reasons. The species is generally easy to procure, easy to handle and easy to draw blood from. Rabbits are small enough to house easily, but large enough to clearly demonstrate the effects of various chemicals or processes. Rabbits have relatively short gestation periods, which facilitates fertility studies, multi-generational studies and the observation of rabbit fetuses or newborns. The fact that rabbits are induced ovulators means that researchers can exactly time not only the rabbit's release of eggs but also the development of rabbit embryos. Rabbits are also sensitive to teratogens (substances that cause developmental abnormalities), and they produce antibodies

Figure 7.1. "Rabbits, too, aid the war effort." Rabbits began to be used intensively as laboratory animals during the 1930s and '40s. In this photograph, William Edwin Morris, histologist for Baxter Laboratories, Inc., conducts research on blood plasma through experimentation on rabbits. 1942. Library of Congress, Prints and Photographs Division. [Reproduction number LC-USE6-D-008618]

that some researchers consider far superior to those of any other "lab animal." Equally important, the rabbit "does not have the emotional stigma often encountered with the use of dogs or monkeys in research," according to training materials from one Army seminar.[2]

It's impossible to know the exact number of animals used in laboratories today, because lab facilities don't have to report the number of mice, rats, birds, reptiles or amphibians used—although these make up ninety-five percent of the animals in labs each year.[3] Still, most people agree that, with the exception of mice and rats, the number of animals used for laboratory research has declined dramatically in the last few decades, both because of vociferous public opposition to animal experimentation and because of the development of viable alternatives. According to the USDA, which regulates the use of live animals in labs, more than 1.3 million reportable warm-blooded animals were used in research, testing or experiments in

1999. This is one half of the number used a decade ago. When the estimated number of rats and mice are included, some fifteen million animals were used for laboratory purposes that year. (The number of mice and rats used is now climbing, however, because of the popularity of "transgenic" or genetically altered animals.)

The number of rabbits used by laboratories has also dropped—by about thirty percent since the 1970s. The USDA estimates that scientists used nearly 300,000 rabbits in 735 facilities in the United States in 1999 (down from 450,000 in 1973 and a peak of about 550,000 in 1987[4]). Most of those rabbits are New Zealand Whites, whose light-colored eyes enable researchers to readily observe ophthalmological changes and whose light-colored ears ease blood-drawing. ("Lop-eared breeds," notes the Web site for the Professional Rabbit Meat Association, "are not desirable due to an automatic association with 'pet' rabbits, as well as the thinner ears causing difficulties in applying the IV."[5]) Most of those rabbits are supplied by either large commercial breeders (like Charles River Laboratories and Covance) or by smaller, independent breeders.

Some of these breeding facilities are quite specialized; they provide "Specific Pathogen Free" (SPF) rabbits who are raised in sterile conditions and guaranteed to be free of a number of viruses, bacteria and parasites. Other researchers may require "Barrier Specific" rabbits, who not only are raised in sterile conditions but are born by caesarean section (so the kits contact no bacteria in the birth canal) and bottle fed with synthetic formulas (to keep them free of contaminants). The prices for commercially bred laboratory rabbits range from $30 to $250 per rabbit, depending on type, size, special features (e.g., whether they are pathogen-free or barrier-specific) and whether they are a "proven breeder."

Breeders who annually sell more than $500 worth of rabbits to laboratories need an Animal Welfare Act permit and must abide by AWA requirements. (The AWA governs the housing, feeding, sanitation and veterinary care of laboratory animals.) Smaller "growers," on the other hand, can sell to labs and universities without these permits. The fact that the numbers of rabbits used in laboratory testing is dropping is heartening, especially given the very real technological advances that now allow researchers to do their work with alternative (non-living) models. But rabbits do continue to be used in laboratory settings across the country, and many of them don't fare very well at all.

Blinded for Beauty: Product Testing

Historically, one of the most common uses for the rabbit has been in product testing. Each year, thousands of new (or "improved") household products—from pesticides to hair dye, from window cleaner to shoe polish and from mascara to new drugs—are released into the marketplace. Over the years, the majority of these products—or their components—have been tested on animals, primarily rabbits, rats and mice, to find out if they can cause harm to humans, including eye or skin irritation, reproductive problems, birth defects and cancer.

Federal law requires that food products, pesticides, medical devices and drugs be tested on animals. No U.S. laws mandate that cosmetics or personal care products be so tested, although the FDA does insist that if a product (or any of its ingredients) hasn't been tested on animals, its label must reflect that. This can serve as a "not so subtle way of forcing the companies to do animal tests," Dr. John McArdle, director of the Alternatives Research and Development Foundation, said in an interview. The Organisation for Economic Cooperation and Development (OECD) does require animal testing, however, so any company that wants to market its products internationally needs to perform them. (Companies that sell "cruelty-free" products are often able to market them internationally because, while they may not conduct animal testing, they use ingredients that were tested in the past.) Many companies have also tested their products on animals for liability reasons.

Rabbits have especially been the animal of choice for the Draize Eye Irritancy Test (DEIT), which measures how various chemicals affect the eyes. The need for such a test became clear in the 1930s, after a material called "Lashlor," which was a lengthening and darkening agent in mascara, caused people to go blind. In 1939, the FDA

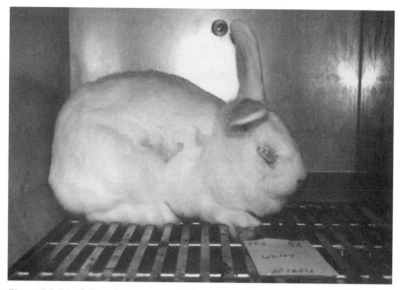

Figure 7.2. People have been protesting the use of rabbits for product testing since the 1970s. Courtesy People for the Ethical Treatment of Animals.

passed the first laws requiring the testing of all cosmetics. In 1944, J.H. Draize developed a test that used the eyes of live rabbits to measure the potential irritability of chemical warfare agents. Within a few short years, that test became the gold standard for monitoring the potential damage that cosmetics, pharmaceuticals, consumer products, industrial chemicals and other products could cause to the human eye.

The test is fairly straightforward. The rabbit is restrained in stocks with the head immobilized. The eye is held open with a clip, while the researchers place the substance (which may be a liquid or a solid) in one eye. (They leave the other eye untreated so it can serve as a "control.") Over the course of several days or weeks, the researchers then measure the amount of tissue damage that occurs after exposure to the substance, and the rabbits are killed at the end of the test.

It is easy to see why rabbits are popular for this experiment. Their eyes are sensitive (in part because the cornea is much thinner than that of a human). Their eyes protrude in a way that facilitates observation of ophthalmological effects. Rabbit eyes also produce tears different-ly than do humans, so it is harder for them to "wash" out the sub-stances. These very same characteristics, however, make rabbits extremely vulnerable to the suffering that can result from these tests—like ulcerating corneas, swollen eyelids, bleeding and blindness—espe-cially when, as is most common, they receive no pain medications.

Twenty years ago, a U.S. Environmental Protection Agency (EPA) staff member admitted to *Science News* that the Draize test was "fairly inhumane" and that "technicians hate to do it, because if you get a very corrosive chemical, it's really cruel." Today, in most countries, the test has been considerably improved—pain medication is often administered, for instance, and technicians use pre-screening protocols to be sure that very caustic materials aren't put in the rab-bits' eyes. Yet the animals can still suffer. "The test is designed to find substances that cause damage to the eyes of the rabbits—which some do," McArdle says. "Even when anesthetics are used, they only last a short time, while the test itself lasts for days."

Equally important, the test is now considered unreliable, as it depends entirely on subjective observations of the damage. In one oft-cited 1971 Mellon Institute study, twenty-five laboratories used the Draize tests for twelve chemicals and reported widely varying results. The researchers concluded that "the rabbit eye and skin pro-cedure currently recommended by the Federal agencies . . . should not be recommended as standard procedures in any new regulations. Without careful reeducation these tests result in unreliable results."[6]

Roger Curran, vice president and chief science officer for the Institute for In Vitro Sciences, told us in an interview, "These researchers did everything they could think of to figure out what the problem with the test was. They finally deduced that the problem was that the animals were fundamentally different. You can put the same chemical in a rabbit from here and a rabbit from there and you'll get two very different results. That's not a good test. It means that the results aren't predictive."

Further, he notes, the test doesn't require researchers to test a reference chemical concurrently as a control. "So you have no way of knowing what that particular researcher normally sees in that rabbit's particular eye," he says. "In the absence of that, you can't even compare results within labs, never mind across labs. So if you're worried about human eye safety, we're using a test that isn't all that dependable."

Henry Spira started a public campaign to stop DEIT in the early 1980s and focused, initially, on Revlon, which had used the test for developing cosmetics. Eventually his coalition included more than four hundred groups, and Revlon agreed to give $750,000 to Rockefeller University to research alternatives to DEIT. Since then, many companies have abandoned the practice—in part because it's cheaper to use alternatives, in part because being "cruelty free" is good PR. Many continue to use the test, although exact figures are unavailable. However, some government programs, including the Office of Pesticide Programs within the EPA, still require it for any new or re-formulated products, which can include everything from citronella candles to crop sprays and antibacterial soap. That the government—and consumers—need to know if these materials will cause human eye damage is indisputable. But Curran and others are hoping that the EPA, too, will move to alternative testing materials soon. "There's still a feeling among many scientists that the animal will tell you the truth about a substance," he says. "An animal does tell you the truth—but it's for its own experience. It can't be extrapolated to everyone else."

The Draize Skin Irritancy Test is equally unreliable—and equally cruel. In this test, technicians shave an animal's skin, sometimes abrade it and then apply substances to the area to see if they corrode it, irritate it or create an allergic reaction. Rabbit skin is sensitive, so if the substance is indeed caustic, it can cause bleeding, infections, ulcerations and tremendous pain. The rabbit is immobilized—to prevent licking—and a patch is sometimes applied to increase the severity of the test. With toxic materials, researchers develop a dosage that will kill half of the rabbits. For less toxic substances (i.e., those that only damage the skin upon acute exposure), researchers apply the substances daily, for as long as ninety days, to monitor the effect.

Figure 7.3. Dermal tests can cause open wounds and significant pain for the rabbit subjects involved. Courtesy People for the Ethical Treatment of Animals.

But again, because the data depend on subjective interpretations, the test results are neither conclusive nor predictive. "In one study, the interpretations of something as readable as a scar were all over the place," Curran says. "One laboratory reported that eight of eight rabbits developed scars from a particular substance. Six of the other labs reported no scars whatsoever on their eight rabbits—and that was for the same substance. This was due to variations among the individual rabbits, as well as variations in how the substance was applied, and whether the tape they used to hold it down could breathe or was occlusive. So what we're seeing is that the gold standard really isn't a gold standard at all."

Adds Steve Zawistowski, senior vice president and science advisor to the American Society for the Protection of Animals, "lots of people in the animal testing world will tell you they're afraid to use alternative methods, that they haven't yet been validated against the animal tests. The truth is, the Draize tests are pretty sloppy. At a time when we've got alternatives that use sophisticated quantitative analysis to measure structural damage in microns, animal testers still want to rely on human observation. In fact, no one ever validated the animal tests either. It's sort of bizarre."

Rabbits have also typically been used for "lot release" or "pyrogenic" studies, which screen batches of vaccine or other injectable drugs to be sure they're not contaminated with bacteria. Researchers inject a rabbit with a sample of the batch; if the rabbit develops a fever, the batch is contaminated. But it turns out that "if you inject ten milliliters of a drug into a rabbit's ear, and then stick a thermometer up its rectum, it's not surprising if the animal spikes a fever, just from the irritation alone," Curran notes. In addition, rabbits can only be used a few times before they have to be destroyed, because they may develop immunity to the bacteria and thus not show a result.

Alternatives to Product Testing
In the past twenty years, hundreds of companies manufacturing everything from household cleaning products to nail polish have chosen to end their use of animal-based toxicity tests. Indeed, the number of products tested on live animals has dropped precipitously in the last few decades. According to the New England Anti-Vivisection Society, today more than 1,500 companies no longer use animal tests. These companies aren't just "progressive," "bleeding heart" or "alternative" establishments. Procter & Gamble has stopped testing about eighty percent of its products (including its beauty, home care and cleaning products) on live animals, although they continue to test new ingredients, even when not required by law, on animals. Colgate-Palmolive, Bristol-Meyers Squibb, Dial, Gillette, Avon, Revlon and Mary Kay have also stopped or limited their animal tests, while smaller companies like Beauty without Cruelty, Tom's of Maine and Kiss My Face have led the way in creating cruelty-free products.

The motto for these companies is the three R's: *replace* living animals in laboratories, *reduce* the number of animals required for statistically valid results and *refine* the actual procedures used so that the animals suffer less physical and emotional distress. For instance, to avoid using rabbits in the DEIT, some companies have begun using cell cultures, corneas from eye banks (although there is a scarcity of these), and computer and mathematical models. The CAM Test or Hen's Egg Test uses egg membranes instead of live rabbit eyes. One researcher at the University of Waterloo is using lenses from cow's eyes harvested from a local slaughtering plant; his test uses a computer, not a researcher, to measure the results.[7] IIVS now uses cow corneas to do similar tests. The EpiOcular test—which uses epidermal cells—mimics the cornea so closely it's actually considered more accurate than the Draize test. These tests are not free of animals. But they are at least using parts or products of animals who have already been killed, or, as in the case of the CAM test, they rely on beings that are not developed enough to feel pain or distress. "Alternative tests that still involve animals to some degree (e.g., hen eggs) are seen as steps in the right direction," says Dr. Martin Stephens, Vice President of Animal Research Issues for the Humane Society of the United States. "Eventually, the hope is to get completely away from *any* involvement of animals, their parts, etc., perhaps with the exception of 'immortalized' cell lines based on animal cells."

To avoid using rabbits for skin tests, some companies have begun using in vitro tests, like EpiDerm, which uses neonatal foreskin cells to test skin irritants. The Irritection Assay uses a protein alteration system to detect how five thousand different materials might affect the skin. The Rat Skin Transcutaneous Electrical Resistance (TER) assay uses pieces of rat skin to test corrosiveness. (The test does involve killing the rats, but is considered preferable to doing painful testing on a live animal.) SKIN and EPISKIN assays have also been used; the latter was actually developed by L'Oreal. Corrositex mimics the effect of corrosives on living skin by using layers of collagen. It also takes just one day, and costs $100; the Draize rabbit test takes twenty-one days and costs $1,000.[8] This test has already been approved by the U.S. Department of Transportation, the Consumer Product Safety Commission and the Food and Drug Administration. No tests have been developed yet for measuring the sort of allergic reactions a product may cause, but several laboratories are exploring such alternatives.

Other new testing alternatives include human cell-based assays (to identify anti-cancer drugs) and simulated human lungs made from human cells (to test aerosols). Charles River Laboratories, a company that is unpopular with animal rights groups because of its high-volume breeding programs, has also developed an in vitro test to replace animal-based "lot release." In this test, researchers place the medicine to be tested into fluid containing the blood of horseshoe crabs, which coagulates in the presence of bacteria to protect the crab from contamination. If it coagulates in the test tube, the batch is contaminated. (One might argue that this isn't a particularly good deal for the crabs, who are caught, bled and then released. There is some debate, however, about whether or not invertebrates, like horseshoe crabs, can feel pain or distress. At the present time, Stephens told us, this procedure is not considered inhumane.) The fact that many ingredients have already been tested—in some cases tested over and over again—can also spare animals. Companies today can refer to the U.S. GRAS (Generally Regarded as Safe), a list of thousands of ingredients found in household products already known to be safe for human use. A few years ago, the cosmetics industry also began developing a Cosmetic Ingredient Review. The goal of this project was to gather previous test results from scientific literature and company files, so that companies could draw on these instead of re-inventing the animal-testing wheel and sacrificing still more animals.

Even the U.S. government, which heretofore has been slow to approve alternative methods, has begun to search for replacements to animal tests. In 1997, the federal government created the Interagency Coordinating Committee on the Validation of Alternative Methods (ICCVAM) to specifically address finding substitutes for live animal testing. In 2000, the ICCVAM recommended that federal agencies stop using the Draize skin tests for measuring corrosiveness, as viable, alternative, non-animal tests currently exist. Animals would still be used to test any chemicals that come up negative in the initial tests, and the recommendations do not cover the Draize Eye Irritancy tests. In 2001, the U.S. also joined the OECD in its decision to phase out the use of the Classic Lethal Dose Percent 50 test or "LD 50" (a test that defines a product's "lethal dose," or the amount that kills 50 percent of the animals tested when it is fed to, injected into, or applied to an animal). The OECD had been ready to ban the test five years earlier, but the U.S. EPA refused to sign on.

Indeed, the Europeans tend to be far ahead of the Americans in all issues related to lab animals. In June 2002, for instance, the European Union voted to immediately ban new cosmetics with ingredients that have been tested on animals if alternative testing methods exist. New cosmetics that have ingredients for which no alternative testing procedures exist will be banned starting in 2005—even though this may cause trade upsets with countries like Japan and the United States, where animal testing is still prevalent. And in 2001, the European Centre for the Validation of Alternative Methods (ECVAM) completed validation studies on three other alternative in vitro test methods for assessing skin corrosivity—EpiDerm, EPISKIN and the Rat Skin TER assay. Unfortunately, even as our federal government is struggling to keep abreast of the European developments, the EPA is sponsoring three of the largest animal testing programs ever. The Endocrine Disruptor Screening Program (EDSP) will evaluate the effects of industrial chemicals on the human endocrine system; in the course of evaluating environmental contaminants, pesticides and other industrial chemicals, the tests will use more than 100 million animals. The voluntary children's chemical evaluation program (VCCEP) will generate toxicity profiles of the chemicals to which children are most commonly exposed. The High Production Volume (HPV) program will test the toxicity of the 2,800 chemicals most widely used in this country.

The HPV program was expected to use one million animals, including rabbits, to test the acute, subchronic, developmental, reproductive and genetic toxicity of these chemicals. But in 1999, the Johns Hopkins University Center for Alternatives to Animal Testing (CAAT) organized meetings to assess the potential of alternative, non-animal-based methods. That same year, the EPA announced both that it would wait two years before testing some chemicals (to research alternatives) and that the National Institute of Environmental Health Sciences, the National Toxicology Program and the EPA would put $4.5 million towards the development of new methods. The EPA also announced that it would allow companies that had withheld testing information in the past to share it in the course of this study (without fear of reprisals), to reduce the number of new tests required. The changes were so broad and relevant that some animal protection organizations stopped their campaigns.[9] (Other activist groups, like PETA and In Defense of Animals, are still vigorously campaigning against the HPV program.)

Rabbits in White: Medical Research

The use of rabbits in product testing has been the most visible (and for some, the most egregious) way that rabbits have been used for scientific purposes. But millions of rabbits have also been used in the course of medical research over the last 150 years. Scientists have used those rabbits to study arteriosclerosis, herpes, ovulation, tuberculosis, nutrition, immunology, embryology and how drugs cross the placental wall and affect fetuses (the rabbit placenta system and the human placenta system, it turns out, are identical). Rabbits were key to Pasteur's development of the rabies vaccine, to an understanding of how bacterial infections cause fevers and to the development of mono- and poly-antibodies. They have been used to study chemotherapy and radiation on tumors in the young, staph infections of the eye, high blood pressure, contact dermatitis and organ rejection, as well as epilepsy, diabetes, induced lupus, orthopedics, brain lesions and drug addiction.

Without question, many rabbits have suffered in the course of these studies. Over the last one hundred years, rabbits have been injected with herpes (resulting in brain inflammations and sometimes seizures), hydrocephalus, inflammatory bowel disease, kidney tumors and campylobacter (to create diarrhea, which becomes so severe the animal eventually dies of dehydration). They have been made to develop acute respiratory distress, endocarditis (inflammation of the membranes that line the heart and heart valves), eye infections, endometriosis, osteoarthritis and cholecystitis (inflammation of the gallbladder). They have had their bodies rotated while their heads remained immobilized (to study eye movements). They have had their eyes wounded again and again, to see how the eyes repair themselves. They have had spermicides injected into their vaginas, so that researchers could gauge said spermicide's irritability, and have had their oocytes removed and injected with human sperm. They have had their coronary arteries tied in order to produce heart attack and death. They have been mated and then killed immediately afterwards (to study post-coital changes in the brain), injected with cocaine while pregnant and had marijuana applied to their eyes. The "forty smoking rabbits" mentioned in the epigraph to this chapter spent three hours a day in a plastic box. "To do their smoking for science," a *Science News Letter* article noted in 1957, researchers held a lighted cigarette two centimeters from the rabbit's nose every hour. One researcher said the rabbits seemed to be enjoying the smoking—proof of this claim wasn't given.

One of the most famous uses of rabbits in medicine was the gonadotropin pregnancy test, popularly known as the "rabbit test." In this test, used since the 1920s, female rabbits were injected with the urine from a possibly pregnant woman. If the woman was indeed pregnant, her urine contained the hormone hCG, which would force the rabbit's ovary to emit an egg. (This would, of course, only be detected after killing the rabbit—thus the popular misconception that only a positive test result killed the rabbit.) The test was quite expensive and required that the woman bring a bottle of urine to her local pharmacist—both disincentives in earlier, more modest times. Still, the general public used the phrase "the rabbit died" as a euphemism for a positive pregnancy test for a long time. The rabbit test has now been replaced with an agglutination test that eliminates the use of animals altogether.

The applicability of other rabbit tests to human health, however, is open to question. For example, rabbits are induced ovulators, a condition that greatly improves their chance of successful fertiliza-

tion and pregnancy. This condition has no parallels to human reproduction. Yet rabbits continue to be used in reproductive studies
aimed at understanding more about problems like human infertility.
Studies that use rabbits to investigate lung damage are also ques-
tionable, as human and rabbit lungs are entirely different.[10] Several
researchers have even noted that the results of tests on rabbit eyes
aren't always relevant to human eyes.[11]

It seems rabbits' usefulness to medical science, then, is starting to
wane. That fact, combined with the public's growing distaste for
using live animals in laboratory settings, would seem to make rabbits
an increasingly unpopular choice. But still odder experiments continue to take place.

Glowing Bunnies, Growing Bunnies

Perhaps one of the oddest in recent years was the creation of Alba,
the green bunny. Eduardo Kac, an American artist, commissioned
the National Institute of Agronomic Research (INRA) in Paris to
create for him a glowing rabbit as a conceptual art piece. According
to Kac, the laboratory filled his request by splicing the albino rabbit's
DNA with that of a Pacific Northwest jellyfish—something they had
done before as part of an effort to learn how to "tag" embryos. The
result? A rabbit who glowed phosphorescent green under ultraviolet
light and whose very existence—as an art piece—was supposed to
make viewers grapple with issues of transgenics, or our modern ability to custom-design creatures by crossing one species with another.
Alba was, Kac claims, "transgenic art," a way of allowing people
other than scientists to use biotechnology, of using that technology
for something other than scientific research and of sparking discourse among scientists, philosophers, artists, lawyers and writers.

Whether Alba was created for research purposes or simply as
performance art is open to debate. Kac claims he and the INRA
researchers had an agreement that Alba would go home and live with
Kac's family in Chicago. (Kac later told U.S. News and World
Report, "It's not about making an object. I invent situations.")
INRA claims that no such agreement ever existed and that Alba was

part of an eighteen-month long line of glowing bunnies. As such, the fate of Alba has become very public. The issues her existence raised, in fact, don't just have to do with the ethics of bioengineering, but with the question of how biotechnology will intersect with our personal lives. Kac has told several newspapers that Alba seemed like a normal rabbit—except for her glowing qualities—and that he is heartbroken that she died without ever being able to live or travel with him. INRA claims Alba died for unknown reasons, but that her lifespan (two and a half or four years, depending on who you talk to) was normal. (Rabbits actually can live up to twelve years or more.) This too is part of Kac's point—that animals who seem like freaks of nature still deserve respect and kindness. "I will never forget the moment when I first held her in my arms, in Jouy-en-Josas, France, on April 29, 2000," he writes on his Web site (http://www.ekac.org/gfpbunny.html).

> My apprehensive anticipation was replaced by joy and excitement. Alba—the name given her by my wife, my daughter, and I—was lovable and affectionate and an absolute delight to play with. As I cradled her, she playfully tucked her head between my body and my left arm, finding at last a comfortable position to rest and enjoy my gentle strokes. She immediately awoke in me a strong and urgent sense of responsibility for her well-being.

Describing this intimate relationship is also part of Kac's artistic purpose. He notes, "What is important is the completely integrated process of creating the bunny, bringing her to society at large, and providing her with a loving, caring and nurturing environment in which she can grow safe and healthy. This integrated process is important because it places genetic engineering in a social context in which the relationship between the private and the public spheres are negotiated."

Critics of Kac have noted that he must have doctored his photographs of Alba to make her whole body glow green; in real life, only the ears and eyes of an animal with the jellyfish gene would glow, because hair is dead tissue, and so can't express a gene. Still, whatever Kac did with his photos—and whatever agreements were made about her creation—Alba represents the furthest extension of our ability to breed animals for certain traits. She is a cross not only between a jellyfish and a rabbit, but also between our sci-fi notions of monstrous transgenic animals and our very real ability to bond with our pets. As such, Kac's experiment has been successful—the very fact that Alba remained in a lab in Paris and Kac can publicly proclaim his heartbreak has allowed him to provoke the public (at least those members of the public who care about his experiment/art) to ponder these issues. Just how successful the experiment was for Alba is not clear, however.

In 2002, researchers at INRA also announced that they had successfully cloned rabbits using genetic material from the differentiated cells of adult rabbits. (Rabbits had been cloned as long ago as 1992 using the nuclei of embryonic cells.) The rabbit is only the second "laboratory animal" cloned (after the mouse), although sheep, cattle, goats, pigs and cats have also been cloned.

The French news excited cloning companies around the world for a number of reasons. Cloning in general allows researchers to examine how cells differentiate. Cloning also allows very specific animals—e.g., those with or without certain genes—to be produced, which can facilitate the study of certain diseases and the effects of chemical compounds. There is some talk, too, of using cloned rabbits to produce pharmaceutical proteins in their milk. But cloning rabbits, in particular, is seen as beneficial because they are seen as such good laboratory animals. "It's a milestone in cloning," Robert Lanza, medical director of Advanced Cell Technology, a biotechnology company in Worcester, Mass., told the *Washington Post*. "Rabbits are easy to handle and breed."[12]

But again, the welfare of these rabbits is unclear. The NIAR researchers created four females, who are already beginning to reproduce. The researchers declined to give the four rabbits names, however, just as they declined to name the adult females who provided the genes and eggs from which the clones were created. As the primary researcher told the *Washington Post*, the animals weren't named because they "are starting to be used for research purposes."[13] Manufactured animals, in other words, are things, not sentient beings. In itself, the lack of a name seems like a relatively small problem. (For all we know, a rabbit can respond to "B1" as well as she can to "Beatrice.") It's the attitude that these animals are objects for us to experiment on—or objects for us to create replicas of—that's most disturbing.

Alternatives to Medical Research

Public opinion polls show that many people support the use of live animals for medical research, even while they oppose it for personal or household products. Surveys by the National Science Board have found that public attitudes towards vivisection have changed since 1985, when the NSB first started measuring them. That year, sixty-three percent of the American public agreed that experiments involving pain to dogs and chimpanzees were acceptable if they led to benefits for human health. In 1996, only fifty percent agreed.

Yet the fact remains that many alternatives to animal-based medical research exist. Indeed, according to the Alternatives Research and Development Foundation (ARDF), two thirds of the Nobel Prizes awarded in the fields of physiology and medicine went to researchers who primarily or entirely used non-animal-based methods for their research, indicating the efficacy of such methods, especially in important fields such as AIDS, Alzheimer's and cancer research. Currently all fields of biomedical research utilize alternative methods, and many fields use only non-animal methods. Those alternatives include clinical research and observation, epidemiological studies, human autopsies, in vitro research, research with human tissues and computer and mathematical models. For example, in vitro methods are being tested to develop and test the efficacy of HIV vaccines. The ARDF has also funded tests that will use human cells and recombinant biotechnology to produce monoclonal antibodies (immune-system proteins used in tests that diagnose diseases), and chicken eggs to produce polyclonals; both of these developments will spare the lives of thousands of rabbits, the species that is most widely used for immune system experimentation.

New imaging technology, like ultrasound and nuclear magnetic resonance, allows doctors to "explore" animal bodies without actually invading them. And using human stem cells (taken from aborted human embryos) could also reduce the numbers of animals used in research, as those stem cells can be grown into muscle, blood, bone or any other organ or tissue on which drugs and vaccines can be directly tested.

Life in the Laboratory

Rabbits don't only suffer in the course of the actual experiments. Many of them also live lives of deprivation, loneliness and frustration. Although they are social animals, rabbits are typically housed alone, in steel cages. And although they are active animals, rabbits are typically kept in cages that are "too small to permit some normal behaviors such as sitting up on the hind legs, hopping, digging and hiding," the authors of one report on the welfare of laboratory rabbits wrote in 2002. Those authors, who work at the Animal Care Center of the University of British Columbia, added that "stereotypical bar licking or chewing, pawing at the corners of the cage," psychologically induced excessive thirst and excessive self-grooming "are frequently seen in such animals and are recognized as indicators of reduced well-being."[14] In addition, single-caged rabbits often "look unhealthy and depressed, sitting in a hunched position for hours on end"; they often either under-eat or overeat to counter their boredom; and many develop deformations of the spine and legs because they can't move freely in their small cages.

Regulations regarding housing, care, treatment and transportation of laboratory rabbits are laid out in the Animal Welfare Act, originally passed in 1966 in response to a public outraged by the treatment of laboratory animals. Still, USDA inspections have found that lab rabbits—like other "lab animals"—don't always live in conditions that meet the standards. USDA inspectors have found rabbits in cages that are too small (even by AWA standards), or that are rusty, caked with manure or crawling with insects. They have also found rabbits caged without water, or with soiled water. They have found rabbits whose toenails were so long they were curving out to the side, whose feed bags were crawling with roaches and whose rooms reeked of ammonia from un-cleaned cages.[15]

The Act also requires "enriched environments"—or environments that allow animals to pursue normal behaviors and social interactions—for non-human primate species. The Act carries no such recommendations for the social housing of rabbits, although in its "Standards" section it does suggest that animals in single cages (for instance, un-castrated bucks or rabbits that need to give urine samples) be able to move freely and see other animals. "That's modest encouragement for enrichment," says Dr. Stephens of HSUS.

That's not to say no one has considered enrichment for rabbits. Dozens of studies have been published on the topic since 1991. Researchers have traditionally housed rabbits alone to prevent fighting, pregnancy and disease transmission, as well as to facilitate observing food and water intake and cleaning the cages. But many studies have found that living in group pens allows the rabbits to socialize and exercise, which is so beneficial that "behavioral disorders, which typically occur in single-caged rabbits, are virtually absent," according to the Animal Care Center researchers, whose article surveyed the scientific literature on rabbit enrichment.[16] Those same studies have found that stress-sensitive variables and susceptibility to infectious disease are not significantly affected. In fact, the studies have found, housing female rabbits together seems to make them less susceptible to stress than housing them alone.

Adult male rabbits do tend to fight when living in groups, but some studies have found that neutering the males or, if that's not possible, letting them at least see and smell other rabbits from their single cages is more humane than keeping them in total isolation. The technicians at UBC's Animal Care Center also found that returning a rabbit to its group after surgery—rather than keeping the rabbit alone, as is standard practice—actually hastens the rabbit's recovery.

"It is our experience that rabbits lie down beside a group member who is returning from a surgery and that this extra warmth and comfort hastens the recovery process," they wrote.[17] Several studies have found that putting rabbits who are used to being alone in a small cage into larger, group cages, however, does not work well, as the animals lack good motor coordination—from living in small cages—and have weak bones that are more vulnerable to breaking.

A number of studies have also recommended that rabbits have hay to dig and forage in, shelves to rest on and under, wooden sticks and other materials to gnaw on, toys like wire balls to play with, crates or boxes to hide in and room to run. Again, studies have found that having such enrichment reduces stereotypical stress-related behavior and increases general levels of activity, but results in no deleterious effects on health or hygiene. The researchers at the Animal Care Center even recommend giving rabbits outdoor runs in which to play:

> The outdoor run allows the rabbits to indulge in "fast running," an activity that we frequently observe, particularly in young animals. A rabbit runs quickly to one end of the pen, stops and then runs quickly to the other. This may be repeated several times. We have never observed a special reason for this exercise, other than that the animals obviously enjoy it.[18]

This is the very same play behavior that wild rabbits and domesticated rabbits living "free-range" have exhibited for centuries, yet it is something that has been denied to laboratory rabbits for decades.

Some researchers have even investigated the effect of kind treatment for the rabbits, and have found that gentle handling, patting, playing, being talked to and being given treats all help rabbits feel secure, develop a bond with their handlers, resist infection and stay calm during what can be uncomfortable procedures. A strong bond with the animal also helps the technicians learn to notice the subtle changes in rabbit behavior (e.g., not playing or not eating) that can signal the beginning of an illness.

The rabbits living in the facilities at the University of British Columbia are relatively lucky. Most research rabbits don't get to run, or leap, or spend a sleepy afternoon lying cheek to cheek with another rabbit, or enjoy the affectionate pats and chatter of a caring handler. "We moved enrichment from an interesting research problem to the practical implementation a long time ago," says Dr. Jim Love, who leads the enrichment studies there. "That was possible primarily through the interest and the efforts of the technicians who wanted to make it work. I think that should be the goal of all enrichment studies, i.e., to get the results quickly to the animals." Curiously, this may be one of the few instances in animal science research where the supposed experts—that is, the scientists—are learning what those who live with rabbits have known for a long time. Rabbits like to play. Rabbits like the company of other rabbits. And rabbits thrive in loving human care.

The Fate of Laboratory Rabbits

By far, the vast majority of rabbits used in product testing or medical research are euthanized at the end of the research, if they don't die in the course of the actual experiments. But some rabbits do experience a different fate. Many laboratory technicians and graduate students involved in the care of laboratory animals, for instance, come to feel affection for the animals in their care. In addition to advocating for their better treatment, they sometimes end up "sneaking" them out of the labs and into their homes, or into animal shelters or foster homes.

The liberation of laboratory rabbits is a complicated ethical issue. Margo recently received an email from an employee of a local pharmaceutical company who was hoping to find homes for six two-year old New Zealand White rabbits who had fulfilled their duty to the company. The employee had taken an active interest in these rabbits and provided them with straw-filled exercise pens, toys and treats. Besides ensuring that the rabbits in her care lived the best possible life while in the lab, this employee was proposing that her department consider "retiring" former lab rabbits, rather than euthanizing them, and was looking for help—not just in placing these six rabbits, but in setting a precedent that would allow for the retirement of a great number of future rabbits.

A handful of universities do have staff who work hard to ensure that some of their lab rabbits are placed into homes after their projects are over, and plans currently exist to create a sanctuary in Colorado for former laboratory animals, including rabbits. But proposals like this are not as simple as they seem. Enabling a university or private company to "retire" its research rabbits with rescue groups or at sanctuaries would not, ultimately, end the use of rabbits at that facility, or in research in general. They might even prolong their use. This same issue has come up in greyhound rescue circles, as some say that a guaranteed "rescue" of the dogs actually enables the racing to continue even in the face of great opposition. In the case of lab rabbits, we believe that if we're going to "rescue" or "retire" these animals in the short-term, moral and financial support for viable alternatives to animal testing also has to continue, because that's what will save other rabbits in the long term.

That's not to say in the least that rescuing or retiring lab rabbits—or advocating for their welfare in the laboratory setting—is a bad or futile idea, because the experiences we have had with lab rabbits show that the rabbits benefit enormously from living out their lives in homes where they have compassionate human attention, rabbit friends and no work to do. Margo's first lab rabbit was Mama, an aggressive New Zealand with a large metal identification clip in her ear. Mama arrived at Margo's house with her three babies. Left over from an unknown experiment at a local laboratory, Mama and her family had been sent to the local zoo to be used as snake food but were rescued by a zoo employee who happened to be a rabbit lover. Mama lived with Margo for three years until she died from myxomatosis. It's tempting to tell a "noble" story about a rabbit who came to love the loving humans who cared for her, even after her laboratory ordeals. But the more telling truth is that Mama never did warm up to Margo or to any other humans. She did come to deeply enjoy her life with the other rabbits, however.

Figure 7.4. After leaving the dark cellar where he lived as a lab rabbit, Stimpy learned to enjoy living inside the house and playing outside in the yard. Photo by Margo DeMello.

Stimpy, one of the six rabbits found in the Bay Area laboratory, lived with Margo for more than three years, until he died at the ripe old age of ten. Despite his health problems, he came to enjoy his new life. At night he slept in a large indoor cage with three other rabbits. During the day he played in Margo's backyard, chewing on the grass, lounging in the sun and digging holes in the dirt with his friends. Stimpy, like Mama before him, was lucky. He got out of the lab and was able, before he died, to run and jump, to groom another rabbit and be groomed, to taste grass and dig in the dirt, to feel the sun and sniff the breeze, to do rabbit things and feel rabbit pleasures. Not all of those rabbit pleasures can be made available to the rabbits still being used in laboratories. But without too much effort and too much expense, more of these kind of species-specific "enrichments" could be built into the lives of laboratory rabbits, even as the culture and industry as a whole work toward eradicating unnecessary animal experiments.

Notes

1. McArdle, John, "Small Companion Animals: From the Lap to the Lab," The Alternatives Research & Development Foundation.
2. Sanders, Ron, "Rabbits: Models And Research Applications," United States Army Medical Research Institute of Infectious Disease, Seminar Series 20, October 1989.
3. Humane Society of the United States, "Science and Conscience: The Animal Experimentation Controversy" (Washington, D.C.: National Association for Humane and Environmental Education, 2000), p. 3.
4. United States Department of Agriculture, "Rabbit Calicivirus Disease, Iowa, April 2000 Impact Worksheet," http://www.aphis.usda.gov/vs/ceah/cei/rabbitcal.htm.
5. Lamar, Pat, "Laboratory Rabbits," at http://www.3–cities.com/~fuzyfarm.
6. Weil, C.S., and R.A. Scala, "Study of intra- and interlaboratory variability in the results of rabbit eye and skin irritation tests" *Toxicology and Applied Pharmacology* 1971, 19:276–360.
7. D'Amato, Lisa, "Cruelty-free Eye Tests," *Kitchener-Waterloo Record*, January 27, 2001.
8. Keville, Kathy, "Compassionate Cosmetics," *Better Nutrition*, Vol. 64, No. 6 (June 1, 2002), p. 58.
9. Humane Society of the United States, "An Overview of the High Production Volume Chemical Testing Program," http://www.hsus.org/ace/Article_Printer_Friendly?Content_ID=12574 accessed August 20, 2002.
10. McArdle, *op. cit.*
11. Animal Welfare Institute, *Beyond the Laboratory Door* (Washington, D.C.: The Animal Welfare Institute, 1985), pp. 123–30.
12. Brown, David, "French researchers add rabbits to list of clones," *Washington Post*, March 30, 2002.
13. *Ibid.*
14. Boers, K., et al., "Comfortable Quarters for Rabbits in Research Institutions," in Reinhardt and Reinhardt (eds.), *Comfortable Quarters for Laboratory Animals* (Washington, D.C.: Animal Welfare Institute, 2002), pp. 43–49.
15. For examples, see pages 7, 20, 22 and 25 in *Beyond the Laboratory Door*, published by the Animal Welfare Institute.
16. Boers, *op. cit.*, p. 43.
17. *Ibid.*, p. 44.
18. *Ibid.*, p. 45.

8. How Much is That Rabbit in the Window?

The Pet Rabbit Industry

———•◆•———

"Thank you, Father," said Dick.
"Thank you for the pet rabbit."

"Come here, Sally," said Father.
"You did not see the rabbit.
Do you want it for a pet?"

"No thank you," said Sally.
"I want a little yellow duck.
Get a yellow duck for me."

From "Two Pets" from *The New Fun with Dick and Jane*, 1950, p. 51.

IN THE LAST few years, several animal protection organizations have publicized the plight of puppies and dogs living in puppy mills— large, often unlicensed facilities used to breed dogs for the wholesale market. Dogs in these facilities spend their entire lives in wire cages and are bred over and over again, producing litter after litter. The puppies from those litters are then sold, via brokers, to pet stores and others. Exposés on *Dateline* and *20/20*, and in publications like *The Atlantic Monthly*, have exposed millions of Americans to the horror that these dogs endure and to the health problems often prevalent in the puppies bred in these mills.

Most people have no idea that other species are also bred in such mills—that, for instance, many thousands of rabbits are created annually by commercial breeders for the pet store market. Nor are most people aware that vast numbers of those rabbits are then euthanized annually at animal shelters across the country, because their caretakers no longer want them. While a good portion of the American public now adopts cats and dogs from shelters, rather than buying the animals from pet stores or breeders, people who want rabbits as pets generally still buy them from these sources. According to the American Pet Products Manufacturers Association, about twenty percent of the people who currently live with rabbits bought them at an independent pet store. Another one percent went to a pet superstore. Twelve percent went to a breeder and five percent went through the newspapers. Another thirty-one percent claim they got their rabbit from a friend. An investigation of where those rabbits come from—and how they were bred, raised and transported before they were purchased—sheds light on a "cute bunny" industry that very few people understand or would feel comfortable supporting for other species.

How Pet Rabbits Are Made

It's hard to know exactly how many pet rabbit breeders exist in the United States today. One 1998 ARBA survey noted that 66.5 percent of its 30,000 members raise pet rabbits, but not all rabbit breeders belong to ARBA, and some meat breeders sell some of their kits as pets. What we do know is that today pet rabbit breeders range from the small backyard or hobby breeders, to sophisticated show breeders (with an extensive knowledge of genetics and selective breeding), to very large commercial rabbitries, some of which we could call "rabbit mills."

These commercial pet rabbit breeders sell large numbers of rabbits at wholesale prices either directly to pet stores or through wholesalers who act as middlemen. The USDA estimates that in 1998 136 such rabbit breeding and dealing facilities were inspected by the USDA. Those facilities contained some 84,000 rabbits. (The USDA does not inspect rabbitries that sell directly to the public.)[1]

Wholesale breeders usually get a low price for each rabbit (generally from $3 to $5 per rabbit) in order to provide some profit margin to both the wholesaler and the pet store, which can sell the rabbits for upwards of $25. Many smaller breeders do not have the facilities for such a large-scale operation, so they sell directly to the customer (via advertisements in magazines like *Rabbits Annual*) or to small, local pet stores. But customers who purchase a rabbit at a chain pet store like Petland or Petco are most likely buying a rabbit who was bred at a rabbit mill and sent to the store via a wholesale middleman.

Rabbit Mills

Whether or not a rabbit breeder is a rabbit mill depends very much on who's doing the analysis. Animal protection groups generally go for a broader definition (e.g., a large-scale breeding operation where rabbits are kept in unhealthy conditions, bred frequently and without regard to their own welfare and sold at low prices to pet stores or wholesalers). Breeders often define the term more narrowly. According to the Rabbit Education Society, whose members are mostly breeders, "A rabbit mill is a business where rabbits are kept in filthy and unhealthy conditions and bred without regard to breed purity, genetic abnormalities, health, or their welfare in great quantities solely for the pet market for profit at ages too young to ensure their survivability."[2] Sometimes those mills are producing other species, as well; often the animals are sick or dying. One breeder writing into the Rabbit Education Society (RES) Web site added, "[Rabbit] mills have to do with conditions, not numbers, not types."

That rabbit mills exist can't be denied—many breeders complain that other breeders are selling three- and four-week-old kits to pet stores (because pet stores, and pet store patrons, want "cute" baby animals) and that many sell mixed breeds that are passed off as purebreds, keep their females pregnant all the time and have poor hus-

Figure 8.1. This Missouri rabbitry kept and bred its animals in miserable conditions. Courtesy Marshall Smith, In Defense of Animals.

bandry standards.[3] "Sadly, rabbit mills really do exist," says Pamela Alley, a breeder of Rex and other breeds in Oroville, California. "I've seen them. And I say sadly because it's just not acceptable to be selling rabbits that are three to five weeks old. But it happens all the time. Pet stores want rabbits that are small and cute. After that, their popularity starts to drop."

Sandy Koi, a House Rabbit Society representative, visited a Florida rabbitry that raised hundreds of rabbits at a time for for the pet rabbit market, for alligator food and for the meat market. Koi reports that the rabbits were housed outdoors, several to a cage, with food provided in large bowls and water in rusty coffee cans. Feces were piled underneath the wire cages, which contained no toys, resting mats or other diversions. The rabbitry was violating no law, as it provided food, water and shelter. But the conditions were miserable and most of the rabbits had nasal discharge, often a sign of respiratory infection. At another rabbitry, this one in Pennsylvania, Koi found similar conditions: one hundred or more Angora rabbits, piled into cages that were too small, with only pellets and water to distract themselves, and with matted, dirty fur. Such conditions are unconscionable—and would probably merit news coverage—for puppies. But "rabbit mills" are far below the radar of the American public. Indeed, according to the news database LexisNexis, in the last thirty years, no newspaper has investigated the issue of rabbit mills, despite the plethora of stories about Easter bunnies that are published each year.

Part of the problem is that getting solid information on these mills is nearly impossible. Any commercial breeder making an annual profit over $500 automatically qualifies for USDA licensing and must provide care consistent with the Animal Welfare Act. However, periodic visits by USDA inspectors notwithstanding, rabbit mills, like puppy mills, are largely unregulated. As Marshall Smith, a former USDA inspector, points out, funds are so tight that inspectors can barely cover their regions. Providing more funding for inspectors—and creating laws aimed at banning inhumane breeding establishments—would help put an end to breeding mills for rabbits, as well as for dogs. (This may be easier said than done, as efforts to ban puppy mills have already been stymied by the powerful pet store lobby.) Another helpful step would be educating potential rabbit caretakers that buying a rabbit from a shelter saves one animal's life and lessens the demand for more mass-bred baby bunnies.

Animal Dealers

The majority of rabbits in pet stores come from larger wholesalers or brokers—also licensed by the USDA—who buy and sell rabbits, as well as other animals, on a weekly basis. Breeders generally don't have a large enough market in their own areas to make a profit, so they sell to brokers, who can transport their animals to stores around the country. According to some breeders, this is where the inhumane treatment begins. On the Rabbit Education Society Web site, one breeder noted that it's the brokers (speaking for pet stores) who demand prematurely weaned animals and then transport baby bunnies in poor conditions over long distances to their ultimate destinations. Because the rabbits purchased by the dealer are so young, and conditions during transportation so difficult, dealers and pet stores generally assume that twenty to thirty percent of the babies will die en route. The system continues, however, because, breeders who refuse to sell rabbits that young will lose their business.

Brokers who buy and sell a number of species for a number of markets are known as Class B (or random source) dealers, and obtain their animals from sources as divergent as shelters, breeders and animal auctions or trade and sale days, and sell them to pet stores, research institutions and for food and fur. Many dealers even buy back the rabbits (and other animals) who are returned to pet stores and then re-sell them at animal auctions and stock sales. Breeders acknowledge that under this system some rabbits go through stock sales three times before they are finally sold.[4]

Pet stores place their animal orders with their dealer about once a week. The dealer then arranges to have all the animals shipped to the store in a large truck. Like commercial breeders, the dealers' facilities are subject to USDA inspections, but as with breeding facilities, this is no guarantee that the animals in a dealer's control will be treated humanely, as inspections are just as patchy, and enforcement just as light. In addition, there is very little oversight during the transportation process, the period during which deaths will be highest.

Pet Stores

A baby rabbit who survives first the breeder facility and then the long truck ride to a pet store is not guaranteed a healthy or happy life. Pet stores that sell live animals are generally not known for excellent attention to their charges. And baby rabbits at pet stores rarely face any kind of quarantine procedure, which means that any disease one rabbit has may very well spread to the others. One Angora breeder suggests that twenty percent of all newly arrived baby rabbits die during the first week at the store, most likely from enteritis—if you add this to an estimated twenty to thirty percent mortality rate during transit, this means that between one-third and one-half of all baby rabbits die before they can be sold.[5] The surviving babies spend their time at the store being handled by large numbers of people and most likely will be cared for by staff untrained in rabbit husbandry. Rabbit lovers across the country have reported dozens, if not hundreds, of instances in which rabbits in pet stores have no water, or no toys, or are in too-small cages, or are on wire floors, or have the wrong kind of food or are clearly sick, stressed or both. "I'd rather kill the rabbits and put them in my freezer than sell to the pet market," Alley says. "At least then I know what happened to them."

What's harder for consumers to see is whether or not animals have received adequate veterinary care, whether they've been weaned prematurely, whether they are housed with animals of opposite sex (which causes pregnancy) and how the unsold animals die. One pet store owner in Madison, Wisconsin told his staff to suffocate excess rabbits by putting them in Styrofoam containers and taping them shut.[6] In Britain, former employees of Petsmart, the country's largest pet store chain, said that sick rabbits were clubbed to death with spades.[7]

Often the staff cannot give even the most basic care information with the rabbits that they sell. No pet stores that we know of provide any sort of pre-sale counseling, nor do they refuse to sell rabbits to people who seem irresponsible. One breeder—who sells her rabbits both as pets and as feeders (that is, snake food)—claims that demand for the latter is actually larger than that for the former, and that many breeders who sell "pet" rabbits to pet stores may be unwittingly turning their animals into snake snacks.[8] (Such callousness is not specific to the treatment of rabbits, of course—Susan once overheard a young man at Petco laughingly complaining that he kept "losing" his mice out his car window. The clerk cheerfully sold him two more mice, seemingly unaware or unconcerned that the man was engaged in some sort of sadistic game.)

Sadly, once the consumer has purchased a cute baby rabbit, the rabbit will often die within a few weeks of going home. Many of these people won't tell the pet store, thinking that it was their own poor care that killed their new rabbit. Sometimes that is the case. More often, the series of stresses and traumas that these young and vulnerable bunnies have had to endure from the time of their birth will have simply killed them.

Pet stores that sell animals are coming under increasing fire from animal protection advocates for the lack of care that they provide to their animals, and to the often brutal conditions in which they live. Groups ranging from PETA to House Rabbit Society, for example, have campaigned against Petco, one of the largest national chains still selling rabbits. According to complaints from customers and district attorneys across the country, Petco stores routinely keep animals without adequate food or water and in cages that are much too small, and they refuse to medicate animals that are sick. (As one Petco employee told an investigator with PETA, "We sell pets; we're not an animal hospital.") The city of San Francisco recently filed a lawsuit against the local Petco after investigators found dead and dying animals throughout the store, as well as dying animals in the freezer. (That particular Petco didn't sell live rabbits, but other complaints have been launched against other Petcos for selling sick rabbits to customers.)

To make matters worse, animals kept at pet stores are not protected by the Animal Welfare Act, which means that once they leave the breeding facility, no rules regulate their care. As of this writing, twenty-four states have enacted laws that cover humane care for animals kept in pet stores, but both the conditions required and the species covered vary from state to state. All of the state laws require food and water for pet store animals. Only four states have laws that cover sanitary conditions, enclosures, temperature, veterinary care and the sale of unweaned animals. Only nineteen states have laws that include rabbits.

Selling Directly to Customers

Breeders who either won't or can't afford to sell to pet stores, but who still cater to the pet rabbit market, sell their rabbits directly to the consumer via advertising and word of mouth. According to ARBA, the majority of pet rabbit breeders sell this way. Rabbits purchased from breeders generally fare better than the rabbits sold through pet stores, because the breeder can better control with whom the rabbits will end up and what kind of care information the buyer gets. The typical price will range from $15 to $25 per rabbit (as opposed to the $5.00 the breeder might get from a dealer or pet store). These breeders often provide care information for their rabbits, and some will screen potential buyers to ensure that the rabbit will go to a good home. Some go as far as to recommend that the rabbit be spayed or neutered, provide information on litter box training and other aspects of house rabbit care and recommend that the new "purchaser" join an education group like House Rabbit Society.

Other breeders, who breed primarily for show purposes, use the pet market as a way to get rid of their "culls," or undesirable rabbits who might otherwise be killed. Not every rabbit born into a breeding facility will qualify for show purposes, and few breeders are able to keep every rabbit born on their premises. This means that there will be "excess" rabbits for the breeder to dispose of. Some breeders simply kill these undesirable rabbits; others sell them for meat or as pets.

The busiest season for selling pet rabbits, of course, is during Easter, when many parents, especially, buy baby rabbits for their children. (Many of them buy dwarf rabbit breeds, because they seem so cute.) But because few of those parents are given good care information, they often end up with rabbits who become sick, timid or even downright aggressive when their hormones kick in at four to six months of age. A great majority of those young rabbits are then either surrendered to animal shelters (where they are most often euthanized) or released in the wild. The number of rabbits killed in shelters can be alarmingly high: in 1998 one Montreal animal shelter noted that it euthanizes ninety-eight percent of the 350–500 rabbits it receives each year after Easter.

Hobby and Show Breeding
Because there is little money to be made by breeders who don't sell to dealers or pet stores, many are hobby breeders, or breed specifically for show. According to one RES survey, a full ninety percent of those surveyed consider themselves hobbyists. Rabbits bred for show

purposes must conform to a breed "Standard of Perfection," otherwise they will be "culled" or killed. Rabbit shows are held year-round, all around the country, and are sponsored by ARBA or 4-H. There people show their own rabbits, but also network with other breeders and buy and sell breeding "stock" as well as equipment and supplies. Having winning rabbits usually increases sales for show breeders, as more people will want to buy the offspring of proven winners, one area where profits can be quite high.

In the last few years, there has been considerable antipathy between show rabbit breeders and rabbit rescuers. While show rabbit breeders do not conform to most definitions of rabbit mills (as they breed less for quantity than "quality"), rescue groups and many house rabbit advocates still find fault with them for several reasons. Besides the basic problem of breeding rabbits when other, unwanted rabbits are dying at animal shelters, "fancy" breeders will breed only purebred rabbits, thus continuing the perception that there is something wrong with mixed-breed rabbits. Show rabbits, like show dogs and cats, are also never spayed or neutered, putting the lives of the rabbits (especially the females) at risk in order to conform to the breed's standard. While the rabbits may be much loved and admired by the breeders, they still spend their lives traveling from show to show, living either in carriers or cages, which can be stressful for a species that, by and large, doesn't like to leave its territory or travel in cars.

In addition, while many "fancy" breeders take good care of their animals, others allow them to languish in horrible conditions. Kirk Lowis, now the Michigan House Rabbit Society chapter manager, encountered terrible conditions when he visited a Michigan rabbitry to investigate cruelty charges. The rabbits bred at the facility were show rabbits who often sold for hundreds of dollars apiece. At the time, Kirk noted:

> Another volunteer and I spent about two hours removing the matted fur, pus and necrotic skin from one large female rabbit. I was absolutely shocked at the magnitude of her infec-

tion. . . . She had clearly had this infection for some time and it was allowed to fester without proper attention and veterinary care. Her eyes were both swollen shut. The fur surrounding the eyes had long since matted to a rock-hard consistency from the copious weeping of the infected eyes. . . . When we removed as much of the matted fur as possible the smell and sight of the rotting, infected skin was unbelievable.

There are many Angora and other long-haired breeds in this case. These rabbits all came to the shelter with severe matting in their fur. Some were so severely matted that they couldn't move their legs. All of them had urine and feces caked in with the mats all over their hindquarters.

Many of them came into the shelter with their noses almost entirely encrusted over with mucus. The rabbits with nasal discharge that I worked with were all wheezing and struggling to breathe; rabbits breathe primarily through their nose. When the tiny nasal passageways become filled with mucus the rabbit cannot breathe properly. I should also point out that keeping rabbits in unsanitary conditions where there is a high concentration of ammonia (from urine) can compromise the rabbits' respiratory system and allow these types of infections to take over. The smell of urine was still quite strong and acrid on these rabbits' fur even after being relocated; this suggests that they were kept in conditions where the ammonia concentration in the air was far too high and certainly unhealthy.

You could clearly tell by looking at the rabbits which ones had been on the top, middle or bottom of the stacks of cages based upon the amount of urine you would find on their heads, faces, shoulders and backs. Rabbits who were kept on the bottom row of cages fared the worst, getting soiled by the urine and feces from the rabbits in cages stacked over their own.

Lowis noted that rabbits to be sold would be cleaned up prior to shows and that the babies would be removed from the squalor before they had a chance to get sick or covered in urine and feces like their parents.[9]

The Breeding Process

In order to be successful, rabbit breeders need to worry about a number of factors that pet rabbit owners generally do not. "Selecting" stock, for instance, involves looking for does or bucks (called "earning units") who have proven that they can deliver large litters, can produce heavy amounts of milk, can be bred frequently, are resistant to disease (given the difficult environment) and have desirable shape and color. "Replacing" stock involves getting rid of certain does who aren't "good mothers" (either because they don't give birth to large litters or because they don't nurture the kits well) to ensure high levels of production. According to Manna Pro (a rabbit food producer), most successful breeders replace fifty percent of their breeding does every year in order to keep production as high as possible. Breeders must also decide which breeding bucks, and which baby rabbits, to keep and which to "cull."

"Culling" doesn't always mean killing. Sometimes baby rabbits who are deemed unacceptable for the show table are sold—or given away—as pets. But most often they are sold to meat processors or as food for other species. According to many small breeders, only those with genetic defects are killed (yet what constitutes a genetic defect—like a tooth problem—does not necessarily preclude a happy and healthy life as a pet). Large commercial breeders tend to kill all of their undesirables, whether the rabbit's markings aren't right, his shape isn't perfect, he's not easy to handle or he has a runny nose. When one member of the meatrabbits@yahoogroups.com listserve posted a panicky note about many of her kits having a nasal discharge (a condition that probably could have been treated with antibiotics), Pamela Alley, the Rex breeder in California, responded: "First step: CULL and HARD!!! Smack all kits that look ill, NOW. Smack every kit that even LOOKS like it might be sick! Isolate associated animals and litters, and check DAILY for more problems and smack them, too...Cull, cull, cull, CULL!! Then cull some more. And I mean kill 'em..."[10]

The culling technique varies from breeder to breeder; as the *Lop Rabbit Club of America Guidebook* notes,

> Culling is emotionally and physically difficult. It's easiest when the kits are tiny, at that time a violent collision with the floor or wall does the job immediately and humanely. Older rabbits are much harder. The USDA approved process is to put carbon dioxide in the bottom of an airtight container and then lower the rabbit into the bottom. Check with experienced breeders and see what else is done in your part of the world.[11]

Most experienced breeders actually use other techniques, as evidenced in one online chat of the Professional Rabbit Meat Association. During that session, one participant asked if there was an "easy way" of culling rabbits, like, she suggested, throwing them, alive, in the freezer. Other participants noted that freezing live animals to death is inhumane, but that shooting them, breaking their necks, or bonking them over the head works well. One participant said his favorite tool was an empty champagne bottle; others chimed in "Who can afford champagne?" and "kinda like christianing [sic] a ship." When one member said he uses "firewood," Pat Lamar, who co-founded the PRMA, punned, "That's been proven to be pretty hard on rabbits, Haw."

A few participants in this chat admitted they felt squeamish about slaughtering their own animals—or selling them live to people with reptiles who, presumably, would also eat them alive. Yet within a few seconds, the online conversation took an even more glib tone, as the chat participants joked about ways that backyard butchering can go awry. One participant, for instance, said that he was afraid of using a stun gun incorrectly and "torturing the poor critter." The host of the chat wrote "ROFL" (for "rolling on the floor, laughing"); another participant wrote: "I got this extreme visual and then fell off my chair!" Humor is clearly subjective.

Some show rabbits experience multiple culling cycles in their lives. Many breeders first cull their litters at five to six weeks, and then at twelve to thirteen weeks, when body "faults" are easier to spot. Show breeders also do one final cull after a rabbit's first show, at approximately twelve months. Manna Pro recommends that each litter be culled as follows: cull the smallest of the litter, the individuals who are mismarked and those with any other visible disqualification. Only then, the company notes, should a breeder start culling for breed standards. This involves, as one can imagine, quite a few rabbits being eliminated. As one breeder writes: "Only 5% of most herds produce 95% of your winners! Why keep the others? Think of the money that can be saved on feed!"[12]

The Debate over Breeding

Unlike organizations that promote pet cat and dog breeding, rabbit breeder groups support the breeding of rabbits both for the pet rabbit and show (or fancy) rabbit industries, and for fur, meat and vivisection. The largest of these groups is the American Rabbit Breeders Association (ARBA), with more than 30,000 members. The association supports all three types of breeders (although the organization's current focus is on show and pet rabbits). Likewise, the Rabbit Education Society (RES), started by breeder Corinne Fayo, promotes breeding for pet rabbits, shows and other purposes (although the organization is primarily aimed at pet rabbit breeders). The RES tends to be more political than ARBA; it claims on its Web site that the organization is "fighting for our rights" against "the radical animal rights movement."

The considerable animosity that exists between rabbit rescuers and rabbit breeders focuses on the ethics of breeding itself. That is, most rabbit rescuers oppose the commercial breeding of rabbits for fur, meat and vivisection. But the debate surrounding the breeding of pet rabbits is a more complicated issue. Many rabbit rescuers (and animal rights activists) argue that pet rabbit breeding should slow down because the country is currently suffering from a glut of pet rabbits, so much so that they are the third most euthanized pet in the nation's shelters. But some industry groups claim no such overpopulation exists. "The RES does not recognize the term 'overpopulation,' " Fayo writes on her Web site, "as it is inaccurate and has not been proven to exist and is a word meant to stir the emotions and demonize rabbit breeders as a part of animal rights propaganda."[13]

The debate sometimes reaches absurd levels. Some rabbit rescuers criticize not only all breeders and the act of breeding, but any breed preferences (which can lead one to feel embarrassed about being crazy for Belgian Hares, say, or for scanning animal shelters for abandoned Giant Chinchillas). Some rabbit industry groups, in turn, claim that rabbit rescue groups, which are generally filled with gentle bunny lovers, are actually terrorist groups. (In fact, many rabbit advocates take a more conservative, welfare-oriented approach.)

Unfortunately, no national statistics exist on how many rabbits end up in animal shelters every year, because animal shelters typically do not keep records on the rabbits who are surrendered, adopted or euthanized. One RES survey estimates that 43,517 rabbits were surrendered to U.S. shelters in 1996; a survey of British shelters suggests that some 24,000 rabbits were surrendered to shelters in the U.K. in 1997. That estimate is probably too low. Rabbit rescuers across the country have long known that the great majority of rabbits surrendered to shelters are euthanized—and that a great many more are dumped in forests, parking lots and city parks. In the Bay Area alone, the House Rabbit Society shelter serves more than two dozen animal shelters and turns down dozens of rabbits from those and other shelters—as well as from the public—every week. Similarly, in the St. Louis area, House Rabbit Society members are in contact with twelve animal shelters, only two of which even attempt to adopt their rabbits out; the rest are euthanized.

Just who is to blame for this problem is also a topic of lively debate. Certainly breeders and pet stores who sell to the public without screening or educating them bear a good portion of the blame for the numbers of rabbits left at shelters every year. But some breeders actually blame "irresponsible pet owners" (for not knowing what no one told them, presumably), while Pat Lamar, president of the Professional Rabbit Meat Association (PRMA), has blamed House Rabbit Society, writing:

> [I]n their effort to re-home more abandoned rabbits, the HRS promotes and encourages house rabbit owners to "adopt a companion" for the existing house rabbit and without informing the adopters of the dangers and difficulties involved in attempting to "bond" two naturally territorial rabbits, even when they have been neutered or spayed. When the "bonding" fails, one of the rabbits usually winds up on the doorstep of a breeder or is, again, abandoned, since the owner is either too disgusted, disillusioned or embarrassed to take the rabbit back to the HRS adoption center.

Ironically, House Rabbit Society is the recognized leader in providing information on rabbit care and is a pioneer in the art and science of safely bonding altered rabbits so they can live together in the home.

The larger issue of breeding and overpopulation may never be thoroughly solved, in part because rabbit rescuers and rabbit breeders tend to come from very different perspectives. But some steps can be taken to ensure greater welfare for the animals. Pet dealers should be monitored more carefully. More laws should be created (and enforced) that call for older weaning times, quarantines, enriched cages and veterinary care for pet shop rabbits. Proper rabbit care guidelines should be distributed when rabbits are sold, to at least give the caregiver a chance at providing proper food, housing and interaction. (Pet store staff should also be required to read and understand those guidelines.) More shelters should advertise their available rabbits, as well as provide good care guidelines, and the public, we believe, should be better educated about both the existence of rabbit mills and humane alternatives to supporting them. Cities and counties that have passed mandatory spay/neuter ordinances for cats and dogs have seen the numbers of cats and dogs euthanized at their shelters go down; similar laws could be passed for pet rabbits. Finally, rabbit breeders should pay attention to the numbers of rabbits in their communities being euthanized, abandoned and otherwise " gotten rid of" and should modify their own breeding practices accordingly.

Military Rabbits
While rabbits have clothed, fed and entertained people for thousands of years, it has only been in the last hundred years that they have represented a source of profit to a wide range of individuals in this country. No other animal's fur, flesh and organs have been used for so many different purposes. And no other animal's products have been marketed to such a broad economic spectrum. Rabbit meat is currently sold as a high-end "white meat" in the United States and as an inexpensive protein source in developing countries. Rabbit pelts are sewn into expensive fur coats and used on cheap cat toys. And rabbits are bred and sold for laboratory use, for $25 or $250, depending on the environment in which they were born and raised.

Rabbits have also been the animal of choice for other revenue- (and adrenaline-) producing schemes. The military, for instance, regularly uses rabbits (as well as goats and chickens) for training in "emergency food procurement," or rather, learning how to kill animals when the soldiers need food. It's a little unclear just how many branches of the military use rabbits, but government documents show that two Air Force bases alone use more than 1,500 rabbits each year. According to the PRMA, color and breed do not matter for survival training, but up-eared (non-lop) rabbits are preferred, presumably because soldiers would see lops as too pet-like to hunt down and slaughter with their bare hands.

Private tracking or survival training schools also offer their paying participants the chance to chase, slaughter and prepare their own domestic rabbit, as do some Boy Scouts of America clubs. In 1998, former scout leader Diana Orr, founder of a rabbit rescue organization in Texas, forced her local Boy Scouts club to stop killing domestic rabbits during their survival training. They switched to chickens instead, which prompted a successful protest by the United Poultry Concerns later that same year.

Dog Bait

Greyhound racing began in the nineteenth century, when farmers brought greyhounds to the United States to hunt jackrabbits who were destroying crops. People began betting on which dogs could catch the rabbits first, and a new sport was born. Traditionally, greyhound racers used live rabbits to train the animals (and to lure them down the track on race day). The National Greyhound Association banned using live rabbits for greyhound training in 1978, due to public opposition to the grisly practice. Today, the NGA claims, both races and trainers use artificial lures, and "industry members who violate this practice may be expelled from the sport for life."[14] Yet several animal protection organizations have found that trainers continue to use the live animals for training. The live rabbits are either allowed to run or are whisked around on a whirligig. If the rabbit survives the chase, he or she is typically tossed to the dogs and torn apart. According to the Animal Rights Foundation of Florida, which is the top greyhound racing state in the country,

> For each of the approximately 17,000 greyhounds registered in one year, at least five small animals, mostly rabbits, are killed in training. . . . Less aggressive dogs are often placed in a cage with a rabbit or other animal and are not released or fed until they kill the cage companion.[15]

In an article on the Adopt-A-Greyhound Web site, Robert Baker, Chief Investigator for the Humane Society of the United States, also noted that using live rabbits is still common, as it is still legal in many states. "I've seen them training these dogs first hand," Baker said. "Ninety percent of them use live lures. They believe the dogs will race faster when they're trained on a live animal rather than an artificial lure." Baker claimed that more than 100,000 animals, includ-

Figure 8.2. Hare coursing, in which greyhounds chase and then tear apart a hare, remains a popular sport in the United Kingdom and in several states in the western U.S. Courtesy Animals Voice Online.

ing jackrabbits, guinea pigs, domestic rabbits and chickens, are used in greyhound training every year. "Most commonly, jackrabbits are used in coursing, domestic rabbits on the whirligig because the animals are tied so they don't have to be fast," Baker said. "For a while, the industry was promoting guinea pigs because they squealed so loud and the dogs like a loud squeal. That's why [trainers] break the jackrabbits' legs. . . . At one place, we went to a trash barrel where they were throwing the discarded rabbits and one was still alive. They didn't even have the decency to put the rabbit out of its misery when they were done using it."[16]

As recently as October of 2002, a greyhound racer in the Phoenix, Arizona area had his racing license temporarily suspended after he was found to be using live rabbits as lures. While it was unclear from the investigation how many rabbits had died during training at the kennel, more than 180 live rabbits were found on the premises, including one dying rabbit attached to a whirligig.[17]

Pulling Rabbits out of Hats
Some breeders sell to the very small and very specialized magic market. Magicians usually want rabbits who are small, docile and easy

to handle, and white remains the most popular color. (These criteria, unfortunately, are somewhat contradictory, as larger rabbits tend to be more docile than smaller ones, and most props are built for smaller animals.)

Today many "live rabbit" tricks have been replaced by tricks involving fake rabbits (such as "Hippy Hop Rabbits," "Multiplying Rabbits" or "Run Rabbit Run"), in part because many cities now ban the use of live animals in performances like circuses. Yet some magicians, particularly those who specialize in children's parties, still use live rabbits in their acts and still defend their choices. When the city of Newcastle upon Tyne (in the United Kingdom) tried to ban Mr. Duffy, a magician, from using his white rabbit, Sapphire, in his act, Mr. Duffy protested, saying, "My act does not involve my rabbit being squashed, dropped from a great height or in any way propelled into the box. It's just an illusion and I take her for check-ups at the vet's every three months." The city council relented.[18]

One California magician, Rick Allen, is also well known for using live rabbits—in his case, rescued Easter bunnies who are thereby given a second life. According to Allen, also known as the Hollywood Magician, his rabbit, Hocus Pocus (a Hotot), is the world's happiest rabbit, with a very large cage and lots of love. While some animal rights activists might say that Allen is exploiting Hocus Pocus, we think that Allen is doing what many rabbit rescuers try to do: giving rabbits that have been abused, abandoned or simply overlooked a chance for a happier life.

◆   ◆   ◆

It's hard to hear about animals suffering. In the course of writing these chapters, in fact, many people told us that they couldn't bear to hear about rabbits being slaughtered, experimented on or even perishing on trucks on their way to pet stores; we suspect that many readers ended up skimming some of the sections where we discussed these issues in detail. We didn't describe these procedures simply for shock value. We did it partly because outside of the meat,

Figure 8.3. The magician Zan Zig performs with a rabbit and roses. Library of Congress, Prints and Photographs Division.

fur, vivisection and pet store industries, it seems that most people have no idea what most domestic rabbits in the world experience in their (usually) very short lives. We also added these details because outside the pet rabbit world (and, more specifically, outside the house rabbit world), it seems that most people don't understand that rabbits are capable not only of joy, love and bonding, but also of profound suffering. That is, one purpose of this book has been to show that rabbits are smart, emotional and social creatures; the other purpose has been to show that for these very reasons, the dominant ways of using them are inhumane. As Peter Singer once wrote, in regard to meat production specifically, "Those who, by their purchases, require animals to be killed, have no right to be shielded from this or any other aspect of the production of the meat they buy. If it is distasteful to humans to think about, what can it be like for the animals to experience it?"[19] That's a harsh statement, but it's also one with which we found ourselves agreeing as we researched these chapters. Supporting—even reinforcing—images of rabbits as happy, cuddly frolicsome beings is dishonest—even illogical—given the miserable conditions in which so many of them are born, raised, and slaughtered. And maintaining silence (or ignorance) about these conditions neither gives rabbits a chance for something better nor allows humans to *do* better in their treatment of this (or any other) species.

Notes

1. United States Department of Agriculture, "Rabbit Calicivirus Disease, Iowa, April 2000 Impact Worksheet," http://www.aphis.usda.gov/vs/ceah/cei/rabbitcal.htm.
2. Rabbit Education Society (RES) Web site, http://www.rabbited.0catch.com.
3. RES.
4. RES, "RES Report On Substandard Commercial Breeding Facilities," http://www.rabbited.0catch.com/Rreports.html.
5. From Angie K. of Angie's Angoras, taken from a discussion on the Showbunny Web site (www.showbunny.com), reprinted on RES Web site.
6. Elbow, Steve, "Owners Charged with Animal Deaths, Neglect," *The Capital Times*, November 2, 2001.
7. "Catalog of Cruelty," *Bristol Evening Post*, December 3, 1999.
8. Kincaid, Molly, "Selling Rabbits to Pet Stores: Is It Really Good Business?" www.Rabbitweb.net.
9. Personal communication with the authors.
10. Posted to meatrabbits@yahoogroups.com on November 29, 2002.
11. Pett, David, Editor's comment in "Culling for Quality" by Lana Gore, in *Lop Rabbit Club of America Guidebook,* 5th edition (Lop Rabbit Club of America, 1996), p. 70.
12. Dill, Marti, "5% Produces 95% Winners," ARBA Web site, www.arba.net.
13. RES.
14. National Greyhound Association Web site, http://www.ngagreyhounds.com.
15. Animal Rights Foundation of Florida, "Greyhound Racing: Death in the Fast Lane," on Animal Concerns Web site, http://articles.animalconcerns.org/arvoices/archive/greyhounds.html.
16. King, Marcia, "Racing Greyhounds: Bred to Run or Born to Die," on Adopt-A-Greyhound Web site, http://www.adopt-a-greyhound.org/about/body_king.html.
17. Pitzl, Mary Jo, "Dog Breeder Gets 60-Day Suspension," *The Arizona Republic*, November 15, 2002.
18. "Council Apologises for Banning Magician's Rabbit," http://www.ananova.com/news/story/sm_658846.html, August 28, 2002.
19. Schleifer, Harriet, "Images of Death and Life: Food Animal Production and the Vegetarian Option," in Singer, Peter (ed.), *In Defense of Animals* (Oxford: Basil Blackwell, 1985), p. 69.

CONCLUSION

The Rabbit-Human Bond

———•·•———

Well—one at least is safe. One shelter'd hare
has never heard the sanguinary yell
of cruel man, exulting in her woes.
Innocent partner of my peaceful home,
Whom ten long years' experience of my care
Has made at last familiar; she has lost
Much of her vigilant instinctive dread,
Not needful here, beneath a roof like mine.
Yes—thou may'st eat thy bread, and lick the hand
That feeds thee; thou may'st frolic on the floor
At evening, and at night retire secure
To thy straw couch, and slumber unalarm'd;
For I have gain'd the confidence, have pledg'd
All that is human in me to protect
Thine unsuspecting gratitude and love.
If I survive thee I will dig thy grave;
And, when I place thee in it, sighing, say,
I knew at least one hare that had a friend.

William Cowper, from *The Task*, Book III, "The Garden"

WHEN WE FIRST started thinking about this book, we didn't
expect to write about the commercial rabbit industries. We knew

domestic rabbits as companion animals; moreover, we knew them very specifically as indoor pets. We were interested in rabbits as wild animals, too, and as icons in both ancient and contemporary societies. Rabbits as commercial "units" seemed very far from our own lives and our own rabbits.

Once we began the book in earnest, we realized that we couldn't write about rabbits without discussing their status and welfare in the meat, fur, vivisection and pet industries, because the rabbits in our homes, in our media and in commercial barns were of the same species. If we were going to advocate for better conditions for *pet* rabbits—i.e., living indoors, with humans, and with rabbit friends, proper food and plenty of room for exercise—how could we possibly overlook the lives of the many millions of rabbits being raised for profit?

Researching these sections wasn't easy. With the exception of vivisection, no one has investigated or written about commercial rabbit industries for a lay audience. That meant we had to start from scratch, in terms of compiling statistics, resources and descriptions of the actual workings of each industry. Much of what we discovered wasn't pleasant. But we also had to individually and mutually sort through our own feelings about creating and raising rabbits for profit.

Our backgrounds would seem to bring us to different conclusions. Susan grew up in a small, rural New England town that still had a strong agricultural base. Her father was (and still is) a judge of dog obedience trials. She and her friends participated in 4-H, and as an adult Susan has continued to spend considerable time around horses. The idea that people work with animals (and that this working relationship can be mutually beneficial and joyful) still makes sense to her, as does the idea of breeding animals for specific traits—as long as it's done responsibly and humanely.

For Susan, then, the initial problem with commercial rabbit industries (with the exception of the rabbit fur industry, which she has never had patience for) was one of *welfare*. She knew many rabbits were suffering, often profoundly. She also knew, in very practical terms, that people would continue to use rabbits commercially.

Yet this often put her in what Harriet Schleifer has described as "the perilous acrobatics involved in dividing animals into two categories: animals that it is unequivocally wrong to abuse and others that it is acceptable to exploit in a benevolent fashion."[1] After months of thinking and writing, and thinking and writing some more, Susan finally came to the conclusion that using these intelligent and sensitive animals for meat or fur is unacceptable and that the pet store industry needs serious reform. Yet she still believes that breeding and showing can be done responsibly and that the humane use of rabbits in laboratories, when no alternative exists, has a place.

Margo's take was a little different. A vegetarian since she was a child, Margo has been involved with both animal rescue and animal rights for over a decade. For her, the use of animals for human gain is more problematic—even when it's done humanely. Margo's feeling is that animals should not be used by humans at all unless both humans *and* animal benefit; a condition that she would be hard pressed to find in any of the rabbit industries discussed in this book, with the exception, perhaps, of some rabbit-savvy magicians. For Margo, then, the issue was more of animal *rights*—that animals shouldn't have to sacrifice their lives for science, human hunger, fashion or a pet store's profit margin.

These divergent philosophies have marked the animal protection movement since the 1970s, when some animal advocates began adopting the language of the civil rights, women's rights and environmental movements to create an animal rights movement. Today, many people still believe that animals shouldn't be used (or, many would say, exploited) to provide food, fur, entertainment or any other service to humans. Other people believe that humans will always use animals, but that the animals should at least be treated humanely. The two groups often bicker, with the animal rights folks accusing the animal welfare folks of being too moderate and the animal welfare folks accusing the animal rightists of being too extreme. Yet together, the animal welfare and animal rights movement have generated tidal waves of public concern about the lives of "working" animals, like horses, pigs, cattle, sheep and chickens, on the one hand, and the experience of "pet" animals, especially abandoned or abused dogs and cats, on the other hand.

With the exception of antivivisection campaigns, rabbits—who have served as both farm animals and family pets—have received relatively little attention from either animal rights or animal welfare advocates. What's more, their plight has not been addressed by either farm animal or pet welfare organizations—despite the cherished status of the "bunny" as both a pet and a storybook hero in this culture. As such, the welfare of rabbits—or rather their lack of welfare—has escaped the notice and concern of the general public, while people within the commercial rabbit industry dismiss the welfare issue by presenting it as a numbers game. Both advocates for farm animal welfare and breeders told us that no one has investigated the rabbit meat industry because it is so small (although 8.5 million rabbits are slaughtered here each year and some eight hundred million are slaughtered around the world annually). No one has investigated the rabbit fur industry, because the number of rabbits killed pales in comparison to the numbers of mink and fox (although, again, millions of rabbits are killed for their pelts each year). The Rabbit Education Society even dismisses rabbit overpopulation as a myth because, according to their very incomplete statistics, only one to two percent of all rabbits in America are surrendered to shelters. Yet that figure, which we suspect is much too low, represents more than 43,000 live animals who are left—and generally euthanized—at shelters each year.

The question then, is how we as a culture decide how many animals can be sacrificed to human needs—or human pleasures—and just which animals we're comfortable with sacrificing. This is a question most people decide based on a number of factors—cost, availability, dominant images, common customs, the animal's status as a pet, religious teachings, taste and our beliefs about the animal's intelligence. Such decisions are hardly conscious—in fact, most people probably don't think about these issues at all. But they're worth considering because they tell us so very much about our ideas about animals and our ideas about ourselves as humans.

The Hierarchy of Animal Worth

One reason that this culture as a whole doesn't acknowledge the commercial rabbit industry is that people don't know about it, so remote is it from their daily experience and from the rabbit images transmitted in popular culture. The other reason is that rabbits still are not considered as smart, emotional or interesting as other pets, like dogs or cats. That is, most people don't acknowledge suffering in commercial rabbits because we don't understand who the rabbit is—what gives it pleasure, what gives it pain, what it's capable of, why it's built the way it is, what frightens it, what makes it feel secure and just how deep the human-rabbit bond can go.

Of course, it's hard to understand rabbits when you've only met them in cages, because generally, caged rabbits, like most caged creatures, don't show a lot of personality. That makes them seem both stupid and boring. Karen Davis aptly shows the error in this thinking, however, in describing a similar prejudice against poultry:

> Rather than showing that chickens and turkeys are stupid, the fact that they become lethargic in continuously unstimulating commercial environments shows how sensitive these birds are to their surroundings, deprivation, and prospects. Learned helplessness, which may as well be referred to as "learned hopelessness," is a pathologic adaptation to pathogenic living conditions from which they cannot escape.[2]

Since the Victorian period, rabbits have also been associated with children. This has made rabbits seem like childish animals that are not to be taken seriously. (By extension, this association has made people who study rabbits—or who even just like them—seem childish, too.) But rabbits have also been associated with women since the Greek and Roman civilizations (when hares and rabbits were attributes of various goddesses), through the medieval and Renaissance periods (when rabbits and hares began to symbolize, simultaneously, both virginity and lustfulness) and into the modern era (when the rabbit has been associated with domesticity, childhood and, conversely, the sexy Playboy Bunny).

Today, women tend, in general, to be more involved with all animals than are men. A survey discussed in *Society and Animals,* the journal of Psychologists for the Ethical Treatment of Animals, found that: women are more likely than men to have companion animals;[3] women make up the majority of donors to animal protection organizations (although women take a back seat when it comes to leadership within the movement); women make up the majority of vegetarians and are thought by many to have a greater empathy for animals and interest in animal issues. This gender pattern is especially clear in the rabbit world, where women dominate the show breeding and rabbit rescue communities and are unquestionably the primary consumers of the bounty of rabbit collectibles offered in the marketplace.

The association between rabbits and women has a dark side, however. Hares were for a long time associated with witches. Rabbits symbolized untamed female sexuality in some Renaissance paintings. Words about women and rabbits—like "dumb bunny" and "cunt"—belittle and degrade women and rabbits simultaneously. And the very success of the Playboy Bunny—a creature that is half rabbit and half woman, after all—reveals a male penchant for a very chilling notion of female sexuality: one that is bound in notions of prey, childishness and submissiveness, on the one hand, and unbridled lust, fertility and even witchery on the other.

Many feminists and animal rights activists believe that the roots of violence toward animals lie in a patriarchal culture that sees humans (especially men) as superior to animals (and women). Mental health experts, animal advocates and law enforcement professionals have long known that animal abuse and human violence are closely linked. Studies by Psychologists for the Ethical Treatment of Animals and the Doris Day Animal League demonstrate that many notorious killers—including "school shooters"—began their careers by abusing animals. But it is only recently that people have understood that in households in which women and children are battered, animals are likely abused as well. Hence, it should come as no surprise that an animal perceived as simultaneously passive, stupid, cunning and sexual—all traits that women too often are accused of combining—would be the target of considerable abuse in modern society. In 1945, Cleveland Amory, late founder of The Fund for Animals, witnessed one scene that brought this connection between women and rabbits into startling clarity. He wrote:

> In defense of the "Bunny Bop"—in which rabbits are killed by clubs, feet, stones and so on—sponsored by the North Carolina American Legion post, one organization explained, "What would all these rabbit hunters be doing if they weren't letting off all this steam? I'll tell you what they'd be doing. They'd be drinking and carousing and beating their wives."[4]

Carol Adams, a feminist theologian and animal rights activist, notes that historically hare hunting has also combined extreme violence toward animals with symbolic violence toward women. She writes: "One animal-rights and feminist writer comments on the English tradition of hunting hares, traditionally female (as in Playboy Bunnies): 'So important was the hare's femininity that breaking its [sic] back, with the foot, was (and still is) called 'dancing on the hare,' the usual erotic movement of courtship being transferred to death.' "[5] This evocative conflation of sexual pursuit of women and the killing of animals is particularly disturbing given the very strong association between women and rabbits throughout history.

Into the Hearts and Minds of Rabbits
Seen as stupid, passive, childish and predominantly female (even "bewitched"), the rabbit appears to be one of the last "pets" to be acknowledged as a worthy animal. This is true even in an era when it is widely acknowledged that pets are not simply diversions but enrich our lives emotionally, physically and mentally. Studies show that living with a companion animal can lower blood pressure and cholesterol, reduce loneliness, increase psychological well-being, aid

in dealing with stress, improve the lives of seniors or those with serious ailments and much more.[6] It's no wonder that sixty-two percent of American households include one or more companion animals.[7] In fact, according to a 2002 survey by the American Animal Hospital Association (AAHA), more than fifty percent of people with pets have more pictures of their animals than their spouse or significant other, seventy-three percent would spend $1,000 or more to save their pet's life, seventy-three percent have signed a greeting card from their dog, and forty-six percent spend all or most of their free time around their pet.[8] The sheer amount of money people spend on their pets is evidence of their commitment and devotion. Statistics from the American Pet Products Manufacturing Association show that Americans spent $28.5 billion on products for their animals in 2001. Equally telling, Americans also give about $203 million in charitable contributions to animal protection organizations per year.[9]

From Object to Subject

This dedication to animals has been supported and boosted by scientific research on the intelligence and emotions of animals. This is all quite revolutionary: for many centuries, animals in general were thought to lack any mental or emotional faculties and were said to act only on instinct. As such, animals were thought to be simply machines, with their bodies interpreting environmental stimuli and translating them into behavior. Humans, on the other hand, were granted a vast array of learned behaviors, individual emotions and particular personalities that are shaped by a myriad of factors— including culture, the local environment, historical conditions, socioeconomic positions and, with the discovery of the modern science of genetics, inherited traits.

More recent research, however, has asserted that animals are far more than machines (or, as the Cartesians contended, little clocks with springs inside), exemplars of a species, unthinking placeholders in a dominance hierarchy or objects to be observed and experimented on. In his introduction to Jane Goodall's *In the Shadow of Man*, Stephen Jay Gould discusses Goodall's groundbreaking descriptions of the chimpanzees in Tanzania's Gombe National Park as individuals rather than as types (e.g., alpha male or lactating female). Goodall also recognized the importance of individual agency and historical specificity in the creation of chimp social structure. Gould writes:

> Thus we learn that an alpha male is not always the biggest or strongest, but may win his rank by peculiar cleverness (Mike, who bluffed his way to the top by banging empty kerosene cans together) or by subtle alliances (Goblin, the present incumbent, who, although smaller than average, knows how to play that oldest game of imperialism— "divide and conquer"). Or we discover that the main outlines of the history of the Gombe chimps during twenty-five years are not set by general principles of chimpness, but by particular events and historical peculiarities.[10]

Goodall also dared to name the chimps she studied, a practice unheard of in early primate research. The "alpha male" became Mike; the "lactating female" became Flo. Additionally, by acknowledging the importance of history in the creation of social structure, Goodall recognized that the defining feature of chimpanzee societies is not always a generalizable "chimp territorial behavior," but can be other factors, like the splitting of one main group into two rival factions. Goodall's work was radical because she refused to honor long-held moral distinctions that placed humans separate from—or far above—non-human animals.

Since that time, Goodall has written at length of her experiences, attempting to gain legitimacy and respect from her colleagues, who saw her work upon her return from the field as unscientific. "Objective" scientists don't name the animals that they study, much less write that they have emotions, personalities or intelligence, as Goodall did.[11] Until recently, if a scientist attempted to describe the behavior of an animal with terms like "sadness," "jealousy," "grief" or "joy," they would quickly be accused of that most dreaded (and

unscientific) of approaches: anthropomorphism. There are valid reasons for this attitude. No human can ever truly get inside the brain
of an animal—without dissecting it—and animals cannot answer
questions if we ask them how they feel, which forces us to interpret
their behaviors. But the belief that animals have no intelligence, emotions or individual personalities has certainly benefited those who
exploit animals. As Jeffrey Masson writes, granting animals the ability to think, to reason and to feel opens up a Pandora's box of issues
regarding how we, as a society, should treat animals:

> The professional and financial interests in continuing animal
> experimentation help to explain at least some resistance to
> the notion that animals have a complex emotional life and
> are capable of experiencing not only pain but the higher
> emotions such as love, compassion, altruism, disappoint-
> ment and nostalgia. To acknowledge such a possibility
> implies certain moral obligations. If chimpanzees can expe-
> rience loneliness and mental anguish, it is obviously wrong
> to use them for experiments in which they are isolated and
> anticipate daily pain. At the very least, this poses a matter
> for serious debate—a debate that has scarcely begun.[12]

Taking this idea further, biologist and feminist animal activist
Lynda Birke objects to the way that individual animals have traditionally been studied as exemplars of their species, rather than as
individuals. This assumption that any animal, or any group of animals, is representative of the larger species is reductionist at best, and
effectively denies individual emotion or feeling.[13] In addition, studying animals in a strictly scientific context (whether in the "field" or
in a laboratory) objectifies them. The animals become depersonal-
ized objects of inquiry, mere sources of data. They are not seen as
subjects who act according to their own wills—or would act according to their own wills if they had any choice.

Birke also believes that the language scientists use to *write*
about animals contributes to their objectification. The use of the

passive voice, for example ("the animals were sacrificed" versus "we killed the rabbits") denies the animal any participation or voice; "it" is simply the object of a procedure.[14] Moreover, such passive construction fails to assign responsibility for the killing to any person; "the animals were sacrificed" sounds as if no human hands were involved at all.

The resulting distance between writer/researcher and subject/object is problematic in two ways. First, the perspective itself results from the rationalist idea that the human world is sharply disconnected from the animal world, with animals constructed as being the Other to the human Self. Second, as Masson notes, it allows the researcher, particularly in laboratory settings where the vast majority of the animal subjects are killed, to feel no guilt or pain at the loss of life, since the researcher perceives neither connection nor similarity to the animal involved.

Eileen Crist, another behavioral scientist, goes so far as to defend anthropomorphism, which she defines as the representation of animal life in the language of the "lifeworld" (i.e., a world populated by actors whose lives are filled with action and meaning). "In rendering action meaningful and authored," she writes, "animals emerge as subjects. In turn, the portrayal of animals as subjects allows the existence of mental life to supervene with forcefulness and credibility."[15]

Intelligence

Just how much subjectivity and agency animals have remains a topic of lively debate. Writers (like Jeffrey Masson, Elizabeth Marshall Thomas and Matthew Scully), scientists (like Jane Goodall, Frans de Waal, Donald Griffin, Cynthia Moss and Marc Bekoff) and philosophers (most notably Vicki Hearne) have all posited that animals have both emotion and intelligence. Many biologists continue to assert, however, that animals are mostly "hard-wired" by their genes and have little intelligence.

Donald Griffin, the modern founder of cognitive ethology (after Darwin), and author of *The Question of Animal Awareness: Evolutionary Continuity of Mental Experience*,[16] was one of the first scientists to posit that animals are capable not only of cognition, but also of thinking, consciousness and conscious (or deliberate) behavior. Using evidence both from the field and from labs, Griffin found that animal behavior is flexible and variable, that it can change when the environment changes. (This is called "adaptive behavior," and for a long time researchers believed only humans were capable of it.)

More recently, researchers have discovered that animals are capable of tasks as complex as tool making and tool use, category formation, spatial memory, deceptive behavior, social sophistication, cognitive adaptability, symbolism, the communication of abstract feelings and "if-then" or "purposive" thinking and behavior.[17] For instance, researchers have documented cases in which an animal would remember where a morsel of food had been placed in the past and would seek it out without being given a sensory cue.[18] Anyone who lives with a rabbit who races into the kitchen to demand a snack from the refrigerator will recognize this ability. In Margo's house, Chester stops at the kitchen cabinet where the cereal is kept, while Helga continues on to the refrigerator, where her preferred treats are stored. In Susan's house, Maybelline regularly does reconnaissance hopping near the children's art table, as she knows that crayons, which are among her favorite toys, often fall on the floor there. As simple as these examples are, the concept that an animal might be able to remember something from the past and use that information in the present, even in the absence of a stimulus, can seem quite novel to people who believe that animals cannot think.

Researchers have also discovered that animals are able to understand abstract categories. Chimpanzees, for instance, can demonstrate the relationship between two sets of objects, such as two red balls and a red and a green ball, or even more amazingly, understand that a key is to a lock as a can opener is to a can of paint, rather than as a paintbrush is to a can of paint.[19] Some animals—like Koko the gorilla and Alex the African Grey parrot—have also learned elements of human communication; others are able to convey important and complex information to others of the same species.

Marc Bekoff discusses the notions of "dog-smart" and "monkey-smart" to differentiate the ways in which different animals possess different kinds of intelligence, based on their own survival needs.[20] Neither of us has tried to test our rabbits in a game of "how is this object not like the others," but we've certainly seen them demonstrate "rabbit smarts" on a daily basis. They've shown the ability, for instance, to compare different categories of objects, by making a choice, say, between a small piece of banana and a larger, but less desirable, piece of banana skin. They've demonstrated the ability to differentiate between humans by the sound of the footsteps—surely a skill that a prey animal needs. Rabbits can also use—but perhaps not make—tools. Many rabbits push their food bowl or drag a toy across the bars of their cage as a way of demanding to be let out; Elmo used to drop his little plastic ball into his food bowl, over and over again, to make Susan get out of bed and feed him breakfast. Rabbits can certainly communicate information to each other, as well; they will, for instance, show their friends the location of a previously undiscovered food source in the living room, and they often appear to "talk" or check in with each other after one has been picked up and then put back down again.

Rabbits also develop a pretty sizeable auditory vocabulary of human words. Most house rabbits know their own names and can understand words like "vegetables," "outside," "raisin," "ok," "just patting," "come inside," "get off the couch" "no nipping" and "What in the world are you up to?" And they convey what seems to be fairly complex information to humans—although not in human language. As an example: about two weeks after Elmo died, Susan felt it was time for Maybelline (and the human family) to get a new, male rabbit. Susan took Maybelline down to the local animal shelter to see how she got along with the rabbits up for adoption there. On that particular day, none of the male rabbits seemed just right, so Susan and Maybelline went home empty-handed. But as soon as Maybelline got into the house, she started racing around in circles around Susan's feet. Then she leapt up on the bed and started dashing toward and then away from Susan. Each time she came close, she'd shake her head merrily, and then do a half shimmy in the air. Maybelline generally hides under the bed after any car ride—never mind a stressful trip to an animal shelter, with all the strange sounds, smells and animal messages it entails. Yet she was displaying what seemed like great joy after this field trip, as if she was truly excited that Susan was trying to find a new rabbit friend for the household. This was not human language, but a very animal form of communication that both humans (who are animals after all) and rabbits can share.

In recent years, a number of animal rights advocates have constructed complex arguments detailing just what sorts of "rights" should be accorded to which animals. Most of the arguments place a value on modes of animal thinking that match or approach human ways of thinking—the ability to count, for instance, or to "speak" or somehow "sign" with humans. In *Drawing the Line*, Steven Wise claims that certain species, like dolphins, bonobos (a very close relative to the chimpanzee), gorillas and humans, deserve "basic liberty rights" based on their possession of "practical autonomy," which he defines as: having a desire, being able to intentionally try to fulfill that desire, and having enough sense of self to understand that one has a given desire and and is trying to fulfill it.[21] Wise is clearly a brilliant legal thinker and a compassionate advocate of animals. But his argument begs a very simple question: what if animals have intelligences that humans can't measure or even imagine? What if rabbits exchange extremely complex information every time they bump heads or lie cheek-to-cheek? What if the scents left by rats carry far more nuances than we've yet discovered? What if, in other words, humans don't yet know everything about how animals think? What, then, will we value? As Karen Davis notes,

> Not only men but women and animal protectionists exhibit a culturally conditioned indifference toward, and prejudice against, creatures whose lives appear too slavishly, too boringly, too stupidly female, too "cowlike." Moreover, we regard conscious logical reasoning as the only valid sort of

"mind." Evidence that chimpanzees possess such a mind is a primary reason why many are now insisting that they should be granted "human rights." Human rights for chimpanzees? Yes. Human rights for chickens? Meaningless.[22]

But perhaps Jeremy Bentham best summarized the problem in his oft-quoted passage on our hierarchies of animal value when he wrote:

> The French have already discovered that the blackness of the skin is no reason why a human being should be abandoned without redress to the caprice of a tormentor. It may one day come to be recognized that the number of legs, the villosity of the skin, or the termination of the *os sacrum* are reasons equally insufficient for abandoning a sensitive being to the same fate. What else is that should trace the insuperable line? Is it the faculty of reason or perhaps the faculty of discourse? But a full-grown horse or dog is beyond comparison a more rational as well as a more conversable animal than an infant of a day or a week or even a month old. But suppose the case were otherwise, what would it avail? The question is not, can they *reason*? Nor, can they *talk*? But can they *suffer*?[23]

Emotions

Scientists studying the emotional lives of animals have also made startling progress. One early discovery was the understanding that animals *anticipate*, and that they then demonstrate disappointment when what they anticipated does not come to pass. To animal lovers, this sounds obvious—a dog gets excited when the human puts on her running shoes; said dog gets dejected when said human walks out the door *alone*. Rabbits expect a pat when a beloved human sits down on the floor; when that pat doesn't come, the rabbit can get insistent (as displayed by shoving his head under the human's hand) or even angry (as shown by nipping the human or digging at her clothes). But the fact that animals can anticipate something means that they also have memory. The fact that they have memory, in turn, suggests that they can experience strong feelings—surprise, anger and disappointment—when they are denied what they expected.

Other new discoveries include the fact that animals can feel pain—and can also carry the emotional scars associated with that pain. Anyone who has worked with animals knows they display evidence of feeling physical pain—consider the yowl of a cat whose tail has been stepped on, the grunt (or nip) of a horse whose girth has been tightened too quickly or the shriek of a rabbit who has been grabbed too tightly or is in the midst of being slaughtered. People who work with abused animals—chimpanzees whose mothers were slaughtered in the bushmeat trade, former circus elephants, once-abused or neglected dogs and former laboratory rabbits—can also testify to the fact that animals will continue to suffer from that emotional trauma for years afterwards. Bea, a former laboratory beagle, showed extreme fear in the presence of men, and especially men in white coats (such as her veterinarian), for years after she arrived in a new home.[24] Some rabbits never get over their fear of small children (if they were in a home that had ill-behaved youngsters) or of being handled (if they were in a situation where handling conferred pain, not pleasure).

Grief is another emotion now attributed to animals, thanks especially to the studies of elephants in the wild and in captivity. Using heart-wrenching detail, Cynthia Moss has described the reactions of elephants when their relatives and friends die—from frantic denial (attempting to lift a dead elephant up to a standing position, even attempting to place food in her mouth) to partial burial of the body to a nightlong vigil. Elephants even recognize the bones of other elephants, and react accordingly when finding them.[25] Jane Goodall has written movingly of the grief of the chimpanzee Olly, who continued to care for her four-week-old baby for days after she died, by carrying her, grooming her, even attempting to nurse her before finally abandoning the body.[26] The fact that rabbits often grieve, and grieve very deeply, is evidence that many animals—not just those that are commonly thought to be "intelligent"—can feel great sadness.

What about joy, love, friendship? Even researchers who grant an animal "negative" emotions are cautious about admitting that animals have a capacity for happier feelings. But for many researchers today, as well as for those who live and work with animals, it is clear that animals do feel pleasure in all of its variations. Some "play," for instance, can be explained as simple evolutionary behavior (for example, kittens play with yarn or chase each other to practice hunting). Other forms of play, however, are less useful in survival and cannot be so easily dismissed. Dolphins who surf, rabbits who throw toilet paper tubes into the air, animals who tease humans and parrots who creatively turn their toys upside down (Margo's conure will wear a toy bell like a hat for hours) are not practicing survival skills, yet the animals clearly enjoy them.

Most house rabbit people have seen their rabbits "binky" or dance as an expression of joy, as well as execute a not-very-graceful "flop," in which they fall to their sides in a gesture of deep contentment. When Margo first introduced Helga to Chester, he would leap, hop and skip when she was first placed (angrily) into the living room every day. Never mind that she was repelled by him; he was so thrilled to have a potential new playmate that he could not contain his joy. For weeks, Chester would lie as close to Helga as he could, staring amorously at her; once she finally agreed to let him touch her, he began to spend as much time as possible scrunched up against her.

Puddles and Muddles, Margo's Angoras, also binky, but for a different reason. Every morning, Margo opens their gate so they can come out to exercise, but one of the first things they do is go to the living room to eat Chester's food and mess up his things. Upon catching them in the act, Margo chases them back out of the living room and watches as they race, skipping and jumping across the house, back into their room. These rabbits seem overjoyed at the fact they once again got away with something funny. Their actions, in fact, look much like a full-body laugh.

Some researchers now believe that animals experience even more complex emotions, such as altruism, compassion, heroism, cooperation, embarrassment, pride and more. Masson describes one instance of elephants joining together to help a fallen comrade stand up (thus sparing him a certain death). Elephants have also been seen to "bury" a dead friend with palm fronds and branches. Female rats will put the young of other female rats into a nest if they fall out. The instances of pets providing comfort to people who are sick or depressed are too numerous to count. Many stories exist of dogs who wake up their humans when a fire starts; most people don't know that parrots, pigs and even a hamster have done the same thing.

Rabbits, too, demonstrate this type of emotional complexity. Many will lick their paws or wash their faces when they are complimented, as if they are very pleased or slightly embarrassed. Marinell Harriman's first rabbit, Herman, even once saved a mouse. When Herman found a cat torturing the mouse, she thumped her foot in protest. When that failed to deter the cat, she attacked her, allowing the mouse to escape.[27] Other rabbits show an amazing amount of compassion towards members of their own species, such as the examples we have cited of healthy rabbits acting as support (both physical and emotional) for their disabled friends.

Kristin Von Kreisler refers to animals who behave heroically or compassionately as animals who "choose to do good." One of her more amazing stories is about Lulu, a 209-pound pig who found her caretaker on the floor after a heart attack. Lulu not only cried over her beloved friend but squeezed herself through a small doggy door, and, bleeding, went out into traffic numerous times to alert drivers to what had happened.[28] Was Lulu choosing to do good, or was there some other explanation for her behavior? When there is no obvious benefit to an animal who goes out of his or her way to help another, as in these stories, what other explanation could there be?

Collections of stories dealing with the emotional complexity of animals, such as *Animals as Teachers and Healers*, *The Compassion of Animals* and *Beauty in the Beasts* also describe animals who demonstrate dignity, strength of character and grace in their daily lives. Von Kreisler, for instance, writes of Justin, a pampered King Charles Spaniel, who was lost from his home for months but survived the winter all alone, until he was found and reunited with his grateful family.[29] Justin's survival demonstrated the grit and strength that many other animals demonstrate under extraordinary conditions: e.g., cats who were trapped in walls and survived for weeks, dogs who were beaten or burned by cruel youths, and the recent case of Hok Get, the terrier mix who was abandoned on an Indonesian tanker and who lived for two weeks alone on the burned-out ship.

Many rabbits, too, demonstrate an amazing spirit when confronting adversity. We have already written about rabbits like Hopper, Pippin and Mrs. Bean—all injured by people and left without the ability to walk. Both Pippin and Mrs. Bean learned to use a custom-built cart to get around, and their personalities blossomed. Mrs. Bean savored her new freedom, using the cart to create a new, independent life for herself, while Pippin used his to get attention and to interact with people. Even before using the cart, Pippin seemed happy to join Margo's household after what he had been through, executing a flop on his first day without the use of his rear legs. Hopper never did learn to use the cart well, but like the others, he adapted to his altered condition with grace and dignity, and charmed everyone who met him with his peaceful, gentle and loving personality.

Some rabbits who have suffered abuse, injury or illness have responded to human kindness and care with what can only be described as gratitude. Many of our own rabbits have lost their aggressive or terrified tendencies after being nursed through serious illnesses or injuries and given kind, consistent treatment. Mr. Bop, for instance, was so ill and so depressed when Susan first brought him home that he barely hopped—he would follow her around the house by taking a few steps and then lying down and staring up at her mournfully. After about a month of good food, plenty of water, medication and many kind words and pats, his depression lifted, only to reveal an alarmingly spastic skittishness. Bop would dive under the bed or behind a chair whenever someone walked into the room; loud noises sent him nearly to the ceiling. It was only after six months that his fearfulness—no doubt a product of his having some sort of trauma (as evidenced by his scars) while a stray on the streets of San Francisco—eased. Today, he can pop binkys and spin wheelies with the best of them. He can doze through the roar of a vacuum cleaner, the shriek of a smoke detector and the wails of a baby. He once even sprawled out on his belly, with his hind legs stretched out behind him, smack dab in the middle of a party of shrieking four-year-old girls dressed like princesses. That's confidence.

Of course, it would be a mistake to ascribe to animals only "noble" characteristics. Like us, nonhuman animals certainly can be selfish or mean and may manipulate or deceive in order to get what they want. Territorial battles, food robbing, infanticide, rape and ostracization regularly take place in a number of species, including rabbits. Domestic rabbits often steal food from a communal plate (or sometimes from another rabbit's mouth!) and race away to eat it alone. Both domestic and wild does will kill other does' babies; bucks are reported to do the same. And for every case we have seen of rabbits caring for a sick or disabled rabbit we have seen other rabbits behave in ways that could only be described as cruel. It's hard not to feel angry when viewing this type of behavior. Still, it's essential to remember that rabbits' emotions are not just limited to positive ones; in fact, it's our own expectation that rabbits will be sweet and passive that makes us overlook what very complex, dynamic animals they really are. It's also essential to realize that rabbits, like all animals, may experience emotions entirely different from ours— that animals, in other words, may actually be more emotionally complex than humans, not less.

The Worth of Rabbits

In the first edition of the *House Rabbit Handbook* (1985), Marinell Harriman dedicated her book to "Herman (October 1981–December 1983), our first house rabbit, whose influence on our lives has forced us to produce this book." Without Herman, House Rabbit Society and the community of rabbit advocates that it set off would likewise not have been created; even the term "house rabbit," which Harriman coined, might not exist today. And while cats and dogs are certainly higher-profile pets than rabbits, and their advocates are greater in number, people who love rabbits are a vocal, active group themselves.

The House Rabbit Society Web site (www.rabbit.org) receives fully one million hits per week. Companies like Busy Bunny, BunnyBytes and BunnyLuv—to name just a few—sell toys, treats and equipment to rabbit lovers. People who live with rabbits also build elaborate "condominiums" for their pets, chat on Internet groups like Petbunny, Housebun and Etherbun, create home pages and even set up "bunnycams"—or video cameras that broadcast their rabbits' daily activities on the web for all to see.

Rabbit lovers photograph, paint, talk and write about their rabbits; a quick look at the "Bunny Randomizer" on the HRS Web site[30] shows the wide range of ways people and rabbits live together. There are pictures of people bringing their rabbits to their college graduations, to the park and on airplanes; it shows rabbits on beds, on couches and under tables; there are photos of rabbits in gardens, on desks and in laps; with dogs, with hamsters and with Santa; and yawning, snoozing, flopping, binkying and eating. These rabbits share their lives with their humans just as dogs and cats do.

The great grief that humans feel when their rabbits die is also evidence of the very remarkable bonds that develop between these two species. Marinell Harriman still chokes up when she talks about Herman's death—which occurred almost twenty years ago. Though veteran rabbit guardians, both Susan and Margo grieve deeply when their rabbits die. Dozens, if not hundreds, of rabbit caretakers have posted memorial Web sites to rabbits who have died. William Cowper's despair at the passing of his hare Puss is moving to anyone who has mourned any kind of pet. In his "Eulogy for Another" he writes:

This also lies in death
Who all of nine years lived
Puss.
Stop a little while
You who are going to pass on

And reflect on yourself also—
This neither hunting dog
Nor lead missile
Nor trap
Nor violent storm
Killed
Still he is dead—
And I will die.[31]

Such mourning is accepted among the caretakers of cats, dogs and horses, because the bond between humans and these species is well understood. People who live with rabbits who express grief at the passing of their pets, however, are often ridiculed. This dichotomy was most clear on one recent thread on the meatrabbits@yahoogroups.com listserve. Several rabbit growers were posting quite moving poems and thoughts on their dogs going to the "Rainbow Bridge," which a growing number of animal lovers construe as cross between heaven and a celestial train station, a place, that is, where the souls of pets and their guardians re-unite after death. Not one of the members of the listserve mentioned their *rabbits* going to the Rainbow Bridge after being slaughtered. In the rabbit growers' world view, rabbits aren't pets, so they don't deserve an afterlife.

A Plea for Welfare

Just how we decide which animals are to be eaten, or experimented on, or slaughtered for fur, and which are to be protected as companion animals is a mysterious process. According to Marc Bekoff, it is "our beliefs about the nature of animals" that most influence how we treat them. "How we represent animals, the conditions in which we study them, and how smart or emotional we assume them to be all influence what we consider to be permissible and non-permissible treatment," he writes.[32]

The fact that a species is unknown—as the rabbit is—means that we as humans can project all sorts of characteristics on the animals that would deem them unworthy of protection. We can even project a trait of blankness on them; that is, because we don't understand the rabbit, we assume there is nothing to understand, that the rabbit is a creature with neither sentience nor subjectivity. And once we assume that, creating what in other species we would recognize as "suffering" becomes acceptable.

It is only by living with, observing and empathizing with rabbits that we can begin to recognize their subjectivity, or, as Lockley put it, the fact that "rabbits are so human." But where do we go from that recognition? Do we decide that rabbits deserve the lives that so many thousands of house rabbit people have given them, lives similar to those experienced by millions of dogs and cats: beds, toys, snacks and litter boxes and a home filled with love? Will we recognize that, to paraphrase Karen Davis, there is more to the rabbit than a meal, or a fur coat, or a laboratory resource? Or do they deserve the fate suffered by the vast majority of rabbits around the world today: short, lonely lives that are sometimes filled with suffering, but that always end with death at a human's hands, for human profit?

If rabbits deserve better treatment, what of all the other animals who so clearly demonstrate the same range of emotions and intelligence? What about cows, pigs, chickens and even the most beloved of all animals, dogs, who are still experimented upon in labs, still slaughtered for fur and meat, still killed by the millions in our nation's shelters? Marinell Harriman told us that her love for and appreciation of Herman and other rabbits inspired her to become a vegetarian and to become active in other areas of animal protection. "It's serendipity," she said. "You become so enamored of one animal that it extends to the entire species and then, little bit by little bit, to all animals." This is not at all an unusual case. Countless other rabbit people have traveled a similar path, as have people like Jeffrey Masson, Jane Goodall, Marc Bekoff and Kristin Von Kreisler, all of whom studied the minds and emotions of animals and then became passionate animal advocates. Marc Bekoff calls this "minding animals" and defines it as "caring for other animal beings, respecting them for who they are, appreciating their own worldviews, and wondering what and how they are feeling and why."[33] Matthew Scully, in his recent *Dominion: The Power of Man, the Suffering of Animals, and the Call to Mercy,* considers such compassion to be nothing less than the measure of the charitable Christian heart: he writes: "Go into the largest livestock operation, search out the darkest and tiniest stall or pen, single out the filthiest, most forlorn little lamb or pig or calf, and that is one of God's creatures you're looking at, morally indistinguishable from your beloved Fluffy or Frisky."[34]

Jeffrey Masson, quoting from Tom Regan's *The Case for Animal Rights,* argues that we must protect "the rights of animals who are 'capable of being the subject of a life.' Every animal used in every experiment in every laboratory has its own life story. It has felt strong emotions, loved and hated and been devoted to others of its own kind."[35] Our goal in writing this book was to demonstrate that rabbits, too, have their own life stories, that those stories are worth listening to and, in Linda Vance's words, can "make us care." It was George Bernard Shaw, after all, who noted, "The worst sin towards our fellow creatures is not to hate them, but to be indifferent to them."[36]

Notes

1.   Schleifer, Harriet, "Images of Death and Life: Food Animal Production and the Vegetarian Option," in Singer, Peter (ed.), *In Defense of Animals* (Oxford: Basil Blackwell, 1985).

2.   Davis, Karen, *More than a Meal: The Turkey in History, Myth, Ritual and Reality* (New York: Lantern Books, 2001), p 67.

3.   Munroe, Lyle, "Caring about Blood, Flesh and Pain: Women's Standing in the Animal Rights Movement," *Society and Animals: Journal of Human–Animal Studies,* Vol. 9, No. 1 (2001).

4.   Adams, Carol, *The Sexual Politics of Meat* (New York: The Continuum Publishing Company, 1991), p. 45.

5.   *Ibid.,* pp. 73–74.

6.   See the Delta Society for more information on the benefits of living with pets.

7.   American Pet Products Manufacturing Association; figure from the 2000 survey.

8.   American Animal Hospital Association, "2002 National Survey of People and Pet Relationships," Colorado: November 25, 2002.

9.   According to Merritt Clifton of *Animal People.*

10. Goodall, Jane, *In the Shadow of Man* (Boston: Houghton-Mifflin, 1988), p. vi.

11. Jeffrey Masson discusses the fact that in scientific fields, like Goodall's, "women have been deemed especially prone to empathy, hence anthropomorphic error and contamination. Long considered inferior to men precisely on the ground that they feel too much, women were thought to over-identify with the animals they studied."

Moussaieff Masson, Jeffrey, and Susan McCarthy, *When Elephants Weep* (New York: Delta Books, 1995), p. 33. A woman's empathy toward animals, then, is said to lead to her being less qualified to understand them!

12. *Ibid.*, p. xx.
13. Birke, Lynda, "Exploring the Boundaries: Feminism, Animals and Science," in Adams, Carol and Josephine Donovan (eds)., *Animals and Women: Feminist Theoretical Explorations*, (Durham: Duke University Press, 1995), p. 40.
14. *Ibid.*, p. 44.
15. Crist, Eileen, *Images of Animals: Anthromorphism and the Animal Mind* (Philadelphia: Temple University Press, 1999), p. 4.
16. Griffin, Donald, *The Question of Animal Awareness: Evolutionary Continuity of Mental Experience* (New York: Rockefeller University Press, 1976).
17. Page, George, *Inside the Animal Mind* (New York: Broadway Books, 1999) p. 54.
18. *Ibid.*, p. 57.
19. *Ibid.*, p. 76.
20. Bekoff, Marc, *Minding Animals: Awareness, Emotions and Heart* (Oxford: Oxford University Press, 2002), p. 91.
21. Wise, Steven M. *Drawing the Line: Science and the Case for Animal Rights* (Cambridge: Perseus Books, 2002), p. 32.
22. Davis, Karen, "Thinking Like a Chicken: Farm Animals and the Feminine Connection," in Adams, Carol and Josephine Donovan (eds)., *Animals and Women: Feminist Theoretical Explorations*, (Durham: Duke University Press, 1995).
23. Bentham, Jeremy, *Introduction to the Principles of Morals and Legislation*, 1823, Chapter 17, Section 1.
24. Von Kreisler, Kristin, *Beauty in the Beasts: True Stories of Animals Who Choose to Do Good* (New York: J.P. Tarcher, 2002).
25. Moss, Cynthia, *Elephant Memories* (New York: William Morrow and Co., 1988), pp. 269–271.
26. Goodall, *op. cit.*, pp. 214–217.
27. Harriman, Marinell. *House Rabbit Handbook: How to Live with an Urban Rabbit*, 2nd edition (Alameda, CA: Drollery Press, 1991).
28. Von Kreisler, *op. cit.*, pp. 26–27.
29. *Ibid.*, pp. 129–130.
30. http://www.rabbit.org/fun/net-bunnies.html.
31. Cowper, William, "Epitaphium Alterum," in Spiller, Brian (ed.), *Cowper: Verse and Letters* (Cambridge: Harvard University Press, 1968).
32. Bekoff, *op. cit.*, p. 133.
33. *Ibid.*, p. 10.
34. Scully, Matthew, *Dominion: The Power of Man, the Suffering of Animals, and the Call to Mercy* (New York: St. Martin's Press, 2002), p. 26.
35. Masson, et al., *op. cit.*, p. 231.
36. Shaw, George Bernard, *The Devil's Disciple*, 1897.

Index

Ackerman, Diane (*The Moon by Whale Light*), xv
Adams, Carol, 333
Adams, Richard (*Watership Down*), 16, 27, 194–195
advertising, 219–222, 260–261, 272
Aesop, 146–151
African-American dialect, 158, 163
aggression. *see also* biting: domestic rabbits, 99–100, 109–118, 313; laboratory rabbits, 299; wild rabbits, 13, 27–30
Alexander, Neil, 207
Alexander the Magician, 208
Alice's Adventures in Wonderland, 133, 142, 171, 173, 192
Alilepus, 8–9
Allen, Rick, 324
Ally, Pamela, 263, 308
Alternatives Research and Development Foundation (ARDF), 283, 297–298
alternative tests, 281, 288–292, 297–298, 302
altruism (animal), 343–344
Amani rabbit, 12
American Animal Hospital Association (AAHA), 334
American Pet Products Manufacturers Association, xix, 306, 334
American Rabbit Breeders Association (ARBA): beginning of, 70; on breeders and breeding, 306, 318; pet owners and, 58, 312–313; on rabbit breeds, 72; rabbit shows and, 231, 314
American Veterinary Medical Association (AVMA), xix, 249–252
Anderson, Alex, 188
animal abuse and violence toward people, 192, 332–333
Animal Care Center, 300
Animal Equality: Language and Liberation (Dunayer), 218
animal protection groups, xx, 292, 307, 319, 332. *see also specific groups*
Animal Rights Foundation of Florida, 322
animal rights/welfare: breeders and, 254–255, 318–319; fur and, 275; meat, 261–262; pets, 320–321, 330; philosophy, 328–330, 340–341; plea for, 348–350; rabbits and, 241, 247, 255–257, 262, 325–326; sentimentalism and, 2–3; vivisection, 281
animal testing. *see* vivisection
Animal Welfare Act (AWA), 244, 282, 298–299, 309, 312
Animal Welfare Institute, 257
anthropomorphism, 336–337
Aphrodite, 134, 143
arctic hare, 11, 17
Amory, Cleveland, 332–333
arrogance, rabbits symbolizing, 149–152, 164, 184–185
art: fear of hares in, 133; hunters, rabbit revenge on, 32–34; moon-rabbit connections, 136–137; naturalistic paintings of hares, 62; rabbits and hares, 15–16, 33, 62, 67; sexuality, rabbits symbolizing, 142, 147; suffering of rabbits, 33–35

astrology, 132, 143
Augustus, 37
Australia: population, rabbit, 36–37, 39, 49; rabbit fences, 44–46, 198; viruses, rabbit, 50–53, 55
Avery, Tex, 187

babies, human. *see* children
babies, rabbit, 25–26, 242–243, 248
Baker, Bart, 47
Baker, Robert, 322–323
Baker, Stephen, 129, 213
Beaumont, Frederick, 67
Beaver, Bonnie, 249–250
Bekoff, Mark, 337, 348–350
Belgian Hares, 70, 72, 232, 237
Bentham, Jeremy, 341
Bettelheim, Bruno (*Uses of Enchantment*), 183
Bible, 20, 190. *see also* Jesus Christ; religious symbols, rabbits as
binky, 18, 160, 179, 343
biological warfare on rabbits, 49–59, 196
biomechanical study of rabbits, 16–17
biotechnology, 294–296
Birke, Linda, 336–337
biting, 89, 91, 92, 114–118. *see also* aggression
Blackstone, Harry Sr., 207
Boinger, 172, 190
Boy Scouts of America, 321–322
Braddon, Russell (*Year of the Angry Rabbit*), 195–197
Branckaert, René, 260
breeders, rabbit, 62. *see also* farming, rabbit meat; *specific breeds*; advice on aggressive behavior, 114–115; breeding process, 62, 240, 316–318; changes in animal morphology, 61; culling, 316–317; debate over breeding, 254–258, 318–321, 329; for fur, 268–269; glowing bunny, 294–296; group living for rabbits, 247–248; hobby and show breeders, 313–316; meat, 226, 231, 237, 252–254; pets, 306–310; rabbit hemorrhagic disease (RHD) and, 58; for vivisection, 280, 282–283
breeding, wild rabbits. *see* reproduction, rabbit
breeds, 63–64, 66, 70–72, 319
Brer Rabbit, 146, 157–163, 171, 185–186, 188
Brothers Grimm, 146, 151
Brown, Margaret, 172, 175–176, 208
Buddha and Buddhism, 136, 146, 203–204
Bugs Bunny, 171, 172, 186–188
"Bunny Bop," 333
bunny collectibles. *see also* advertising: Bunny Museum, 170–171, 204–205, 217; distancing from real rabbits, xviii–xx, 213, 222–223; Oswald the Lucky Rabbit, 189
bunny-proofing, xiii, 85
burrows, 24–25, 144, 181, 200–201
"Buy-back schemes" for rabbits, 237–238, 272–273

cages: laboratory rabbits, 279–280; pet rabbits and, 83–84, 86–87, 89, 311, 312; rabbit aware-

ness of, 98; rabbit farming and, 126, 242–248; "rabbit mills," 308
calicivirus, 53–56, 57, 240
cannibalism on rabbit farms, 244
CARE, 258
Carlson, Laurie Winn, 212–213
Carter, Jimmy, 10
CAT (Johns Hopkins University Center), 291
cats: dominance hierarchy of, 120–121; feline calicivirus, 57; protest at use of, 226, 275; rabbits and, 40–41, 97–98
cells, alternative tests using, 289–290, 297–298
Center for Alternatives to Animal Testing (CAT), 291
cervical dislocation, 249–250
Charles River Laboratories, 290
Chase, Mary, 193
Chicken Little, 148
children. *see also* virginity/innocence: Aboriginal, 198; decorative items for, 208–210; pets and, 67–68; rabbits and, 88–89, 331; rabbits as, in fiction, 173–184
chimpanzees, 335–336, 338
China, rabbit meat and, 239–240
chinchillas and Chinchilla rabbits, xxi, 45, 254, 269–270
Chinese astrology, 132
Christianity, 202–204, 209, 350. *see also* Easter; Jesus Christ
cigarettes (rabbit research), 279, 293
Classic Lethal Dose Percent 50 Test, 290–291
classification of rabbits (origins), 6–8, 12
climbing, 10, 97
cloning, 296–297
clothing on bunnies, 174–177, 183–184, 210–212
Coalition for Consumer Information on Cosmetics, 219
coccidiosis, 247
colony breeding, 247–248
communication (rabbit), 19–24, 85, 91–93, 114
Compassion in World Farming, 256–257
conservationists, 1–2, 12. *see also* ecosystems
Consumer Product Safety Commission, 289
Cook, James, 36
Copenhagen Fur Centre, 273–274
coprophagy, 20–21
Corrositex, 289
Cosmetic Ingredient Review, 290
cosmetics (animal testing), 283–284
cottontails, 10–12
country simplicity, 211–212, 272–273. *see also* bunny collectibles
cowardice/timidity: rabbit as symbol of, 147–149; of rabbits in fiction, 158, 163–164, 173, 193, 199–200
Cowper, William, 65–66, 79, 327, 347–348
Coxe, Julian, 153
crepuscular nature of lagomorphs, 14–15
Crist, Eileen, 337
Crosby, Alfred (on ecological imperialism of Europe), 38
crowding of farmed rabbits, 242–246, 248, 255
cruelty-free companies and products, 283, 286, 288
Crusader Rabbit, 188

culling, 316–318
culture: in animals, 123–125; art and folk tales, 162, 164, 198; rabbits as icons of, 129–130, 171–172, 205, 213, 227
cuniculus species, 6–7
Curran, Roger, 285, 287, 288

Dalai Lama, 202
Davis, Karen, 219, 331, 340–341, 349
dealers, rabbit, 309–310
decapitation, 251–252
de la Fontaine, Jean, 150
De La Mare, Walter (*Hare*), 131
del Cossa, Francesco (*Allegory of April: Triumph of Venus*), 142
DeLille, Armand (painter), 51
dialect, African-American, 158, 163
Diana (goddess), 137, 143
disabilities, physical (in rabbits), 92, 105–107, 345
diseases and rabbit farms, 244, 245, 247
dog bait, 322–323
dogs, 120, 226, 275, 297, 302
domestication, 61–65, 73–74
domestic rabbits. *see* rabbits, domestic
dominance: domestic rabbits and, 87–88, 109–110, 113; in rabbits, generally, 100–107, 120–123; wild rabbits/warrens, 26–27
Doris Day Animal League, 332–333
Draize Eye Irritancy Test (DEIT), 283–290
Draize Skin Irritancy Test, 286–288, 290
Duffy, Mr. (magician), 324
Dunayer, Joan (*Animal Equality: Language and Liberation*), 218
Dürer, Albrecht, 15–16, 62
dwarf rabbits, 183–184, 313

ears, 15, 144–145
Easter, 137–141, 180, 187–188, 190, 238
ecosystems, 1–2, 12, 38, 53
Edwards, Stephen, 250
elephants, 342
Elizabeth I, 31–32
embryo resorption, 26, 30
emotions, animal, 83, 334, 335–336, 341–346. *see also specific emotions*
endangered/rare species, 10–11, 53, 265–266, 271, 275
Endocrine Disruptor Screening Program (EDSP), 291
enuration, 20, 23, 93, 121
Eostre, 138, 154, 215–216
EpiDerm, 289, 291
EpiOcular test, 289
EPISKIN, 289, 291
equinox, spring, 138
Europe, 31–40, 51–55, 62, 235–236, 291
European Centre for the Validation of Alternative Methods (ECVAM), 291
euthanasia, 301, 306, 313, 319
evil, rabbits symbolizing, 152, 154, 163, 208
evolution, 13, 73–74. *see also* history of rabbits
extinction. *see* endangered/rare species
eyes, xx, 14–15, 132, 283–286, 294

Fagen, Ken, 273

Fairfax, Edward (*Daemonologia: A Discourse on Witchcraft*), 153
Fairfax, William, 153
fake rabbits for magicians, 207, 324
FAO (United Nations Food and Agriculture Organization), 231, 243, 245
Farmer's Bulletin, 267–269
farming, factory, 236–237, 241, 243–245, 248, 255–256
farming, fur. see fur
farming, rabbit meat. see also meat, rabbit (the meat); rabbits, meat (the animal): backyard, 233–237, 248, 257–258; history, 30–32, 62, 232–238; investigation of, 244; organization, lack of farmer, 58; pet rabbits and, 66–67, 226, 262–263; in the Third World, 258–261
farming (non-rabbit), 1–2, 11, 51–52, 55
Fatal Attraction, 192
Fayo, Corrinne, 58, 318–319. see also Rabbit Education Society (RES)
fear of rabbits and hares, 133–134, 191–192, 195–198
feces, 20–21, 121
Federal Bureau of Investigation, 241
feline calicivirus, 57
felt, 265, 274
fences, 44, 46, 60, 198
feral vs. wild rabbits, 34–35
fertility: of the female rabbit, 13; Playboy bunny, 216; rabbit as symbol of, 134, 139, 141, 143–144, 203; rings (jewelry), 206
FIAWR (Food Industry Animal Welfare Report), 256
fights. see aggression
filthiness, believed of hares and rabbits, 20, 134
Finster, Howard (*Us Poor Rabbits*), 33–35
fleas (myxoma virus), 50–53, 59
folk tales, 130, 143–165, 194–195, 258–259
Food and Drug Administration, 283–284, 289
Food for Freedom campaign, 233
Food Industry Animal Welfare Report (FIAWR), 256
foolishness, rabbits symbolizing, 147, 157, 163–164, 193
foot stomping/drumming, 91, 148, 173–174, 203
Ford, Henry, 235
4-H Program, 233, 314, 328
Frazee, Candace, 170–171, 204–205, 217
Frederick, Wilhelm, 32
freezing: defense mechanism, 16; rabbit meat, 239–241
friendship and love, 26, 90, 99, 101–107, 127
frustration/boredom of rabbits, 243, 298
Fun With Dick and Jane, 305
fur: farming, 225, 265–268, 271–276, 318, 330; markets, 47–49, 268, 272, 321; rabbit lives and, xx, 328, 329; viruses, rabbit, 50, 58; wild rabbits, 10, 14
Fur Information and Fashion Council, 272
Fur Trade Review, 267

Garis, Howard (*Uncle Wiggily* books), 171, 189
gender differences (rabbits), 19, 24–25, 121–122. see also reproduction
genitalia, female, 141–142, 143, 217, 218

Gentlemen's Magazine, 66
geographic distribution of rabbits and hares, 9–10, 36–37. see also population, rabbit
gin traps, 39, 50
glowing bunny, 294–296
Goforth, Dean, 250
Goodall, Jane, xxi, xxii, 334–336, 342, 349
Good Night Moon (Brown), 172, 175–176, 208
Gould, Stephen Jay, 334–335
Grandin, Temple, 256
Grauer, Dan, 8, 184
greyhounds, 302, 322–323
grief and mourning, 107–109, 342, 347–348
Grier, Katherine, 65
Griffin, Donald (*The Question of Animal Awareness: Evolutionary Continuity of Mental Experience*), 337–338
grooming, 23, 26–27, 96
Ground Game Act, 38–39
group living, 24–30, 45, 117, 118–125, 247–248
growling, 92–93
guinea pigs, 323

habitat, 11–12, 39, 60
harelips, 135, 145, 148
hares. see also jackrabbits; *specific hares*: ancient beliefs, 133–135; classification (origins), 6–8; coursing, 323; in fiction, 176–178; rabbits, differences from, 7, 15, 25, 31, 60–61; relationships among, 7, 141–142; women and, 152, 333
Harriman, Bob, 84
Harriman, Marinell: Herman (first house rabbit), 344, 346–347; *House Rabbit Handbook*, xx; house rabbits and, 84–85, 99–100; on vegetarianism, 349
Harris, Joel Chandler, 146, 157–163, 187
Harvey, 172, 193–194
health benefits of pet ownership, 333–334
hearing, 15
heart rates and dominance, 27
Hefner, Hugh, 10, 214–215. see also Playboy bunny
Heifer Project, 258, 260–261
Henry IV, 32
hermaphrodites (hares as), 134
"hierarchy of animal worth," xiv, 331–333, 340–341
High Production Volume (HPV) Program, 291–292
history of rabbits: domestic, 1–3, 30–32, 61–68, 73–74, 83–84; morphology, as prey, 13; origin and evolution, 6–9
hopping, 16–18, 160, 179, 181–182, 199–200
horror movies, 195–198
House, C. A., 195–198
House Rabbit Handbook (Harriman), xx, 84–85
house rabbits, xiii, xix, 81–90, 328, 346
House Rabbit Society (HRS): breeders and, 308–309, 313–314, 319–320; history and purposes of, 85–87, 346–348; Petco, 312; pet owners and, 58; rabbit meat and, 257, 259
Howard, John, 154–155
Humane Farming Association, 256–257
Humane Slaughter Act, 249, 254

Humane Society of the United States (HSUS), 289, 322

Humans Against Rabbit Exploitation (HARE), 257

Hummel figurines, 206, 210

hunting: endangered/rare species, 11; in folk tales and nursery rhymes, 145, 152, 265; fur market, 271; images in art, 34, 143; images in popular culture, 188, 210; opinions about, 32–35, 66; pest control, rabbits, 2, 49; rabbit distress calls used for, 93, 241; rabbit meat, 235–236; viruses, rabbit, 51, 53, 55

Hurd, Clement, 176

hutches. *see* cages

hyrax, 9

Idol of the Moon, 137

illnesses: laboratory rabbits, 299–300; pet rabbits and, 313; at pet stores, 310; rabbit farms, 244, 245, 247; "rabbit mills," 308

imaging technology, 298

In Defense of Animals, 244, 292

innocence. *see* children; virginity/innocence

inspections. *see* USDA (United States Department of Agriculture)

Institute for In Vitro Sciences, 285–286

intelligence: animal, 257–258, 262, 334, 336, 337–341; rabbit, 132, 143, 158, 164, 339–340

Interagency Coordinating Committee on the Validation of Alternative Methods (ICCVAM), 290

Intercolonial Commission on Rabbits, 36–37

intuition and prophecy, 132, 191–192, 194

invading species, 36–40

investigation, undercover, at rabbit farm, 244

in vitro tests, 289–290, 297

islands, rabbit, xxi, 31–32, 37, 44–46

jackrabbits, 5–6, 10, 11, 43, 323

Jataka, 146

Jesus Christ, 137, 139–141, 180, 202

John Hopkins University Center for Alternatives to Animal Testing (CAT), 291

"just so" stories, 144–148, 151–152, 156, 162–163, 195

Kac, Eduardo, 294–296

kangaroos, 17–18, 24

Knowles, George S., 67

Koi, Sandy, 308

Koons, Jeff, 222–223

laboratory rabbits, 279–280, 298–303, 321, 328. *see also* vivisection

lagomorph order, 7–8, 12, 14–15

Lamar, Pat, 320

Landseer, Edward, 67

Lashlor, 283

Last Judgment, 133

Lawson, Robert (*Rabbit Hill*), 180–183

Leach, Edmund, 218

learned helplessness, 331

Leporidae family, 6, 7, 9, 24–25

Lepus genera, 6–7, 9

liberation of laboratory rabbits, 301–303

Life magazine, 226, 233

life span of a rabbit, 13

literature: agriculture, history, 30–31; animal appreciation, xix, xv; animal rights, 218–219, 334–337, 340–341, 344, 349–350; demonology, 153; fiction, 68–70, 171–185, 189–195, 226, 305; folk tales, 130, 143–165, 194–195, 258–259; *House Rabbit Handbook* (Harriman), xx, 84–85; hunting, nonfiction, 32; magicians, 207; *Picturing the Beast: Animals, Identity and Representation* (Baker, Stephen), 129, 213; poems, complete, 131, 270, 347–348; poems, excerpted, 5, 229, 327; *Private Life of the Rabbit* (Lockley), xxi, 1–2, 18; rabbit farming, 232–233, 243, 255; scientific, 2–3; *Uses of Enchantment* (Bettelheim), 183

litter-box training, 84, 121, 126, 313

Lockley, Ronald: on aggression, rabbit, 28–29; on gait, rabbit, 81; influences on *Watership Down*, 194; personalizing rabbits, 2, 217–218, 349; on pest control of rabbits, 44–46, 51–52; on population, rabbit, 21, 38–39; *Private Life of the Rabbit*, xxi; on warren/family life, 23, 26

Lop Rabbit Club of America Guidebook, 317

Lorenz, Konrad, 123

Love, Jim, 301

love and friendship: domestic rabbits, xiv, 90–91, 99–107, 127; laboratory rabbits, 299–300; wild rabbits, 26

Lowis, Kirk, 314–316

Lubansky, Steve, 170–171, 204–205, 217

Lucina, 135

luck, 132–133, 204, 207

lungs (research on human), 279, 290, 293–294

macaques, 123

Mackey, Margaret, 208–209, 211

Madonna and Child with Saint Catherine, 147

magicians, 207–208, 323–325

Manna Pro, 316, 318

March hare, 13, 142, 171, 192

Marsh, Charles, 229–231, 246, 274

Marshall, Frances (*Bunny Book for Magicians*), 207

marsh rabbits, 10–11, 17

Masson, Jeffrey, xiii–xv, xxii, 336–337, 343–344, 349–350

Master Henry's Rabbit, 68

mating. *see* reproduction

McArdle, John, 283

McBratney, Sam (*Guess How Much I Love You*), 176–178

meat, 325–326

meat, rabbit (the meat). *see also* farming, rabbit meat; rabbits, meat (the animal): animal consumption, 240–241, 252; byproducts, 241; "disguising," 238–239; human consumption, 225, 231, 257; industry, 229–263, 330; markets, 47–49, 232, 238–240, 321; nutrition and taste, 232; taboos against eating, 261; unacceptability of, 329; viruses, rabbit, 50, 58, 240

medical research, 288, 292–294, 297–298

Meek, Marcellus, 233–235, 265–268, 270–271

Mendel, Gregor, 63

mice and rats, 37, 56, 226, 282, 283

Mickey Mouse, 189, 226

military rabbits, 321–322
milk-hare, 153–154
Milne, A.A., 184–185
monogamy, 24
monsters, rabbits as, 195–198
Monty Python and the Holy Grail, 197
moon: collectibles and, 206; in fiction, 202; in folk tales, 146, 159–160; rabbits, association with, 135–137, 143, 156
morphology of rabbits and hares, 12–17, 217
Morris, Desmond (*Dogwatching*), xix
Morris, William Edward, 281
mortality rates, rabbit, 13
mosquitoes (myxoma virus), 50–53, 59
Moss, Cynthia, 337, 342
movies and television, 186–189, 192–198, 226
mutilations (factory farms), 255–256
Myers, Ken, 12
Myktowycz, Robert, 29–30
myxoma virus, 2, 50–54, 59

National Belgian Hare Club of America, 70
National Council of Chain Restaurants, 256
National Greyhound Association (NGA), 322
National Institute of Agronomic Research (NIAR), 294–297
National Institute of Environmental Health Sciences, 292
National Pet Stock Association, 70
National Science Board, 29
National Toxicology Program, 292
NesQuik Bunny, 171, 219
nets, 39–41, 200–201, 203
neutering, 86, 99–100, 313–314
New Zealand, 36–38, 47–49, 52, 55–56
Night of the Lepus, 195–197
Nobel Prizes, 297
nocturnal nature, rabbits, 14–15, 136
nursery rhyme, 265

objectification of animals, 334–337. see also products, animals as
Office of International Affairs of the National Academies, 231
Office of Pesticide Programs, 286
Of Mice and Men (Steinbeck), 190–192, 235
Omori, Emiko, 198
Operation Feed Yourself, 258–259
Organisation for Economic Cooperation and Development (OECD), 283, 290–291
Oryctolagus genus, 6–7, 34–35
Ostara, 138, 154, 215–216
Oswald the Lucky Rabbit, 189
ovulators, induced, 13

pain (animal), physical and emotional, 342
Palmer, T.S., 42, 43
Panchatantra, 146
parenting, 24
Parsons, Richard, 238–239
Pasteur, Louis, 292
patriarchy, 332–333
Pat the Bunny, 208, 276
Peace Corps, 258–259
pejoratives, 7, 18–19, 218–219, 221, 332

Pel-Freez, 235, 246, 257
Pendelfin, 210–211
Penez, George, 32
People for Animal Rights, 244
Pepin, Jacques, 238
personal care products, 283–284
pest, rabbit as, 26–27, 30–59, 196, 212, 261
PETA (People for the Ethical Treatment of Animals), 219, 256–257, 292, 312
Petco, 311, 312
Peter Rabbit, 171–172, 174–175, 201, 262. see also Potter, Beatrix
"Peter Rabbit Syndrome," 238
pets: breeders, rabbit, 306, 318–319; history of rabbits as, 65, 67–68; meat and, 241, 262–263; rabbit lives as, xx, 311–312, 328; rabbits as feeders (snake food), 311; rabbits as, 49, 64–68, 225, 333–334; sales, 309; viruses, rabbit, 52, 58
Petsmart, 311
pet stores, 310–312
Phoebus, Gaston (*Book of the Hunt*), 32
Picturing the Beast: Animals, Identity and Representation (Baker, Stephen), 129, 213
pikas, 7–9
play, rabbit: games, 93–99, 343; "hopping like crazy," 18, 160, 179, 343; humor, xiv; laboratory rabbits, 299–301; meat rabbits and, 246–247; "wildness" of, 126
Playboy bunny, 10, 154, 169, 214–217, 331–332
Pliny the Elder (*Natural History*), 37–38
poems: complete, 131, 270, 347–348; excerpted, 5, 229, 327
poisoning, 44
Policy and Global Affairs Division of the NA, 231
polygamy, 24
population, rabbit. see also pest, rabbit as: estimating, 21; geographic distribution, 9–10, 36–37; glut of pet rabbits, 318–319; human introduction of rabbits, 11, 31, 34–40; natural controls, 26–27, 40; overpopulation, 36–39, 47–49, 59–60
Potter, Beatrix: books, 72, 171–172, 174–175, 201, 262; collectibles, bunny, 208–209, 211; house rabbits and, 72, 73; on rabbits' gaits, 16; sentimentalism and, 2–3
poultry, 219, 238–239, 322
Powell, Jody, 10
predators, 39–41, 187
pregnancy tests, 293
prey, rabbits and hares as, 12–19. see also cowardice/timidity; collectibles, bunny, 206–207; in fiction, 147, 156, 173; Playboy bunny, 216; protection, in warrens, 25
products, animals as, 212–213, 225–227, 297. see also cloning; fur; meat
Professional Rabbit Meat Association (PRMA), 231, 241, 282, 317–318, 320–321
profits of rabbit farming, 232–235, 240–241, 270, 274
prophecy, 132, 191–192, 194
Psychologists for the Ethical Treatment of Animals, 332
puppy mills, 305–306
pygmy rabbit (*Brachylagus idahoensis*), 6–7, 11–12

quickness, rabbits symbolizing, 132, 206

rabbit calicivirus (RCV), 53–57, 240
Rabbit Education Society (RES), 307, 309–310, 313–314, 318–319, 330
rabbit hemorrhagic disease (RHD), 53–57, 240
Rabbit in the Moon, 198
"rabbit mills," 306–309, 314
Rabbit Nuisance Amendment Act, 47–49
Rabbit Proof Fence (fence), 44, 46, 198
Rabbit Proof Fence (movie), 198
rabbits, domestic. *see also* house rabbits: aggression and, 99–100, 109–118; collectibles, 210; greyhound racing and, 323; group living, 118–125, 247–248; history, 1–3, 6; mating, 99–100; *Rabbit* (Updike), 200; released, 74, 79–83, 221–222; wild rabbits, differences from, 6–7, 31
rabbits, meat (the animal), 257. *see also* farming, rabbit meat; meat, rabbit (the meat); in art, 33; Belgian Hares, 70; farm living conditions, xx, 242–247, 256–257, 328; humane standards, 257; military food procurement training, 321; public concern, lack of, 257; slaughtering methods, 249–254
rabbits, wild. *see also* hares: ecosystems and, 12; humans and, 1–3, 31, 210; nature of, xxi, 6–7, 10, 14–15, 34–35; *Rabbit* (Updike), 200, 204; relationships among, 24–30, 99, 113, 117
rabbit's foot, 132–133
Rabbit tetralogy (Updike), 198–204
rabies vaccine, 292
Raeburn, Henry, 67
rats, 37, 56
Regan, Tom (*The Case for Animal Rights*), 350
relations (communication), 19–24, 85, 91–93, 114
religious symbols, rabbits as, 131–132, 135–141, 180
Remus, Uncle, 157–163, 185–186
reproduction, rabbit. *see also* breeding; population, rabbit: babies, 25–26, 242–243, 248; controls of, 26, 59; at farms, 31, 232, 254–255; mating, 19–20, 21–22, 23–24; vivisection, 280, 293–294; wild rabbits, 13–14
rescuers, rabbit, 58, 314, 318–319. *see also* House Rabbit Society (HRS)
Revlon, 286, 288
Rex rabbits, 272–273
Richardson, Barry, 49, 55, 59
Rockefeller University, 286
rodents, 7–8
Roger Rabbit, 192–193
Rolke, Daniel, 244
Roller Bunny, 169–170
Rose Bowl Parades, 170–171
Rountree, Harry (*Wicked Tim*), 68–70
Rowland, Beryl, 139, 141
Royal Society for the Prevention of Cruelty to Animals, 51–52
Runaway Bunny (Brown), 176

sacrificing hares and rabbits, 133–139, 143–144, 330, 336–337
Sadler, Eugene, 240, 247
scent glands, 19–20, 111

Schaper, John, 32–33, 34
schedules, 88, 108–109, 124
Schleifer, Harriet, 329
Schlesinger, Felix, 67
Science News, 279, 285
Scott, William (*Letters on Demonology and Witchcraft*), 153
Scully, Matthew (*Dominion: The Power of Man, the Suffering of Animals, and the Call to Mercy*), 337, 350
Seely, Beth, 262–263
selfishness, rabbits symbolizing, 157
Selig, Marion, 244
sensitivity, rabbits symbolizing, 143, 258
sentimentalism, 2–3, 238–239
Serpell, James, 61–62
sexism, 216, 218–219. *see also* witches
sexuality. *see also* Playboy bunny: advertising, 221; collectibles and, 206–207; hares as symbols of, 133–134, 154, 332; rabbits as symbols of, 139, 193, 201, 203–204
Shakespeare, William, 219
Shaw, George Bernard, 350
Simons, Rachel, 16–17
Singer, Peter, 325–326
size of domestic rabbits, 62, 121–122
skins, rabbit. *see* fur
skin tests, 289–291
slaughter, 230–231, 241, 245–246, 249–254, 256
slavery, xiii, 164–165, 185–186
Smith, Alvin, 54, 59
Smith, Susan, 259
snowshoe hare, 10–11
sociability: farms and, 243, 255; laboratory rabbits, 298–301; natural, of rabbits, 7, 87, 118–119, 258
Solis, Virgil, 32
Song of the South, 185–186
spaying and neutering, 86, 99–100, 313–314
species, invading, 36–40
spine deformities, 243–244, 298
Spira, Henry, 286
spirituality/morality, 189–190, 199, 201–203
Stahl, Edward, 254, 270
St. Andre, Nathaniel, 155
Steinbeck, John (*Of Mice and Men*), 190–192, 235
Steinem, Gloria, 169, 216
Stephens, James (*The Snare*), 229
Stephens, Martin, 289
stereotypical behavior in laboratory rabbits, 298, 300
Strabo, 37
stress. *see also* transportation: breeder rabbits, 254; laboratory rabbits, 298–301; meat rabbits, 243, 245–246, 256; pet store rabbits, 311–312; "rabbit mills," 306–309; show rabbits, 314
stunning before slaughter, 249–250, 253
Subaru, 221–222
superfoetation, 24
swamp rabbit, 10
Sylvilagus genera, 6–7, 10–12
symbolism, 131–157, 164, 173, 190–194, 206

tar baby, 146, 162–163
Taurens, Ilsa, 215

teeth, 28
Teletubbies, 172
television. *see* movies and television
Templeton George (*Domestic Rabbit Production*), 243, 255
teratogens, 280
territory, 19, 26, 29–30, 121
Third World, 258–261
Thomas, Elizabeth Marshall, xxii, 120–121, 337
Thompson, Henry, 2–3, 39, 60
Thorn, Jennifer, 240
Thumper, 171–174
Tierra del Fuego, 37, 51
Titian (*Madonna and Child with Saint Catherine*), 142
Toft, Mary, 154
tool making and use (animals), 338
Tortoise and the Hare, 149–151
transportation of rabbits, 245–246, 309–310, 314
Trans-Species Unlimited, Inc. (TSU), 257
trapping: fur, 275; in literature, 200–201, 229; pest control of rabbits, 41–44, 50; public opposition, 271; of rabbit predators, 39
trickery, rabbit symbolizing, 155–164, 185–186, 194, 207
Trix rabbit, 171, 219–220
turkey, 219. *see also* poultry

Uncle Remus, 157–163, 185–186
Uncle Wiggily, 189
United Nations, 258
United Nations Food and Agriculture Organization (FAO), 231, 243, 245
United Poultry Concerns, 322
United Rabbit Growers, 240
United States, 6–7, 54, 57, 230–231
University of British Columbia, 301
Updike, John (*Rabbit* tetralogy), 198–204
urine, 20, 23, 93, 121
U.S. Army, 240
USDA (United States Department of Agriculture): breeding facility inspections, 306–307, 309; fur, 255, 267–269; Humane Slaughter Act, 249, 254; laboratory rabbits, inspections, 298–299; licensing of pet sellers, 309–310; poultry, 238–239; Rabbit Experiment Station, 255; rabbit hemorrhagic disease (RHD), 57, 58; rabbit meat, inspections, 239–241, 244; *Rabbit Production* bulletin, 274; statistics on rabbits, 225, 231
U.S. Department of Transportation, 289
U.S. Environmental Protection Agency (EPA), 285–286, 290–292
U.S. GRAS (Generally Regarded as Safe) list, 290
U.S. News and World Report, 294
U.S. Pet Ownership and Demographic Sourcebook, xix
uterus, rabbit, 24

vaccines, 53–54, 57, 288, 292
Vance, Linda, xxiv–xxv
Varro, Marcus Terentius (*De re Rustica*), 30–31
Velveteen Rabbit, 171–172, 178
Venus, 134, 143
viral hemorrhagic disease (VHD), 53–57, 240

virginity/innocence: bunny collectibles, 206, 213; Playboy bunny, 216; rabbit as symbol of, 134–135, 140, 142, 192; women, 218
viruses, rabbit, 49–59
vision, 14–15, 132. *see also* eyes
vivisection: alternative tests, 281, 288–292, 297–298; common species used, 226; debate over, 336; decrease in, 288; Draize tests, 283–288; laws requiring, 283; medical research, 288, 292–294; public opinions, 297; rabbits, xx–xxi, 225, 227, 279–303; unreliability of animal tests, 285–288, 293–294; welfare of animals and, 329
vocalizations, 21–22, 92–93, 241
volcano rabbit (*Romerolagus diazi*), 6–7, 10–11
Volkswagon rabbit, 219, 221
voluntary children's chemical evaluation program (VCCEP), 291
Von Kreisler, Kristin, 344–345, 349

Walt Disney, 185–186, 189
Walters, Barbara, 216
Ward, Jay, 188
Warner Brothers, 186–187
warrens, 24–30, 34, 44, 201
Washburn, F. L. (*Rabbit Book*), 232–233
Washington Post, 258, 297
Watership Down (Adams), 16, 27, 194–195
weaning prematurely, 242, 308–311
Wells, Rosemary, 174, 184, 208
"wheelchairs"/carts for disabled rabbits, 92, 106–107, 345
White Rabbit, 171, 173
wildlife centers, 61
Wildlife Services leaflet, 235
wild rabbits. *see* rabbits, wild
William of Wykehan, 65
Williams, Marjorie (*Velveteen Rabbit*), 171–172, 178
Wise, Steven (*Drawing the Line*), 340
witches, 131, 133, 152–155, 216, 332
women. *see also* genitalia, female; Playboy bunny; sexism: animal involvement and, 331–332; bunny collectibles, 210–213; rabbit farming, 63, 260, 271; rabbits, link with, 134, 141–144, 154, 217–218, 331–333
Wordsworth, William ("All Things That Love the Sun"), 5

Zan Zig (magician), 325
Zawistowski, Steve, 287
zoning, 232
zoos, 57, 61, 171, 240–241